NEW PLAYWRIGHTS
The Best Plays of 2008

NEW PLAYWRIGHTS

The Best Plays
of 2008

Edited and with a Foreword
by Lawrence Harbison

CONTEMPORARY PLAYWRIGHTS
SERIES

A Smith and Kraus Book
Hanover, New Hampshire

A Smith and Kraus Book
Published by Smith and Kraus, Inc.
177 Lyme Road, Hanover, NH 03755
www.smithandkraus.com

Manufactured in the United States of America

Cover and text design by Julia Gignoux, Freedom Hill Design, Cavendish, Vermont
Composition by Kate Mueller, Electric Dragon Productions, Montpelier, Vermont
Front cover photos: Marisa Wegrzyn by Charlie Olson, Brett C. Leonard by
Monique Carboni, Kate Fodor by Doug Macron, Jennifer Haley by Robin Dicker,
Jim Knabel by Rosey Strub, Josh Tobiessen by Eduardo Placer, and
David Wright Crawford by Veronica Smith.

First Edition: December 2008
10 9 8 7 6 5 4 3 2 1

Library of Congress Control Number: 2008940846
ISBN-13 978-1-57525-618-4 / ISBN-10 1-57525-618-5

CONTENTS

FOREWORD

No one I think can disagree that the theatrical season 2007–2008 was one of the strongest in terms of new plays in recent memory. Amazingly, more than a handful escaped the critics' clutches, though some fine new plays deserved better than the drubbing they received. One thinks of Theresa Rebeck's *Mauritius*, Stephen Adly Guirgis's *The Little Flower of East Orange*, and Roberto Aguirre-Sacasa's *Good Boys and True*—though none of these excellent plays would have made this book, as none are by new playwrights. Of the plays included herein, only one was produced outside New York. Usually, I try to include at least three plays produced by regional theaters. This year I read several, but I just couldn't get as worked up about them as I did the plays I selected. It was also a good year for comedy, lately generally unwelcome on our stages unless it's dark, satiric, and cynical. It is hard for me, usually, to find comedies worthy of inclusion in my new playwrights book. Not this year!

The Butcher of Baraboo, Election Day, and *Spain* are comedies. The first two plays were produced by Second Stage as part of their summer series. *The Butcher of Baraboo* is about a small-town woman whose husband has disappeared under mysterious circumstances, and the town gossips suspect that she done it. *Election Day* is about a local mayoral election and examines with amusing dexterity why we vote the way we do. *Spain* was produced Off Broadway by MCC at the Lucille Lortel Theatre. It's about a young woman who believes that there's a sixteenth-century Spanish conquistador in her living room. *Harvest* is a touching drama about a farmer who refuses to give up his farm, even as he is going under. He manages to hold onto his farm but not his wife, who didn't bargain for a life of poverty and struggle. *Neighborhood 3: Requisition of Doom* is a drama about a group of teenagers in a suburban neighborhood obsessed with an online video game set in their community, who come to believe that they are being invaded by aliens from outer space— who look suspiciously like their parents. It was produced to acclaim by Actors Theatre of Louisville at their 2008 Humana Festival and subsequently at the 2008 Summer Play Festival in New York. *100 Saints You Should Know* comes to us from Playwrights Horizons and is about a single mom looking for something to believe in and a Catholic priest who has decided to leave the church as he has lost his faith. *Unconditional* was produced by LAByrinth Theater Company at The Public Theater. Of its three disparate stories, the central one is about a human resources worker who becomes enraged when he is laid off after many years on the job and just a short while from retirement and the pension he was counting on.

All these plays represent the best of American playwriting. I hope you like them as much as I do, but more important, I hope you produce them!

—Lawrence Harbison
Brooklyn, New York

INTRODUCTION

Ben Hecht wrote in his memoirs that that too much "cerebration" can "ruin" a play. He actually stated that "a good playwright needs little mind," that playwrights are guided by "the burn of experiences of the heart," and that they write plays because they know how to wear "make-up on their souls as expertly as on their faces."

I am willing to bet that the playwrights featured in *New Playwrights: Best Plays of 2008* might well agree with Mr. Hecht—not because they aren't capable of some heavy-duty cerebration, and certainly not because cerebration isn't necessary to writing plays. It's clear that these writers thought long and hard about what you're about to read. But they probably *did* feel that they had *less* than a "little mind" as they made their plays. In fact, they probably *lost* their minds completely as they wrote them. They probably sat alone as they began to write, moved by the "burn of experience of the heart" to tell a story. Then they slathered some "make-up on their souls" and became possessed by the brand-new, fantastic and horrible, lovely and nasty, cruel and kind souls that inhabit their plays. And when these make-believe souls start talking to each other—and to all of us—about the world we live in, they do something very real to us: They move us to think differently about our world, maybe even inspire us to change it or fix it—or at least hope for what Hecht calls "an unreal or possibly better one." It's downright miraculous to me that these fictional souls have the power to make us feel and think almost as deeply as the nonfictional souls in our real lives do. Because when these make-believe souls come together and start talking—very real stories are born. And we, the audience, feel very real things.

When I was approached about writing this foreword, I was asked to write specifically about the plays contained in this collection. I didn't know how to do that without being a spoiler—and without offending the playwrights! (What if I totally didn't "get" their plays?) So I decided that the best way to introduce these fine writers was to introduce you to the souls they have created with their very own hearts, minds, and souls. Here's an introduction to some of the folks you're about to spend some time with.

In *The Butcher of Baraboo* by Marisa Wegrzyn. you'll meet a butcher, her daughter, her sister, her brother, and a fecund sister-in-law. Fate made them family and plagued them with mistrust. As Wegrzyn gets these people talking, you'll find yourself laughing, but there's a chill in the air. Because it can be just as cold indoors as it is outdoors in the middle of a Wisconsin winter.

In *Election Day*, Josh Tobeissen will introduce you to a mayoral campaign volunteer, her apathetic boyfriend, his sister, a radical organizer, and a mayoral candidate. It's election day in a seemingly unimportant city, and when these people get jammed together, they learn more than they want to about what they believe and whom they love, and heartbreaking hilarity ensues.

In *Harvest* by David Wright Crawford, you'll meet Rick, a singularly determined farmer, who gives up the first woman he loves for the land he loves. The years pass, and you'll meet the other women in Rick's life. Ultimately, the past meets the present—in human form—and all this makes for an uncertain, achy future for a farm in the Texas panhandle.

In Jennifer Haley's *Neighborhood 3: Requisition of Doom*, you'll spend time with some American sons and daughters who are fully absorbed by what seems to be the new American pastime: the video game. You'll meet their fathers and mothers, who want desperately to connect with their kids and keep them safe and happy in that safest of places, the suburbs. As fathers, daughters, mothers, and sons attempt to communicate, you'll find yourself in decidedly unsafe and bone-chillingly unexpected territory.

In *100 Saints You Should Know* by Kate Fodor, you'll get to know a troubled priest, his mother, a single mom, her daughter, and a fragile boy who will come together and grapple with questions of faith, fate, belonging, and morality—and, ultimately, the devastatingly unexpected.

In *Spain*, playwright Jim Knabel will introduce you to Barbara, a betrayed, modern woman; a conquistador; a mystical presence; a "diversionary friend"; and the betrayer, all of whom come together across time and space to teach Barbara that, in order to *do* in this world, you have to know what you want.

And in *Unconditional* by Brett C. Leonard, a menagerie of lonely, interconnected urban and suburban souls jockey for connection, for dignity, and for their place in this world. As they do so, racial and cultural boundaries are crossed, sex and violence ensue, and one wonders if all was for naught, because the dull ache of loneliness and disconnection pervades.

Now—I don't think I have been a spoiler. I really don't. It's difficult to write about plays without giving anything away. But I hope I have intrigued you, piqued your interest—because what a collection of fictional souls you're about to meet!

To the playwrights featured in this volume: I thank you for your creations. I thank you for using and losing their minds; for listening to the burning in your hearts; for wearing makeup on your souls; and for populating the fictional world with a bunch of brand-new souls. I also want you all to know that I wore makeup on my soul as expertly as I could as I read these plays. Seriously. In meeting all the souls you've created, I found that I had to stop reading—and *do*! What a great treat for an actor or a director to start thinking about breathing life into these people. And I did just that! I got some actors together, and we read the plays out loud—a completely different experience from reading them to myself!

And now I ask you, the reader, to do just the same. Right now. Don't be lazy. Don't just read these plays to yourself. You're short-changing yourself and the playwrights. They were ambitious enough and brave enough to write these plays. Now it's your turn to be ambitious and brave: Read these plays out loud with people who are eager to put some makeup on their souls—actors! Plays have to be spoken; they have to be done. So do them! Activate the incredible ache in these plays, and thank the stars for these wonderful playwrights who have hungered publicly for an "unreal and possibly better world." That's about as noble as it gets.

—John Cariani

Mr. Cariani is the author of Almost, Maine, *included in* New Playwrights: The Best Plays of 2006.

THE BUTCHER OF BARABOO

Marisa Wegrzyn

PLAYWRIGHT'S BIOGRAPHY

Marisa Wegrzyn was born and raised in Evanston and Wilmette, Illinois. She is a graduate of Washington University in St. Louis and lives in Chicago. Her plays include *Killing Women, Psalm of a Questionable Nature, Hickorydickory, Ten Cent Night,* and *Diversey Harbor.* Her work has been featured at Steppenwolf Theatre Company, Second Stage, Actors Theatre of Louisville's Humana Festival, Geva Theatre Center, Lucid by Proxy, Magic Theatre, CenterStage Baltimore, Available Light Theatre, Nice People Theatre Company, Washington University in St. Louis, Hourglass Group, HotCity Theatre St. Louis, Theatre Seven, Chicago Dramatists, and Rivendell Theatre Ensemble. She has been commissioned by Steppenwolf Theatre and Yale Repertory Theatre. Wegrzyn is a resident playwright at Chicago Dramatists and a founding member of Theatre Seven of Chicago.

ORIGINAL PRODUCTIONS

The Butcher of Baraboo was developed and produced in Steppenwolf Theatre Company's First Look Repertory of New Work (artistic director, Martha Lavey; executive director, David Hawkanson; director of New Play Development, Edward Sobel) in Chicago, Illinois, summer 2006. It was directed by Dexter Bullard; set design by Jack Magaw; lighting design by J. R. Lederle; costume design by Tatjana Radisic; sound design by Martha Wegener; dramaturged by Sarah Gubbins; stage managed by Lauren V. Hickman. The cast was as follows:

CAST

VALERIE . . . . .Annabel Armour
MIDGE . . . . .Rebecca Sohn
GAIL . . . . .Natalie West
DONAL . . . . .John Judd
SEVENLY . . . . .Danica Ivancevic

The Butcher of Baraboo was premiered Off Broadway by Second Stage Theatre Uptown (artistic director, Carole Rothman; executive director, Ellen Richard), New York City, summer 2007. It was directed by Judith Ivey; set design by Beowulf Boritt; lighting design by Jeff Croiter; costume design by Andrea Lauer; sound design by Ryan Rumery; stage managed by Lori Ann Zepp. The cast was as follows:

CAST

CHARACTERS

VALERIE: female, fifties. A butcher
MIDGE: female, thirty-two. A pharmacist, Valerie's daughter
GAIL: female, mid- to late forties. A cop, Valerie's sister-in-law
DONAL: male, fifties
SEVENLY: female, thirties

SETTING

A house in Baraboo, Wisconsin.

TIME

February. The present.

THE BUTCHER OF BARABOO

SCENE 1

The kitchen and living room of Valerie's small house in Baraboo, Wisconsin, on a cold February morning. The room is comfortable, accented with kitchen kitsch: cow potholders, souvenir mugs, a wall calendar of puppy dogs, etc. There's an impressive array of cutlery. A meat cleaver juts from a butcher block. Valerie sits at the table with a mug of coffee. She reads the morning paper. Midge enters, pajamas, bed-head. She sets out a bowl, a spoon, and a box of Count Chocula. She opens the fridge and takes out a gallon of milk. There is only a splash left. She holds it out for Valerie to see, shakes it.

VALERIE: You know where the grocery store is.
(Midge puts the milk back in the fridge. She pulls out a two-liter bottle of pop and sits at the table. She opens the cereal box and fishes the prize out; this will be the highlight of her day. She pours the cereal in the bowl and pours the pop on the cereal and eats.)

VALERIE: Why's it you're coming in so late now, no explanation to me, why is that, Midge, hm? When I've gone and made dinner and you're not even here. I heard a rumor from Mary Berwyn and I'm not one to believe gossip straight out, especially from that woman, so why don't you tell me direct. What were you doing behind the junior high school last night?
(Midge gets up and opens the can of Maxwell House coffee. It's almost empty, so she gets a full bag of Starbucks coffee and prepares to pour it in the Maxwell House can.)

VALERIE: The heck you're doing? What are you doing to my coffee.

MIDGE: Was empty.

VALERIE: In my Maxwell House?

MIDGE: Where I always put my coffee.

VALERIE: Always?

MIDGE: Yeah.

VALERIE: The heck can't you scoop it out of the bag, why are you putting it in my . . . that's not decaf. You know I don't drink caffeine.

MIDGE: Yeah, I guess.

VALERIE: Yeah, you guess? Mess up my coffee again and yeah you can guess how many chops it takes my cleaver to chop your hand clean off.

MIDGE: Starbucks is a step-up. Seattle refined the coffee drinking experience.

VALERIE: This is not Seattle. This is America.

MIDGE: Seattle is in America.

VALERIE: But are we in Seattle?

MIDGE: We're in Wisconsin.

VALERIE: We are in Wisconsin.

MIDGE: Which is also in America like Seattle which is also in America.

VALERIE: You know I don't drink caffeine.

MIDGE: You do now.

(Valerie takes the coffee bag, picks up her meat cleaver, slams the Starbucks bag on the butcher block, and cleaves the Starbucks with her meat cleaver.)

MIDGE: *(Smoldering.)* That is fair trade coffee.

VALERIE: What is fair trade coffee?

MIDGE: Fair trade coffee is expensive is what fair trade coffee is.

VALERIE: How much does it cost?

MIDGE: It is very expensive. That particular bag I got for free. But normally it's twelve dollars a pound, plus tax, so thirteen dollars about.

VALERIE: Well it's half off now.

(Midge salvages her coffee then returns to her breakfast.)

VALERIE: These folks moving in next door, you'll see out there the moving trucks, these are nice and respectable people and I'd like it for you to be nice and respectable in return. Do you know what a nice and respectable person doesn't do? A nice and respectable person doesn't sell stolen pharmaceuticals behind the junior high school to twelve-year-old children.

MIDGE: They're not twelve-year-olds, Mom. They're fourteen.

VALERIE: They are children, and stealing is wrong.

MIDGE: You steal stuff from work all the time.

VALERIE: Meat is different, meat is food. I am speaking the differ between food and drugs. Food and drugs have nothing in common.

MIDGE: The Food and Drug Administration.

VALERIE: Do you know what sort of law you could be dealing with if you get caught?

MIDGE: Aunt Gail, oh yeah, she's a regular CSI: Baraboo.

VALERIE: Not nice to make fun. Your Aunt Gail has feelings.

MIDGE: I have feelings too when she throttles me with the newspaper, you know what that feels like? Maybe you don't think current events hurt, but when they're all rolled up? And for no reason at all she hits me.

VALERIE: Oh, no reason?

MIDGE: None that I'm aware of.

VALERIE: None that you're aware of. Not even the time you made a crack about her hair, then asked which cop she thought she was, Cagney or Lacey? Or the time you plastered her squad car in neon Post-It notes? And she certainly had no reason to give you a smack when you replaced the bullets in her gun with jelly beans. Now I won't say a word to Gail about the drugs and the junior high kids. I won't turn this into a matter of police business if you say you'll stop selling drugs to children. And I want you to say it like you mean it.

MIDGE: I will stop selling drugs to children.

VALERIE: Did you mean it?

MIDGE: Yep.

VALERIE: You're a young woman, Midge. Get over this juvenile carry-on and find a nice man, have some nice kids of your own. You can find a good man. You're . . . attractive . . . in your own . . . unique way. For god sake, you are thirty-two.

MIDGE: You said I was a young woman.

VALERIE: Well you're thirty-two. Just about everyone you went to high school with is married. Even that boy who walked with you at graduation, that retarded boy. He's getting married. If a retarded boy can get married, it bodes well for you. You can do better than this.

MIDGE: What's "this"?

VALERIE: *(gestures to whatever.)* This. There's a whole world out there for you. You don't need to be living at home with me.

MIDGE: You don't appreciate my company.

VALERIE: Sweetheart. Sometimes I don't, you're right.

MIDGE: Thought you were lonely now that Dad is gone.

(Gail appears at the kitchen door, knocks, lets herself in. Gail is in her cop uniform and winter cop gear.)

GAIL: You wouldn't have any a those good fillets left, Valerie, would you now?

VALERIE: Not on my person at the moment.

GAIL: Eddie really loves those fillets and when you get any extra T-bones, Eddie really loves those T-bones.

VALERIE: Yes, Eddie loves anything he doesn't have to pay for.

GAIL: That is so true. Cold out there, isn't it! And those poor movers next door, they must be freezing. Although they get warm, moving around like that, lifting heavy boxes and pullout couches and tricycles. You really should lock your door. I walked right in, anybody could walk right in, who-knows-who could waltz in here while you're asleep. Chop you in the neck with one of those dealies *(Points to meat cleaver.)* happens all the time.

VALERIE: When exactly does it happen all the time?

GAIL: Ohhhh right let me pull out my dossier on neck chopping statistics in the greater Sauk County region. Happens all the time in general I'm saying. You and your cutlery. I only have me this here pocket knife, birthday present from Frank years back. Suits me just fine.

VALERIE: What, that little piss-ant thing?

GAIL: You wouldn't be thinking it so piss-ant sticking out of your neck. Oooh Starbucks! I don't drink the stuff myself, the Starbucks, but I could sit inside one of those shops for hours, listening to Norah Jones.

(Valerie has gotten a milk gallon filled with blood from the fridge and sets it in front of Gail.)

GAIL: —what in the holy heck is that.

VALERIE: Gallon of blood . . . The one you asked for?

GAIL: Ohh right right right, but Valerie, I won't be needing it til the Spring.

VALERIE: Made it sound you needed it now, I got it now.

GAIL: I can see you got it now but I don't need it til Spring. Y'know, I don't think you ever raised an eyebrow at my request. Don't you think it strange I request a gallon of blood?

VALERIE: I assumed it was for Eddie. The backwards lout will drink anything, won't he?

MIDGE: Oh snap.

VALERIE: Midge, what did I tell you about making fun.

MIDGE: ? . . . you made fun, I went "oh snap."

VALERIE: Well it's not nice of you to laugh at Gail's stupid husband.

GAIL: Eddie is not stupid. A little not very smart sometimes, but that's far different from stupid. So in order to deter teenagers from the drinking and the driving around prom time, we like to stage the aftermath of a drunk-driving accident on the, uh, *(Points.)* service road runs long the high school there, you know where I'm talking?

VALERIE: No.

GAIL: That road—you know where I'm talking right, that busted-up no-traffic road there, you know where I'm talking right?

MIDGE: I dunno, Aunt Gail, maybe I'll get it you keep pointing at the wall.

(Gail thwacks Midge hard with a bit of rolled-up newspaper.)

GAIL: So we get some crushed-up cars from the junkyard and kids from the drama club role-playing the mangled victims—Always a real hit of the school year—but our morality tale seemed missing an element of nuance. So this year we're gonna spatter the drama kids in blood.

VALERIE: Seems a bit gratuitous.

GAIL: Oh you bet! Kids these days, you gotta shock it into them: don't drink and drive, don't do drugs, don't have sex, or you'll be dead. But kids are still drinking and crashing cars and I'm not convinced this program has any effect, really. Between you and me, I'm not sure it matters. *(Suddenly sullen.)* . . . Not sure anything matters anymore . . .

(Valerie puts the gallon of blood back in the fridge.)

GAIL: Whoa there girly, where you off to?

MIDGE: Getting ready for work.

GAIL: I'll be having a word with you before you're off to the pharmacy. 'K, dollface?

(Midge exits.)

VALERIE: What sort of word you need to be having with her?

GAIL: A matter that may concern her.

VALERIE: Police business?

GAIL: Mm. Police business.

> *(Valerie will pick up her meat cleaver as she speaks, twirl it in her hands. Gail will discreetly put her hand near the gun in her hip holster, just in case.)*

VALERIE: Gail, I know we've had our differences since the day I married Frank.

GAIL: Now I don't begrudge you anything marrying my brother.

VALERIE: I wasn't saying you begrudged me that necessarily.

GAIL: If that's something you thought, I want to clear the air and say I don't begrudge you.

VALERIE: And I don't begrudge you either.

GAIL: *(Offended.)* For what?

VALERIE: For what what?

GAIL: For what could you begrudge me for?

VALERIE: For whatever you don't begrudge me for.

GAIL: You know what I begrudge you for.

VALERIE: You said you didn't begrudge me.

GAIL: And I don't. I'm saying if I begrudged you something you know what I'd begrudge you for, but I don't, so it's moot.

VALERIE: (You're moot.)

GAIL: What?

VALERIE: What?

GAIL: What did you say?

VALERIE: Hearing things.

GAIL: You said something, and I am not hearing things. I don't appreciate an insult to my intelligence. And even further, to take this further as I'm about to do, Valerie, I don't appreciate you waving cutlery in my face.

VALERIE: Was a good four feet from your face and not in your face.

GAIL: Was near enough for a gal who knows how to wield cutlery and butcher people the way you do.

VALERIE: What did you say?

GAIL: I said near enough for a gal who wields cutlery and butcher animals the way you do.

VALERIE: You didn't say animals.

GAIL: I said animals.

VALERIE: No, you said—

GAIL: Animals.

VALERIE: Animals isn't what I heard.

GAIL: Look who's hearing things now, eh.

(Valerie slams the cleaver back into the butcher block.)

VALERIE: What I'm saying is you don't need to take out your grudges on my daughter. Whatever police business you're here to talk to Midge about, let's consider the matter settled. We don't need to bring police business into the mix, I've already talked with her about it.

GAIL: You did?

VALERIE: Yes.

GAIL: And what did she say?

VALERIE: She said she'll stop . . . Because I know it might be a matter of police business, but she'll stop . . . She won't do it anymore because she'll get herself in a mess of trouble canoodling with junior high kids . . . We're not talking about the same thing are we?

GAIL: What are you talking about?

VALERIE: I thought you said you were talking to Midge on police business.

GAIL: But what are you talking about?

VALERIE: Nothing. Noth—I thought we were talking something else.

GAIL: You thought we were conversing on some other matter sure. Sure.

VALERIE: Care for breakfast?

GAIL: I wouldn't say no to a splash of orange juice, would I?

VALERIE: Would you?

GAIL: No I would not.

(Valerie pours some juice for Gail.)

VALERIE: What sort of splash would you say no to? Splash of acid in your face?

GAIL: Careful now.

VALERIE: Figure of speech.

GAIL: There's no figure of speech about a splash of acid in my face.

VALERIE: Who are you, Emily Dickinson?

GAIL: I have read the poetry of Emily Dickinson and not one poem did she write about splashing acid in faces.

VALERIE: She should've though. Might make her poetry less boring.

(Gail laughs and sticks her hand in the cereal box, searching.)

GAIL: She does bore the snot out of me.

VALERIE: Midge got the prize already.

GAIL: *(Removes her hand from the cereal box.)* Now if we're talking poetry you know who's a real poet: Billy Joel. The man is dumped by his first record label, drinks a bottle of furniture polish in a botched suicide, turns his suicide note into the lyrics of "Tomorrow Is Today." And that, Valerie, is the essence of true poetry by a true poet. What was the prize, like stickers or something?

VALERIE: You'll forget what I said about Midge?

GAIL: Would've been well forgotten without that business about splashing acid in my face.

VALERIE: Gail . . . Please.

GAIL: I don't like the word canoodling. But I trust you'll put a stop to whatever Midge is or isn't doing.

VALERIE: Thank you.

GAIL: She wouldn't do anything stupid.

VALERIE: She is a smart girl.

GAIL: Not so smart enough to keep from setting her hair on fire making soup. Out of a can, condensed. How's a person do something like that? I don't know. She managed.

VALERIE: Was twenty years ago, leave her alone.

GAIL: To be completely honest, Valerie, I'm not entirely comfortable thinking it's people like her who dispense pharmaceuticals to the population. Makes you wonder about all the incompetence in those professions we put our good faith in. *(She drops her gun.)*

VALERIE: Mm.

GAIL: And Midge is a little not very nice at that too, the way she treats people. If you're not very attractive, the least you could be is nice. You're forgiven an ugly mug if you have a good soul. You turned that girl of yours into a real B dash itch, pardon my French, and I'm not just saying that because I'm still sore about the jelly beans.

VALERIE: Midge could be nicer, I suppose. She switched my Maxwell House for Starbucks.

GAIL: Oh but that's a step up.

VALERIE: She knows full well I don't drink caffeine. Full well. Does it anyway, does whatever she wants. Some days I could kill her.

GAIL: You don't mean that, sure.

VALERIE: Some days. Some days.

GAIL: If you were me and I were you, I wouldn't be saying such things, Valerie. And I wouldn't be saying them in such a way that it sounds like I could well mean it.

VALERIE: *(Pause.)* Have people been talking about me?

GAIL: Now, now.

VALERIE: I've been taking notice. My regular customers not being so regular.

GAIL: Now, now.

VALERIE: Now now what "now, now," has there been gossiping?

(Gail moseys over to the wall calendar.)

GAIL: Puppy dogs are cuter than the old calendar you had up here what was that last year's calendar you had up here what was that.

VALERIE: John Deere tractors.

GAIL: Puppy dogs are cuter than John Deere tractors.

VALERIE: Was Frank's calendar.

GAIL: Frank did love his John Deere.

VALERIE: He did, sure.

GAIL: He did. He did, sure . . . There we are. The seventeenth of February. Spot on. Guess the day had to come around sooner or later, didn't it. Poor Frank. What're you going to do with yourself today?

VALERIE: What I do with myself every Wednesday. Go to work.

GAIL: Hm.

VALERIE: Is there something you want to say to me, Gail? You say it to my face.

(Donal appears at the door and knocks. Valerie opens the door.)

DONAL: Hey there neighbor.

VALERIE: Was wondering when you'd finally knock on my door.

DONAL: Busy morning, I was looking for a quick escape from the moving chaos. Of course saw Gail's squad car out there, hi Gail.

GAIL: Hi.

DONAL: This really does have to be a quick hello and get back, but I wanted to thank you for your invitation, Valerie, that's nice of you. My wife is insisting on bringing something. Sevenly is terribly excited to meet you.

GAIL: What invitation?

VALERIE: I invited Donal and his wife over for dessert, coffee.

GAIL: Why?

VALERIE: Because I'm nice.

GAIL: So you're all having a little get-together kinda thing, huh, little dessert, little coffee thing? *(To Donal.)* So that's why you asked me if I knew any babysitters, huh, you needed a babysitter so you could come here for a little dessert.

DONAL: Well . . .

GAIL: Suppose I was going to be having a word with Midge about that this morning. But clearly I wasn't invited to this family gathering, so.

DONAL: I'm sure Valerie wouldn't mind, would you Valerie, if, em . . .

VALERIE: Babysitting? That's the word you needed to have with Midge? Exactly how is babysitting a matter of police business?

GAIL: Well I am in uniform. So it was police business.

VALERIE: Not at all was it police business is more like it.

GAIL: It, yes, it did lean a bit towards not at all, didn't it. But it would be a shame if I had to mention the word canoodling to the chief of police, he just hates the word canoodling and especially hates people who engage in acts of canoodling.

VALERIE: *(Pause.)* Would you like to join us for dessert, Gail?

GAIL: Oh, I dunno . . .

VALERIE: Please, Gail, join us for dessert Friday night.

GAIL: Well if you insist.

(Midge enters, ready for work.)

DONAL: Hi, Midge.

VALERIE: You remember your Uncle Donal?

DONAL: Been a long time, huh Kiddo. You were yay tall last time I saw you.

VALERIE: Would it kill you to give your uncle a hug?

(Midge complies.)

GAIL: Midge, you wanna babysit for Donal?

VALERIE: It's a couple hours and it's only six kids.

MIDGE: No.

VALERIE: Well you don't have to drag us to your dark place, you could just say no.

MIDGE: I did say no.

VALERIE: Well you could say it nicer, with some nice inflection.

MIDGE: *(With jazz hands.)* No.

VALERIE: Don't forget milk on your way home.

MIDGE: Yeah right.

VALERIE: Yeah right right, don't forget.

(Midge exits.)

DONAL: I'm sure we'll find somebody to watch the kids, it's no problem. I should get back to the house. If there's anything I can do for you . . . I realize today must be hard for you. How are you holding up?

VALERIE: I'm doing OK.

DONAL: If you need anything . . .

VALERIE: Thank you, Donal.

DONAL: Gail, can I speak to you later about the parking ticket you left on the movers' truck.

GAIL: Law's the law, Donal.

DONAL: But I'm your brother.

(Lights.)

SCENE 2

Later that week. Evening. Valerie, Gail, Donal, and Sevenly are in the midst of dessert.

DONAL: . . . and so this story begins oh, let's see. This is like something something years ago I'm at. This was high school, and I know that was when you first met Frank wasn't it, Valerie. I remember clear as a bell Frank at the kitchen table. Has his notebook doing homework, and he looks up at me says there's this girl, and the look in his eyes goes all soft—I remember this one moment so clear about my brother—this girl. He says just like that. This girl in my biology class and we're lab partners and she's excited to dissect the frog. And then he blurts: and I'm going to marry her.

VALERIE: He did not say that.

DONAL: As God is my witness.

GAIL: I highly doubt Frank blurted anything.

DONAL: So Frank, as you know, was a quiet boy. Shy. Christmas vacation rolls around, I ask him, so have you even asked her on a date yet? I haven't said one word to her, he tells me. You're her lab partner, how can you not say one word to her? I don't know, he says, she seems to be OK with it. Frank! You like her! Ask her something! So what did ask you?

VALERIE: Asked me if I wanted to go ice fishing.

DONAL: Who asks a girl to go ice fishing on a first date? Who does that?

VALERIE: I said yes, didn't I?

DONAL: You did. Do you remember that day, Gail? That day ice fishing and Valerie came with us. I was just thinking. So we were technically all on your first date with Frank. That's funny.

GAIL: Dad didn't like to take me ice fishing.

DONAL: He did take you.

GAIL: Took me that once, wouldn't take me again.

DONAL: You complained.

GAIL: I did not so.

DONAL: "Oh my toes. I have frostbite. There's a bear."

GAIL: I never said there's a bear, was Frank saying there's a bear when it was just fat Mr. Harris sitting on a bucket looking fat and bearlike. Boy Glenn's dad was fat wasn't he? Freak Show is what we called him. Morbidly obese is the polite term now. He had a heart attack on the toilet last year had to knock down a wall to get him out. That was Frank saying "there's a bear." I never said there's a bear.

DONAL: All right, Gail, you never said there was a bear, I was mistaken.

GAIL: I think you were mistaken, Donal.

DONAL: I don't suppose Frank kept up with the ice fishing, did he.

VALERIE: Was the odd time he'd pick up and go. Fish the day and that was enough for the year.

DONAL: Did he ever get you out on that cold lake with him again?

VALERIE: No. No.

(Silence.)

SEVENLY: I love to hear stories of how people met. Me and Donal met through my brother, when they were on their missions in Brazil.

DONAL: Honey, they know how we met.

SEVENLY: Valerie doesn't. Valerie and Frank didn't come out to the wedding.

DONAL: I'm sure she knows, we don't need to bore them.

SEVENLY: Are we boring you?

VALERIE: No, no.

GAIL: I'm a little bored.

SEVENLY: Oh no. You are?

GAIL: Little bit.

SEVENLY: Gail, how was it you and Eddie met?

VALERIE: Yes, tell her how you met Eddie.

SEVENLY: Do tell!

GAIL: They know how me and Eddie met.

SEVENLY: Oh, I don't.

VALERIE: Sevenly doesn't know.

DONAL: You have to tell it now.

GAIL: I was a rookie cop, I get a call to go on over to Mrs. McGinty's house on Surrey Lane. Says she's hearing a thump coming from the roof, like a *(Thumps fist on table)*. Every half hour or so a *(Thumps fist on table)*. Thinks there's a burglar and would I check it out? So I go around the house, inside and out. I hear it . . . *(Thumps table)* . . . Then way across the way on 18th Street, there's a whoopin' and a hootin', some fellas got something going on. Eddie and Tommy Laroux and Jessie Berwyn and . . . they got this contraption set up in the backyard. *(looks to Valerie)* . . . you're just busting to tell what it was.

VALERIE: This thing looks like something Wile E Coyote would order out of the ACME catalogue.

DONAL: The infamous squirrel catapult.

VALERIE: Eddie likes to break it out on the foruth of July.

GAIL: I pull up and Eddie's smearing peanut butter in the bowl because you gotta lure the squirrels before you launch 'em onto rooftops *(Thumps table)*. And I say, y'know, we got a complaint and you can't be launching squirrels onto Mrs. McGinty's roof. So that's how I met Eddie. And then we got married.

SEVENLY: Were the squirrels OK?

GAIL: Squirrels bounce.

DONAL: I'm sure they were fine.

GAIL: Midge said she'd make an appearance tonight? Right Val?

VALERIE: Don't call me Val. I don't call you Gay.

GAIL: Don't call me Gay.

VALERIE: Then don't call me Val.

GAIL: How about I call you Ms. Grumpy Pants, would you like that instead? Huh, Ms. Grumpy Pants, who irons her trousers with grumpy starch and a hot grumpy iron.

SEVENLY: *(looking at Valerie's meat cleaver.)* That's a big one! Sharp too, I bet, huh. Sharp. Donal, do you remember those knives I bought from the shopping channel and how dull and flimsy they turned out to be.

DONAL: Mm.

SEVENLY: They were so dull and flimsy I couldn't believe how dull and flimsy they were, they weren't sharp and sturdy like this. Those QVC knives were just, oh, disappointing's the word.

VALERIE: Would you like to pick it up?

SEVENLY: Oh no, but thank you for the offer.

GAIL: What a weird thing to offer.

VALERIE: She was admiring it.

GAIL: Kids admire my gun, I don't let them take potshots at squirrels.

SEVENLY: I used to use a meat cleaver all the time. Everybody is so nice here! Donal had me worried, saying, now, Baraboo is not at all like Provo. And it's true, it's not at all like Provo, but everybody has been very welcoming.

DONAL: I'm sorry, honey, did you say you used to use one of those all the time?

SEVENLY: Oh yes! Don't you remember? I told you.

DONAL: No . . .

SEVENLY: I told you about the chickens. I didn't tell you about the chickens?

DONAL: Well I know your family raised chickens.

SEVENLY: *(To Gail and Valerie.)* We raised chickens! I had a chicken and I named her Lulu. Lulu the Chicken. Oh she was a sweetheart. I'd read books to her.

GAIL: You read books to chickens?

SEVENLY: Well sure. To soothe them. They're not too critical if you read slow or mispronounce words or skip the boring parts to get to the good parts even if that means the book doesn't make sense. Chickens aren't so worried about narrative. *(Then self-conscious.)* Silly, I know. Reading to a chicken, who reads to a chicken.

VALERIE: That's not silly.

SEVENLY: I couldn't be the one to . . . my father took care of Lulu when it was her time to go.

(Quiet.)

DONAL: Thank you for having us over. It's very kind of you.

SEVENLY: Yes, thank you for having us, Valerie. It's nice to feel welcome.

VALERIE: Ohh sure. Good brownies.

SEVENLY: These are Katherine Hepburn's brownies. Katherine Hepburn used this same recipe.

DONAL: I could eat a whole pan of these.

SEVENLY: Sometimes you have.

DONAL: Oh, now.

VALERIE: Tell me about your name, Sevenly. Does it mean what I think it means?

SEVENLY: I was the seventh child in my family.

GAIL: What's your younger sibling called? Eightly?

SEVENLY: There are no more after me. I'm the youngest in my family. *(Slight pause.)* We all have big families. All my brothers and sisters I mean. And we always talked about having a big family.

DONAL: We're still deciding on the name for our next one. We've been thinking if it's a boy we'll name him Frank, you know. After, well, after Frank.

GAIL: You're expecting?

DONAL: No, no. No. Not yet. We're just planning ahead, right honey?

SEVENLY: Planning ahead.

DONAL: I suppose if it's a girl we could call her Frankie. What do you think of that?

SEVENLY: That's nice.

DONAL: We'll have at least one more when the time comes. I'd want to honor my brother's memory.

(Gail rolls her eyes at this, scoffs.)

DONAL: Something you want to say, Gail?

VALERIE: I think it's a fine idea you're thinking to name the baby after Frank. Was a nice funeral you missed, Donal.

GAIL: This one didn't cry. I cried. This one didn't.

VALERIE: I don't need to make a public display.

GAIL: Well. At least you were there.

DONAL: I told you I couldn't leave Provo, and Sevenly couldn't travel being almost nine months along at the time, I explained all this to you.

GAIL: Donal, I'm not accusing you of anything. I'm not trying to make you feel guilty. When we find the body, then you can see Frank off proper. We can all see Frank off proper when we find the remains of him.

VALERIE: "When we find the body." Something I blame on shoddy police work.

GAIL: The heck you say shoddy police work, our police work is thorough and sound.

VALERIE: Thorough and sound like when the Petersen boy went missing.

GAIL: That wasn't a gaff in police procedure.

VALERIE: It took the circus cops a whole day to find him drunk asleep under a squad car in the police station parking lot.

GAIL: Well who sleeps under a squad car?! And we did find him. And it wasn't Jim running over his neck that killed him, but the transmission fluid dripped in his mouth he swallowed drunk asleep. All I'm saying is Devil's Lake is hardly a Great Lake. It's a great lake for fishing, sure, but where could a body go? We would've found it if that's where he was.

VALERIE: If you haven't found his body by now, you're not going to find it.

GAIL: Oh?

DONAL: Enough! . . . Enough . . . It's a terrible thing that happened. Frank is at rest—wherever he is. Let's leave it at that for tonight.

GAIL: I won't leave it at that, Donal, when I know full well she had some hand in our brother's death. How about that, Val?

VALERIE: You call me Val one more time I will cut your throat.

(Silence.)

SEVENLY: Excuse me, where is your restroom?

VALERIE: Down the hall there, on the left. Hold the flush down, so.

(Sevenly exits. Gail gets her coat.)

VALERIE: I said I don't like you calling me Val. Donal, didn't I say I don't like her calling me Val. Gail, you push my buttons sometimes, you push and you push. I apologize for saying what I said about the throat cutting, I didn't mean it.

GAIL: *(To Donal.)* Don't ever say I didn't warn you.

VALERIE: Warned him, you warned him? There's no need for warnings here.

(Midge enters. She has a plastic shopping bag filled with boxes of Sudafed.)

MIDGE: Oh—hi.

GAIL: Whatya got there, Midge?

MIDGE: Nothing.

GAIL: Heard you've been getting in some trouble. Canoodling at the junior high? *(Gail takes the bag from Midge, looks through the contents.)* All this cold medication. Wow, Midge. You must have the world's worst cold.

MIDGE: Oh, it's terrible. *(cough.)*

GAIL: *(To Donal.)* Can you give us a minute here?

DONAL: Where do expect me to go?

GAIL: Go check on your wife make sure she's not reading to chickens.

(Donal exits.)

GAIL: So who are these junior chemists you supply? Ohhh surprise surprise, you didn't think I knew a darn thing about your druggy buddies and the meth labs? I want names, I don't care who you feel obligated to protect. Is it that Gordy Laroux who works at the Starbucks. *(Midge doesn't respond.)* Yeah. That's what I thought.

(Gail leaves with Midge's bag, slamming the door.)

MIDGE: *(To Valerie.)* You said you weren't gonna tell her about the canoodling.

VALERIE: I didn't mean to use the word canoodling.

MIDGE: Aunt Gail is going to get me in trouble.

VALERIE: I didn't know you were mixed up dealing methamphetamines but I'm sure as heck glad I know now. Hooked on meth, the first thing to go is hygiene, I have seen the segments on 20/20.

MIDGE: I thought me and you were going to look out for each other? I watch your back you watch mine. What happened to that?

(Sevenly and Donal enter. Midge and Sevenly have a moment of recognition—they've met, briefly, before.)

DONAL: Sevenly, this is my niece, Midge. Midge, my wife Sevenly.

SEVENLY: Hello.

VALERIE: Midge? Wasn't I saying something the other day about nice and respectable?

MIDGE: Golly, it sure is nice to meet you, Aunt Sevenly!

SEVENLY: Nice to meet you too.

DONAL: Midge is a pharmacist, at the what, the Walgreens?

MIDGE: Mm hm.

SEVENLY: Oh terrific, OK, sure.

MIDGE: You need anything from the pharmacy, you let me know. I get a good discount on Flintstones vitamins. For the kids.

DONAL: That's kind of you, Midge.

MIDGE: Sure I'll be seeing you around the neighborhood.

(Midge exits.)

SEVENLY: Donal, I think we should go home.

DONAL: You're right, it is getting to be about that time. Here. Why don't you go on ahead and pay the babysitter. *(Gives some money to Sevenly.)*

SEVENLY: You're not coming with?

DONAL: I'm going to help Valerie clean up. I'll be there in ten minutes.

SEVENLY: OK. Don't forget the brownie pan. Thank you so very much, Valerie, this all was wonderful.

(Sevenly exits. Valerie cleans up. Donal looks at the brownies.)

DONAL: Gosh, I'm sick of these things. Sevenly makes them all the time. They're too rich for me.

VALERIE: You said you could eat a whole pan of them.

DONAL: She thinks I like them, so I say I like them. I don't want to hurt her feelings. The kids like 'em, though. Especially Lucas who's going through a phase about food that looks like poo.

VALERIE: How old?

DONAL: Five, he's five. That age, y'know.

VALERIE: Bet they keep you feeling young.

DONAL: Ahh well, some days.

VALERIE: Bet they're wonderful.

DONAL: Oh, they're terrors.

VALERIE: Terrors sure, that's why you're going for lucky number seven.

DONAL: God willing. They are wonderful kids. They really are.

VALERIE: Mm.

DONAL: Do you like Sevenly?

VALERIE: She's . . . very nice.

DONAL: Valerie . . .

VALERIE: You think I'm not being sincere I say that? She's a nice girl, she reads to chickens, you're a lucky man.

DONAL: You're never going to drop those chickens, are you?

VALERIE: Donal. I'm happy for you.

(He hugs her, a warm embrace. She melts into it.)

DONAL: I don't believe one word of what Gail says. I know you had no hand in his death. Gail is upset, and when Gail gets upset she stays upset. She'll never forgive me for throwing her teddy bear into a lit barbeque and that was forty-some years ago. I was never very nice to her. She isn't the easiest person to love. Doesn't mean she's undeserving though . . . Valerie, you wouldn't happen to have any, em . . .

(Valerie gets a glass and a bottle of whiskey.)

DONAL: What's Midge still doing here?

VALERIE: She lives here.

DONAL: Imagine she makes a good salary at the pharmacy.

VALERIE: You have some concern with my daughter?

DONAL: Just saying she could afford to be out of your hair. Or out of your house at least, nevermind your hair. Which is very nice, by the way.

VALERIE: My house?

DONAL: Your hair. Looks nice.

(Valerie pours a drink for Donal.)

VALERIE: She's not going anywhere.

DONAL: She might, some day, want to.

VALERIE: . . . I don't think you need have concern with Midge, you mind your own kids.

DONAL: *(About drink.)* Have one yourself.

VALERIE: Oh, offering me my own liquor now?

DONAL: Will you have a drink with me, Valerie?

VALERIE: I don't drink.

DONAL: Since when?

VALERIE: Last year.

DONAL: Well I don't drink anymore either. Don't tell. *(Drinks. Coughs.)* Good lord.

VALERIE: It's a harsh brand. I keep it for the sentiment. Was Frank's favorite.

DONAL: You're not dwelling too much on it now?

VALERIE: No. No, not too much. *(Pause.)*

DONAL: Do you think he wanted to kill himself?

VALERIE: Would've been too big a commitment for Frank.

DONAL: What does that mean?

(Valerie waves it off.)

DONAL: Now I want to know what you meant.

VALERIE: Well he could hardly commit to having a piece of toast. Like the easiest question in the world "do you want toast?" Either you want toast or you don't want toast. It's toast. But with Frank it was all hemming and hawing, "ohhhhh . . . I don't know. Maybe. Is it you're making some is why you asked? I just, ohh, I just don't know." And this was a lousy piece of toast and not a suicide, so you can stop thinking that way, suicide. He may have been a touch melancholy but that's all. That's all. Have another if you're going to have one.

DONAL: Ohh, I don't know . . .

(*She pours him another. He doesn't drink it.*)

DONAL: Can't shake the odd feeling that my brother is still out there. That feeling, y'know. Creeps up in the night.

VALERIE: You didn't come to the funeral and that's what funerals are for. Good-byes and all.

DONAL: *(Getting his coat.)* Sevenly doesn't know anybody in town, and it would mean a lot to her to have a friend next door. She's a gentle soul. Would you be a friend to her? . . . I'm sorry, you don't have to . . .

VALERIE: I can be a good friend.

DONAL: If she mentions anything you think I should know . . .

VALERIE: Like what?

DONAL: I don't know.

VALERIE: Worried about her?

DONAL: We've always been so open with each other, now it's all, 'em. The move has been stressful, you know?

VALERIE: Sure.

DONAL: *(Pause.)* If I had been the one to ask you to marry me, would you have said yes?

VALERIE: You didn't ask me to marry you. Was Frank who asked.

DONAL: But would you have said yes if I had asked?

VALERIE: You never asked. *(Pause.)* Would you ever consider remarrying?

DONAL: Is that something you're thinking about now? Remarrying?

VALERIE: I'm saying if something were to happen to Sevenly. Would you remarry?

DONAL: I don't want to think about that.

VALERIE: *(Regarding the whiskey.)* Not going to finish?

DONAL: No.

VALERIE: Tell Sevenly I enjoyed meeting her, would you?

(*Donal exits. Valerie downs the whisky in Donal's glass. She picks up her meat cleaver, sharpens it, and then thunks it back into the block.*)

SCENE 3

Later that evening. The lights in the kitchen are out. Sevenly opens the door and peeks her head into the kitchen.

SEVENLY: Hello? *(Sevenly enters. She picks up her brownie pan from the table. She senses someone in the room.)* Hello.
(Midge turns on a light.)

SEVENLY: The door was unlocked. Donal forgot to bring home the brownie pan.

MIDGE: We would've returned it.

SEVENLY: I just thought . . . I would get it tonight.

MIDGE: Good brownies.

SEVENLY: Oh. I'm. Glad you liked them.

MIDGE: They're very rich. Chocolatey. Like fudge almost.

SEVENLY: They're Katherine Hepburn's brownies . . . I didn't want to wake anybody.

MIDGE: You didn't.

SEVENLY: And the door was unlocked, so . . .

MIDGE: We don't lock our doors.

SEVENLY: You should lock your doors. We always lock our doors. Err on the side of caution. Have faith that God will keep you safe, but a sturdy deadbolt never hurts.

MIDGE: We have that stitched on a pillow.

SEVENLY: I. It's getting late and Donal doesn't know I left the house.

MIDGE: You need his permission to leave the house?

SEVENLY: No, but.

MIDGE: But.

SEVENLY: If he wakes up and I'm nowhere to be found, I don't want him to worry that something happened to me.

MIDGE: He'd worry something had happened to you?

SEVENLY: Yes.

MIDGE: Something bad had happened to you.

SEVENLY: He's a worrier. He worries enough for the both of us. I worry too, but I'm not . . . "a worrier." In quotes. Not so much. How long have you been a pharmacist, Midge?

MIDGE: Two years.

SEVENLY: That's great, that's really great.

MIDGE: Junior pharmacist. I'm not one of the big dogs. I'm a peon. The big dogs peon me.

SEVENLY: I know what that's like. I used to work in an office. Accounting. I wasn't an accountant. I filed. I was good at filing. Very quick, accurate.

MIDGE: Are you cold?

SEVENLY: Ah. No. A little.

MIDGE: I bet your house is warmer than this.

SEVENLY: Yes.

MIDGE: That must be nice. *(Pause.)* I had a dog liked to sleep on my feet kept my feet warm. Dog's been gone couple years now.

SEVENLY: What was your dog's name?

MIDGE: Steve.

SEVENLY: *(With a little laugh.)* Steve? *(Pause.)* Steve is a very nice dog name. *(Pause.)* Pharmacists are sworn to customer privacy. Is that so? I read that somewhere. *Time* magazine, *Newsweek*.

MIDGE: It would be unprofessional to disclose information to outside parties.

SEVENLY: Oh. I was just curious when I inquired the other day at the pharmacy. I read about it and I was curious. That's all. I would appreciate it if you . . . if I could be sure you wouldn't . . . you wouldn't say anything to anybody. I would appreciate it very much.

MIDGE: It would be unprofessional of me to say anything.

SEVENLY: Thank you.

MIDGE: But . . . For future reference. If you want to be absolutely safe? Should make your inquiries at a pharmacy in another town. Here, people talk. They're terrible gossips. I hate everybody in this town. You'll probably like them, but I hate everybody.

SEVENLY: Hate is a strong word. It's a word I tell my children not to use.

MIDGE: Do you hate when your kids use it?

SEVENLY: Yes. No. Ooh, you got me.

MIDGE: I got you.

SEVENLY: Are you sure your mother's asleep, she can't hear us?

MIDGE: MOOOOOOOOOOOOOOM!!!!

SEVENLY: Sssshhhh!!! Oh no, don't wake her.

MIDGE: Once she's down she's down for eight hours. Eight hours exactly. Ideally, adults should get eight hours. Ideally. What time do you need to get up tomorrow?

SEVENLY: Six.

MIDGE: *(Checks her watch.)* Tomorrow is not going to be an ideal day for you.

SEVENLY: I am a very very nice person. That's what everybody at home says about me, that I'm very nice, that I'm a very nice good person who would never ever hurt anybody. And here I am. I feel terrible. I haven't been sleeping.

MIDGE: I can help you sleep.

SEVENLY: How can I sleep when I know I am going to hell.

MIDGE: You're not going to hell.

SEVENLY: I am, I am, it's people like me who go to hell.

MIDGE: You're not going to hell.

SEVENLY: I am, I am, I'm going to hell.

MIDGE: No you're not. Stop saying that. It's annoying.

SEVENLY: Have you ever killed anybody? Have you?

(Pause.)

MIDGE: Here, have one of Katherine Hepburn's brownies.

(Sevenly knocks the brownies away.)

SEVENLY: Fuck Katherine Hepburn's brownies! *(Shocked pause.)* Oh my goodness. Oh my. I don't really feel that way about Katherine Hepburn's brownies. They're really very good brownies. I don't know what came over me. I'm not usually this way.

MIDGE: It's all right. Would you like some coffee? I have some made.

SEVENLY: I don't drink coffee.

MIDGE: Cream? Sugar?

SEVENLY: I don't . . . what do you usually put in it?

MIDGE: Two sugars, two and a half.

SEVENLY: That's fine.

MIDGE: How far along are you?

SEVENLY: I don't know.

MIDGE: You don't know for sure how far along you are?

SEVENLY: Not. Exactly. No.

MIDGE: Can you maybe take a guess? Makes a difference, I'm saying, what I can do for you.

SEVENLY: I don't know.

MIDGE: All right.

SEVENLY: Donal has been through this six times already. He'll know soon enough. I need to do something soon. I wouldn't be doing this if it weren't absolutely imperative.

(Midge sets the mug in front of Sevenly.)

MIDGE: Here's what I can do. The pill you asked about the other day, it's emergency contraception. It's not abortive, it only prevents conception. The drug you need to terminate your pregnancy is RU-486, medical abortion. The manager of my pharmacy "forgets" to stock RU-486. So what I'm saying is I can't get it from my pharmacy. You need a doctor's prescription to . . . Hey. Hey. It's all right. Sevenly. Look at me. It's going to be all right. I know someone who will get it for you without going through a doctor. Nobody but me is going to have to know. OK? OK?

SEVENLY: Yeah, OK.

MIDGE: I'm not gonna tell, and don't you be having a breakdown either, feeling like you gotta tell somebody, especially don't let it slip around my mother because she's, like, this close to slapping a bumper sticker on her car, if you know what I mean.

SEVENLY: Who is this person, this someone you know.

MIDGE: Another pharmacist. Don't worry, I'll get it for you. It'll be a little more expensive then it would be otherwise, just so you know.

SEVENLY: Midge. Are you religious at all? Do you believe in God, in God's plan, in his will? Do you? I don't know you. I don't know anything about you. What kind of person are you?

MIDGE: I'm a very cool person.

SEVENLY: Does God think you're a very cool person?

MIDGE: The coolest.

SEVENLY: I've told you my biggest secret. Do you have anything you want to tell me?

MIDGE: Why. Like . . . why? Like, to reciprocate?

SEVENLY: Sure.

MIDGE: You might not like my biggest secret.

SEVENLY: Did you like my biggest secret? You didn't have to like it, it is what it is.

MIDGE: But I understand your secret. I understand fear. You're easy to comprehend.

SEVENLY: What is your biggest secret?

MIDGE: I like you.

SEVENLY: That's your biggest secret, that's, that's it? You like me, that's your biggest secret. Well that's not much of a secret.

MIDGE: You're OK with it that I like you?

SEVENLY: Well sure.

MIDGE: Would you want to do something sometime?

SEVENLY: What do you mean?

MIDGE: Would you like to go to lunch or see a movie sometime?

SEVENLY: Oh. Um. I don't know. I have six kids. If I want to do anything I need to get a sitter.

MIDGE: If I got you that sitter, if I paid for it, would you want to go to lunch and a movie some time?

SEVENLY: Um. Perhaps. Perhaps we can do that.

MIDGE: Perhaps perhaps or perhaps not a chance stop asking.

SEVENLY: Perhaps . . .

(Pause.)

MIDGE: You don't want to finish the coffee? It's very good coffee. It's fair trade coffee. It's expensive. But whatever. You want to leave so leave.

(Midge takes Sevenly's coffee to the sink.)

SEVENLY: No, wait—I'll—it's cooled down some, I can drink it.

(Midge returns the coffee mug to Sevenly. She drinks.)

MIDGE: It's very good coffee.

SEVENLY: It is, yes. Thank you . . . What about . . .

MIDGE: What.

SEVENLY: Your pharmacist friend.

MIDGE: He's not my friend. He's someone I know who gets me things.

SEVENLY: Midge.

MIDGE: Come back tomorrow. We'll talk about it tomorrow.

SEVENLY: I can't get away from the house.

MIDGE: You got away from the house tonight.

SEVENLY: Everybody's asleep.

MIDGE: Then come back when everybody's asleep, I mean, fuck, this isn't rocket science. Go home. Come back tomorrow. We'll talk about it tomorrow.

SEVENLY: Do you promise you won't say a word to anybody about this?

MIDGE: It would be very unprofessional for me to say a word to anybody about this.

SEVENLY: OK. OK. *(Sevenly puts her coat on, goes to the door.)*

MIDGE: But I've never been much of a professional.

(Pause.)

SEVENLY: I think we should talk some more.

MIDGE: Oh, you want to talk more?

SEVENLY: I do, yes.

MIDGE: OK. What would you like to talk about.

SEVENLY: What would you like to talk about?

(Sevenly stands with her mug, getting groggy.)

MIDGE: *(Lulling, careful.)* Have you been to the Wisconsin Dells? You should go. It's really close. Your kids will love it. It's like Las Vegas for Kids. Water parks. Go Karts. Bungee Jumping. Miniature Golf. The Wonder Spot. A futuristic house made entirely of styrofoam. And: The Famous Wisconsin Dells Ducks. They're military vehicles that can go on land and water. They take you on a tour all over and there's this joke the driver says driving down the winding road with a steep drop off fenced by chicken wire. And the driver says, "If it can hold a chicken, it can certainly hold a duck."

(Midge kisses Sevenly on the mouth. Sevenly drops the mug, her legs go weak, limbs heavy, eyes bleary. Midge catches her.)

SEVENLY: Oh my. Oh goodness.

MIDGE: You smell like soap.

(Midge helps her sit.)

MIDGE: Told you it's good coffee. Two sugars.

SEVENLY: What's . . .

MIDGE: Sssshhh, relax. You'll get some good sleep now. I'll get you the thing you need. I'll take care of you. *(Midge touches Sevenly's stomach.)* You don't have to have this baby if you don't want it. I do have one more secret. Haven't told anyone. Sevenly?

SEVENLY: . . . mmm . . .

MIDGE: My father's not dead. Not really.

(Lights to black.)

SCENE 4

Early the next morning. Sevenly is sound asleep in the kitchen. Valerie sits at the kitchen table, drinking coffee, working on the newspaper crossword. Pop music from a mix-tape plays on a tape recorder.

VALERIE: Actress Turner . . . Lana . . . Jai blank. J-A-I, then a blank, four letters . . . Don't worry yourself, I know it, I just thought you may want to chime in. Jai alai, in just about every morning's crossword being it's a boon for vowels, A-L-A-I, three out of four letters being vowels. Jai alai. Whatever that is. You know, I do these things every single morning and every single m— *(Sevenly wakes)* . . . hello. Gail keeps at me for not locking my doors, so funny it's you the first break-in I have, though not the first time I greet the day to someone asleep here. Midge has this no-good acquaintance, Gordy Laroux, works at the Starbucks, found him strung out asleep right here on the kitchen table. He has a bit of a mouth on him. I was forced to go after that stubble-chinned candyass with my meat cleaver.

SEVENLY: What time is it?

VALERIE: Near five-thirty.

SEVENLY: In the morning?

VALERIE: In the morning. You must've had some night, huh, you weren't drinking were you?

SEVENLY: No. No. I need to get home before Donal and the kids wake up. They'll be expecting breakfast and . . .

VALERIE: Have a sit there, take it easy. Just sit a moment . . . You wouldn't happen to know where Midge went, would you?

SEVENLY: No.

VALERIE: Her car's not here, thought that was a bit strange. Not like her to be the least bit productive before nine in the a.m. You see Midge earlier?

SEVENLY: Earlier?

VALERIE: Whenever you came in and before you conked out, you see my darling daughter Midge?

SEVENLY: I did, yes.

VALERIE: She didn't say where she was going?

SEVENLY: No.

VALERIE: Will she be back?

SEVENLY: I don't know.

VALERIE: Seems you two had a little talk over coffee last night or such.

SEVENLY: How—did you know?

VALERIE: Coffee mugs out, I saw.

SEVENLY: Ohh.

VALERIE: It's just not like her to take off. You know? Midge doesn't take off, she's very stagnant, like a pond. It's one thing Midge doesn't come home at night, because that's failure to return. Another thing entirely to be here one night then not the next morning because you know what that is? Success in leaving. I can make you some breakfast. Toast?

SEVENLY: No, thank you.

VALERIE: You sure now? Donal is worried about you. Seems to think something's wrong. Now you don't have to tell me anything, but if there happens to be something on your mind, well. Here I am. Somebody to talk to. I am a good listener, you know.

SEVENLY: Thank you, Valerie, but—

VALERIE: But you need to go home, OK then. Out of curiosity, because I know Midge isn't a social creature, you mind telling me what you talked about? She happen to say anything about her father?

SEVENLY: She . . . may have. I can't really . . . recall what she said.

VALERIE: You must've been tuckered out.

SEVENLY: I should go.

VALERIE: My door is open and unlocked if you ever need to talk about the baby.

(Sevenly halts.)

VALERIE: *(Valerie claps her hands.)* I knew it, dang I'm good! I'm right, right. Right? I am right, aren't I, you're going to have a baby?

(Gail enters the kitchen. She's dressed in most of her cop uniform for the cold weather—hat, gloves, boots—but she's not wearing a coat and her shirt is sweat through. She's high on crystal meth. She'll root through the cabinets, drawers and get cereal and a bowl and spoon.)

GAIL: So, ah. This waitress. Um. *(Laughs.)* Some waitress. SallyShirleySusie some "s" name some name starting with "s." Sssssandra? This waitress. Works at the Blue Squirrel you ever been to The Blue Squirrel the bar slash restaurant though it's not a restaurant restaurant they just serve buffalo wings on Friday night. You can throw your peanut shells on the floor do you like peanuts? Do you like peanuts?

SEVENLY: Peanuts are all right.

VALERIE: What in the blast is wrong with you?

GAIL: What in the blast is wrong with me what in the blast is wrong with you!

VALERIE: Where's your coat. It's freezing outside.

GAIL: I'm hhhhhot. I'm burning up. Here I'll show ya. *(gets a meat thermometer from the drawer and sticks it in her mouth.)* Check it out. Check out how hot I am. Feel my pulse. No really feel my pulse. My heart's gonna explode.

VALERIE: Are you on drugs?

GAIL: Am I on what?

VALERIE: Drugs.

GAIL: *(Nervous laugh.)* Look. Look. OK, look, OK. Look. OK. Look. If I don't know, ah. The baseline of narcotics, the, you know, what the kids are using, what good am I? If I don't know these things, these things we confiscate? Signs to look for in an individual who may be using such and such this, or such and such that. If I don't know these things intimately, personally, well. What good am I? I want to be the best police officer I can be. I have to know things.

VALERIE: What are you on?

GAIL: Nothing. crystal meth.

SEVENLY: What's crystal meth?

GAIL: I run the D.A.R.E program at the elementary school. Dare to keep kids off drugs, lemme know if you ever want me to have a chat with your kids. Me 'n' McGruff the Crime Dog are like THIS: *(Crosses fingers. Then dead serious.)* It's just a guy in a dog suit. *(Gail starts doing the crossword.)*

VALERIE: Gail.

GAIL: If you don't like peanuts, there's popcorn, which you can also throw on the floor I imagine, but, like, why would you do that? Why throw perfectly good popcorn on the floor. Why? I don't recommend eating the popcorn. I do not think they wash those popcorn baskets. I do not think those popcorn baskets are very sanitary.

VALERIE: That's not tic-tac-toe, that's a crossword puzzle.

(Gail throws the paper and pen aside.)

VALERIE: I think you ought to go home.

GAIL: I can't go home. That slut is in my home. That shit-eating taint-licking cocksucking slut is in my home that SallyShirleySusie with my husband and the two of them have the the the audacity to do it in my marriage bed.

VALERIE: This isn't the first time this has happened, Gail.

GAIL: No but by god it's the last time! *(Gail checks her gun.)*

VALERIE: Why don't you leave the gun here?

GAIL: I'm supposed to have my gun, Valerie, I'm supposed to have Rosalinda with me at all times. At all times! I am supposed to have Rosalinda with me AT ALL TIMES.

VALERIE: Sure but are you supposed to use Rosalinda for shooting husband-stealing sluts? Is that what the department issued her for. Yes or no.

GAIL: Yes?

VALERIE: No.

GAIL: No.

VALERIE: They did not issue your gun for shooting husband-stealing sluts. They issued it for other things.

GAIL: I shot that coyote in your backyard that one Thanksgiving.

VALERIE: I know, you did. And that wasn't a coyote but Midge's dog Steve, so give me the gun before you hurt someone.

GAIL: No. No way, no hoo-how. Hoo-how.

VALERIE: If you won't give it to me, let Sevenly take it from you.

SEVENLY: Guns make me feel very uneasy, Valerie.

VALERIE: I don't like guns either and I'm not asking you to use it. Just take it from Gail and set it down over there. You'll give it to Sevenly, won't you?

GAIL: Sure, yeah, sure. I'll give it to Sevenly, I'll give it to her. Come and get it.

(Sevenly approaches. Gail jabs the gun in Sevenly's stomach.)

GAIL: I'm just messin'.

(Gail holds the gun in her palm for Sevenly to take. Sevenly takes the gun. Valerie takes Gail by the hair and wrenches her head back.)

VALERIE: I am sorry for the way Eddie treats you, but you win little sympathy from me when you go all freewheeling with your firearms, pointing your gun like that when she's going to be having a baby.

GAIL: Ohh congratulations a baaaaybe, just what the world needs another baaaay—

(Valerie gives Gail's hair a tugging twist.)

GAIL: —hey!

SEVENLY: I'm. Not.

VALERIE: You said you were having a baby.

SEVENLY: You implied I was.

VALERIE: Oh. Well. It's just that Donal is worried about you, and I thought maybe that was a good guess being so fertile the way you are. It's not at all because I think you're fat.

SEVENLY: You think I'm fat?

VALERIE: No no no, you have a respectable figure, it's just that maybe I thought you were walking a little funny.

SEVENLY: You think I walk funny?

GAIL: I remember a time when you didn't have your hand in my hair, those were nice times.

VALERIE: Apologize to your sister-in-law for pointing your gun, and pray to whatever you need to pray to that she learns to tolerate you as much as I've tolerated you all these years.

GAIL: Yeah right.

(Valerie twists Gail's hair.)

GAIL: Ow. Sorry.

VALERIE: To her.

GAIL: You got my head wrenched back I can't exactly direct my apologies to anything but the cracked plaster in your dumb ceiling, you called me an idiot, well who's the idiot now—

(Valerie twists Gail's hair.)

GAIL: —ow! Is all I'm sayin is who's the idiot now—

(Valerie twists.)

GAIL: —ow! I'm just sayin—

(Valerie twists.)

GAIL: —ow!

(Valerie directs Gail's head toward Sevenly.)

GAIL: I'm sorry.

VALERIE: Go soak your head in the shower.

(Valerie releases Gail.)

GAIL: You're crazy, Valerie. I'm calling the cops.

VALERIE: You are the cops.

GAIL: Well good! I'm glad I know about this! *(Gail exits, immediately reenters.)* Going to grab my cereal I'm super hungry.

VALERIE: Grab your cereal.

GAIL: I'm super hungry.

VALERIE: I've heard that rumor.

GAIL: Who told you that???

VALERIE: Get what you need to get.

(Gail gets her cereal, opens the fridge, grabs the milk. There's only a splash left. She shakes it, then chucks it across the kitchen.)

GAIL: What am I supposed to do, eat this raw?

VALERIE: Do what you want.

GAIL: "Do what you want." Do what I want, I will do what I want. *(Stands there.)*

VALERIE: Well?

GAIL: I'm overwhelmed by the possibilities.

VALERIE: How about you pick up that flung milk gallon and put it back from whence it came.

(Gail does so, and looks through the fridge.)

VALERIE: Donal said he was worried about you and I assumed unrightly about what it was was bothering you. If the implication upset you, I apologize. It would be nice if we could be neighborly like. I'm not saying we have to. But if it's something we could work on, it might be nice to have a, you know, a . . .

SEVENLY: Friend?

VALERIE: Sure. One of those. And I don't at all think you're fat.

(Gail takes the milk gallon—the one filled with blood—from the fridge and pours it on her cereal and eats. Sevenly notices the peculiarity, but Valerie's back is to it.)

SEVENLY: Do you keep milk containers of blood in your refrigerator?

VALERIE: Sometimes, yes, don't you? One moment. Gail.

GAIL: What?

VALERIE: Probably don't want to be drinking that milk, Gail.

GAIL: What?

VALERIE: That funny-looking milk, Gail, probably don't want to be drinking that, it's going to taste as funny as it looks . . . Gail!

GAIL: What?

VALERIE: Excuse me.

(Valerie grabs the bloody gallon, trailed by Gail who has blood dripping down her chin.)

VALERIE: Sit.

GAIL: But—

VALERIE: Sit.

GAIL: No, but—

VALERIE: Sit!

GAIL: I'm going to sit but not because you say so. *(Sits.)*

VALERIE: This is blood.

GAIL: Well that's nuts.

VALERIE: Sit there. Relax.

(Gail sits, still, relaxing.)

VALERIE: OK? Good. *(Valerie wipes the blood off Gail's face.)* What I'm understanding is that you're a little vague about last night, am I right?

GAIL: I'm kinda vague about last night too.

VALERIE: I'm really not talking to you.

SEVENLY: There are certain vague parts.

VALERIE: Let me help you suss out your memory here. What's the last thing you remember talking about.

SEVENLY: The Wisconsin Dells. The Ducks.

VALERIE: The Ducks. That it? You can't remember what she said about Frank.

SEVENLY: Why do you want to know?

(Midge enters from outside. She has a pharmacy bag. Gail approaches her.)

GAIL: Hey do you have Gordy's number, phone number?

MIDGE: What's wrong with you?

GAIL: Nothing nothing.

VALERIE: Seems she got into some meth.

MIDGE: Did you confiscate meth from Gordy? That stuff's really not good for you. His recipe is wacky. *(To Sevenly.)* You OK? You wanna, uh. Meet me later.

VALERIE: Meet you later, you two are buddies now?

MIDGE: Yeah.

VALERIE: What have you been talking about.

MIDGE: We're just . . . friends. Right?

VALERIE: Well, seems you had an interesting conversation last night?

MIDGE: I thought we were keeping all that about the baby between me and you?

GAIL: *(Finally figuring it out.)* Ohhhhhh.

VALERIE: Gail, why don't you go lay down in my bedroom. Have a shower, lay down a bit, OK?

GAIL: *(To Sevenly.)* You're a liar. *(Gail exits.)*

VALERIE: Suppose you haven't told Donal about the baby.

MIDGE: Mom, don't . . .

VALERIE: It's none of my business, is it.

MIDGE: Well, OK. Good.

(Valerie grabs the pharmacy bag from Midge.)

MIDGE: Give that back.

VALERIE: You can't be feeding her drugs if she's going to have a baby. Sevenly, don't get mixed up in things like this.

MIDGE: Give me the bag. Mom. I'm warning you.

VALERIE: You're warning me?

MIDGE: I am.

VALERIE: You're warning me, oh, OK, I can see you've got your "I'm warning you face" on you, sure.

MIDGE: I'm going to count to three. One. Two. Three . . . Four . . . Don't make me count five, Mom.

(Sevenly, with Gail's gun.)

SEVENLY: Would you please give me the bag please!

(Pause.)

MIDGE: Here, Sevenly, give me the g—

SEVENLY: Sit down. Both of you. *(They do.)* What did you put in my coffee last night?

VALERIE: Midge, did you drug Sevenly? How many times have I told you not to do that to guests?

MIDGE: You don't mind when I do it to Uncle Eddie.

VALERIE: Eddie doesn't count.

MIDGE: I just gave her something to help her sleep some. Doesn't she look less tired?

VALERIE: You do look fresh.

MIDGE: I wanted you to not feel so bad.

SEVENLY: Give me the bag.

VALERIE: Sevenly, drugs aren't the answer. I don't know if you watch *20/20*.

MIDGE: Your notions concerning pharmaceuticals are antique so I'll forgive you your faux pas.

VALERIE: Faux pas.

MIDGE: It's French.

VALERIE: For?

MIDGE: It's just French—god—can't I say something French without you being all up in my grill?

SEVENLY: Give me the bag!!!

VALERIE: What sort of drug is this?

SEVENLY: We all have big families. Lots of children. It's just how it is, it's what's expected. Our faith. Our faith in God. I love my children, I love them dearly. Please understand that.

I have four sisters, two brothers. I'm the youngest in my family. Five years ago my oldest sister Susan died giving birth to her seventh child. Four years ago my second oldest sister Helen died giving birth to her seventh child. Three years ago my third oldest sister Debra died giving birth to her seventh child.

I was my mother's seventh child. My name was chosen in a resigned sigh. My name was chosen in the way you chose the wood finish of your own casket. There is no number beyond seven. It's something else. Something bigger that's striking us down. And if it's God, why would he do that to us? Why?

This will be my seventh child. I have to do something. Now. Give me the bag.

(Valerie doesn't release the bag. Sevenly puts the gun to Midge's head.)

MIDGE: Mom?

(Valerie gives up the bag to Sevenly. Sevenly puts down the gun, takes her brownie pan, and exits.)

VALERIE: Go check on your Aunt Gail. See she's all right.

(Midge exits. Valerie goes to the phone, dials.)

VALERIE: Donal? Hi, it's Valerie. You're sure right to be worried about your wife.

SCENE 5

Late that night. Gail at the kitchen table with a tape recorder and gun.

GAIL: *(Hits record button.)* OK. Hey. If my handwriting weren't all chicken scratch I'd leave a note but, uh. Crud. That's stupid. *(Stop, rewind, record.)* Hi. This is Gail. Um. If you're listening to this, it means, um. y'know, I'm probably dead. On the floor. Or something. No. *(Stop, rewind. record.)* Hi. Um. Blehhh. Poop. *(Stop, rewind, record.)* Let's see, uh. Hi. Gail here. These are my last words. Um, first to Eddie. You're a bastard for sleeping around with cocktail waitresses that Shirley or Susie or Sally. I let you follow your dreams and you didn't give two halfshits about my dreams and I had dreams, whole dreams, not just halfshits of dreams, and you better believe I would not have encouraged your baseball dream had I known the steroids would squash your little sperms. To Valerie. You were never good enough for my brother and if you didn't kill him then you drove him to it and that's all I have to say about that. Though you do bring me good cuts of meat and you don't make me pay for them. So, thanks. Midge, you irritate me. A lot. But I know how much you like Billy Joel so you can have my records *Glass Houses* and *52nd Street*. You're welcome to *Piano Man*, but it has a big scratch. And, also, have my collection of souvenir ashtrays, I've collected one from every state except Montana and Hawaii. And Delaware but *(Scoffs)*. Sevenly, if you want my Peter Paul and Mary record your kids might like that, it's very wholesome. Donal: I don't have anything for you. You made fun of me when we were younger and you made me feel stupid and you set my teddy bear on fire. It's you who should've died instead of Frank. And if the lot of you think I haven't been very nice, then that's just the way I am and what I felt is what I felt and I can't change things now. The crystal meth I did gave me clarity and perspective, mostly on the ineffectiveness and wrong-headedness of our school district's antidrug programs. *(Pause.)* I loved Frank and I miss him. I miss him so much. The other day, I drove to the lake, late, and the lake, it was frozen, and out there, I thought I saw Frank give me a wave before going under. It was my imagination I suppose. I'll have to live and die with that I suppose. And . . . Despite all the stuff I've said, I love most of you somehow, for some reason. That's it. Good-bye. *(Stop. Pause. Rewind. Play.)*

TAPE RECORDER: "Let's see, uh. Hi. Gail here. These are my last words. Um, first to Eddie. You're a —" *(Tape abruptly cuts to a pop song.)*

GAIL: Aww noooo. No no no no no no no! You didn't record any of that! My final words are lost! . . . You know what? Fine. This is good. I'm glad you didn't get that. *(She stops the tape.)* Here are my final words that nobody is going to hear: I'm going to kill myself and nobody is going to know why. This'll be just one more mystery. *(Gail puts the gun under her chin and pulls the trigger. Click—empty. She tries again. Empty chamber. She puts the gun to her head and is about to pull the trigger.)*

MIDGE: Bang. *(Midge enters, having been lurking the whole time.)*

GAIL: You weren't going to stop me from killing myself?

MIDGE: What about your Billy Joel records?

GAIL: What about my Billy Joel records.

MIDGE: You said I could have them.

GAIL: I said that when I thought I was going to be dead.

MIDGE: Right.

GAIL: And I'd have no use for them anymore.

MIDGE: Right.

GAIL: But I'm not dead so you see what I'm getting at? I'm alive and I still like Billy Joel so you can't have my Billy Joel records.

MIDGE: Not even *Piano Man* with the scratch?

GAIL: Not even *Piano Man* with the scratch and the fact that I want *Piano Man*, scratch and all, is a testament to Billy Joel's talent.

MIDGE: What about the ashtrays?

GAIL: Are you thick? I'm not dead!

MIDGE: So?

GAIL: So no. I have a duplicate Indiana, you can have Indiana.

MIDGE: I don't want Indiana.

GAIL: Well who does? What do you want?

MIDGE: New Hampshire.

GAIL: Get outta here. Go to bed. Look, I'm fine. I'm not going to do anything. I was in a bad way before. I feel better now. Like I needed to cleanse myself of that. You know? I don't know what got into me. Like that was a sign. That my gun didn't even go off.

(Midge opens the chamber and empties the contents of the gun on the table— jelly beans.)

GAIL: That's real good of you taking the bullets out of my gun. I'm rather fond of my brain, and I'm glad it's not all over the ceiling. You're my brother's daughter and I've treated you like just another no-good pistol whipped kid in the back of my squad car. I owe you an apology if you think I've been too hard on you.

MIDGE: That's nice of you, Aunt Gail.

GAIL: Apology accepted?

MIDGE: Yeah, yeah, apology accepted.

GAIL: Good. Great. Also owe you an apology for shooting your dog.

(Midge tenses, shocked, angry. Stares at Gail.)

GAIL: OK, here's what happened. It was Thanksgiving at your house, and you were at work, and I thought there was a coyote in the backyard. But after a six pack of Milwaukee's Best, pretty much everything looks like a coyote. I feel so much better telling you this! Like a two-ton weight's been lifted off my shoulders! Phew! . . . Midge? Now you're not mad, are you? I'm real sorry. I thought it would be better you thinking that he just ran off in the woods or something. No?

MIDGE: I would rather've known the truth.

GAIL: Is there anything I can do to make you feel better? *(Pause. Gail takes off one of her socks, puts it on her hand as a sock puppet.)* "Hello, Midge. Do you like cheese?"

(Midge stares at Gail. Then snorts a stifled laugh through her nose.)

GAIL: See, everybody likes sock puppets.

MIDGE: Nobody likes sock puppets.

GAIL: But you're smiling now, so, that's something. That's something, at least. Steve was a good dog, and it was quick and painless. Probably. You ever do meth?

MIDGE: Why?

GAIL: You wanna get high with me sometime, that might be fun. Something we can do together, like family bonding. I don't ever spend much time with you.

MIDGE: I don't do drugs.

GAIL: Well that strikes me as a bit hypocritical.

MIDGE: Do you know how dangerous meth is?

GAIL: I am an officer of the law. I run the D.A.R.E. program.

MIDGE: *(Overlap.)* You run the D.A.R.E program, yeah yeah yeah.

GAIL: You got anymore stuff in your stuff, *(Midge's backpack.)* fun stuff, just, you know, for fun and laughs. The night is young.

MIDGE: You should lay off the junk, Aunt Gail. I don't want to be the reason you don't wake up in the morning.

GAIL: Only person ever seemed to care about me was Frank. And he's gone. Least I know you inherited some of his goodness.

(Pause.)

MIDGE: What do you know about my mom and Donal?

GAIL: Valerie and Donal.

MIDGE: Yeah.

GAIL: *(Pause, uncomfortable.)* What do you want to know?

MIDGE: Everything.

SCENE 6

Next morning. Valerie at the kitchen table, newspaper, coffee. Gail has her head down in her arms, asleep on the table. Valerie rewinds the tape in the tape recorder, presses play.

TAPE RECORDER: "Let's see, uh. Hi. Gail here. These are my last words. Um, first to Eddie. You're a—" *(Tape abruptly cuts to a pop song.)*

(Valerie stops the tape.)
VALERIE: That was my favorite mix tape.
(Midge enters, beginning her breakfast routine.)
MIDGE: Can you be honest with me, Mom?
VALERIE: I've always said, honesty is best.
MIDGE: You've never always said that.
VALERIE: I've sometimes thought that's something I should've always said.
    That would've been a good something to always say. If I'm going to be
    honest with you Midge, I think if you ever want to find a decent man
    you need to make the effort.
MIDGE: *(Overlap.)* Ohhhhhh stop, just stop, stop talking, god.
VALERIE: I'll be damned if I see you spend the rest of your life alone. Maybe
    you'll get the inspiration to find a knot to tie yourself after you go to that
    retarded boy's wedding.
MIDGE: He didn't invite me.
VALERIE: You can probably go anyway.
MIDGE: But I didn't get an invitation.
VALERIE: What's he going to do, kick you out? He's retarded.
    (Donal enters with Sevenly.)
DONAL: Did you give my wife some illicit pharmaceuticals? Valerie called, told
    me you may have given her some pills.
    (Midge looks at Valerie.)
VALERIE: You know how I feel about it. I can't just stand by let something like
    this happen.
DONAL: I don't know who you think you are or what you said to my wife to
    make her consider this as an option. You are never to speak to her again.
    Do you understand?
MIDGE: *(To Sevenly.)* Did you take any?
DONAL: Was I unclear, the part where I said you're never to speak to her?
    (Midge looks at Sevenly, Sevenly looks away. Midge gets up.)
    I'm not done talking to you, you stay right here.
MIDGE: Oh, who are you now? My dad?
DONAL: You let this happen in your own house?
VALERIE: I was asleep when it happened. Seems to me you don't communicate
    so well with your wife there.
DONAL: We communicate just fine.
VALERIE: If that were so, I don't think you'd have to ask me to act the spy.
DONAL: What all went on here behind my back?
SEVENLY: Donal, I asked her for help.

DONAL: You don't need her help.

SEVENLY: You know what happened to my sisters . . .

DONAL: What happened to your sisters is not going to happen to you.

SEVENLY: How can you know?

DONAL: Because it's not going to happen. It's not. You're nervous. You were nervous with the other six, remember how nervous you were? She can't help you.

SEVENLY: You're wrong.

DONAL: I'm not.

(Gail falls out of her chair, passed out on the floor. Everybody looks at her.)

MIDGE: Maybe she took something.

VALERIE: Oh maybe you think? What did she take?

(Donal attends to Gail.)

DONAL: *(To Midge.)* This is your doing?

MIDGE: I told her not to do anything. She got into my stuff.

DONAL: Face down on your kitchen table and you don't do anything?

VALERIE: She was face down and she groaned a bit, and that's not far different from her usual demeanor.

DONAL: Gail? Wake up.

GAIL: *(Wakes.)* Mm. Frank?

DONAL: No, I'm not Frank . . . Gail? . . . Gail!

SEVENLY: She needs to go to the hospital.

DONAL: What did she take? Midge, what did she take.

MIDGE: Sleeping pills. Same stuff you use to help you sleep.

VALERIE: Oh geez, how many did she take?

MIDGE: Enough to kill her.

DONAL: Come on, give me a hand here. Valerie, help, please. Help me get her to the car.

VALERIE: Course.

DONAL: Jesus, this unbelievable.

(Valerie and Donal exit with Gail.)

SEVENLY: He flushed the pills in the toilet.

MIDGE: What do you want me to do?

SEVENLY: Get me more.

MIDGE: I'll get you the phone and address of a doctor. He'll take good care of you. It's the best way.

SEVENLY: Will you go with me?

MIDGE: Thought you didn't want to go anywhere with me.

SEVENLY: I need somebody there. You're the only one.

MIDGE: Really? Of course I'll go with you if you—

(*Donal enters. Sevenly moves away from Midge.*)

DONAL: Valerie went on ahead with Gail, we'll meet her there. Let's go.

SEVENLY: Donal, the kids.

DONAL: What ab—OK—mm—you'll have to go home then. I'll call you from the hospital, let you know.

SEVENLY: OK.

DONAL: It'll be all right. Go on home. I'll call soon.

(*Sevenly looks to Midge.*)

DONAL: I said go home.

(*Sevenly exits. Donal reaches into his coat, pulls out a checkbook, and writes her a check.*)

DONAL: Your mother and father may have turned a blind eye to your wicked behavior, but I will not. My wife is upset and fragile and confused. My sister clearly has emotional problems and you shove pills down her throat. Who do you think you are you can do this. Who do you think are? (*Hands the check to Midge.*) That should cover your expenses well enough.

MIDGE: Expenses for what?

DONAL: I want you to go away and that will cover your expenses for travel, living, anywhere, anywhere other than Baraboo. Fold that up, take it to the bank. You need more, give me a call. I'll send you more on the condition you don't set one toe back here.

MIDGE: This is a lot of money.

DONAL: It is, yes.

MIDGE: If I take this and use it to get a boob job, you'd keep sending me more as long as I don't come back?

DONAL: I don't think you need one of those.

MIDGE: You checking out my rack?

DONAL: No.

MIDGE: Yeah you were.

DONAL: I was not.

MIDGE: You totally were checking out my rack.

DONAL: There was no rack-checking-outing going on. Now take the money, Midge. Go, and don't ever come back. (*Pause.*) Are you crying?

MIDGE: I'm not crying.

DONAL: You don't need to be having a bit of a cry.

MIDGE: I'm not having a bit of a cry.

DONAL: Oh you're not, now? Then what's that leaking out of your eyes and your nose?

MIDGE: Tears and snot.

DONAL: *(Fatherly.)* Tears and snot, ohh, well, tears and snot. If that's not the recipe for a bit of a cry, I don't know what is. Here now. Here. *(Holding out a tissue.)*

MIDGE: No.

DONAL: Take it.

MIDGE: I don't want your stupid Kleenex and I don't want your stupid money. You're gonna need it for your wife's funeral when she has your stupid seventh baby. *(Midge slams the check down on the table.)* But you can't watch her all the time, can you? Who knows where she'll go next.

(Donal hands her a tissue. Midge dabs her eyes, wipes her nose.)

DONAL: Stay away from her. I meant what I said, I don't want you speaking to her.

MIDGE: She's lonely. She's scared. Round here, lonely and scared people have a habit of disappearing.

DONAL: Is that so?

MIDGE: Unfortunately.

DONAL: What lonely and scared people have disappeared? *(Pause.)* Do you know something about what happened to your father?

MIDGE: My who?

DONAL: Don't—Midge—I'm through playing games, you understand me now? What happened to Frank. *(Donal grabs her arm, hard.)* Did you do something to him?

MIDGE: *(Shakes him off.)* Don't touch me! Don't.

DONAL: Please, just, Midge.

MIDGE: Wasn't me did anything. He and mom had a fight and he left for the lake. He couldn't stay here anymore, knowing the truth. Was real low what mom said to him. He wasn't strong enough for truth.

DONAL: What did your mother tell him.

(Pause.)

MIDGE: Is it true?

(Pause.)

DONAL: You're Frank's girl, that's that. We are not speaking of this ever again. Understand?

MIDGE: Fine.

DONAL: You're Frank's girl. OK?

MIDGE: OK.

DONAL: This is what drove him out to the lake that night, hearing that?

MIDGE: No, that didn't drive him out there. Was me drove him out there. In my car. He needed a ride, couldn't get his car started.

DONAL: You were with him that night.

MIDGE: Yeah.

DONAL: What were you doing out there?

MIDGE: Fishin'. I got cold. Went home. Left him out there. And he never came home.

DONAL: You just left him out there on the lake?

MIDGE: He wanted me to go away.

DONAL: Is that the truth. You left him out there and he never came home?

(Pause.)

MIDGE: I can show you where he was. Where I left him, on the lake. Would you like that? If I showed you where I left him?

DONAL: All right. Show me where you left him.

MIDGE: It's cold out there, you know. Always colder that you expect. Bundle up.

DONAL: I'll meet you outside.

(Donal exits. Midge puts on her coat, picks up Valerie's meat cleaver, and exits.)

SCENE 7

The next morning. Valerie at the kitchen table. Midge enters, breakfast routine. She's limping on a sprained ankle.

VALERIE: Gave a call over to the hospital this morning, Eddie says your aunt is doing fine today, just fine. Eddie was worried about her. Nothing like a near fatal overdose to keep a marriage together. *(Pause.)* Funny that Donal didn't show at the hospital. Or last night. Or this morning, for that matter.

MIDGE: That's weird.

VALERIE: Wonder what happened to him.

MIDGE: He didn't show up this morning?

VALERIE: No.

MIDGE: Yeah that's weird.

VALERIE: Is weird, isn't it. Also called Sevenly. She's a bit distraught.

MIDGE: Oh yeah?

VALERIE: Husband up and vanished, of course she's upset.

MIDGE: I have to get ready for work.

VALERIE: You seem a bit gimpy this morning, sweetheart. Why don't you have a seat. What's the matter with your foot?

MIDGE: I sprained it.

VALERIE: Doing what? *(Pause.)* Remember when you were a little girl and you had that subscription to *Highlights Magazine for Children*. You remember that, *Highlights Magazine* . . .

MIDGE: Yeah, yeah.

VALERIE: And in every issue they had that "What's Wrong with This Picture?" game and there was, oh, a dog with a boot on his head or the sun outside the kitchen window was square or maybe it was, instead of square, it was purple, a purple sun, or something, right? And you had to stare at this picture. Had to figure out what was wrong with it, circle all the things that were wrong with a particular domestic scene. Is this ringing a bell or am I just talking . . .

MIDGE: Yeah, yeah.

VALERIE: *Highlights Magazine,* very educational, OK. Well. What's wrong with this picture, Midge?

MIDGE: What picture?

(Valerie gestures indicating the entire kitchen.)

MIDGE: I don't know.

VALERIE: You didn't even try. *(Valerie draws a circle in the air around her cleaver in the butcher block.)* You don't see what's wrong with this here? How 'bout now? How 'bout now? Now? If I keep circling you think you may get it? . . . a little ding in the blade that I know was not there yesterday. I can account for all the other dings in my cutlery, but this teeny tiny little ding is not one I can account for.

MIDGE: You account for your dings?

VALERIE: Mm hm.

(Midge stands.)

VALERIE: Sit.

MIDGE: I dropped it, I dropped your meat cleaver, I'm sorry, OK. Sorry.

VALERIE: When did you drop it?

MIDGE: When I was running through the woods.

VALERIE: OK, let's go back, because I'm running into a little problem with your storytelling here. What I understand is—and feel free to jump in, help me fill out the details where you can—While I was at the hospital with your aunt—

MIDGE: Aunt Gail.

VALERIE: Really don't need help with the obvious stuff.

MIDGE: Fine.

VALERIE: While I was at the hospital—

MIDGE: Don't need my help, fine.

VALERIE: Are you done? At the hospital, with your aunt who overdosed on pills you let into this house.

MIDGE: I didn't force Aunt Gail to do anything.

VALERIE: But you enabled her, isn't that so. You're an enabler as John Stossel would say.

MIDGE: Is it my problem she's inherently flawed?

VALERIE: No, it's not, but it's your problem she's going to stay that way, and I have an idea that maybe you weren't running through the woods for exercise. Why did you bring my meat cleaver to the woods?

MIDGE: For protection. Out in the woods. I knew I'd be coming back alone, again.

VALERIE: Well the woods can be scary, sure. Whatever you have to do to feel safe, I understand.

MIDGE: You're not mad I took your cleaver?

VALERIE: No, 'course not.

MIDGE: But I dinged it.

VALERIE: Accidents happen. Just, in the future, please ask me if you'd like to borrow my cutlery, all right?

MIDGE: All right.

(Valerie hits Midge with a stunning blow upside the head with a coffee mug.)

MIDGE: AAAAAOOOW!!! OW! FUCK!

VALERIE: That always works in the movies, I don't understand. *(Valerie grabs Midge by the neck and wrangles her in a sleeper choke hold to compress the carotid artery and black her out.)* Did you see in the paper this morning, city council voted to abolish the beer tent at the Old-Fashioned Days Festival. Didn't I say that was going to happen sooner or later, because it's a family event? You said it wasn't going to happen, but from my mouth to God's ear. *(Midge goes limp.)* . . . I'm sorry, sweetheart, just a bit of necessary prep work.

MIDGE: *(Wakes.)* What the fu—?

(Valerie slams Midge's head on the table and pushes her on top of the table. Midge is finally unconscious. Valerie hog-ties Midge's feet with her robe tie. Sevenly enters with her brownie pan.)

SEVENLY: Valerie, have you heard from D . . . ?

VALERIE: Oh! She's fine. Midge has these spells. Are those more brownies for us?

SEVENLY: I had leftovers.

VALERIE: That's really nice, I've never had a next-door neighbor as nice as you before.

SEVENLY: Why are you doing that?

VALERIE: She'll be wily and I don't want her hurting herself. Really, it's for her own safety and comfort.

SEVENLY: Have you heard from Donal yet?

VALERIE: Mm, no.

SEVENLY: This isn't like him at all.

VALERIE: Disappearing on you.

SEVENLY: He wouldn't just . . . not come home. He wouldn't just not call me, even going to be the least bit late. I should call someone but the only other person I know is Gail in the hospital and—well unless that's where Donal went this morning, do you think that's where he is?

VALERIE: There's an off-chance that Donal may not be coming back.

SEVENLY: What are you talking about?

VALERIE: Well . . . things happen. You know?

SEVENLY: No, Valerie, I don't know, what are you talking about?

VALERIE: The way it was with Frank is . . . was a couple days before we all figure out what happened. So you think maybe he's just . . . out. Until he's not just "out" but gone. Gone. You start thinking thoughts you'd never thought you'd think. The things you'd miss if he didn't come walking through that door like he did day after day. Like Frank could grill a good steak. Always said it was because the quality cuts I brought home from the shop, but I could grill that same exact meat and it would taste like shoe. Frank could probably grill a shoe and make it taste like filet mignon. I don't know how he did it. He was a vegetarian. Such is a person's contradictory nature.

SEVENLY: Valerie, where's my husband?

VALERIE: Midge knows the answer to that question. I'm glad you dropped by. Gimme one sec, I'll be right back.

(Valerie grabs her cleaver and exits. Sevenly looks at Midge, brushes back Midge's hair to see the coffee-mug welt.)

MIDGE: *(Wakes suddenly.)* . . . the fuck just happened . . . ? Wh—? Ohhh my fucking god my head . . . You need to go away. Don't be here. This is gonna be bad. This is gonna be really bad. Um. Yeah, this is gonna be bad. But you could untie me first.

SEVENLY: Valerie said you know where Donal is.

MIDGE: Untie me and I'll tell you.

SEVENLY: Tell me and I'll untie you.

MIDGE: How 'bout instead of that, you untie me then I'll tell you.

SEVENLY: You already said that.

MIDGE: I know you don't like me but I'd do anything for you. Please. Help me. Please.

(Sevenly starts to untie her.)

MIDGE: Hurry.

(Valerie enters with the book Goodnight, Moon. *She stands watching Sevenly work at the difficult knots.)*

VALERIE: See, what I haven't mentioned yet is that Midge took Donal out to the lake. Little field trip to the lake. Just her, Donal, and my meat cleaver.

(Sevenly stops untying.)

VALERIE: How 'bout you fill us in on the details.

MIDGE: I took him to the lake. I left him out there.

VALERIE: You didn't just leave him. I know you did something to him.

MIDGE: How do you know that?

VALERIE: I know you, Midge. I'm your mother and I know you best. You did something to him. *(Valerie pulls out Donal's check, shows Midge.)* Found this on the table. You want to tell me why Donal wrote you a check for a large sum of money?

MIDGE: He wanted me to go away.

VALERIE: Uh huh.

MIDGE: He did, he wanted me to go away, so he wrote me a check.

VALERIE: Uh-huh.

MIDGE: It's the truth!

VALERIE: But you're here . . . and Donal is not . . . which seems contrary to that truth. Sevenly? What do you think?

SEVENLY: It seems contrary.

MIDGE: Well sorry if it seems odd.

VALERIE: Well sorry you're gonna look odd if I tear one of your ear flaps off the side of your head.

(Valerie twists one of Midge's ears.)

MIDGE: Gaaaahhhhhh!!! Stop!!!

(Valerie stops.)

VALERIE: I'm just noting this morning felt familiar, don't you think? Similar to a morning last year when your father didn't come home, don't you think? Am I having unreasonable thoughts or am I suffering a stunning case of déjà vu.

MIDGE: You think I killed Dad?

VALERIE: I don't know, did you?

(Midge shakes her head, sadly.)

VALERIE: Suppose you didn't get a good look at the ding you left in my blade, but you see it there now, good and close. Riiiiight there. And you see how sharp this is too, dontchia? It would be one swift chop right here *(Indicates Midge's neck.)* and maybe I'd have some peace to see the red cascade of you wash over the floor. Now what do you have to say to me about this *(Indicates check.)*

MIDGE: I like the way Donal signed the check. Me and him write with a similar lilt. Did you see the segment on *20/20* about how parents and kids often have similar handwriting?

(Valerie slams the book on the table.)

VALERIE: How dare you imply that! How dare you! Frank adored you.

MIDGE: He could barely speak to me.

VALERIE: You answer me now: what did you do to Donal?

MIDGE: Would it make you feel better to hear I sunk your meat cleaver in his neck before I ran off? Fine. So I did.

(Valerie hands Goodnight, Moon *to Sevenly.)*

VALERIE: Looks like my little chicken may need some soothing from the chicken-reading expert. Was always Midge's favorite at bedtime. Start reading . . . Said start reading.

(Sevenly starts reading Goodnight, Moon *out loud.)*

VALERIE: Remember, now, when you were a little girl and you'd sometimes come to the butcher shop Saturdays to watch me chop chickens. And you asked where they went when they died? And I said they went to heaven . . . just remember when you believed my stories with all your heart and you'll hardly feel the pain elsewhere. *(Valerie holds Midge's head down, cleaver at the ready.)* You tell me the truth now or this blade is going through your neck.

MIDGE: Was your fault he left, Mom! Was always your fault!

(Valerie raises the cleaver to chop Midge's neck, and Midge cries in terror. The kitchen door flies open, and Donal roars into the kitchen. Valerie halts, stunned. Donal is bundled up in scarf, hat, hood, obscured under layers, near frozen.)

DONAL: Can't feel my hands. They're there, I know. I see them. But if I can't feel them it's like they're not even there. Feel my hands, please, feel them, tell me they're there.

(Sevenly squeezes his frozen hands. He yowls in pain. She lets go.)

DONAL: No no don't stop it's all right. It's all right. I'm cold. It hurts.

SEVENLY: Where were you?!

DONAL: The lake! The woods! I was out there a long time searching! I thought maybe I could find my brother out there but I got lost. She left me and

I got lost on the lake in the woods through the night. The only thing that kept my legs moving was you, thinking of you, getting back to you.

SEVENLY: I thought you were dead.

DONAL: I'm alive. My joints are burning. It's beautiful out there. The lake, at night. All those stars. Silent and cold and empty. *(He collapses on the floor.)*

SEVENLY: Donal!

DONAL: I thought I'd find him out there but there was nobody out there but me walking on the frozen water.

SEVENLY: Donal, please, get up.

DONAL: God I'm tired. I could sleep for a thousand days.

SEVENLY: Can you stand?

DONAL: I just want to sleep here.

SEVENLY: I'll get you home to bed. You're not sleeping on the floor.

DONAL: Sweetheart lemmie just take a nap.

SEVENLY: Come on.

DONAL: Just a quick nap.

SEVENLY: You're getting off the floor and getting home to bed. On your feet, soldier. Up. You made it this far, just a little bit further to bed . . . Donal! Get up!

(She helps pull him to his feet.)

Are you steady?

DONAL: I'm OK. Yeah.

SEVENLY: Look, you're off the floor.

DONAL: I am, it's way down there now.

(Gail enters. She has a teddy bear.)

GAIL: Eddie was asking about the T-bones again, and if you have any T-bones again . . . *(Looks at Donal, Sevenly, Midge, Valerie.)* Something happen here? *(Pause.)* So I've been discharged. Didn't overdose nearly enough for a longer stay according to my insurance policy. Hey, you hear me ask you about the meat?

VALERIE: Eddie, T-bones, yeah.

GAIL: *(Gives the teddy bear to Sevenly.)* For you! Well, for your baby. I remembered something about the other day when I was in my drug wackadoo. And if you and Donal do name it after Frank, that would be great. It really would. In the hospital there was this little boy, little bald-headed boy. Leukemia. That's why he's bald. Had this big box of teddy bears. Gave one to me. So there ya go.

SEVENLY: Thank you. Thank you. Donal. Let's go home.

DONAL: Oh God I love you. You're so beautiful.

SEVENLY: Time to go home.

(Sevenly and Donal exit.)

GAIL: Thanks for driving me to the hospital yesterday, I really appreciate that. I'd like to return the favor, so feel free to give me a call if you need a ride home from the hospital today.

VALERIE: A ride home from the hospital today?

GAIL: For the stitches.

VALERIE: For the stitches?

GAIL: For when I stuck you with my pocket knife.

VALERIE: For when you what?

(Gail sticks her pocket knife in Valerie's side.)

GAIL: Not so piss-ant now, eh?

VALERIE: You stabbed me!

GAIL: Ohhh is that what I did, 'cause I thought I baked you a cake.

VALERIE: The heck?

GAIL: For my poor brother Frank. The Gail of last week would've stuck this in your neck, but I'm a better person now. I even asked at the hospital, if I were to hypothetically stab somebody, where would be a good place so I wouldn't kill them. Say what you will about health care in this country, I have found doctors nothing but courteous and helpful. So that's that. We're fair and square now, Valerie. I forgive you for whatever you did to Frank. I forgive you.

(Gail holds her hand out to Valerie. Valerie takes her hand and they shake.)

GAIL: Yeah . . . that's what I thought. *(Gail tosses Valerie's hand aside, disgusted.)* You wouldn't've shook my hand for forgiveness if you didn't feel the need for my forgiveness, so you know what I'm forgiving you for? I'm forgiving you for nothing. I don't forgive you. You did something and you feel guilty and I will never forgive you.

(Gail exits the kitchen, slamming the door. Valerie unties Midge. Midge jumps off the table and grabs her stuff to leave.)

VALERIE: *(Feeling her stab wound.)* Ah geez. Ow. *(Realizing Midge is leaving.)* Midge? Midge? You'll be back for dinner yeah?

MIDGE: No. *(Heads to the door.)*

VALERIE: Wait. Wait please. Please don't go! . . . please . . .

(Midge stops. She gets the gallon of blood from the fridge.)

MIDGE: Heard a rumor round town you butchered him. Chopped off his hands, mailed 'em to Hong Kong. Chopped off his feet, fed 'em to polar bears at the zoo. Stabbed him in the neck with a meat thermometer. Wrenched open an artery, drained the hot blood out of him. Didn't spill a drop. *(Midge sets down the gallon of blood.)*

VALERIE: Well, I loved every drop of him . . . Didn't always seem so, did it?

MIDGE: No.

VALERIE: No. It didn't, I suppose. *(Pause.)* The gossip in this town. Shouldn't believe everything you hear, you know that. *(Pause.)* You never told me what happened out on that lake with your dad. You came home and he wasn't with you. You never told me what happened.

MIDGE: You know why I didn't tell you?

VALERIE: Why?

MIDGE: You never asked.

(Pause.)

VALERIE: What happened?

MIDGE: He just left, Mom.

VALERIE: That's it?

MIDGE: Walked off into the night.

VALERIE: God. Lots of ways to kill a person, no death worse than a heartbreak to drive them away into that cold lonely night. I am guilty. And I'm going to get away with it.

END OF PLAY

ELECTION DAY

Josh Tobiessen

PLAYWRIGHT'S BIOGRAPHY

Originally from Schenectady, New York, Josh Tobiessen studied improv in Chicago with Del Close and Charna Halpern and received an MA in theater and drama from the National Univesity of Ireland, Galway, and an MFA in playwriting from the University of California. He is a founding member of the Irish theater company, Catastrophe, which produced his plays at such venues as the Galway Arts Festival and the Dublin Fringe Festival. *Election Day* was a finalist in the Kendeda Graduate Playwriting Competition at the Alliance Theatre in Atlanta, Georgia. His other plays include *Brandy Bean's Big Break, Red State Blue Grass,* and *Spoon Lake Blues.* He lives in Brooklyn, New York.

ORIGINAL PRODUCTIONS

Election Day was first performed at UCSD's Baldwin New Play Festival 2006 in San Diego. The production was directed by Jerry Ruiz. The stage manager was Jinny Parron, with set design by Nikki Black, light design by Christian DeAngelis, and costume design by Emily DeAngelis. The cast was as follows:

CAST

EDMUND	Rufio Lerma
CLEO	Liz Jenkins
ADAM	Brandon Taylor
CLARK	Larry Herron
BRENDA	Hilary Ward

Election Day was produced by the Second Stage Theatre on August 1, 2007. The production was directed by Jeremy Dobrish, with lighting by Michael Gottlieb, sets by Steven Capone, costumes by Mattie Ulrich, and sound design by Jill BC DuBoff. The cast was as follows:

CAST

EDMUND	Michael Ray Escamilla
CLEO	Halley Feiffer
ADAM	Adam Green
CLARK	Lorenzo Pisoni
BRENDA	Katharine Powell

CHARACTERS

ADAM: Graphic designer. Brenda's boyfriend. Cleo's adopted brother.
BRENDA: Public-defense lawyer. Adam's girlfriend.
CLARK: Mayoral candidate.
CLEO: Adam's adopted sister. Cat lover.
EDMUND: Waiter at the Pine Nut Café. TREE leader.

SETTING

A small American city.

TIME

November. The present.

ELECTION DAY

SCENE 1

Brenda's apartment. Adam, just out of bed, enters from the bedroom door while a more energetic Brenda runs around the living area getting dressed for work.

BRENDA: *(With some fanfare.)* Happy Election Day!

ADAM: Is that today?

BRENDA: You know it is. It's 7:30. You should get dressed so you can vote before work.

ADAM: *(Tired.)* Oh man.

BRENDA: Wakey wakey! Pick out a work shirt so I can put a campaign button on it.

ADAM: I'm not going to work. Mr. Singh said we didn't have to come in today.

BRENDA: Really?

ADAM: Yeah, so we wouldn't have him as an excuse for why we didn't vote.

BRENDA: But you are going to vote.

ADAM: Yeah, of course. Just now I have all day so there's no rush. You want me to make you some coffee?

BRENDA: We only need to go down the road. It's in that church.

ADAM: I know. You printed me a map, you big dork. I already knew anyway.

BRENDA: But what if they need you to print up some posters or flyers at the last minute?

ADAM: I don't use the printers, I just design stuff. Albert is probably going to be there.

BRENDA: If you're going to skip work today, you might as well be productive and help me hand out flyers downtown. You haven't done much for the campaign so far.

ADAM: I'm not skipping work. I got the day off. And I was actually hoping that we could move most of my stuff over here today. If that's productive enough for you.

BRENDA: Today?

ADAM: Well, I need to be out by this weekend.

BRENDA: This weekend? *(Checks her Blackberry.)* Ohmigod, yeah, you're right.

ADAM: I thought it might be fun if we did it together. Like the people in that bank commercial.

BRENDA: Sorry, I've just been so busy with the campaign.

ADAM: You're just volunteering. What are they going to do if you don't show up?

BRENDA: Adam, I'm not using my vacation time on this campaign because I like to punch clocks. I'm doing it because I believe that Jerry Clark would be a disaster as the mayor of this city.

ADAM: So what am I supposed to do? Just move all the stuff by myself?

BRENDA: It's the day of the election. I can't help you today.

ADAM: Well—

BRENDA: Ok, be quiet and let me think for a second. *(Thinks and solves problem.)* Does Cleo still have a job? Call her. It'll give her something to do.

ADAM: I don't want to call her.

BRENDA: Well, you don't have a lot of options. She's your sister so she has to help.

ADAM: And the reason that we're together, as she always points out.

BRENDA: I don't think that was her intention when she got arrested. I thought of her because she still has that truck, right?

ADAM: I assume so.

BRENDA: There you go. That'll help. And then when you're done you can both hand out flyers downtown. And make sure she votes.

ADAM: You do like your politics.

BRENDA: I was student council president my senior year of high school.

ADAM: I know, you told me, why do you think I love you? *(He kisses her. Briefly at first but then tries to get something going.)*

BRENDA: What are you doing?

ADAM: Come on, I have the day off. You can be an hour late. I'll make us some omelets. We can eat them in bed.

BRENDA: I already ate a muffin. These posters and flyers need to get out there ASAP for the morning commute.

ADAM: Well maybe you can come back here for lunch at least?

BRENDA: I'll try.

ADAM: Good. Hey, you might as well take the car today since we'll have her truck.

BRENDA: Your car?

ADAM: It's our car now. We live together right? Mi auto su auto. Just like I could use your computer or your shampoo.

BRENDA: Don't use my shampoo.

ADAM: OK.

BRENDA: It's scientifically formulated for my hair type. And you'd smell like a girl. And you really shouldn't use my computer either. I have a lot of confidential information dealing with the cases that I'm working on. You have your own anyways.

ADAM: Well if mine broke and I needed to check my e-mail. I could use yours then, couldn't I?

BRENDA: Sure.

ADAM: You OK?

BRENDA: Yeah. I'm sorry. Stress. Just don't forget to vote today.

ADAM: Who are we voting for again?

BRENDA: Don't joke.

ADAM: Yes ma'am.

BRENDA: I'm serious. Look at me. *(He does.)* Now promise me you'll vote.

ADAM: I promise you that I'll vote.

(Brenda slaps him across the face.)

ADAM: Wow, what was that?

BRENDA: That's so you remember.

ADAM: All righty, well . . .

(Adam tackles Brenda and starts to playfully spank her.)

ADAM: That's so you remember to put away the milk, and that's so you remember to tivo *The Daily Show*—

BRENDA: Get off me.

ADAM: That's so you remember to shave your legs—

BRENDA: Adam, get the hell off me!

ADAM: . . . Sorry. I thought we were . . .

BRENDA: We're not.

ADAM: Sorry.

BRENDA: Take a picture of your ballot with your phone when you vote and send it to me.

ADAM: Is that even legal?

BRENDA: Adam.

ADAM: I'll vote, OK. Do you not trust me?

BRENDA: Can I? This is a serious runoff. The polls have them in a dead heat. It's going to be a handful of votes that win this one.

ADAM: *(Under his breath.)* It's just the mayor.

BRENDA: Adam!? The next mayor is going to have an awful lot of extra money to decide what to do with if they log the forest and put up that casino they're thinking about—

ADAM: There's going to be a casino?

BRENDA: Are you reading the articles I cut out for you?

ADAM: Some of them. You cut out a lot of articles.

BRENDA: Adam, you're supposed to know this. That's the whole reason we vote. We learn the facts and then we help decide what's best for the community. If you don't know the facts then what are you voting for? This is important to me.

ADAM: Absolutely. I've read most of them. I can read the rest before I vote.

BRENDA: Good. Do that.

ADAM: Just try to relax, Brenda Bear. It's going to be fine.

(Adam kisses Brenda and tries to get something started again.)

BRENDA: Adam, please. You know I can't. Not with the election being so close. Are you not stressed out?

ADAM: I'm not that stressed.

BRENDA: Well you should be. God. Sometimes when I see someone drive down the street with a "Vote Clark" bumper sticker I wish I had a rocket launcher.

ADAM: Wow.

BRENDA: Jerry Clark does not deserve to be the mayor of our city. He's just using this city as stepping stone so he can follow in his daddy's footsteps to Washington. And he's an asshole.

ADAM: Hey, come on. Don't get so worked up about it.

BRENDA: This is who I am. This is the person that you're moving in with.

ADAM: I know who you are, Brendy. Don't worry, OK? It's going to be all right. *(Thinks and tries to solve problem.)* Here's what I'm going to do for you. I'm going to fix us something nice for dinner tonight. That Indian chicken you like? And we'll have a romantic little celebration.

BRENDA: That sounds nice. Hopefully we'll have something to celebrate.

ADAM: Hey Brenda Bear. I'm moving in.

BRENDA: Right, obviously that, but hopefully the election will go well too.

ADAM: Sure. If we win we'll have something extra to celebrate.

BRENDA: I have to go. Call me when you and Cleo are ready to come hand out flyers.

ADAM: OK, I love you.

BRENDA: Please please please remember to vote.

(A kiss on the cheek and Brenda leaves.)

ADAM: You love me too.

(Adam looks around a little bit and goes back to bed.)

(Lights.)

SCENE 2

Cleo is sitting on a bench on the sidewalk. Edmund enters and sits next to her holding a paper bag. They sit for a moment enjoying the fresh morning air.

EDMUND: The sun is up. But the birds of the morning, sing a sad lament.

CLEO: Hey Running Bear!

EDMUND: Cleo.

CLEO: What?

EDMUND: Oh for the love of god, just say it.

CLEO: It's me, Eddie.

EDMUND: We've been over this. If you don't say it, that means your situation's been compromised. Has your situation been compromised?

CLEO: No.

EDMUND: So say it.

CLEO: Something about sad birds.

EDMUND: No, that's what I say. What do you say?

CLEO: Eddie—

EDMUND: What?

CLEO: I forget, all right?

EDMUND: Do you want to be a part of my group or not?

CLEO: That's not the fun part for me, all the secret stuff. That's not why I hang out with you guys.

EDMUND: You know, I shouldn't even be giving you this package without hearing the password.

CLEO: Come on. Don't be like that. Your hair looks good today.

EDMUND: No. I'm serious. This is serious. An organization like this, like the one that you and I belong to, has to maintain a certain level of discipline.

CLEO: Sure, I know that.

EDMUND: Not because we need to keep our profit margin from dipping, but because if we slip up we're fucked. You, me, Raymond, Lakisha, and Moonstar are all fucked.

CLEO: It's just the passwords, Eddie. That's the only thing I think is silly.

EDMUND: Silly?

CLEO: Not silly but—

EDMUND: This is a big day for you. For all of us. It's not going to be like last time, this is the real deal.

CLEO: I know.

EDMUND: So you'd better be pretty sure about this.

CLEO: I am, I really am.

EDMUND: Good. The earth thanks you.

CLEO: Cool. I like how in touch you are. With the planet and all that.

EDMUND: It's a big green pulsating planet we're on, and she has a lot to say. You just have to listen.

CLEO: I can do that.

EDMUND: *(About a passing vehicle.)* Like this guy out here: not listening.

CLEO: Asshole.

EDMUND: Fucking Humvee. Choking up our traffic arteries, drinking gasoline like a frat boy at a beer keg. That's a military vehicle, you know, on the streets of our city. Who's he at war with?

CLEO: Really.

EDMUND: I'll tell you who: Us. He's at war with everyone trying to live here. That vehicle is a tool for domination by the rich and driving it is an act of violence. He's the reason the planet is shriveling up like a scrotum in cold water. How many miles per gallon is he getting in that thing?

CLEO: Like zero.

EDMUND: Zero miles per gallon? You can't get zero miles per gallon. Your car wouldn't move.

CLEO: I was just exaggerating.

EDMUND: Come on. I'm serious. You know how many miles per gallon?

CLEO: How many?

EDMUND: Did you read that packet I gave you?

CLEO: I haven't had a chance.

EDMUND: You're supposed to know this. That's the whole reason we're doing this. We learn the facts and then we become outraged by them and we do some scary shit. It's that cause-and-effect situation that makes this all logical. If you don't learn the facts, then why are you outraged?

CLEO: I don't have time to read everything you give me. I trust you guys.

EDMUND: You trust us?

CLEO: If you're outraged, I trust there's a good reason . . . There is right?

EDMUND: Yes but . . . *(Gives up.)* It's ten. It gets ten miles per gallon.

CLEO: That's bad.

EDMUND: Yes it is. It's very fucking bad.

CLEO: Nice color though. The yellow.

EDMUND: Are you joking?

CLEO: Yellow's my favorite color.

EDMUND: So what?

CLEO: So I'm just trying to be friendly. We are going on a date after all.

EDMUND: After we do this I said.

CLEO: Sure after, but doesn't hurt to be nice.

(The two of them watch some birds for a while.)

EDMUND: *(Softening.)* In the evening the shadows reclaim all things in a cool embrace.

CLEO: Hm?

EDMUND: That's what you were supposed to say. Your part of the password. They're a pair of haikus. I write poetry sometimes.

CLEO: I like it. It's pretty.

EDMUND: Thanks.

(Edmund slides the bag over to her on the ground with his foot.)

CLEO: So where do you think you'll take me on our date?

EDMUND: Let's see how this goes first.

(Lights.)

SCENE 3

(Later in Brenda's apartment. Cleo is rifling through Brenda's refrigerator.)

CLEO: Can I have one of these mini-muffins?

ADAM: Those are Brenda's.

CLEO: You don't share?

ADAM: I don't like mini-muffins so she buys her own. There's six to a box.

CLEO: I do like mini-muffins, so can I have one?

ADAM: *(Looking in the fridge.)* I have some apples in here you can have. Or, what did you bring in the bag?

CLEO: Nothing. Just bottles. Wine. It's too early for wine. I'm having a mini-muffin.

ADAM: . . . All right. I can buy some more later.

CLEO: *(Back in the refrigerator.)* How about this juice? That hers too?

ADAM: It's fine. I'll go shopping later.

CLEO: I bet she'd be all pissed off if she knew I was in her apartment.

ADAM: What are you talking about? She likes you. She was the one who suggested I call you.

CLEO: Really? So she's not scared to have you home alone with a sexy woman?

ADAM: No, I don't think she's worried.

CLEO: Why? You don't think I'm sexy?

ADAM: No, it's not that. It's because you're my sister.

CLEO: We're both adopted.

ADAM: Yeah, but legally you're my sister.

CLEO: Oh, you and your laws. Is this because Brenda's a lawyer?

ADAM: No.

CLEO: You used to be fun.

ADAM: When was I ever that kind of fun?

CLEO: I don't mean that. I just mean . . . Look at this place.

ADAM: What? This is a really nice place.

CLEO: I know. All decorated. And clean. How are you going to deal with that?

ADAM: What?

CLEO: You're not clean.

ADAM: I'm clean when I'm around Brenda.

CLEO: That's the least of your worries. Brenda's like this hyperactive little monkey and you're like one of those things that doesn't move.

ADAM: A sloth?

CLEO: Or a hippopotamus or something. And she's going to get fed up with that one of these days. She might not say anything straight out, but maybe she starts vacuuming at six in the morning, or maybe she loses interest in sex all of a sudden.

ADAM: Yeah.

CLEO: So it's the sex?

ADAM: No—what?

CLEO: You're having a bit of a dry spell?

ADAM: That's not any of your business.

CLEO: I hear that. Me too. A bit of a dry spell. Fucking desert. I got tumbleweed blowing through my bedroom. It's just funny that we would have the same problem at the same time.

ADAM: Brenda wants us to hand out flyers downtown later by the way, and you need to vote.

CLEO: Tell her hi for me too.

ADAM: Yeah, of course she says hi too, and hope things are going well at . . . Are you still at the cat shelter?

CLEO: Six months next week.

ADAM: Oh, congratulations. Is that a raise?

CLEO: No, still minimum. But free cats.

ADAM: Oh.

CLEO: Your birthday's coming up, isn't it?

ADAM: I don't want a cat.

CLEO: Well, I don't make a whole lot of money, so I hope you're not expecting anything fancy for your stupid yuppie apartment.

ADAM: That's fine. It's the thought that counts.

CLEO: If you're telekinetic. I guess all I have to offer is my body.

ADAM: Can you quit it?

CLEO: It'd be a good present, Adam. Solve both our problems.

ADAM: No no. What is that? No. Why do you say stuff like that!?

CLEO: God Adam, it's a joke. You're not even my type. You're like my brother.

ADAM: I am your bro—OK, what are we doing here? You're helping me move.

CLEO: That's good. Be like Brenda. Take charge.

ADAM: Right. Getting all my stuff and bringing it back here and that's our plan for today. Let me get some pants and we can take your truck over to my place.

CLEO: I don't have a truck.

ADAM: You don't?

CLEO: It's gone. I sold it.

ADAM: You sold it? That was sort of the reason I called you.

CLEO: Oh, gee thanks.

ADAM: So how did you get here?

CLEO: I got Eddie to drop me off.

ADAM: Who's he?

CLEO: He's one of my friends.

ADAM: Friends?

CLEO: Yeah, I have friends too.

ADAM: People friends?

CLEO: Yeah, of course. I joined this nature club.

ADAM: Nature? Really?

CLEO: Yeah, it's great, it is really great. We do all kinds of stuff together: hikes, bird watching, protests. They count on me to make most of the signs 'cause I have a good eye for art.

ADAM: You could have asked me. I'm really more of the artist of the family.

CLEO: No you're not. You're too busy with your job now anyways. We hang out a lot. Pretty much every weekend we're doing something. Sometimes during the week.

ADAM: *(Indicating bag.)* Is that what the wine is for?

CLEO: We're having a little thing today. Because of the election.

ADAM: What'd you get?

CLEO: Nothing, just the cheap stuff.

ADAM: Actually, you can get some really good quality wines these days for pretty cheap. Brenda and I took a tasting class last month at the community college. I can tell you if you bought anything good.

CLEO: It doesn't matter, they don't care.

ADAM: They should care. I'm sure given the choice they'd rather drink a wine that doesn't taste like—

(Adam takes a bottle out of the bag. It's a Molotov cocktail.)

ADAM: This is . . .

CLEO: OK, before you go freaking out on me, I just want to say that I really like these guys so don't start acting all superior like you know what you're talking about.

ADAM: What is this?

CLEO: It's not even illegal, OK? It's just a bottle, some cloth, and some gasoline. Those are all things that you can buy perfectly legally anywhere in the world.

ADAM: But these are bombs right? I mean, basically, that's what these are?

CLEO: But what does that even mean? And is that even a bomb? What do you really call this? It's just a way of carrying gas around. Maybe my car ran out of gas. You don't even know what's going on.

ADAM: So what's going on?

CLEO: Just let me tell you OK. Jesus Christ. It's a political protest thing. You go to protests with Brenda. We're going to protest some law that gives people tax breaks for driving big gas-guzzling SUVs. So if that law passes, which may not even happen, but if it does, maybe, we're going to burn a few of them.

ADAM: You're really gonna do this?

CLEO: You know what? So what? What the hell do you care? I've finally found some friends that get me, that actually want to hang out with me. So if they need me to help out with a little petty vandalism, then, yeah, I'm going to help them out all right?

ADAM: Why are you getting mad at me? I just don't want to see you go to jail.

CLEO: Eddie would never let that happen. He used to be in this other group that would do this all the time.

ADAM: You can't just go blowing up cars. People these days are very touchy about that kind of thing. Please, don't do it . . . For me.

CLEO: For you?

ADAM: For yourself. Please just call your friend up and say you can't do it.

CLEO: . . . You want me to call him up?

ADAM: I think you should, don't you?

CLEO: . . . Where's your phone?

ADAM: *(Bringing over the phone.)* I think you're making the right move. I mean, who knows what could happen really. Wait—

CLEO: What?

ADAM: You should probably use a pay phone. To be safe.

CLEO: Is there one in this building?

ADAM: No, and if there is don't use it. There's a Starbucks down the street I think has one.

CLEO: Whoa no. Fuck that. I am not patronizing a Starbucks.

ADAM: Just for their phone.

CLEO: I don't have any change.

ADAM: *(Giving her a handful of change.)* Here. I don't know how much it is, these days, but this should do it.

CLEO: Eddie's gonna be pissed.

ADAM: If he's a real friend then, you know, he'll still be your friend.

CLEO: You'll make a great father.

ADAM: Well, thank you. Maybe you can say that sometime when Brenda's around.

CLEO: Maybe she'll pick up on the sarcasm.

(Cleo grabs her coat and leaves.)

(Lights.)

SCENE 4

Pine Nut Café. Brenda enters with a handful of flyers and posters. Edmund is working. Sort of.

EDMUND: Welcome to the Pine Nut Café.

BRENDA: I've been here before. Do you mind if I put up some posters?

EDMUND: You in a band?

BRENDA: It's for the election today.

EDMUND: Well, check that wall. I think some of those shows are over. Check the dates.

BRENDA: Thanks. I have some flyers too if there's some place that you put those.

EDMUND: I can just put them by the counter.

BRENDA: That would be great. It's just for today.

EDMUND: Are you going to get something to eat?

BRENDA: Ah, I probably should, shouldn't I?

EDMUND: I think so.

BRENDA: OK, let me just think . . . *(Checks her watch.)* Yeah, I have time. If you could just tell them in the kitchen that I'm in a bit of a hurry.

(Brenda sits down at one of the tables.)

EDMUND: Busy day huh?

BRENDA: Busy busy busy. Because of the election.

EDMUND: OK.

BRENDA: Don't forget to vote!

EDMUND: Sure, right. You working for one of the guys?

BRENDA: Sure am. Don't worry I'm working for the good guy.

EDMUND: Good to hear.

BRENDA: Just thought you should know so you don't spit in my food or anything.

EDMUND: OK.

BRENDA: Sorry, that was a stupid thing to say. I'm not trying to imply that you would ever actually spit in anyone's food.

EDMUND: No, I do sometimes.

BRENDA: Oh, well then I'm glad I told you.

EDMUND: So our special today is a mushroom and leek lasagna. Were you ready to order?

BRENDA: Yes. Sorry, did you say you had voted or were going to vote?

EDMUND: Not yet. I've been here all morning. I will.

BRENDA: Make sure you do. It's important.

EDMUND: Sure. I mean, voting's fine, I agree. But I usually like to get a little more involved.

BRENDA: Oh good, what do you—

(Edmund holds up his wrist, which is bandaged.)

BRENDA: Ouch, what happened?

EDMUND: You want to know what happened?

BRENDA: Can you tell me?

EDMUND: Don't see why not. It was on TV. It's from handcuffs. I was chained to a tree in the Tolowa Forest for twenty-nine hours. That's why I wasn't at work Friday.

BRENDA: Yeah, I remember that. How did it go?

EDMUND: Well, some of the trees were marked and some weren't, and we didn't know which ones were getting the saw so . . . We guessed wrong. You ready to order?

BRENDA: Sorry, yes. I'll have the barbequed eggplant and lentils.

EDMUND: All right.

BRENDA: I was actually at that protest also.

EDMUND: Yeah?

BRENDA: Just so you know I sympathize with what you're doing. I mean, I wasn't up a tree or anything. That looked kind of dangerous.

EDMUND: It was. I used to write a ton of letters to the papers trying to get my point across, but no one reads anymore. Americans—and by Americans I mean everyone in the world who owns a TV—love a spectacle. That's why they used that shot on the news. You want an iced tea with that?

BRENDA: Oh, you remembered—You know what? Maybe a glass of wine. One glass isn't going to hurt, right? I'm just putting up posters. Do you have a pinot grigio?

EDMUND: We have a house red and a house white.

BRENDA: The white sounds nice.

EDMUND: *(Writing.)* White wine.

BRENDA: So had you ever done that before? Chaining yourself to trees?

EDMUND: Yeah, we do that kind of thing a lot.

BRENDA: We, as in a group?

EDMUND: Yeah. *(Edmund shows Brenda his T-shirt with the letters TREE on it.)*

BRENDA: Tree?

EDMUND: Total Reclamation of Endemic Ecology.

BRENDA: Wow.

EDMUND: I'm the leader. I started it.

BRENDA: Good for you. So are you not a part of . . .

EDMUND: We were, but my group is better. We made these bracelets too.

BRENDA: *(Reading bracelet.)* Cool. "Running Bear"?

EDMUND: That's my Native American name.

BRENDA: Oh, are you Native Ameri—

EDMUND: No. Not by blood.

BRENDA: Yeah I think I've heard of you before.

EDMUND: Wouldn't be surprised. I'm fairly active in the community.

BRENDA: That's crazy. I've been coming here for months. I didn't know that you were . . . I thought you were just some coffee guy. You have this whole other thing going on. Anything coming up with your group?

EDMUND: Maybe.

BRENDA: Maybe? Well, what I mean is, I'm fairly politically minded myself, so—

EDMUND: *(Shows her his shirt.)* Check out our website.

BRENDA: Hang on. *(Brenda takes out her Blackberry and types the address.)* All right, I will.

EDMUND: So the eggplant with lentils and a white wine?

BRENDA: That's right.

EDMUND: And I won't spit in it.

BRENDA: Thanks.

(Lights.)

SCENE 5

Brenda's apartment. There is a sustained knocking at the front door, which brings Adam out of the bedroom to answer it. He opens the door to find a man in a sharp-looking suit. As soon as he opens the door, he remembers Cleo's bag of bombs on the counter.

CLARK: You're not Brenda.

ADAM: No, she's not here. Are you—

CLARK: No, the mailbox downstairs says Brenda Zerkowski on it.

ADAM: I'm Adam, her partner, boyfriend, whatever.

CLARK: Boyfriend, say boyfriend. Partner could mean anything.

ADAM: You want to leave a message or something? She should be back for lunch soon.

CLARK: Yeah, I got a message, but it's a message for everyone. I'm going door to door today, around your neighborhood, trying to get people to come out and vote.

ADAM: Yeah, thanks, I'm not interested.

CLARK: In voting?

ADAM: No, I'm definitely voting. But you're trying to tell me who to vote for, right?

CLARK: I can't tell you to do anything, Adam, Can I?

ADAM: Well, right.

CLARK: So what are you worried about?

ADAM: I just have a lot to do. I'm busy.

CLARK: I respect that, it's good to keep busy. And because I see you're a busy man, I'm going to keep this brief.

ADAM: I'm really busy.

CLARK: I'll be quick.

(Clark moves past Adam into the apartment. As he begins his speech, he takes out a hand-held tape player that plays patriotic music and gives it to Adam to hold.)

CLARK: Our city is facing a plague, my friend, a plague of fiscal irresponsibility and corruption at all levels of leadership. Our children's futures are compromised, our public safety is ignored, and all the while taxes continue to rise like a rocket, hurting our local industries and kicking hard working citizens like you and me right in the wallet. It's time to bring respectability back to our local government. It's time to bring smiles to the faces of our innocent little children. It's time for Americans everywhere to be proud to see their flag waving high over our city hall. I'm the man that's going to make that happen this time, and I hope that you'll vote for me.

ADAM: You?

CLARK: Yeah. Jerry Clark.

ADAM: You're Jerry Clark?

CLARK: Yeah.

ADAM: I thought you were older.

(Jerry takes back his tape player and stops the music.)

CLARK: That was my dad.

ADAM: That makes sense.

CLARK: But you're right. I'm young, like you. Not your typical politician. So do I have your vote?

ADAM: Well, probably not . . . I'm not actually supposed to vote for you.

CLARK: You're not supposed to?

ADAM: I mean, I don't think I'm going to.

CLARK: You don't think so?

ADAM: No. I'm sorry. But thanks for stopping by.

CLARK: Wow, that's . . . OK. I mean, that's your choice of course. That's the beauty of this wonderful country in which we live. Freedom to make bad decisions.

ADAM: I'm sorry.

CLARK: Yeah. You and me both. Wow. Hey listen: you think I could get a glass of water? Just all this walking I've been doing today, probably should have brought a bottle.

ADAM: Ah . . .

CLARK: Come on, it'll only be a minute. You think I don't have other places to be today?

ADAM: Sure sorry, come on in.

(Clark picks up a photograph from a shelf.)

CLARK: This is you and Brenda here?

ADAM: Yeah.

CLARK: She is cute. Are you guys serious?

ADAM: Well, I'm moving in today. So, yeah, pretty serious.

(Adam goes to the kitchen to get Clark a glass of water.)

CLARK: Actually, you got anything besides water?

ADAM: *(Looking in fridge.)* Let's see. We have some juice?

CLARK: You know what? Give me one of those beers in there. It's been a hard morning. You're not going to vote for me, you can at least give me a beer.

ADAM: I guess that's fair.

CLARK: This is the only kind you got?

ADAM: Yeah.

CLARK: Have one with me. Be social.

(Clark comes in and sits on couch. Adam gets a beer but stays standing.)

CLARK: So, Adam. You always vote how Brenda tells you?

ADAM: What?

CLARK: Well, she's the reason, isn't she? The reason you're "not supposed" to vote for me?

ADAM: No, that's not it.

CLARK: No?

ADAM: No.

CLARK: Good. Because, vote for me, don't vote for me: that's one thing, I respect that, but doing something just because your girlfriend wants you to?

ADAM: It's not like that.

CLARK: Good. Thanks for the beer by the way.

ADAM: Sure.

CLARK: So, if it's not her, then why aren't you voting for me? If I can ask.

ADAM: No, of course, that's fair enough. I . . . just think your views on certain social issues are . . . wrong.

CLARK: Like what?

ADAM: Like your policies.

CLARK: Which ones?

ADAM: Well, like I don't think your environmental policies are very good.

CLARK: How?

ADAM: Not good for the environment.

CLARK: In what way are they not good for the environment?

ADAM: Lots of ways.

CLARK: So tell me. I want to know. I want to know what I'm doing wrong. *(Beat.)* You say you're going to vote for the other guy, I kind of take it as an insult if you can't give me a good reason. I mean that makes sense to you doesn't it?

ADAM: It's not meant as an insult. At all.

CLARK: But you see what I'm saying though. The point I'm making. You don't like me, but you can't give me any reasons why you don't like me. Does that sound fair?

ADAM: It's not about liking you. I'm sure you're a very nice person.

CLARK: I am.

ADAM: It's just a question of your politics.

CLARK: You don't seem to know my politics.

ADAM: Not off the top of my head.

CLARK: Should we wait for Brenda to get back? I'm kidding. You know what? That's fine. You don't actually know who to vote for. That's what we've established here. Right? You're an undecided voter.

ADAM: I'm not undecided.

CLARK: Adam, Adam. Listen to me. You're not an idiot, right?

ADAM: What?

CLARK: I think that I'm right in assuming that you are not an idiot. You agree?

ADAM: Yeah.

CLARK: Politics just isn't your thing. Which is fine, which is absolutely fine. I'm sure that there are things that you care very much about, things that you're very knowledgeable about. What do you do?

ADAM: I'm a graphic designer.

CLARK: Oh, yeah? Like posters?

ADAM: Posters, advertisements mainly.

CLARK: OK. There you go. That's your thing, your specialty. Graphic design. I need some posters, I'll come to you. You have a card?

ADAM: Yeah, um, here. *(Adam gives Clark a card.)*

CLARK: See, I'm taking your card. You just got some business. I need an ad designed, some posters, I go to you. Right? Good. Now, I need a steak.

ADAM: A steak?

CLARK: Yeah, a big juicy steak. I got this girl coming over for dinner, a theoretical girl of course because in real life I'm happily married, but suppose I want to make this girl some steaks. They've got to be the best I can get because I'm looking to impress. Do I come to you?

ADAM: No?

CLARK: No, of course not. That's not your thing. Posters is your thing, I go to a butcher. That's his thing. And I don't go to a butcher I haven't met before. I go to a butcher that I know, that I have a relationship with. I'd better be looking good for this date too right? This hypothetical date. I need a haircut. Do I come to you?

ADAM: No.

CLARK: Of course not. Where do I go?

ADAM: Barber.

CLARK: Exactly. That's his thing. A barber that I know, one that I've met before. Now you're getting the picture. So now. You need someone to run your city. Do you go to the butcher or the barber?

ADAM & CLARK: No!

CLARK: The graphic designer?

ADAM & CLARK: No!

CLARK: All smart people but running a city is not their area of expertise. It is, however, my area of expertise. I'm a politician. And now I'm a politician you know. You know the other guy?

ADAM: No.

CLARK: He's an asshole. And that's fine if you don't believe me, but do you really want to vote for a guy that you don't even know?

ADAM: I guess that's a good point.

CLARK: It is a good point.

ADAM: Yeah.

CLARK: So . . .

ADAM: You've made some good points, and I think you've convinced me to read some more about the issues before I decide who—

CLARK: I'm telling you who. Me.

ADAM: OK, that's your—

CLARK: You don't trust me? You think I'm not a trustworthy person? I'm telling you who the best man for the job is. It's not a hard decision, all right? Vote for me. Vote Clark.

ADAM: *(Beat.)* All right, fine. I will . . . Thanks for stopping by.

CLARK: You trying to get rid of me?

ADAM: No, I just know you have other people to see today.

CLARK: You're not going to vote for me, are you?

ADAM: I will.

CLARK: You are fucking lying to me.

ADAM: I'm not.

CLARK: I can't believe this. Because of your girlfriend. You told me you were your own man. Did we not establish that earlier?

ADAM: I am.

CLARK: I don't know, Adam. It sounds to me like you're not. Like you were lying to me. And you know, I can take it that not everyone is going to vote for me. I disagree with them, but they have their reasons and I can respect that. But this. This is just wrong, and what kills me is that you know it's wrong. You make me want to take a shit. Where's your bathroom.

ADAM: Through there.

CLARK: You're being weak, Adam. This city needs people who are strong. Think about that while I'm in there.

(Clark grabs his beer and goes to the bathroom. Adam runs to the bag of bombs and tries to hide them in the freezer; he is only able to fit a few of them in and hides the rest of them in his backpack by the door. A moment of rest, then Cleo returns.)

CLEO: All right.

ADAM: You found it?

CLEO: Yeah.

ADAM: Everything go—

CLEO: Yeah. I told him that I didn't want to blow up the—

ADAM: *(Trying to cover up what she's saying so Clark doesn't hear.)* OK, OK! Good so everything's sorted out!

CLEO: He just wants me to give the bombs ba—

ADAM: OK, that's fine! Good!

CLEO: Are you drinking a beer?

ADAM: Well, kind of.

CLEO: Are you OK?

ADAM: Yeah yeah. We just have—

(The toilet flushes. Clark enters. Cleo tenses up.)

CLARK: That's a nice shower curtain you have in there, the ducks. *(To Cleo.)* Who's this?

ADAM: This is my sister.

CLEO: Who the hell is this?

CLARK: Hi I'm Jerry, it's a pleasure to meet you.

CLEO: Adam, who the hell is this?!

ADAM: Jesus, relax all right.

CLEO: Adam, what did you do?!

ADAM: Nothing, calm down. He's just trying to get people to vote for him.

CLARK: Maybe you read the paper? I'm Jerry Clark and I want you to make me your mayor.

CLEO: Oh. I thought you were a cop.

CLARK: Would that be a problem?

CLEO: What?

CLARK: If I was?

CLEO: No.

ADAM: Not at all. She just gets jumpy. You know how when you're driving and a police car pulls into traffic behind you and you get all nervous even thought you know that you haven't done anything wrong.

CLARK: You shouldn't be nervous. If anything you should feel safer. We should all be so lucky to have a member of our city's police force in such close proximity. I didn't catch the name of this beautiful woman.

CLEO: It's Cleo.

CLARK: Wonderful. And you're friends with Brenda too?

CLEO: Sure, we're best friends. I was the one who introduced them. You're the Jerry Clark that's running for mayor?

CLARK: The very same.

CLEO: Is it him we're supposed to vote for or the other guy?

CLARK: Wait, Cleo, don't do that. You're an independent woman. Am I right?

CLEO: Yeah.

CLARK: So don't ask him. Independence is an attractive feature in a woman. Decide for yourself who you feel you should vote for. You don't want to do something just because your brother tells you to.

CLEO: I don't. Besides I'm not going to vote.

CLARK: Another undecided voter!

ADAM: I am not undecided!

CLARK: Adam, have you voted yet?

ADAM: No.

CLARK: Well until you take that number two pencil and fill in the little boxes, you haven't really decided. Am I right, Cleo?

CLEO: They use pencils?

CLARK: OK, lets all have a seat.

(Clark grabs three more beers from the fridge.)

CLARK: You know, the two of you are lucky enough to have me here today to ask you, personally, what you need from me, for you to give me your vote. By the way Adam, you're out of beer.

ADAM: If you seriously wanted me to vote for you, your stance on some of the issues would have to—

CLARK: What? No, no, no, fuck that. You've already established that you have no grasp of the issues at all. I'm talking about something that I can give you that will make you give me your vote. A trade.

ADAM: Like money?

CLARK: Or something else. Do you like basketball? I could get you some tickets.

CLEO: What else?

CLARK: Your road out front is in pretty bad shape. I could have it repaved.

CLEO: I don't live here.

CLARK: You want a job on my staff?

CLEO: I don't like working.

CLARK: Maybe you don't need to show up too much. You have any traffic tickets you want erased? Or maybe there's someone you don't like very much?

ADAM: You're going to do all that for one vote?

CLARK: Two votes. Two votes in a very close runoff election.

ADAM: So you're just whoring yourself out to be the mayor of this crappy little city?

CLARK: Whoring myself out? Is that what you want? You hitting on me?

(Clark takes off his jacket and loosens his tie.)

ADAM: No.

CLARK: Come on, Adam. Why not? Let's get it on.

ADAM: What?

CLEO: Go for it, Adam, Brenda's not putting out.

CLARK: Is that true? Well, hey, I'll solve your problem right here.

ADAM: Stop it!

CLARK: Sex for votes, that's what I'm offering.

CLEO: I'll take that deal!

ADAM: Stop it.

CLEO: Why not? I need the orgasm. Besides, what difference is one vote going to make?

ADAM: Cleo, he's joking.

CLEO: Were you joking?

CLARK: *(Thinking.)* Ahh . . . no. You?

CLEO: No.

CLARK: All right then.

ADAM: Cleo.

CLARK: You registered?

CLEO: Yeah, you work out?

CLARK: Oh yeah. So we'll have sex and you'll vote Clark?

CLEO: Sounds fair.

ADAM: Wait a minute.

CLARK: All right. Let's do this. I've got places to be.

ADAM: Wait a minute! Cleo?

CLEO: Adam! Grow up.

(Cleo and Clark move back toward the bedroom.)

CLARK: Adam, you're not off the hook yet, buddy. I want you to stay here and think about what I can do for you.

(Lights.)

SCENE 6

Brenda's apartment. As the lights come up we hear the sounds of sex mixed with the loud sounds of angry punk music that Adam is playing in a failing attempt to drown out the sex noises. Finally the noises in the bedroom end, and a short while later Cleo emerges from the bedroom putting on her clothes.

CLEO: *(Yelling over the music.)* Adam. Adam!

ADAM: What? Hi.

CLEO: We're done. You can turn off the music.

ADAM: *(Turning off the music.)* No, I was just, listening to some music.

CLEO: Loud music.

ADAM: It's better loud.

CLEO: Yeah. Thanks. Had a good rhythm to it.

ADAM: Did you seriously just have sex with a stranger in my bed?

CLEO: That was the deal. What did you think we were doing?

ADAM: That was my bed!

CLEO: It's still your bed, Adam. You might want to change the sheets though.

ADAM: I can't believe that you just did that. This is unacceptable.

CLEO: Sorry I forgot to read your rules. *(Cleo puts on her coat.)*

ADAM: Wait, are you leaving?

CLEO: Yeah, I gotta go vote.

ADAM: You're actually voting?

CLEO: Yeah.

ADAM: For him?

CLEO: I said I would.

ADAM: You don't even follow politics.

CLEO: We had a deal. It's one vote. Who cares who's mayor anyway?

ADAM: It's important this time. There's some kind of casino or something. Read these articles that Brenda cut out.

CLEO: So you want me to go back on my word? He more than kept his end of the deal. Really I should vote for him a few times. Come on, let's go.

ADAM: Where?

CLEO: Have you voted yet?

ADAM: No.

CLEO: So come with me. You can cancel out my vote. It'll be fun.

ADAM: We're not leaving him alone in Brenda's apartment.

CLEO: Adam, where would you rather have him be? In your apartment in bed or out there convincing people to vote for him? He can be very persuasive in case you hadn't noticed. *(Beat.)* All right, I'm going. You coming?

ADAM: Cleo.

CLEO: Fine . . . Oh and where's you're closest Planned Parenthood?

ADAM: Oh Jesus.

CLEO: OK, I'll be back.

(Cleo leaves. Adam wants to look into the bedroom but doesn't. He walks around the apartment tidying up. Suddenly Clark calls from the bedroom.)

CLARK: Hey Chloe! Chloe! . . . Chloe baby, you out there?

ADAM: Her name is Cleo!

CLARK: Right. Sorry. Hey, Adam, send her back in here.

ADAM: She's not here.

CLARK: What?

ADAM: She left.

CLARK: She's gone?

ADAM: She went to go vote.

CLARK: Is she coming back?

ADAM: Probably.

CLARK: Soon?

ADAM: I don't know.

CLARK: What'd she say?

ADAM: You mean, about you?

CLARK: No, when she left what'd she say?

ADAM: Nothing, just she was going to vote.

CLARK: And not when she was coming back?

ADAM: No.

(Pause.)

CLARK: Did she say anything about me?

ADAM: No.

CLARK: She probably doesn't talk to you about that kind of stuff. Hey, did Brenda make it back?

ADAM: No.

CLARK: Well, I can't stick around here all day. I gotta get a move on.

ADAM: That's probably a good idea. We've all got things to do.

CLARK: All right.

ADAM: Whenever you're ready.

CLARK: I'm ready.

ADAM: OK, thanks for stopping by.

CLARK: Do you have the keys?

ADAM: What?

CLARK: Did she leave the keys with you?

ADAM: Your keys?

CLARK: No the . . . You don't see any keys sitting out there on the counter or anything?

ADAM: No.

CLARK: Can you look?

ADAM: I looked. I don't see any keys.

CLARK: . . . Hey Adam, listen, I'm in kind of an awkward position here.

ADAM: Yeah?

CLARK: Do you have any tools here? Maybe a hacksaw? Buddy?

(Adam goes to bedroom door, looks in.)

CLARK: Hi.

(Adam slams the door.)

(Lights.)

SCENE 7

Behind the Pine Nut Café. Edmund is smoking a joint. When Brenda enters, he considers hiding it but doesn't bother.

BRENDA: Hey.

EDMUND: You leaving?

BRENDA: Yeah, I have to get back to it. Shape the future of our city.

EDMUND: I find it kind of ironic that you're promoting a platform that supports restrictions on logging by printing out thousands of sheets of paper products.

BRENDA: Well, I guess I hadn't really . . . I mean, I hope people will recycle these things once the election is over at least.

EDMUND: I know I will.

BRENDA: Good. Listen, the food was delicious. Of course. As always.

EDMUND: Glad you enjoyed it. Those two glasses of wine probably helped.

BRENDA: Two? No, you're right, 'cause you brought me that second one.

EDMUND: Complimentary.

BRENDA: Yes, thank you. That was very nice. You have a nice place here.

EDMUND: I don't own it.

BRENDA: But you're the manager?

EDMUND: No, I just work here.

BRENDA: Oh, I'm sorry, you just act . . . very confident.

EDMUND: The owner's a friend of mine.

BRENDA: Well, I should probably let you get back to work.

EDMUND: I'm on a break. I take breaks whenever I want.

BRENDA: I guess it's not very busy.

EDMUND: *(Offering his joint.)* You want a toke?

BRENDA: Ah, no, that's all right.

EDMUND: Come on, I thought you were cool.

BRENDA: Well, OK.

EDMUND: *(Holding the joint away from her.)* I was kidding.

BRENDA: Oh, I know . . . But maybe I should, you know? *(Takes joint.)* It might help me relax.

EDMUND: You tense?

BRENDA: Well, yeah. The election. Mainly, and . . . You know what it is? It's just that, sometimes I feel like I'm the only one who cares about what happens around here. Like no one else is putting in any effort to make things better. I don't even feel like I'm doing enough, so if I'm still doing more than everyone else, then what the heck chance do we have?

EDMUND: You look tense.

BRENDA: Well I am. I just think it's very important that we do something, and I wish more people would. And on top of that, I come out of the office to go to lunch and some . . . idiot's put a "VOTE CLARK" sticker on the back of my car.

EDMUND: Sucks.

BRENDA: I'm going to file a police report. I don't need this.

EDMUND: Police won't do anything.

BRENDA: Probably not. Which is exactly my point. No one does anything. No one stands up anymore.

EDMUND: I do.

BRENDA: Yeah. You're one of the few people who actually—

EDMUND: Puts his money where his mouth is?

BRENDA: Yeah.

EDMUND: Gives a shit?

BRENDA: It's nice to find someone who does.

EDMUND: Turn around.

BRENDA: What?

EDMUND: You look tense.

(EDDIE walks behind her and touches her shoulder.)

EDMUND: Don't worry, I have trained in massage.

BRENDA: Really?

EDMUND: I took a class at the community college. Just turn around and relax your shoulders.

(She does and he starts rubbing her shoulders.)
BRENDA: Oh.
EDMUND: God, your back is like a bag of rocks.
BRENDA: Ow.
EDMUND: Sorry.
BRENDA: No, it's a good ow.
EDMUND: Good.
(Edmund starts kissing her neck. Brenda moves away.)
BRENDA: Oh, that's—I'm sorry.
EDMUND: What?
BRENDA: I have a boyfriend and he's moving in with me today. *(Brenda starts to leave.)*
EDMUND: Why did you come back here?
BRENDA: To tell you how much I liked the eggplant.
EDMUND: The eggplant is crap. Tracy always cooks it with too much salt.
BRENDA: Mine was actually—
EDMUND: You didn't even finish yours. I cleared your plate.
BRENDA: Well, I enjoyed talking to you and I wanted to say good-bye.
EDMUND: OK. Good-bye.
BRENDA: Because you seemed cool.
EDMUND: I am cool.
BRENDA: And maybe I wanted to join your group.
EDMUND: All right, you're in.
BRENDA: Oh. Or at least learn more about it.
EDMUND: *(Handing her a flyer.)* Here's a flyer.
BRENDA: OK. Thank you. I guess I should . . .
(Edmund throws his joint away and kisses her.)
BRENDA: You're not making this very easy.
EDMUND: What?
BRENDA: You know what.
EDMUND: *(Standing right up against her.)* No, I don't. What am I doing?
BRENDA: It's not that I don't want to do this.
EDMUND: Good.
BRENDA: But . . .
EDMUND: Don't think so hard.
BRENDA: You remind me of this guy I used to date.
EDMUND: Yeah?
BRENDA: You remind me of a couple guys I used to date.
EDMUND: All rolled into one? I must be quite a guy.

(Edmund kisses her again. She doesn't stop him. His phone rings.)

EDMUND: Goddammit. *(Takes a cell phone out of his pocket.)* Keep those lips warm. *(Answering and speaking into the phone.)* What? OK, hang on hang on hang on. Shut up for a second. I'm going to get to a pay phone and call you back in one minute, OK? Just don't . . . OK. I'm calling you right back. *(Edmund hangs up the phone.)* That was . . . someone I know. I have to go. This is my phone number.

(Edmund takes a bag of marijuana and a pen out of his pocket and writes his phone number on the bag. He gives Brenda the bag.)

EDMUND: Call me later if you want to help out with our protest. Feel free to smoke some of that too if you feel like it. Helps with the thinking too much.

(Edmund runs off. Brenda exhales.)

(Lights.)

SCENE 8

Brenda's apartment yet again. Cleo is back from voting. Adam has been waiting for her.

CLEO: Well that was fun. I've never done that before.

ADAM: I can't believe you did that.

CLEO: What? Did my duty as an American citizen?

ADAM: Voted for the wrong guy.

CLEO: The main thing is that you vote. It's important to have your voice heard, Adam. You should have come. There were these really nice old ladies there who walk you through the whole process, and they had oatmeal chocolate chip cookies there if you wanted to have some. I had three. Usually I'd take as many as I could, but I kind of felt like the other people deserved some too, 'cause, I mean we're all there for the same thing right? Seemed unpatriotic or something to take more than my share. You should go before they run out. And stickers, free stickers that say that you voted. People look at you a little different if you're wearing one of these. I would have gotten you one, but this is one of those stickers that you have to earn.

ADAM: I think you have some keys that we need.

CLEO: For . . .

ADAM: The naked politician chained to my bed.

CLEO: Oh, yeah right. Whoops. He's still here?

ADAM: Yes, he is still here and hoping that you have the keys. And what are you doing carrying around handcuffs anyways?

CLEO: They're my protest cuffs, Adam. Eddie says we need to keep them on our person at all times in case we suddenly need to chain ourselves to a tree, machine, or endangered species.

(Suddenly there is the noise of Edmund running through the hall outside, banging on doors, and yelling Cleo's name.)

CLEO: I'M IN HERE!!

EDMUND: *(Storming into the apartment.)* Cleo! Thank the gods, you're still here. We have a potential situation on our hands. Everyone else is flaking out on me. Tell me you're still in.

CLEO: What do you mean everyone else?

EDMUND: Tell me you're still in.

CLEO: Sure, yeah, of course.

EDMUND: Who's this?

CLEO: My brother.

EDMUND: Hi, um. Cleo and I work together at the pet store.

CLEO: It's a cat shelter. And besides he already knows, I told him.

EDMUND: Secret plan! It's a secret plan!

ADAM: This is the guy? Your friend who wants to—

CLEO: *(To Edmund.)* It's OK. He's cool.

EDMUND: You don't think he's going to crack under interrogation and turn you in?

ADAM: I'm not going to turn her in because she's not going to do it.

EDMUND: She just said she was.

ADAM: I thought you called him up.

CLEO: I didn't want to go into a Starbucks.

ADAM: I thought that we agreed that you weren't going to—

CLEO: Well I don't know now, OK? Maybe I should.

EDMUND: Fucking yes you should. Cleo, listen to me. I need you on this, it's important that we stick together, as a team. We're the only two left on this job. Cormac got cold feet and called Lakisha and then she called Moonstar, Shemp, and Xander, and they all freaked each other out.

CLEO: No one called me.

EDMUND: I need you on this one.

CLEO: If you need me.

EDMUND: I do, I need you.

ADAM: You're going to go to jail.

CLEO: Eddie wouldn't let that happen.

ADAM: It's terrorism! You're using bombs to blow up cars.

EDMUND: Oh, for fuck's sake man. It's not the same thing. Just because a bunch of Saudis are hogging all of the industry attention with their Wal-Mart of political violence it doesn't mean we're all the same.

ADAM: Listen. I'm not saying anything against you or whatever you're trying to do. I mean, I'm down with all the antiestablishment stuff, I love punk music. But Cleo is just not that type of person.

EDMUND: I think she is.

ADAM: Well, she's not. She's not going to go blow up trucks.

EDMUND: She already has.

ADAM: Is that what she told you?

EDMUND: I've seen her do it.

ADAM: Is this true?

CLEO: Yeah, but—

ADAM: I don't believe you.

EDMUND: It was on some logging road, hunters probably.

ADAM: Cleo doesn't always tell the truth.

EDMUND: I was there, my friend. A green Ford Explorer. She walked right up to it and smashed a Molotov cocktail on the windshield.

ADAM: Green Ford Explorer? . . . Cleo, don't you drive a green Ford Explorer?

CLEO: No, I told you I sold it.

ADAM: You torched your own truck.

EDMUND: You owned an SUV?

CLEO: Owned.

ADAM: You burned your own truck just so you could be in his little club.

CLEO: It got, like, ten miles per gallon.

ADAM: Cleo what the—

CLEO: Oh, there you go again about how much you love my truck.

EDMUND: That was your truck?

CLEO: Does it matter?

EDMUND: Well, yes, it does matter because . . . This doesn't inspire much confidence. You don't inspire much confidence. TREE is an organization that is trying to up its profile around this city. We want to be known on the national scene as an organization willing to do anything to get our point across, this means more civil disobedience, higher profile activities, and more risk for ourselves. The whole point of destroying property is that it's not yours. You led me to believe that you had what it took, Cleo. I have to say I'm a little disappointed in you. I want you to give me back the petrol bombs.

CLEO: Eddie, come on. Please.

EDMUND: Cleo. I'll let you stay in the group if you want to, you make good-looking and easy to read signs, but give me back those bombs.

CLEO: I want to help you.

EDMUND: Not this time. Give me the bombs.

(Cleo goes into the kitchen and finds her bag isn't there.)

CLEO: Adam, where's my bag?

ADAM: I hid it. And I'm not sure I should—

CLEO: Adam.

EDMUND: What's going on, Cleo?

CLEO: Where'd you put them, Adam?

EDMUND: I don't have time for this. Help me find them Cleo.

ADAM: No, no, no, don't . . .

(Cleo and Edmund start to tear the place apart looking for the bag, opening cupboards, pulling the cushions off the sofa, until Edmund swings open the bedroom door.)

CLARK: Hi sir, how are you today?

(Edmund closes the door. Thinks, is about to speak, then opens it again.)

CLARK: Hey buddy, you wouldn't happen to have a hacksaw on you?

(Closes the door.)

EDMUND: Is that who I think it is?

CLEO: I think so.

(Edmund opens the door again for another look.)

CLARK: Still here.

(Closes door.)

EDMUND: What have you done?

CLEO: I don't know, Eddie. It all happened pretty fast. I don't know if I can really be held responsible for my actions. I'm not exactly proud of what I've done.

EDMUND: You should be proud.

CLEO: I should?

EDMUND: That's Jerry Clark.

CLEO: Yeah.

EDMUND: You kidnapped a mayoral candidate.

CLEO: I did.

EDMUND: That's what I've been talking about. Why didn't you tell me about this?

CLEO: It was a surprise!

EDMUND: Holy shit. You planned this whole thing yourself? Dakota, Raymond, Lars, Krystal, the rest of them who bailed, it doesn't matter now. Turns out all I ever needed was you.

CLEO: Thanks.

EDMUND: This is just the kind of high profile act that our organization needs to get us on the front pages.

ADAM: Hang on a second—

CLEO: Shut up Adam.

ADAM: This isn't a kidnapping.

CLEO: Shut up, you're just jealous because I didn't tell you about my plan before.

EDMUND: I didn't think that you had this in you.

CLEO: I guess I do.

EDMUND: I guess you fucking do. And to think, just a few weeks ago I was struggling to get you interested in setting fires. Right, we've got a lot of work to do. I'll make a call and list off some demands. And if they don't meet our demands, then we start chopping off his fingers and toes and mailing them to his family.

ADAM: Wait a second!

EDMUND: No, you're right. You're absolutely right. We should wait. I mean who do we have in there right now? Just a former car salesman with a rich daddy. But, if he wins the election, we've kidnapped the mayor!

CLEO: So we want him to win?

EDMUND: Oh yes. We want him to win very much. My god I've been telling everyone to vote for the other guy, I have to go vote. Did you vote?

CLEO: Yes.

EDMUND: Shit.

CLEO: For him!

EDMUND: Aha! You've already thought this out. You're amazing. When were you going to tell me?

CLEO: After he won?

EDMUND: This is incredible. *(Goes to bedroom door.)* Hey guess what you un-lucky bastard! You got my vote after all!

CLARK: *(From off.)* God bless!

EDMUND: Cleo, you're beautiful. I've got to go vote and make some calls.

ADAM: Guys, seriously.

EDMUND: I assume you can handle your brother?

CLEO: Don't worry.

EDMUND: You and I are going to change the world. *(Edmund runs out the door.)*

ADAM: He's going to chop his fingers off!

CLEO: Not if they do what he wants.

ADAM: Does he have his own knife? I need to hide Brenda's knives. We need to get him out of here.

CLEO: No. Eddie wants me to keep him here and he's my friend.

ADAM: You guys are going to end up in jail . . . What about blowing up the trucks?

CLEO: What about it?

ADAM: That was a better plan. You have a better chance of getting away with that. How about this? You give me the keys to the cuffs and I'll give you back your bombs.

CLEO: I don't have the keys.

ADAM: Why not?

CLEO: I don't know, they're probably at home.

ADAM: Why do—

CLEO: They're my protest cuffs. If you carry the key around also, then the cops find it straight off and the protest is over.

ADAM: OK, that's fine. Tell you what. There's a hardware store down the street. I'll run down there and get a hacksaw, and we'll have him out of here before he even knows what's going on. Then you and Eddie can go and blow up your trucks or whatever. Sound like a deal?
(There is a lot of banging from the bedroom. Then the door opens and Clark enters wearing only a pair of boxer shorts. He is handcuffed to a bed frame that he drags out the door with him.)

CLARK: Cleo, you're back. You voted?

CLEO: Yeah.

CLARK: Good girl. You have the key? We've been looking for it.

ADAM: She doesn't have the key.

CLARK: Are you serious?

ADAM: But I'm going to run out and buy a saw.

CLARK: Well hurry up, Adam. I'm in the middle of a political campaign here. I have another fifty-six homes to hit today. I don't have time for this shit.

ADAM: There's a place just down the street.

CLARK: Wait a second. Did you vote yet, Adam?

ADAM: No.

CLARK: Then let Cleo go buy the saw.

CLEO: I don't have any money.

CLARK: Adam, give her some money then have a seat there and while we wait and I'll sway another undecided voter.

ADAM: No, we're not doing this again.

CLARK: You got any aspirin? I think I sprained my wrist taking your bed apart.

ADAM: Brenda finished them off.

CLARK: Fine, I'll just have another drink. Cleo, you want to hustle up and get that saw?

ADAM: You drank all our beer.

CLARK: But I'll bet your girlfriend is the type to keep a bottle of vodka chilling in the freezer.

(Clark opens the freezer and pulls out a Molotov cocktail.)

CLARK: Or something harder.

ADAM: My car ran out of gas.

CLARK: And . . .

ADAM: And I had to fill up wine bottles with gas to—

CLEO: We're part of an eco-terrorist organization and you're our hostage!

ADAM: Cleo, shut up!

CLEO: We're a highly organized and moderately trained group called TREE.

CLARK: Tree?

CLEO: The letters stand for something.

ADAM: I have nothing to do with this.

CLARK: Right, you just keep their Molotov cocktails chilled.

ADAM: I was hiding them from her. I'm the good guy here.

CLARK: So what kind of dastardly plot have I just uncovered? Who was your target?

CLEO: No one. We were going to set fire to some trucks.

CLARK: Jesus Christ! What kind of a sick person sets fire to a man's truck?

ADAM: Cleo, don't say anything else.

CLARK: That is really messed up, people.

CLEO: And now you're our hostage.

CLARK: *(Amused.)* Your hostage? This is ridiculous. I'm calling my people.

CLEO: No. No phone calls. You're not going anywhere. *(Cleo runs to the phone and rips it off the wall.)*

ADAM: Hey! That's not even your phone.

CLARK: You guys? Are you serious?

CLEO: That's what we here at TREE do.

CLARK: I'm leaving. *(Clark moves toward the door dragging the bed frame with him.)*

ADAM: That's my bed.

CLEO: Yeah, are you going to go out there half naked and chained to a bed frame?

CLARK: I guess it doesn't matter now, does it? You guys are some terrorist cell who's holding me hostage. Took my clothes, chained me up. They'll throw me a parade and name a street after me. I'll be a hero for exposing you. You, you're indecisive brother, Brenda.

(Adam moves between Clark and the door.)

ADAM: What? No No. Brenda has nothing to do with this. I don't have anything to do with this either really. Despite how this looks.

CLARK: Getting people to vote for me is my job. Stand aside, I'm leaving.

ADAM: Come on. You're totally misunderstanding the situation. This is silly.

CLEO: Hostage means you can't leave.

ADAM: No, you're not our hostage.

CLARK: So get out of my way.

ADAM: No, you don't understand.

CLARK: You guys have guns? You going to be able to defend yourselves from a twelve-man SWAT team armed with fully automatic assault rifles? Last chance.

ADAM: We'll let you go.

CLEO: No we won't.

ADAM: We will, but you just have to let me explain.

CLARK: I'm not going to let you cloud my mind with your lies.

ADAM: No no, this is actually kind of a funny story, you might enjoy it.

CLARK: HELP! SOMEBODY FUCKING HELP ME! CALL THE POLICE!

(As soon as Clark starts yelling, Cleo jumps to the stereo and cranks up some loud music, and she and Adam sing along to cover his shouts. She turns it down when he stops.)

CLARK: OK, I guess I'll just have to—HELP ME FOR FUCK'S SAKE! I'M BEING BEATEN AND TORTURED AND . . .

(Same as before with the music until he stops.)

CLARK: Clever, but eventually your neighbors will get annoyed and call the police.

ADAM: No, they're mostly students.

CLEO: *(To Adam.)* . . . So we're cool?

ADAM: No Cleo, we're not "cool." I think that you've done a great job of ensuring that we are definitely not cool. I ask you for a simple favor, and you come over here armed with explosives, take a high profile hostage with an Ikea bed frame, involve me in a federal crime, and vote for the wrong guy. I'm calling Brenda.

CLARK: Yeah, she works too hard. Tell her to come home.

(Adam goes into his bedroom and slams the door just as Edmund returns through the front door, slightly flustered.)

CLEO: You voted? Where's your sticker?

EDMUND: Yeah, I'm not actually registered to vote. I forgot. I made some calls but everyone I got in touch with already voted. *(Noticing Clark.)* What's he's doing out here?

CLEO: Why can't he be out here?

EDMUND: Well, don't get too comfortable.

CLARK: I'm not comfortable. My wrist is killing me. I've been handcuffed to this bed for three hours.

EDMUND: Three hours, that's nothing. You should try locking yourself to a tree for a day and a half.

CLARK: Why the hell would I want to do that? Look at my wrist. Can you at least get me some ice?

EDMUND: Ice? We don't use ice in the field. It would melt in two hours.

CLARK: Is this how you treat all of your high-profile hostages?

EDMUND: God, fine. Quit whining and take some of these. *(Edmund takes a pill vial out of his jacket pocket and gives it to Clark.)* These are left over from last Friday.

CLARK: At least someone comes prepared. *(Clark opens it and takes a handful.)*

EDMUND: Dude, those aren't breath mints.

CLARK: And not that I mind, but why are you telling people to vote for me?

EDMUND: Well, if you must know, we're trying to increase your value to us as a hostage.

CLARK: Oh . . . Well, calling up your friends at this point isn't going to do it.

EDMUND: Don't tell me how to do my job.

CLARK: Getting people to vote for me is my job.

EDMUND: . . . Well, OK then preppie. What would you do?

CLARK: Well, what time is it? *(Checks watch.)* OK, the polls are only open for a few more hours. You're in luck because this neighborhood has a lot of undecided voters. They'll be coming home from work soon and they probably haven't voted yet, they're waiting until the last minute to decide. Two things to remember about people. One, if we look at something for long enough we believe it, and two, we all just want to fit in. Here's what you do, I've got a shitload of signs in the trunk of my car, the keys are in my jacket. It's the black sedan parked outside in front of the fire hydrant. How ethical are you?

EDMUND: Not very.

CLARK: Good. Put my signs up in front of every house on the street leading up to the polling station, if you see signs for the other guy, chuck them in a ditch. If anyone comes out to complain, tell them that if they take away my sign you'll burn down their house. As people drive home, they'll be overwhelmed by the sight of the posters and vote for me just to get along with their neighbors.

EDMUND: OK, I can do that.

CLARK: Every house on that road needs a sign.

ADAM: *(Returning from bedroom.)* OK, Brenda's not answering. But you know what? I don't need her. I want everyone out of my apartment. Ed, Cleo, you're leaving. Jerry, Mr. Clark whatever, I'm going to get a saw and get you out of here.

CLEO: We can't do that, he'll have us arrested.

ADAM: That's your problem, you brought this on yourselves, and you tried to bring it on me, but Brenda is going to get me out of this. You guys are on your own. Mr. Clark, I apologize for any inconvenience that this day may have brought you, but now I'm letting you go.

CLARK: I don't want to go.

ADAM: Well you . . . What?

CLARK: I'm fine here.

ADAM: So you can get back to campaigning.

CLARK: Actually, this gentleman here has volunteered his services to my cause.

EDMUND: My cause.

CLARK: Well we happen to share a cause, and his roguish outlaw political strategies are going to do more good than I could do in the time we have left. I don't mind sitting around and having a few drinks while he does my job.

ADAM: So . . .

CLARK: I'm staying. We're all going to stay here a little while longer.
(Edmund leaves.)

ADAM: Brenda is not going to like this at all.

CLARK: Well I can't wait for her to get here. *(To Cleo.)* Would you mind turning on the television? I'd like to see how I'm doing.
(Lights.)

SCENE 9

Brenda's apartment. Cleo and Clark are sitting on the couch, Clark is still handcuffed to the bed frame. They are watching the television election results. Adam is in the kitchen getting some food from the fridge.

CLARK: Yo, Adam. You got anymore of that guacamole dip?

ADAM: Hang on.

CLARK: Don't forget to squeeze some lemon on it again. That was good.

ADAM: Maybe you can cut some up?

CLARK: Adam, I'm handcuffed to your bed frame. Normally I'd help. *(Noting wrist.)* Hey, you know what else is good? Those pain killers that Eddie gave me. I don't feel a thing.

CLEO: I need a refill on my drink too.

ADAM: What are you chained to?

CLEO: You're already up.

(The door opens and Brenda enters. She's stoned. She walks to the kitchen and starts rummaging through the cupboards.)

ADAM: Hi, listen, before you say anything—

BRENDA: Did you votey vote vote today?

ADAM: Things got a little crazy here.

BRENDA: I wanna eat something. Is there something to eat?

ADAM: Honey bear, I'm so sorry, I didn't get a chance to get to the store to get the stuff for dinner. I'll take you out somewhere if you like.

BRENDA: I'm taking some of your Frosted Flakes.

ADAM: That's fine.

BRENDA: Oh no, we're almost out of milk.

CLARK: You're also out of beer.

BRENDA: What?

ADAM: I guess we need some beer too.

BRENDA: You drank all of our beer?

ADAM: No . . .

(Brenda notices the other people in her apartment.)

BRENDA: Are you having a party?

ADAM: Some people are here.

BRENDA: Did we talk about a party?

ADAM: I told them you were going to be mad.

BRENDA: I'm going to name some people and I want you to tell me if they're at this party.

ADAM: OK.

BRENDA: Your slacker sister.

ADAM: Cleo's here.

BRENDA: A naked man handcuffed to our bed.

ADAM: Yeah, I actually need to talk to you about that.

BRENDA: Channel ten news anchor Diane Brown.

ADAM: She's on the TV.

BRENDA: That's what I thought . . . Wait a second.

CLARK: Brenda! There she is. We were wondering when you'd be getting in. Tough day at the office?

BRENDA: Is that Jerry Clark?

CLARK: Brenda Zerkowski, my arch nemesis! No, I'm kidding of course, you'd have to actually win a round or two to be my arch nemesis. I like that you never quit though. Tenacity, I think they call that.

ADAM: What's going on?

CLARK: All right, you got me. I'm sorry I wasn't exactly forthcoming about all of this, Adam, but, Brenda and I, we go way back. Ever since I got back into politics, she's been against me.

BRENDA: The logical position was opposition.

CLARK: Of course we go back even further than that. Don't we, Brenda? I didn't want to tell Adam earlier, because I thought it might make him uncomfortable. Should I tell him why?

BRENDA: No.

CLARK: I was her first boyfriend back in high school. Isn't that right?

BRENDA: No.

CLARK: I think it is.

BRENDA: Second.

CLARK: You told me you didn't count Tommy Lin!

BRENDA: I do now.

CLARK: You two didn't even kiss!

CLEO: Ugh, you two used to date?

BRENDA: Until I beat him in the student council president election. He dumped me that night with a note wrapped around a brick though my window.

CLARK: You should have dropped out of the race.

ADAM: He's the guy that you beat?

BRENDA: I was a good president.

CLARK: Oh, sure. Of course you were. I certainly wouldn't want to take any of the shine off of the high point of your political career. I mean—wow, that really has been the high point of your political career now that I think about it.

ADAM: That's awesome. How come you never said that he was the one—

CLARK: That was over a decade ago! Did you not get that I don't care anymore? Besides, I was the one who broke up with her. Look at me now. Fit and vibrant. And look at her. She looks like she's on drugs.

ADAM: Hey, watch it.

BRENDA: No, it's OK, Adam. I am on drugs.

ADAM: What?

BRENDA: OK now, hang on and hear me out. There was this big bag of narcotical materials, that I may have eaten. Unintentionally.

ADAM: By accident?

BRENDA: Well, no, fine, intentionally, but because of the police.

CLARK: What?

BRENDA: OK, OK, OK. Earlier today, I found myself to be in possession of a sandwich bag, containing no sandwich, but rather a certain quantity of a controlled substance. When I was in the car later on, a police officer of the law attemptedly tried to pull me over, and I reacted in such a way as to not go to jail. So, I ate, and eventually consumed, the inner contents of the aforementioned sandwich bag, therefore inebriating the evidence.

ADAM: Did the cop find anything?

BRENDA: In a sense he didn't pull me over and actually was probably not following me, just driving on the same road. As me. Not impossibly in the opposite direction. But, however, it is important to note that for the previous half hour I have been locationed in Starbucks drinking shots of espresso, so I'm fine.

CLARK: I have to say, Brenda, when I saw your name on the buzzer downstairs I did not expect to come up here and find a drug-addicted member of a terrorist organization who's in a serious relationship with a guy who doesn't vote.

BRENDA: Didn't vote?!

ADAM: Well, obviously things got a little complicated.

BRENDA: What did you do all day?

ADAM: Cleo blew up her truck!

BRENDA: You don't need a truck to vote.

ADAM: No, that's why I couldn't move my stuff.

BRENDA: So you did nothing all day?

CLARK: I mean, granted, I'm coming in here from an outsider's perspective, but I'm looking at this guy, and I just can't believe that he's doing it for you. Someone like you I figured would end up with someone a little more dynamic, someone with passion, someone—

(Edmund returns with some boxes of Clark posters.)

EDMUND: OK, polls are closed. I put up all the posters, made the appropriate threats, I guess now we just wait.

BRENDA: Is that the cute guy from the café?

ADAM: That's Cleo's friend Eddie. You wanna blame someone for all this, he's the guy you need to be talking to.

EDMUND: *(Seeing Brenda.)* Hey, welcome to the party. Glad you could join us.

ADAM: This is my girlfriend Brenda. And this is her place.

EDMUND: Girlfriend? Oh, I get it, you're the boyfriend. That's awkward.

ADAM: Yeah, I'm . . . what do you mean "I'm the boyfriend," who else— *(To Brenda.)* and why did you call him "the cute guy" from the café?

BRENDA: He lives in a café where I sometimes go to eat food and drink drinks.

ADAM: So why does that mean you have to call him the "cute guy" from the café?

BRENDA: Adam, calm down, OK? Is this some kind of, I don't know, inquisition or something? Am I on trial here or something? Because none of this proves anything.

CLARK: OK, OK. Now this makes a little more sense. I admit that I was a bit dumfounded to find you shacked up with this vanilla-on-white-bread sandwich here, but a jalapeno pepper like this guy on the side, that makes more sense for you. This is more your kind of guy.

ADAM: You're on his side? This is the guy who's keeping you chained to a bed. This is the guy who wants to blow up people's trucks.

CLARK: And what do you do for what you believe in? Do you even believe in anything? You were only going to vote because Brenda told you to and you didn't even do that. I don't agree with this guy at all, but at least I can respect him.

ADAM: I do stuff.

CLARK: Like what?

(Adam takes some folders out of a bag.)

ADAM: Like these posters. I designed all of these posters. Which wasn't easy because to get the color contrast right on these images I had to import a color scale from a different program.

CLARK: Adam, that's your job. You're a graphic designer, you make whatever people tell you to.

ADAM: Some of those fonts I created from scratch.

CLARK: Cool . . . I mean somebody probably thinks that that's cool. I don't. And I don't think that Brenda does either.

ADAM: You want to help me out here a little bit, Brenda? Stand up for me maybe?

EDMUND: Look, dude, I didn't know who's girlfriend she was. But we did kiss. A lot. I may have gotten to second base, I'm not sure, it was all in the heat of the moment.

ADAM: You kissed him?

BRENDA: He kissed me.

ADAM: OK. This is all OK. I mean, I understand if he kissed you against your will.

BRENDA: Well, it was against a wall.

ADAM: But I mean he just came up to you and mashed his dirty hippy mouth up against yours. Right? 'Cause that would be assault. You could press charges against him for that, right? Are you going to press charges?

BRENDA: Oh god.

ADAM: Are you?

BRENDA: No Adam, I'm not going to press charges.

ADAM: But . . . Is this because I don't—

CLEO: *(Finally figuring out what's going on.)* Hang on! Back up one motherfucking minute here. You kissed her?!

EDMUND: What?

CLEO: I've been throwing myself at you for three months. You said you weren't interested in that kind of thing.

EDMUND: Not with you.

CLEO: Not with me? What about our goddamn date? What about me being the only one that you need? I want to know exactly what's going on with us.

EDMUND: Hey, you're a good agent but . . .

CLEO: Agent? Fuck you, "agent." And don't look at me like I'm crazy. Lots of guys would love to get with me. Jerry did. Adam would if he wasn't my brother.

ADAM: I didn't say I'd sleep with you—

CLEO: If I weren't your sister, yes you did. And you know what? Maybe we are sleeping together. Did you ever think of that?

EDMUND: What?

CLEO: Sure, what's the big deal? Maybe every time we get together to hang out and think nothing of it because he's my brother, maybe we're actually having the greatest sex you could imagine.

ADAM: Cleo! Goddammit, can you please shut the hell up!

BRENDA: What's going on, Adam?

ADAM: What's going on? I'm supposed to be asking you that.

CLEO: Come on Adam, let's go. If they want to go play tonsil hockey together that's fine with us. You don't need Brenda.

ADAM: Yes I do.

CLEO: You can stay at my place, I have a couch you can sleep on. You're not still allergic to cats are you?

ADAM: I'm not going anywhere with you. Brenda, can we go somewhere to talk?

EDMUND: That's her whole problem with you, dude. All you do is talk.

CLARK: Maybe you could make Brenda a poster.

ADAM: No, I'm not going to make a poster! I'm gonna . . . You want to know what I'm going to do? I'll show you what I'm going to do, and then you'll have seen it and you'll know.

CLARK: Well said.

ADAM: Fuck off!

(Adam grabs his backpack and runs out the door. There is a brief silence that is awkward for some and satisfying for others.)

BRENDA: I think everyone should leave so I can finish my Frosted Flakes.

CLARK: I'd love to. Brenda, it was a pleasure seeing you again.

EDMUND: Brenda, no. I think at this point we would be ill advised to move our hostage due to the risk of drawing unwanted attention. I believe the proper next course of action is to chop off one of his thumbs and deliver it to his offices.

BRENDA: What? That's disgusting.

EDMUND: This will let them know that we mean business as well as giving them the fingerprint proof that we've got their man.

CLARK: Eddie, I was serious when I said that I respected you. And I want you to know that I appreciate the work that you've put into my campaign today. But do you seriously believe that she's going to let you stay here and chop off my fucking thumbs in her apartment?

EDMUND: I'll put down some newspapers.

CLARK: It's not going to happen.

EDMUND: Have you not been paying attention? Brenda's with me. She's a part of my organization so the joke's on you.

CLARK: That's not the kind of girl she is. Tell him Brenda.

BRENDA: I really don't want to deal with this right now.

CLARK: Brenda? You want to sober up a little bit here?

BRENDA: Actually, no. I don't think I do.

CLARK: OK, but we both know you're not going to let this guy carve me up.

BRENDA: You're an asshole.

CLARK: Maybe, but I'm an asshole you know.

EDMUND: Cleo, find me a knife.

CLEO: Why?

EDMUND: Just do it, Cleo.

(Cleo takes a big knife out of a kitchen drawer.)

CLEO: Is this a finger knife?

CLARK: Cleo, come on now sweetheart.

EDMUND: Give me the knife.

CLARK: Don't do it. Give it to me.

EDMUND: You don't have to do it. I'll do it. Just give me the knife.

CLARK: Cleo, listen to me. We shared something special earlier, didn't we?

EDMUND: Just give it to me now.

CLARK: Brenda?!

EDMUND: You don't have anything to worry about Cleo.

CLEO: I don't like this anymore, Running Bear.

BRENDA: That's it! Running Bear, Running Bear Running Running Bear Bear. It's all . . . Yup. That's where I heard of you before. At the Court House about half a year back. Right? They were prosecuting this group of guys that had burned up a bunch of new houses they were building on Peach Street. What were they? . . . Right, they were called something like LEAF, or . . . No, that was it, Leave the Earth Alone Forever. The cops had a pretty decent idea about who was involved, but the only evidence they had was—what do you call it? Circumstantial. Good. So they start leaning on the suspects, playing like they have more evidence then they do and offering deals to anyone who wants screw over the rest of them. And, I mean, you were one of the LEAF members weren't you?

EDMUND: I . . . Yeah.

BRENDA: So, like, why is it that you're now the only one who's not in jail?

EDMUND: I'm not the only—Well, maybe I am. So what?

BRENDA: So you should be in jail.

CLEO: You ratted out all your friends to save yourself?

EDMUND: What? Come on. Who are you gonna . . . Will you give me the goddamn knife?

CLEO: You told me I didn't have anything to worry about, that you had experience.

EDMUND: Right, and she just proved that I do. That's not what's important, who's in jail and who isn't. We're doing something here. I can't not do this, I already sent a letter to the papers with a copy of our manifesto and a list of demands. If we haven't actually done anything by the time they get those letters, our manifesto is going straight in the trash. Cleo, give me the knife.

CLEO: No, Eddie. Fuck you. I trusted you. I blew up my truck for you! And why? What the hell was the point? *(To CLARK.)* Here, you take it.

(Cleo tosses the knife to Clark a little too hard. It sticks into the table that Clark has been leaning on and a finger drops to the floor. There is a brief pause, then Clark lets out a loud scream.)

CLEO: Ohmigod, I'm so sorry!

EDMUND: It's mine! I got dibs on that finger!

CLEO: No, don't you touch it.

BRENDA: Ooh, shitty shit shit shit.

(Cleo and Edmund scramble on the floor for the loose finger. Brenda runs around the kitchen looking for something to help with the bleeding, finds a roll of paper towels, and runs over to help Clark.)

CLEO: Let go!

EDMUND: No, I need that!

(Cleo breaks an empty beer bottle over Edmund's head and takes the finger away from him. He retreats to the other side of the room while Cleo holds him off with the broken bottle.)

EDMUND: Goddammit! What the hell is wrong with you? That really hurt.

CLEO: This isn't your finger!

EDMUND: What the fuck is the big deal? It's already off. Let's accomplish something with it.

BRENDA: No no no, we're giving him back his finger and letting him go.

EDMUND: You can't let him go now. He knows things. He—What are you doing?

(Cleo takes off an artsy-looking earring that has a bunch of crap hanging from it and uses it to unlock Clark from the bed frame. He begins to dress.)

EDMUND: Those are your protest cuffs, Cleo. You're not supposed to have the key on you!

CLEO: Come on, Eddie. I can't be stuck to a tree for three days. Who's going to feed my cats?

(Adam bursts back in through the door.)

ADAM: Ladies and gentlemen, boys and girls, if I could please direct your attention out the front window. *(He walks straight to the window to look outside.)* Oh my god, will you look at that?

(The others join him around the window looking out.)

BRENDA: Oh no.

CLEO: Hey Eddie, there's a car on fire.

EDMUND: Well all right! Game on!

BRENDA: Ohmigod. Call someone. *(Looking at the wall where Cleo ripped out the phone.)* What happened to our phone?

CLEO: I'm sure someone has already called.

BRENDA: We need to do a something. I have a fire extinguisher around here somewhere.

ADAM: It's OK. Relax. Just enjoy it.

BRENDA: Are we under attack?

ADAM: We're not under attack.

BRENDA: You know this?

ADAM: I know this.

BRENDA: How can you . . . ?

ADAM: Notice anything about that car down there?

CLEO: It's on fire.

ADAM: No, look at the back there, the bumper. The sticker? See that? "Vote Clark." Huh? Oh, there it goes. Did you see it?

EDMUND: Yeah.

ADAM: I was talking to Brenda.

BRENDA: I saw it.

ADAM: How about that? You still think I don't do anything?

BRENDA: What?

ADAM: The car.

BRENDA: The car?

ADAM: I . . .

BRENDA: You . . .

ADAM: Did the car . . . For you.

BRENDA: You set the car on fire?

ADAM: For you. Remember you said you wish you had a rocket launcher every time you saw one of those—

BRENDA: Where did you get a rocket launcher?

ADAM: No, it was these Molotov cocktails. But it's the same general result.

EDMUND: My Molotov cocktails?

ADAM: Yeah, Eddie. Your Molotov cocktails. You weren't doing anything with them so I decided to step up. You have a problem with that? You have a problem with me making a bold and beautiful political statement in the middle of the street? You have a problem with me showing the world what I think?

BRENDA: That's your car.

ADAM: Where?

BRENDA: The one that's on fire. Next to the blue one.

ADAM: It's a common make of car, don't worry, that one had a Clark bumper sticker. You saw it.

BRENDA: When I was parked downtown today, somebody slapped that on the back.

ADAM: Yeah, but we park our car in the garage anyway, right?

BRENDA: Well, I couldn't find the clicker for the door.

ADAM: It's always clipped to the sun visor.

BRENDA: Oh yeah.

ADAM: That's always where it is.

BRENDA: If I had known you were going to be out here vandalizing cars on the street, I would have looked harder.

CLEO: It's OK, I blew up my car too. I can teach you the bus schedule.

CLARK: *(Laughing.)* You just blew up your own car?

EDMUND: Nice one, Adam, well done. Way to make a statement.

ADAM: You know what? You can get the fuck out of here right now. I want all of you out of here right now!

CLARK: You can't kick us out, this is Brenda's apartment.

ADAM: No it's my apartment. I live here now too and— *(Noticing Clark's injury for the first time.)* What the hell happened to your hand?

CLARK: Your sister cut off my finger.

CLEO: I have it right here.

(Adam takes Clark's finger from Cleo.)

ADAM: Good, I'm glad she cut off your finger. You're an asshole. Now get the fuck out of my apartment.

CLARK: Don't be pointing my own finger at me, kid. I'll leave when I want to leave.

(Adam goes to the door to his apartment and throws the finger outside.)

CLARK: Hey! Do you realize how much trouble you're already in?

ADAM: I don't think I'm in any trouble, Jerry. Unless you want everyone to know that you were having an adulterous relationship with a known member of a terrorist organization?

CLARK: Her? I didn't know that at the time.

ADAM: Is that what you want to tell your wife and your dad when the press finds out? When they get a hold of the DNA evidence?

CLEO: That's right, DNA baby.

CLARK: I'll pay you five thousand dollars for those sheets.

CLEO: Deal!

ADAM: No, Cleo. We're going to hold the sheets it, and he's going to leave us alone.

CLARK: Ten thousand dollars.

CLEO: Make it twenty.

ADAM: Cleo! Help Jerry find his finger. And put him in his car.

CLARK: All right. I shouldn't even here be anyways. I should be watching the election results at my campaign headquarters. Cleo, could you please find my finger.

(Cleo leaves while Clark collects his things.)

EDMUND: Hey do you have any of those cocktails left?

ADAM: Yeah I do, Eddie. But I think I'm going to hold onto them. In case I ever see you driving around this neighborhood.

EDMUND: 'Cause, I mean, I actually made them so . . . *(To Clark.)* Hey listen, you're going to the hospital right? Do you think you could give me a lift? My head is feeling weird and you finished off my pills.

CLARK: All right, just give me a hand with those boxes.

EDMUND: I don't know man. I'm feeling kind of dizzy.

ADAM: Help him with the boxes, Eddie.

EDMUND: *(Picking up boxes.)* All right, god. But my head seriously hurts. Hey Brenda, stop by the café sometime if you want.

ADAM: Eddie!

CLARK: Brenda, always a pleasure. I'll have to be sure to have you over to my place next time.

(Edmund and Clark leave. Adam slams the door. A moment of calm.)

BRENDA: Some day, huh?

ADAM: Are you fucking kidding me?

BRENDA: It's OK, they're gone.

ADAM: I just bombed my own car for you.

BRENDA: I know.

ADAM: Am I just the world's biggest idiot?

BRENDA: No.

ADAM: I should go.

BRENDA: Adam, please, I'm scared. I'm high. I've committed crimes today. I cheated on my boyfriend with a guy who likes to chop off fingers. You need to be here.

ADAM: Why?

BRENDA: Because you blew up your car for me. No one's ever blown up their car for me before.

ADAM: Well . . . Happy Election Day.

BRENDA: Thank you.

ADAM: You know, we still have a few of those bombs left . . .

BRENDA: Adam, can we please just sit here. Watch TV or something. I just need you to be here with me.

ADAM: OK.

(Adam sits down on the couch next to Brenda. She leans over on his shoulder and he puts his arm around her. Cleo reenters behind them and notices that it is a tender moment so stays quiet. Brenda turns up the volume on the TV.)

TV: . . . with forty-seven percent of the votes. And in the mayoral race, it now seems safe to announce that Jerry Clark has come through as the winner in a landslide victory with over seventy percent of the vote.

(Brenda drops her head into Adam's lap and covers her face with her hands.)

CLEO: How about that? I fucked the mayor.

(Lights.)

END OF PLAY

HARVEST

David Wright Crawford

PLAYWRIGHT'S BIOGRAPHY

David Wright Crawford received an Off-Broadway production of *Harvest* at the Beckett Theatre by the Alchemy Theatre Company of Manhattan. Previoulsy, "Doc" was selected to receive an Off-Broadway reading at the Ensemble Studio Theatre in their Octoberfest after being accepted to their summer workshop at Lexington. Another script, *Borrowed Plumage*, played at the Provincetown Playhouse. His most recent work, *Night Cries*, received a reading by Theatre East in Theatre Row. Regional works include *Seedling, Doors, McDono, Artesia* (winning the Texas Educational Theatre Association's Playfest), and *Tangled Garden* (winning the Texas Playwriting Contest). He has written three scene books: *Moments, Timelesss,* and *Gallery.* Crawford's works are represented by Players Press, Studio City, California.

He has been a theater instructor at Tyler Junior College (TJC) for thirty-two years, twenty-five of those as chair of the Speech and Theatre Department. During his tenure at TJC, he has won numerous awards for teaching and development. He is a founding board member of Texas Dramatist.

A Tyler, Texas, native, Crawford received his AA from Tyler Junior College, BS from the University of North Texas, MA from Stephen F. Austin State University, and PhD from Texas Tech University.

ORIGINAL PRODUCTION

Harvest was produced by the Alchemy Theatre Company of Manhattan and opened December 2007 at the Beckett Theatre in Theatre Row. Act I was directed by Benard Cummings; Acts II and III by Judson Jones. The cast and crew were as follows:

CAST

ACT I

RICK CHILDRESS . . . . .Judson Jones
TONI CHILDRESS .Christa Kimlicko Jones
COPELAND . . . . .Doug Sheppard

ACT II

RICK CHILDRESS . . . . .Jeremy Stuart
RAFAEL LAMAS . . . . .Morgan Baker
AGGY TAYLOR . . . . .Shorey Walker

ACT III

RICK CHILDRESS . . . . .Richard Mawe
MAGGIE FALLS . . . . .Kymberlie Stansell
TONI CHILDRESS . . . . .Kathleen Huber

Productio Stage Manager . . . . .Joseph Mitchell Parks
Scenic Design . . . . .Terry Gipson
Scenic Design Assistants . . . . . Michele Donner, Christopher Ward,
Scott Aronow
Scenic Construction . . . . .Cigar Box Studios
Lighting Design . . . . .Jessica M. Burgess
Composer/Sound Design . . . . .Scott O'Brien
Voice and Dialect Coach . . . . .Kohli Calhoun
Casting . . . . .Laura Maxwell-Scott, CSA
Technical Director . . . . .Greg Bellon/Production Consolidated of NY
Master Electrician . . . . .Keith A. Truax

CHARACTERS

RICK CHILDRESS: a man in his late twenties

TONI CHILDRESS: his wife, in her late twenties

COPELAND: a neighboring farmer, in his late fifties to early sixties

RICK CHILDRESS: a man in his forties

AGGY TAYLOR: a woman in her late thirties

RAFAEL LAMAS: a farm worker, in his forties

RICK CHILDRESS: a man in his late sixties to early seventies

MAGGIE FALLS: Rick's daughter, in her mid-twenties

TONI CHILDRESS: a woman in her late sixties to early seventies

SETTING

On a farm near Estelline, Texas. The action takes place on the front porch and yard of the Childress farm house, an older frame home. Though weathered, the house is sturdy, solidly constructed. The rising sun's light filters through the only trees for miles, those grouped near the house, acting as a brake against the elements.

TIME

Early summer.

HARVEST

ACT I

Rick Childress is sitting in an old, weathered wooden yard chair, on a towel. He is a young man of twenty-seven, wearing worn jeans, work shirt, and muddy boots. An old "gimme cap," a pair of work gloves, and various tractor parts rest on a small table that accompanies the chair. Another chair is empty. Periodically, he looks up at a bird call or to listen to the wind or other sounds only he can hear or stares at the distant horizon and loses himself in thought. Toni enters. She is a pretty woman of twenty-seven, yet the five years of struggling with the constant work of a failing farm have had their effect on her. Yet, this morning she appears renewed. She wears a worn, grayed, short summer sleeping gown. She is bright and cheerful. She drinks in the morning air and spies Rick. She tiptoes behind him and "gooses" him.

TONI: Jumpy this morning.

RICK: *(Startled.)* I didn't hear you.

TONI: Obviously. Good morning, Mr. Childress! *(She kisses him. He allows it but is tentative and winces with slight pain. She smiles, knowingly. Teasing.)* Something wrong? *(Touching his lip.)* A little sore?

RICK: Someone bit me last night.

TONI: Oh?

RICK: Yeah.

TONI: You didn't wake me.

RICK: No.

TONI: Going to let me sleep all day?

RICK: It was early. . .

TONI: You're sweet . . . and tender, and gentle, and forever passionate. I love you so much. Have I told you lately?

RICK: Last night, about four hundred times.

TONI: I could live last night over again.

RICK: I'm not sure I could.

TONI: Oh, you. I do love you. For all you said . . . and did. Rick, you just don't know. I'll never ever forget it. Smell, will you? How fresh . . . real sunshine and no rain. Just for us. A brand new start with everything washed clean.

RICK: Toni, it's not washed clean. It's washed away. Most of the sections are under water.

TONI: It doesn't seem to matter anymore . . . after last night.

RICK: *(Not responding.)* It's crazy. Perfect timing. No rain in sight. And then a hurricane of all things.

TONI: Our luck, baby.

RICK: It's a first for me. A hurricane that begins off the coast of Africa, rolls across the Atlantic, and hits the gulf. Comes straight off the coast of Texas into the high plains. And just stalls here. For three days it doesn't move. Just rain and more rain. Everything was looking so good.

TONI: Nothing ever looked good here. I think it's a message.

RICK: From who?

TONI: God. Mother Nature. Anybody. Get out while you can. Tomorrow you'll need a boat.

RICK: It's not funny.

TONI: Oh, but it is. You've given me that. Before last night, I would've stayed in bed. Now I have something to get up for. There are plans to be made. I can't wait to get to Dallas. We'll look for a house, a small one of course. But one with an extra bedroom. And I want to talk to Daddy—tell him we're coming. He and Momma'll be beside themselves. He'll set you up in one of his stores. And I want to call everyone I can still remember or who remembers me. I'll be on the phone for days. I want to see a movie . . . eat out . . . sleep in air conditioning . . . ice cream . . . *(Her excitement crescendos, and she stops suddenly.)* Am I being silly?

RICK: *(Moved.)* I haven't seen you like this in a long time. It's good to see you laugh.

TONI: And I have you to thank for it. To tell the truth, I didn't think I could last another day here. But when you finally agreed to sell the farm and move to Dallas, I thought I was dreaming. I've made it five years and knew any minute I might die. I really didn't think life would go on. *(She embraces him. He is distant.)* Rick? Where are you? I'm babbling away and you haven't heard a word. Not that you ever do. *(Jokingly.)* Has the good weather spoiled your mood?

RICK: I never can match your excitement. You know that.

TONI: After so long, I guess I am hard to swallow.

RICK: No, it's OK. You deserve to act anyway you want.

TONI: But what about you?

RICK: What about me?

TONI: Don't answer a question with a question.

RICK: What do you want to know?

TONI: You're exasperating.

RICK: No, just tired. I didn't sleep well. I didn't sleep at all.

TONI: Well, I slept like a log. I don't remember when I slept . . . *(Sinking in.)* Why didn't you sleep? I mean, were you sick? You seemed fine after we . . .

RICK: No, I'm fine. It's just that . . . it's so hard to talk. You're so happy and . . .

TONI: *(Moving to him.)* Rick? What's wrong? Honey? Talk to me.

RICK: After . . . last night . . . when I told you I'd sell . . . I guess I began to realize what it all meant.

TONI: Go on.

RICK: *(Moving away.)* I mean, what would happen. What's going to happen to me? How I would deal with so many changes. Can I really be anything outside of farming?

TONI: *(Relieved but concerned.)* Oh, honey. I know you. You'll be fine. You are so gifted. If I have faith in anyone, it's you. I've seen you adjust before.

RICK: That's not the question.

TONI: *(Surprised.)* Then what is?

RICK: *(Terribly difficult for him.)* It's not a matter of whether I can adjust . . . but do I want to.

TONI: *(All of her energy comes to a sudden end. She becomes silent and still.)* Could you explain?

RICK: After you fell asleep, I got up. I walked the farm. All night. Because if I didn't, I might never get another chance. Some of my best memories are of this place. It's . . . a part of me . . . of everything I am. I walked it . . . through the mud and water . . . and I know *(Struggling to tell her.)* I just can't up and leave it. *(Carefully.)* I . . . don't want to sell. I want to stay here. *(He waits for her reply. She can't.)* I know what this means to you. How disappointed you are. But maybe such a drastic change isn't the best thing for us right now.

TONI: *(In shock.)* The best for us.

RICK: For both of us. There's got to be a solution that both of us can live with. Selling the farm's not good for me. I can't stand the thought of leaving. I grew up here. This farm has been in my family for years. I grew up in this house . . . did chores when I was old enough to learn how. It's the reason I went to college and the reason I came back. Dad told me never give it up. There would be times when I was tempted, but save it for my sons. When he died, I became owner. It was natural. I don't know any other way of life . . . and I don't want to learn.

TONI: I see.

RICK: I know this is hard for you.

TONI: You do?

RICK: After last night, yes. It's been hard to tell you.

TONI: I'm sure.

RICK: I didn't know how . . . or what to say to make you understand. It's the hardest thing I've ever had to do.

TONI: Oh, yes. It must be awful . . . terrible. How difficult for you. So hard. After last night. After watching me make a total fool of myself. To let me go on and on . . . to get my hopes up . . . after years . . . just to drop this bomb on me. To let me plan . . . dream . . . the future looked so promising. And last night . . . how . . . how can you? How can you just shove it out of the way? You said you'd take me away from here. You promised . . . you lied . . .

RICK: Toni, honey.

TONI: No! What went wrong?

RICK: What?

TONI: Everything was discussed. We exhausted the topic. You agreed. You said so.

RICK: I know.

TONI: Aren't we in debt enough? Haven't the crops failed enough? Haven't three years taught you anything?

RICK: I know.

TONI: All we own is a seventy-five-year-old house that needs a roof and new plumbing, a fifty-three pickup needing constant care with parts too expensive to replace . . . outdated farm equipment . . . the bank owns the tractor. We had to borrow for seed and more just to pay bills until next harvest.

RICK: I know.

TONI: You know? Do you remember that any profits on the next harvest, if there are profits, are spoken for? Remember? Two good harvests to get out of the red. What about the fields now? How much profit this year? Does that mean two more? Three?

RICK: I don't know.

TONI: You have three standing offers to buy this place. Rick?

RICK: I know things look bad. But think. I spent all night thinking. The positives really outweigh the negatives.

TONI: I don't see any positives. Rick, if it's the responsibility to your dead parents, that's not a positive. Not when we can't afford groceries or clothes or any kind of luxury of the modern world.

RICK: Luxury?

TONI: I don't care what it sounds like. Yes, luxury. I want more out of life than

TV static from Amarillo. I want a glass of water that doesn't taste or look like the sewer. I want to flush the commode without constant fear of rejection. I want more than what Estelline, Texas can offer.

RICK: I know. And you deserve them. How do you think I've felt not being able to give you those things? The past few years . . . I've wanted to so much. It's still not out of the question. A couple of good crops of cotton and we're home free.

COPELAND: *(From far offstage.)* Hello, the house. *(Both are startled at the interruption.)*

RICK: Copeland?

TONI: I called him . . . when I got up. Being an old friend of your family and always offering to buy, I called him over to talk.

RICK: To come talk? About buying my farm? Without asking me?

TONI: After last night . . .

RICK: But to call Copeland? To call anyone. Without talking to me? Now what? You know I hate surprises.

TONI: So do I. *(Rick understands. Mr. Copeland enters. A man in his late fifties to early sixties, he wears khaki work clothes. Toni goes to the door and steps inside. She is still in her gown.)*

COPELAND: Morning, Mrs. Childress. Rick. *(A long, awkward pause. All stand and stare at each other. Copeland attempts to break the ice.)* Is this a bad time?

TONI: Sorry for the way I look. I'll get dressed. Mr. Copeland? With what we talked about over the phone? There's some problems. Rick, you explain. *(She exits.)*

RICK: Morning, Cope.

COPELAND: Rick. *(Both are uncomfortable as neither knows what to say.)* Your wife called me this morning.

RICK: Yeah, I know. Just found out.

COPELAND: I see. *(Silence. Changing the subject. He moves downstage looking across the horizon.)* Got a lot of acreage under water.

RICK: Sure do.

COPELAND: Had to get the big wheels out to make it here. Road's covered.

RICK: Thought as much.

COPELAND: Can we sit?

RICK: I'm sorry. Sure.

COPELAND: *(Another moment of awkwardness.)* Rick, you have a change of heart?

RICK: I guess so.

COPELAND: Now don't feel any pressure from me, son. I don't want you to do anything you're not ready to do.

RICK: Cope? How can I just up and sell it? I was born here. My dad and his wife both died here. They all could have left, but they loved it. That's what got them through all the hard times. Grandpa always talked about bad times coming and going but the land is always here.

COPELAND: Well, I admit you've had your share. *(Points out to the fields.)* How are you going to deal with that?

RICK: Pray for a dry August.

COPELAND: I noticed you planted cotton this time. Probably should've stayed away from sugar beets. Never seen 'em work too good.

RICK: I know cotton. Studied it. Grew up with it. If it doesn't rot, this crop could save everything.

COPELAND: *(Pause.)* I don't mean to pry. Why'd you leave it?

RICK: Momentary insanity.

COPELAND: For three years?

RICK: Toni's always affected me that way. She gets excited . . . I get carried away. She talked me into trying a section. Her dad studies stock market reports and discovered sugar beets. The first year, the price went through the roof. We did so well, the next planting I gave up most of the sections to it. *(Beat.)* And the market fell.

COPELAND: So did the rain.

RICK: I tried again the next year. The prices looked promising. Then a late killing frost. Replant. Drought. *(Pause.)* Cotton made it both years. Now, I'm just hoping to break even, if I can release some of that water.

COPELAND: I've got to do the same.

RICK: You get hit bad?

COPELAND: No. I'm a bit higher than here. But if we get any more rain, I'm looking for the plug.

RICK: Huh?

COPELAND: The plug . . . to the drain.

RICK: Oh. *(Changing the subject.)* I'm sorry about all this.

COPELAND: Don't be. *(Starts to leave.)* I've known you all your life and I hate to see you having to make this decision. But . . . if, and I say if, you decide to sell, remember I know this land. Worked it for more years than I care to say, by horse and tractor. Explored every foot of this country, when I was just a pup. Me and your dad. People don't seem to understand anymore. The smell, the taste . . . I always knew I'd be buried here. Wouldn't have it any other way. I want you to know I'd care for it. But, enough of that. Now, you talk to your wife. Take all the time you need.

I'll hang around awhile, just in case. I saw your truck down the road, up to the hubs in mud. I'll pull it out.

RICK: You don't have to do that.

COPELAND: I know. *(Copeland exits. Rick watches him go. Toni enters, unknown to him. She watches him as he paces.)*

TONI: He'll buy the farm.

RICK: Probably.

TONI: And he'll love it.

RICK: Wouldn't doubt it. So?

TONI: So . . . Rick, why did you agree to sell? Why let me get my hopes up?

RICK: These past few months have been hell-on-earth. I began to doubt the farm and myself. Everything seemed to be giving up. No matter how I tried, I couldn't make it work. Yeah, I thought about giving up . . . about a hundred times. Then this storm hit. I felt like I was at the end of the row. Couldn't take another set back. I just caved in.

TONI: But today?

RICK: I needed distance . . . to think about how I really felt. Now, I see it's not the right thing for us . . . both of us, together.

TONI: You mean, that if what's good for one is not good for the other, we just drop it?

RICK: Yeah, something like that.

TONI: What about me, Rick? What's good for me? If the farm is good for you and not me? What about that? Where does that leave us?

RICK: I'm not blind, Toni. I've watched you. It hurts to see you so unhappy. And I feel it's my fault. You're isolated out here. You don't have anyone to talk to and we've had to "make do" with just about everything. I just wanted you happy again. And then last night. I figured that whatever it took, I'd make it happen. I could fix it.

TONI: The farm is not the remedy.

RICK: Five years ago you made a promise. To make a life with me. Here.

TONI: Five years ago I was junior league material—fresh out of A&M with an Ag. graduate on my arm. I loved you the moment I saw you. I loved your dreams, your plans, the way your eyes lit up when talking about your endless horizon. You weren't like anyone I'd ever met. The day you won that professor over with your paper on cotton production . . . I saw you actually giddy with excitement. I fell in love with you. Not your way of life, or your love for the farm, or the reality of what this place has done to us.

RICK: I tried to tell you what it'd be like.

TONI: No, nothing could have warned me. I couldn't begin to understand. I saw it as a challenge. I wanted to please you. I was in love. I wanted to make you a home, make you happy, to have your children . . . *(A beat.)*

RICK: And? So? Where are they? You keep saying, "Not now, not yet, the time isn't right."

TONI: It's not.

RICK: Then when is?

TONI: How are you going to pay for them?!

RICK: What are you talking about?

TONI: Just to get them home from the hospital . . .we can't even afford new clothes for us. What about children?

RICK: If we wait till we can afford them, we'll never have any.

TONI: And for what?

RICK: What?

TONI: Why do you want children? You've always wanted them, but never told me why.

RICK: I . . . we need a family . . . I want us to have kids . . . to . . .

TONI: Oh, Rick. You want heirs.

RICK: Sure. There has to be someone to give all this to. My dad gave it to me and his to him.

TONI: I don't want children for the sole purpose of carrying on a name or force-feeding a life of farming down their throats.

RICK: I never felt that way.

TONI: You were destined. You never had a chance to know anything else. It was fed to you from day one.

RICK: This is the only life I ever wanted.

TONI: You were never offered a choice. You said the first night you spent out of the county was at college. There's a big world out there with thousands of things to choose from. But you won't consider it. Only the farm. And that's why we're still here and why we're broke, in debt, and childless.

RICK: Do you really think you're being fair?

TONI: Do you?

RICK: After five years . . . five years you suddenly wake up and hate the farm. Five years we work together to make this place work and you, all of a sudden, give up.

TONI: I never loved the farm! *(Beat.)* It just took five years to build the courage to tell you.

RICK: What can I say? This is what I do. *(Beats.)* I love this.

TONI: More than me? *(Pause.)* You have to answer, Rick.

RICK: *(Pause.)* I had a tree house up there. I spent hours . . . the day I learned to drive that tractor . . . right through that fence . . . and through the wall of the barn. Then, I learned construction . . . how to mend fences and build walls. I learned to swim in the creek, when the water was deep enough . . . caught tadpoles, lizards, horned toads. The old Border collie had eighteen puppies under the house and I got to watch. I remember the first time Dad let me work on the Ford. Catching fireflies, counting shooting stars . . . all that I remember. And it happened here. *(He considers carefully, moving away from her.)* These past five years with you being here have been wonderful. You are my wife. I love you with all my heart. *(Beat.)* But I've only known you six years. The farm and I go back generations.

TONI: *(Shaken, she sits.)* It's no surprise, really. I always felt it. I just never thought I'd hear you say so. Now I know how a mistress must feel.

RICK: *(To her, kneeling.)* No. Not a mistress. I want you to be with me. A partner, to share this, not compete with it.

TONI: You're a dreamer. But I've watched the sun bake the ground or the rain drown it. I watched the weather, alone, strip the fields of anything living.

RICK: But that's the weather—a constant inconstant. An early killing frost. A late spring freeze, tornadoes, drought. That's nature. Your objections can't be based on weather. It goes deeper. It's not what I've done or what I don't feel. It's about what you're not and what you wished you were.

TONI: I need more.

RICK: Toni . . .

TONI: I've done everything I knew to do. Everything you asked. I helped in the fields, driven machinery, helped you repair the tractor and truck. When we couldn't afford help, which was most of the time, I played farmhand and still, I cooked meals, cleaned house, washed clothes, even when my legs felt like lead and I couldn't move a muscle.

RICK: You never said a word.

TONI: Until last night. When I saw a speck of hope, there was something to grab onto. My old life died last night when you said you'd sell. I can't go back. I won't.

RICK: So. You've made up your mind. Without me. You're leaving? *(A moment of panic attacks both as they realize the ramifications of the events. They embrace, in fear.)*

TONI: No, not without you.

RICK: But you said—

TONI: I said the only feeling I have left is love for you.

RICK: You know I love you. You scared me. I'd hate to face this place without you.

TONI: I was afraid you'd want to.

RICK: But it'll get better. I know. Doesn't it always? You'll see. Things'll work out. One good crop of cotton . . . *(She pulls away, hurt and dazed.)* I know cotton. I feel good about it. I never should have left it.

TONI: You're blind or deaf. I don't know which. Haven't you heard a word I said? One good crop of cotton? This one's under water. Wait another year? Just to break even? That means no profit for another. Then borrow to plant for another? Another year to pay that off. Then another and another. Where does it end? How many years?

RICK: It doesn't matter. It's a life I want.

TONI: With or without me?

RICK: With you, of course.

TONI: Then tell me. All I need . . . is to know that you love me more than this piece of dirt. Tell me! Now! I've got to know.

(He desperately tries to say something. He desperately wants to tell her what she wants to hear. He cannot. Toni doesn't react. She stands a moment in silence, then moves to the front door of the house. She exits for a moment and reenters carrying a small suitcase and her purse.)

RICK: Toni? What are you doing?

TONI: Two days ago I packed . . . to take a vacation. *(Laughs.)* Imagine. A vacation. We've never taken a vacation. Never could find the time or money. I was going to catch a bus to Dallas to see Dad and Mom. I couldn't scrape together the bus fare. I didn't tell you. You'd be hurt . . . or ashamed. But after last night I thought we'd be going together. I didn't even unpack. Just taking this. There's not much anyway that I could be seen in.

RICK: If that's all you want, I'll go. We'll go visit your parents! OK? Just let me get the fields dried out. Only a few days! Then, we can take a little time off!

TONI: *(Emotionless, dulled. She moves slowly to exit.)* It seems easy now. And the right thing for me. You've emptied me, Rick. One day I may hate you for that.

RICK: Toni. You can't go! You just can't quit like this! Don't leave me! There's got to be another way!

TONI: *(With feeling.)* Come with me. Please.

RICK: I can't leave.

TONI: *(Spoken or unspoken: I guess I've always known that outside of the farm, you couldn't exist. You couldn't be just a number in a large city of nameless faces. What would you become? Could I love that person the way I love you now? Maybe I wouldn't. But you've loved me and the person I've become, even when I couldn't.)*

(She exits. He watches her go. At a loss, he stands in disbelief. Copeland enters slowly.)

COPELAND: *(Awkwardly.)* Rick . . . son? I'm not sure what's happened here . . . but your wife has asked me for a ride into Estelline. I don't want to butt in where it's not welcome, but she's asked me for bus fare.

RICK: *(Struck dumb.)* It's OK. I'll pay you back.

COPELAND: That's not my worry here. *(No reaction from Rick, who is staring down the road at Copeland's truck.)* Are you all right?

RICK: I'm losing her, Cope! She's leaving, right in front of me . . . and I can't get my hands out of my pockets. What am I supposed to do?

COPELAND: *(Hurting for him and is in a very awkward position.)* I can't tell you, son. This has got to be your decision.

RICK: She's sitting in that truck down there and I can't reach her. *(Spoken or unspoken: Am I wrong? What do I do? I can't give her what she needs. I can't. Is that wrong? Everything tells me so, but there she is.)* And I love her, Cope. *(Gaining control. With full understanding.)* *(Spoken or unspoken: How can I leave? And how can she stay?)*

COPELAND: What now?

RICK: *(Rising and putting on his hat and gloves.)* I've got most of my sections under water. I'm going to get on my tractor, and go out, and . . . try to find the plug. *(Rick moves to the porch. Copeland watches, then moves to exit. He hesitates, looking at Rick, who has stopped at the front door. Copeland exits. Rick turns, returns to the edge of the porch and stares into the distance as the lights fade.)*

END OF ACT I

ACT II

Near midday, in July, twenty years later. The action takes place in the front yard of the Childress farmhouse. New chairs have replaced the old ones and new features reveal the change in time. The hot summer sun beats straight down through the trees casting the yard in intense shadows. At rise: Beginning of incidental music. Rick Childress, now in his midforties, is wearing clean but worn jeans, a short-sleeved work shirt worn over a T-shirt, and work boots. A clean "gimme" cap is on the table. He is seated in one of the outdoor chairs writing in his journal. There is a table between the two chairs with a carburetor and tools lying on it. He is totally absorbed. Rafael, a man in his forties, sits in the other chair. The two sit in silence for a long time. This is a ritual.

RAFAEL: You finish your writing for the day?

RICK: What do you mean?

RAFAEL: You writing a book? Maybe another one of them articles?

RICK: *(Uncomfortable.)* Don't you have anything to do?

RAFAEL: I finished in the barn. I can change the oil on the Deere. It's time, you know.

RICK: The door slides?

RAFAEL: Just like it did before you smashed it with the tractor.

RICK: *(Defensive.)* I didn't smash it. I merely bumped into it.

RAFAEL: Whatever you say. You're the boss. But your little bump knocked the door completely off the runners, split the frame, and rearranged part of the tractor.

RICK: OK, OK . . . thanks for reminding me.

RAFAEL: Anytime. Want me to disc the perimeters? Most don't care but I know you like 'em clean and level. Or I can thin out the plants? Or I can get a head start on the spraying?

(Aggy Taylor "drifts" onstage, unseen by Rick: She is an attractive thirty-something woman in khakis. Her short-cropped hair and somewhat masculine demeanor support her tom-boyish tendencies. She is lost in her thoughts as she views the landscape. She is carrying a clipboard by her side as she works her way along the stage, noticeably affected by the farm.)

RICK: *(Laughing.)* Yeah, go ahead and disc. That'll take the afternoon. Check the traps as you go.

RAFAEL: *(Delighted.)* All right. *(Rising, seeing Aggy for the first time.)* Hey, didn't the state boll weevil guy come by earlier this week?

RICK: *(Not seeing her.)* Did you watch him?

RAFAEL: *(Perplexed, he continues to watch her throughout this scene.)* Nope. Just saw him driving the perimeters.

RICK: And he never got out of his truck. Just drove by each trap. Nobody's eyesight is that good.

RAFAEL: You don't trust him?

RICK: Not with my cotton.

RAFAEL: And you trust me? A compliment from Mr. Rick Childress. I may have a heart attack.

RICK: The traps?

RAFAEL: Done.

RICK: It's Friday. Stop by on your way home.

RAFAEL: My pleasure. *(As he prepares to leave and unable to leave the unfolding mystery.)* I don't mean to be nosy, but who's your lady friend?

RICK: *(Seeing Aggy for the first time. He's uneasy with strangers.)* What? Where did she come from?

RAFAEL: Don't you know her?

RICK: See what she wants.

RAFAEL: Nice looking, don't you think?

RICK: Let's not think. Just go ask her.

RAFAEL: Why me?

RICK: Well, let's see. Maybe because you work here and I pay well. Maybe you just feel loyal, working for me these ten years. Or maybe because I asked you to. *(Rick begins to exit.)*

RAFAEL: It's your farm she's inspecting.

RICK: *(Stopping abruptly and returning to him, hushed.)* Inspecting?

RAFAEL: She's filling out some sort of forms or something.

RICK: Why would she do that?

RAFAEL: I don't know, why don't you ask her?

RICK: I don't like strangers.

RAFAEL: Rick, you don't like anybody.

(Rick is just focused on Aggy.)

RAFAEL: That's just the talk. I think you're one sweet guy.

RICK: Rafe, after all these years, I think more of you than just a hired hand. However, just to prove all that talk is correct, I may grab you by the scruff of your neck and throw you under my pickup and roll over you a couple of times.

RAFAEL: If I were you, I'd check her out.

RICK: I'm going. What's the big deal?

RAFAEL: I bet a week's wages that's she's single.

RICK: *(Flustered.)* What are you doing?

RAFAEL: Maybe I can fix you up.

RICK: Hello. Can I help you?

(Aggy is on one knee, which is supporting her clipboard. She is writing furiously. Rick sees she didn't hear him and looks back at Rafael who motions him forward. He moves a few feet.)

RICK: Excuse me, ma'am?

(Again, nothing from AGGY. He looks at Rafael who motions again, having fun at Rick's uneasiness. Rick moves forward.)

RICK: Can I help you? Can I help you, ma'am?

AGGY: No, but I can help you, Mr. Childress.

RAFAEL: She knows your name.

RICK: OK, what's it going to cost?

AGGY: You believe in love at first sight?

RICK: *(Taken aback.)* What?

RAFAEL: She likes you.

RICK: Would you stop?

RAFAEL: Ask her out!

RICK: What?

RAFAEL: I'm only looking out for your welfare.

RICK: Don't!

AGGY: This place is wonderful!

RICK: Excuse me?

AGGY: *(Rapturously.)* I love your farm! It has life . . . a soul all its own.

RICK: *(To her.)* That's nice but it's not for sale.

AGGY: Oh, I don't want to buy it. I want you to give it to me.

(Rafael laughs.)

RICK: What?

AGGY: *(Laughing.)* Just joking, Mr. Childress. Just a joke. *(Offering a handshake.)* Hi, I'm Aggy Taylor. I'm the new county extension agent.

RAFAEL: Rafael Lamas, at your service.

AGGY: Pleased to meet you, Mr. Lamas.

RAFAEL: Just RAFAEL: This is Mr. Rick Childress, proprietor of this small empire.

RICK: *(Following the news that she's the county agent, he is anxious to get rid of her.)* Happy to meet you, Mrs. Taylor. If there isn't anything else, Rafael and I've got to get back to work. Right, Mister Lamas?

RAFAEL: *(Sorry to leave.)* Good to see you, ma'am. Call me if he gives you trouble. *(Going to Rick.)* Ask her out! She's nice. *(Rafael exits.)*

AGGY: *(As Rafael disappears behind the house.)* I'm sure I'll see you again, Rafael. *(To Rick.)* I'm meeting all the farmers in the county. The way I figure it, I'm more likely to catch you here than in a meeting.

RICK: You have a point—

AGGY: *(Interrupting. Sitting on the porch.)* You're not an easy man to catch.

RICK: Oh?

AGGY: I've been by several times but you're never home.

RICK: I rarely leave.

AGGY: And I've called.

RICK: I rarely answer.

AGGY: Why?

RICK: I have the phone to call, not be called.

AGGY: *(Rising.)* You're my last, you know?

RICK: Last what?

AGGY: I've met everyone. Took me a month but I checked everyone off my list, except you. I began to think you were a myth.

RICK: It's a good size farm. I'm out on it somewhere every day.

AGGY: *(Playfully.)* A lot of places to hide.

RICK: *(Clearly unhappy with the exchange and losing patience.)* Yeah, I hide . . . from nosy neighbors and zealous county extension agents.

AGGY: Mr. Childress—

RICK: *(Interrupting.)* So, the list is complete. We've met. You can leave with a clear conscience.

AGGY: *(With a growing curiosity and interest.)* Uh-huh . . . who is Rafael?

RICK: I hired him to help me out.

AGGY: Permanent help?

RICK: As I need him.

AGGY: So, the myth is only a myth!

RICK: Myth?

AGGY: You're not a total one-man operation?

RICK: Who said I was?

AGGY: Your klatch buddies.

RICK: My buddies? "Klatch"?

AGGY: Colleagues . . . peers . . . they meet . . . socialize . . . talk . . . over coffee. Ever heard of it?

RICK: *(On the porch. He thinks about the name and laughs. He becomes serious again.)* "Klatch," I like that. Nope, got better things to do than drive all the way to town to drink coffee, smoke a few packs, and bellyache and complain why my crops are failing.

AGGY: You're not a very social person are you, Mr. Childress?

RICK: You surprise me, Mrs. Taylor. You learn quickly.

AGGY: My feelings could take a beating if I stayed around here too long. *(Rick says nothing, just looks at her. Then, he moves to pick up the carburetor and begins wiping it with an oil rag.)* I see. So . . . it's been said that you have the most productive farm in the county.

RICK: Who said that?

AGGY: County Ag newsletter.

RICK: Never heard of it.

AGGY: *(Taking one off her clipboard and giving it to him.)* It's new. Ought to read one. I'm very proud of it. I bet you'll find it useful. *(Pause.)* And you're not going to read a page of it, are you?

RICK: Now that you mention it, no.

AGGY: Just like they said, a self-made, single-minded man.

RICK: It's just that whenever someone takes the time to drop-in this far out, they want me to buy something I don't want or do something I don't want to do. So, before you go any further, I'm not interested.

AGGY: I don't want a thing. I want to help you.

RICK: Oh! Well, that's a change. *(He thinks for a moment then tosses her the carburetor.)* OK, put this carburetor in that pickup?

AGGY: Nope.

RICK: No, huh? OK, I've got some warping boards on this porch.

AGGY: Can't do.

RICK: No, again. OK, I got a bed that needs making. Dishes? Floors?

AGGY: *(The beginning of a little anger at the turn of the conversation.)* I'm not a hired hand or maid. Besides, I hate housework.

RICK: So, I gather you don't do windows?

AGGY: Or dust your furniture or darn your socks or wash your clothes.

RICK: I guess cooking is out of the question, too?

AGGY: That's not why I'm here.

RICK: You're the one who wanted to help.

AGGY: Why not let me do what I'm paid to do?

RICK: *(Exasperated.)* Who's stopping you?

AGGY: *(First signs of her crumbling. She tosses the carburetor back to him.)* Forget it, just forget it! *(Aggy, losing her patience, begins an exit. Rick moves to the table, leaves the carburetor, and picks up the journal. After several steps, she catches herself and thinks of a new tack.)* I see your plants have "squared."

RICK: *(Reading his journal.)* Yep.

AGGY: "The structure of the plant has appeared and now you're waiting for them to bloom."

RICK: Set boles.

AGGY: What?

RICK: Set boles, not bloom.

AGGY: Same thing, right?

RICK: Yep.

AGGY: I like . . . "bloom." Why were you late in your planting?

RICK: Excuse me?

AGGY: That's the way it appears. Look at the size of the plants and the time of the month.

RICK: I wasn't late. I waited for one more March freeze.

AGGY: You knew it was coming?

RICK: Does that look like alfalfa?

AGGY: So, in reality, your neighbors planted too early?

RICK: I'm not one to point out another's mistakes. Let's just say their cotton didn't come up.

AGGY: And had to replant something else . . . like alfalfa?

RICK: It gets expensive not paying attention to Mother Nature.

AGGY: So, Mr. Childress . . . you're a weatherman, too.

RICK: No, I'm a farmer.

AGGY: But the others . . . they watch the weather.

RICK: I don't depend on a second-string meteorologist to tell me how to farm.

AGGY: So . . . how do you know when . . .

RICK: *(Beat.)* There are signs.

AGGY: What kind of signs?

RICK: You should know this. Ground temperature, upper wind patterns . . . and a bird.

AGGY: A bird?

RICK: A little bird . . .

AGGY: *(Laughing.)* A bird.

RICK: That stops by on its migration from Alaska.

AGGY: You're kidding me. A bird?

RICK: Sandpiper . . . I never plant without her.

AGGY: Have you ever told anyone?

RICK: It's no secret, lady.

AGGY: *(Annoyed.)* But, you never shared this?

RICK: I mind my own business. You want it known, put it in your newsletter.

AGGY: I will.

RICK: *(Moving away.)* And how will you put it? Rick Childress stakes his crop on the migration of a sandpiper? I can imagine what they'll say.

AGGY: *(Leaning against a porch support.)* So you do care?

RICK: *(Flustered.)* That's not the point.

AGGY: It would be to your advantage to keep this quiet.

RICK: How so?

AGGY: Less competition, better market price.

RICK: Oh, so now I'm a crook.

AGGY: I didn't say that. Maybe you're a shrewd businessman.

RICK: One farm is not going to affect the market. Lady, I'm a cotton farmer. I mind my business, do my work, and leave the rest alone and I'm not about to ask another man to gamble his livelihood on my idiosyncrasies.

AGGY: *(Pressing.)* You don't mix with your neighbors much.

RICK: Why ask?

AGGY: It seems everyone knows everyone else. In fact, they know each other quite well. Then, there's you. You are acquainted, mind you, but have few friends. Why keep to yourself?

RICK: Maybe that's none of your business.

AGGY: Maybe because you're not like them. Maybe because you're a helpless romantic who wouldn't be understood. And you know it.

RICK: Now that I've used my lunch break for analysis, I can make it through another day. And just in case it comes up, I loved my dad. Now, can I please get back to work?

(Rick moves to the table and picks up the carburetor and places the journal on the table. He begins to exit.)

AGGY: Are you going to write me off or are you the kind of man who'll at least give me the chance to prove myself?

RICK: I don't know. Depends . . . just how are you going to prove yourself?

AGGY: *(Thinking.)* OK . . . how's this? Cotton was fifty-two cents this morning.

RICK: Yes it was. Last week it was forty-eight.

AGGY: I'm no fortune teller, but I think the market is at a two year high.

RICK: It'll drop around August and drop again in November, which is why I'll harvest in October.

AGGY: Which is still a reasonable price.

RICK: Depends on China.

AGGY: What?

RICK: It will depend on the price set for foreign markets. Why do you think American farmers are such a happy lot? Do your homework.

AGGY: Fine. OK . . . I see you have a fallow southeast section.

RICK: You don't miss a trick, do you?

AGGY: *(Testy.)* Don't make this harder than it is.

RICK: It's your nickel.

AGGY: Ever try corn?

RICK: Nope.

AGGY: Why not?

RICK: Why should I?

AGGY: You'd have an added crop, soil nutrient, and ground cover.

RICK: Lying fallow will do the same without the added expense.

AGGY: Minus the crop.

RICK: I don't know corn.

AGGY: I'll introduce you. We can work together.

RICK: Corn is not my choice crop.

AGGY: Afraid to learn?

RICK: I grow cotton.

AGGY: What type of seed? BT or UNR?

RICK: Conventional.

AGGY: But BT is treated.

RICK: And produced well . . . in Africa . . . for the African farmer . . . and researchers . . . under controlled experiments. It's not proven here.

AGGY: *(Thinking.)* Fine. I noticed you used the "skip-row" planting technique in half of your sections. Why not the rest?

RICK: Did someone pay you to come here and torture me?

AGGY: Why do you say that?

RICK: I grant you, you have a book's eye view of cotton. That can be learned in a few days of reading at the library. So don't come here expecting to compete with me.

AGGY: I'm not competing.

RICK: Then why twenty questions?

AGGY: It's not that at all. I'm merely showing you that I know something, too. You don't like me very much, do you?

RICK: Mrs. Taylor, you make my teeth itch. I don't even know you.

AGGY: *(Offering her hand.)* Ok, then. Let's start over. I'm Aggy Taylor, Hall County Extension Agent, come calling to meet the neighbors and offer my resources and perhaps friendship.

RICK: *(Ignoring the offered hand.)* Just like that?

AGGY: Just like that.

RICK: You come out here to save this dumb ole farmer? Is that really why you're here? *(Knowingly.)* Or did the job play out in Kansas?

AGGY: How did you know I'm from Kansas?

RICK: I learned to read at a very early age, Mrs. Taylor. I do take the newspaper. I make it a point to concern myself with things that will affect this farm and how to cope with them. And I saw you coming all the way from Salina.

AGGY: What are you driving at?

RICK: You had the same job in Kansas. Right? Now you take on the same job in Hall County. I'd call that a step down. What'd you get out of it? Wasn't a raise. Wasn't power or prestige. Come all the way from Kansas corn to high plains cotton and you want me to defend my choices. What do you bring to the table? How are you going to help me? You wanna be my buddy? Answer my questions.

AGGY: *(Stunned and feeling very uncomfortable.)* Have we gotten off on the wrong foot or what?

RICK: You asked to prove yourself. And you have. *(Beat.)* You county people never change. How many have there been . . . six, seven? Come in, gladhanding, making a pitch about fulfilling everything we farmers could ever hope for, how you got all the answers, gonna smarten us up, and then poof, you're gone, using this tiny county as a step up . . . or who knows in your case. The first one . . . I don't remember his name . . . was a real nice guy. We talked hours. Walked the fields . . . had a great friendship, real buddies, you could say. I even tried a few things he suggested. Three months and he was in Lubbock. I don't blame him, I guess. The second one stayed six months. He's in San Angelo. The third quit and teaches in Arkansas. The fourth didn't even stay—

AGGY: So it's the office you hold against me?

RICK: You people move in with all these fresh ideas right out of journals and papers and lectures cornering the market on know-how and experience when it comes to planting some crop I know nothing about or care to. I made two bad mistakes on this farm. Sugar Beets from a previous life . . . and some new "guaranteed" strain of alfalfa from a county guy who promised his personal service until he took a job in Tennessee. He forgot to tell me about a possible blight. I lost every section I planted.

AGGY: And you blame him?

RICK: Oh, no, I blame me for not sticking to what I know and allowing him to talk me into something I don't.

AGGY: And being a woman doesn't help either?

RICK: You know, I noticed that right off. The fact is, it doesn't bother me at all. You hear me complain? You hear me make any sexists remarks?

AGGY: Well, no . . . except those cheap shots about housework.

RICK: *(Caught.)* Well, you have me there. That was out of place.

AGGY: Well . . . you can be charming!

RICK: Don't get used to it.

AGGY: I won't.

RICK: Good.

AGGY: And I'm not wet behind the ears, right out of college, and on my
way up.

RICK: So?

AGGY: So, it seems that I'm more experienced and have more stability than my
predecessors. I'm not a climber. I want to settle here.

RICK: *(Sarcastically.)* Well, welcome to Hall County. Lady, I don't care if you
are man, woman, or somewhere in between. I don't care if you are
twenty, sixty, or cold in the ground. And unlike what I said, I really don't
care if you're from Kansas, Nebraska, or Timbuktu. This is my farm. It's
not in hock or lien. I don't ask for help and I think less of those who depend on it.

AGGY: Like me?

RICK: If you like.

AGGY: I agree.

RICK: You . . . with what?

AGGY: I agree.

RICK: Doesn't anything rile you, lady?

AGGY: Sure, you do it very well.

RICK: I wish you'd let me know.

AGGY: I'm not that easy to get rid of.

RICK: I'm beginning to find that out.

AGGY: And you're a gentleman. You won't walk off and leave a lady standing
alone in your front yard. And it's not "lady," "hey you," or Mrs. Taylor.
The name's Aggy.

RICK: And?

AGGY: I just wanted to get that straight. And I agree with you that I don't view
myself as anyone's savior or that no one should depend on me to make
or break their crop. And I don't see myself in the same league with my
predecessors. What I do is provide a resource and support. And that's it.

RICK: And?

AGGY: And?

RICK: So far, there's always another "and."

AGGY: That's it.

RICK: Really?

AGGY: Really.

RICK: That's it?

AGGY: Yep.

RICK: Then, we're done?

AGGY: Interview's over.

RICK: *(Relieved.)* Can I show you to your pickup?

AGGY: *(She is very aware of his journal.)* It's not about the office at all, is it?

RICK: What?

AGGY: *(Realization.)* It's not that I'm the county extension agent. You have a pet peeve, sure, but it really has nothing to do with me. And it's not me personally. Wow! For a minute, you really had me going. I get it now. You're a hermit . . . a recluse.

RICK: When you're right, you're right.

AGGY: *(A full stop, with insight, fully intrigued.)* I don't think so. Man, you're everything they said . . . and more.

RICK: "They" again?

AGGY: Ole Childress, they say . . . tough, strong, stubborn, and single-minded to a fault.

RICK: Is that why you left me to last?

AGGY: They said nothing about you being insightful, sensitive, a die-hard romantic and idealist.

RICK: *(Laughing.)* Where'd you get that?

AGGY: Just from listening to you.

RICK: You haven't heard a word I've said.

AGGY: It's not what they said. It's what they didn't say. Idle coffee chatter doesn't begin to tell your story. What a challenge! That's why I'm still here. I liked you before I even met you.

RICK: *(Thinking, then retrieving the journal and pen.)* I tell you what. What is your telephone number?

AGGY: 552-2212.

RICK: *(He writes it down and leaves the journal on the table.)* I'll call if something comes up.

AGGY: Is this your idea of a brush-off?

RICK: Sure, if that's how you want to put it. Now, against my better manners and upbringing, I'm going in that door, leaving you here alone. I won't be anyone's challenge!

(RICK exits into the house, slamming the door. She stands there a moment, stunned. When he doesn't return, she moves about the yard, reproaching herself. She moves to the porch and knocks on the door. She checks the windows. She moves back to the chair and sits, frustrated. She repeatedly glances back to the door. She decides to try the door again and crosses up to the porch. She opens the door to enter but losing her courage, returns to the chair. She sits on his journal. She places it on the table. She stares at the journal and then realizes she gave him the wrong phone number.)

AGGY: Stupid! *(She looks for a pen and paper, which she doesn't have. She opens the journal, takes his pen, and begins to write the number. She discovers the poetry inside. She is amazed and turns page after page.)* "The rain came, liquid crystal shadows of what can never be. For waters flood the barren fields where once we planted dreams."

(She is deeply moved and quickly emotional. She turns the page, unable to stop. Rick comes to the front door, looking through the screen door for her. Unable to see her from his angle, he is confident she left. He steps onto the porch and sees her in the chair with his open journal.)

RICK: What are you doing? *(He takes the journal. She remains seated.)* What gives you the right? What makes you think . . . come up here uninvited, interrupting my routine—

AGGY: *(Not meeting his glare.)* I . . . I . . . am so . . .

RICK: I was thinking you were different. You almost had me there, too.

AGGY: *(Very soft and genuine.)* I never meant to invade your privacy. I did. I am sorry. I am so sorry.

RICK: *(Incredulous.)* I don't get you at all! Why?

AGGY: *(Still, very softly.)* I got the phone number wrong. And I wanted to leave you an apology for the trouble. When I opened the journal, I saw your writing. *(She hesitates for his reply. He's stumped and speechless.)* I'm sorry. I never meant to intrude. *(Beat.)* It's just that, I've driven your farm for a week. I sat in the fields . . . hoping you'd see me. Waiting to drum up the courage to meet you . . . to introduce myself . . . I fell in love with it. After all that's been said about you . . . all the warnings and all the revelations . . . I was scared to death. But sitting there in your fields . . . *(Long moment.)* I remember the smells, the feeling of the wind ever blowing in my face. My mother puttering about the kitchen and the cleanest house you ever saw. Every day was another day to impress Papa. And Papa . . . he couldn't wait to get into the fields every morning. Never complained when I chose to follow him. He'd let me ride with him plowing . . . or sit with me in the middle of a section just staring across the landscape. We'd be there forever. He'd tell me stories, explain why we did this or that to the crops, or just be still. Those were my favorite times. And when I read your poetry . . .

RICK: So, you grew up on a farm?

AGGY: *(Continues, lost in thought.)* Kansas corn and wheat and whatever. Lived there till I was fifteen. That was the year we lost the place. Papa tried everything. The debt was too great. We lived hand-to-mouth for two years but the writing was on the wall. Poverty was bad enough but losing the farm was devastating. After the public auction, we moved to town, but Papa never was the same. He was heart-sick . . . never found his place. He died from a heart attack two years later. After that, Momma went out like a light. She died that winter. Some great senior year, huh? *(Where Rick was distant, he slowly relaxes. She breaks the silence, discovering his attention on her and is embarrassed and cries.)* I don't know why I told you all this. I don't know why I've allowed myself to intrude into your private life. I'm crying and I don't know why. I'm embarrassed and . . . *(Moving to exit.)* I'm sure I can find my way and leave you to your farm.

RICK: *(Hesitant, not ready for her to leave but not knowing why.)* Oh, sure . . . there's always something to do. Earlier, I was mainly trying to duck out on your visit.

AGGY: I can accept that. You know, this is the first honest thing you've said to me. Thank you.

RICK: *(Uncertain.)* Honest?

AGGY: Real.

RICK: I see.

AGGY: What I was saying earlier about cotton . . . I was trying to impress you, you know.

RICK: I know.

AGGY: And I can't.

RICK: *(Smiling, knowingly.)* I know.

AGGY: It shows that much?

RICK: Yep.

AGGY: But you do have a very healthy crop.

RICK: I'm a good student.

AGGY: No you're not. You're an expert. *(Beat.)* Can I put your articles in my newsletter?

RICK: How'd you know about those?

AGGY: I learned to read at a very early age. *(With a guilty smile.)* Sorry. When I learned I was coming here, I read everything I could get my hands on. After I read your article, I knew I could either hide or devote myself to "soil surface temperatures and residue management." I thought you were some college professor with a test field.

RICK: Doesn't say much for the universities.
   (They laugh.)

AGGY: You have a nice laugh, Mr. Childress.
   (They share an awkward moment.)

RICK: *(Realization.)* So, you knew I was here before you ever moved?

AGGY: Had me scared to death.

RICK: I never thought about anyone actually reading those.

AGGY: Yep. Farmer, author . . . *(Carefully.)* poet.

RICK: *(His mood darkens, he moves away.)* I'm not a poet.

AGGY: *(She notices the change and follows, not to lose the moment.)* If you wrote this, you are.

RICK: Maybe . . . if I meant it to be read.

AGGY: I see. I'm sorry.

RICK: *(Honestly.)* Forget it. It's done.

AGGY: *(Carefully.)* She must have hurt you terribly.

RICK: *(Decisively, after a long, painful pause.)* It wasn't like that.

AGGY: I'm sorry. Did she pass away?

RICK: *(He picks up the journal and pages through it. He replaces a rubber band around it, in effect, sealing it.)* No.

AGGY: You obviously loved her a great deal.

RICK: A story for another time.

AGGY: Sugar beets?

RICK: What?

AGGY: Sugar beets. One of your two mistakes . . . from a "previous life."

RICK: *(Pause.)* I was young and impressionable . . . and just plain stupid.

AGGY: Or in love?

RICK: *(Unsure of his emotions.)* The time wasn't right, nature wasn't right . . . neither was I. I almost lost everything.

AGGY: "For the rains flood the barren fields, where once we planted dreams." It must have been painful.

RICK: *(Very uncomfortable and self-conscious, attempting to laugh it off. Looking up at the sun and moving to the table and picking up the carburetor.)* Will you look at the time. I've got to get this installed or the truck will wonder where I've been.

AGGY: Paraphrasing Thoreau, nature can be wonderful and yet so awful.

RICK: Wilder.

AGGY: What?

RICK: Wilder. Thornton Wilder.

AGGY: *(Caught.)* You don't hide it well.

RICK: Hide what?

AGGY: Your previous life . . . her . . . the pain. How long—

RICK: *(Having had enough.)* I tell you what. I gotta go to Amarillo on Monday. I'll hire an analyst to help me out.

AGGY: No you won't. You get on your tractor or walk or just go sit in the fields. It's a great place for peace and solitude, but not patching up your soul.

RICK: *(She comes too close and he is almost overcome. He becomes defensive turning on her.)* What are you doing?

AGGY: What?

RICK: *(Intense.)* This a new . . . "behavioral method in crop management"? Agent Taylor travels to the high plains of Texas, meeting and treating the mentally anguished farmer. It'll make a great article in your newsletter.

AGGY: *(Taken by surprise.)* That's not . . .

RICK: *(Emotionally.)* You can't do this. Don't you get it? I don't want you here! I don't know why I've put up with you this long. I tried to be nice. Maybe because you're a woman, maybe because you try so hard, maybe because I was a jerk and felt guilty. Maybe because there's something about you that's likeable and I enjoyed your company. And maybe it's wearing thin.

AGGY: *(Finally beaten.)* Well, I accomplished what I came for. I've introduced myself. And I'm sorry for the inconvenience and intrusion. I hope you'll forgive me and it won't affect our professional relationship. *(She begins her exit.)*

RICK: Why?

AGGY: Why?

RICK: Why? Why did you come? Why now? Don't you see? I did it . . . finally. Put it all in the past . . . made peace with it. And guess who shows up asking questions that's none of her business?

AGGY: I didn't know. I'm sorry.

RICK: "I'm sorry" and it all goes away. "I'm sorry" and everything's back to normal. I had it taken care of, lady! I was content for the first time in ten years. Stupid female questions! *(Back to her as the focus of his emotions.)* What do you know about it, Agent Taylor?

AGGY: *(Taken offguard.)* That's not fair.

RICK: No? Then what is? Let's see. You can delve into my personal life but I leave yours alone, right?

AGGY: *(Stung. She makes her decision.)* I'm starting over.

RICK: *(Loudly, getting the wrong idea.)* No, we are not!

AGGY: *(Painful, yelling at him.)* No, I am! I'm starting over. *(Quietly, with mounting emotions.)* That's why I'm here. *(Long pause.)* You see, he was picture perfect. I have no regrets, nothing to blame, no awful memories of a relationship gone bad. I met him in college and married him the day after graduation. The rest was a storybook. I loved him, Mr. Childress. I always thought I'd die without him. At times, I wish I had. He was my husband, best friend, my hero. I guess looking back, my one constant, unspoken fear was how could something this good go on forever. When would it end? And so it did . . . last January 15th, on an ice-covered highway out of Wichita. Randy was on a respirator for two days, *(Beat.)* then he left me. I tried to keep up the appearance of a single, independent woman on the mend. Friends helped as much as possible, but the job was a dead-end and life had no meaning. I was lost. Three months ago this job appeared in a journal, so I took a chance and applied. The rest is history. That's what I know about it.

RICK: Any children?

AGGY: He couldn't. Life can be wonderful . . . and awful, all at the same time. *(She cries softly.)*

RICK: *(After a long, awkward moment; conciliatory, handing her his handkerchief.)* And it only took this long to find something we both can agree on. *(They laugh.)*

AGGY: And you are a nice man, Mr. Childress.

RICK: Gonna put that in your newsletter?

AGGY: And spoil your reputation? *(They laugh.)* Every so often . . . every once in a great while . . . I meet someone that I want to get to know. Then, I start in, going where I shouldn't. I want to know everything too quickly, and here I am, alienating and intruding. I'm so sorry for all of this.
(Rick and Aggy take a moment staring into the fields. This is a long moment of understanding.)

AGGY: *(Soberly.)* Your wife, she never understood, did she?

RICK: *(With difficulty, but forthcoming.)* She tried. *(Pause.)* Heck, she probably laid it to rest years ago.

AGGY: Had to ask.

RICK: I know. You have a million questions and I haven't talked so much in ten years.

AGGY: *(Pause. Offering her hand.)* Hi. I'm Aggy.

RICK: *(Laughs.)* Just . . . Aggy?

AGGY: Just Aggy.
(The incidental music fades up gradually under the dialogue.)

RICK: *(He smiles and takes her hand. They hold hands in this position for a long important moment. He looks into her eyes and recognizes feelings long forgotten but also sees those feelings returned from her. He slowly releases her hand.)* Nice to meet you, Aggy. I'm . . . Rick. *(Thinking and picking up the carburetor.)* I actually do need to install this thing.

AGGY: *(Quickly.)* I can help. *(Beat.)* I don't know anything about . . . but I can learn.

RICK: Yeah, um . . . so can I . . . *(Nods, tries to say something . . . nods.)*
(He holds the carburetor in one hand offering the tools from the other hand. She moves to him, taking the carburetor as she passes, brushes against him, looking deeply into his eyes. She moves on to the side of the house, turns, and waits on him. As he turns to see her, she cocks her head meaning, "come on." He laughs and follows. Rafael enters. Smiles. Sits in his spot. Laughs lightly as the lights fade.)

END OF ACT II

ACT III

Fall, near sunset, twenty-five years later. Present day. The same as in Act I and Act II. The action takes place in the front yard of the Childress farmhouse. Several old outdoor chairs are placed around an old serving table, used to collect "stuff." The yard is littered with pieces of farm machinery and scrap. The setting sun's light is filtering through the overhead trees casting colorful shadows across the farmhouse and yard. At rise: Rick Childress is sitting in one of the chairs, staring out over the landscape. He is upset, unhappy, and brooding. The years as a farmer have had their effect on his body as he is tired, stiff, and moves with arthritic pain. The decision he faces leaves him feeling very old. Maggie appears at the front screen door. Her spirit, drive and intensity for life are superseded only by her love for her father. She is looking for something in the distance. Not finding it, she looks at her father, watching him for a moment.

MAGGIE: *(Entering onto the porch and sitting on the step. She studies him, notice-ably concerned. She's follows his gaze and they both sit in peaceful silence a moment.)* This is how I'll always remember this place . . . at sunset, magic hour. Night-sounds beginning to wake and day-sounds tucking them-selves in for their long night's sleep. "When all the sounds of the earth are like music" . . . that's my favorite musical. You and mom took me when I was four. Remember? I had to sit in your lap to see. *(No reaction from Rick.)* I guess growing up, you never realize you had it so good. One day you're grown and you sit on the porch steps and look out where you grew up and suddenly realize that it was pretty good. On days like today, I wish I could stop the earth turning, reverse it, and be a kid again. I loved rid-ing behind you in the tractor. You'd plant or spray or cultivate all day long and never complain at my never-ending questions. Or I'd sit under a tree and watch you in the fields grow smaller, finally into a small dot I could hide behind my thumb. I loved the deer playing in the mornings, turkeys chasing each other, the wild hogs tearing up the furrows you planted the day before. You never seemed angry. You just made "wild hog" bacon. *(He still doesn't react.)* I thought you said you'd be OK with this.

RICK: I am . . . but you're carrying on like I've already sold it.

MAGGIE: Isn't that the point? To sell?

RICK: I agreed to this inspection because you said it wouldn't cost anything and we would know the current market value. That's all. Maggie, I have no intention of selling this place.

MAGGIE: *(Moving to him.)* But what if he gives us a great price? Wouldn't now be a good time?

RICK: Why would now be a good time?

MAGGIE: *(With great sensitivity, sitting next to him.)* Because it's going to happen sooner than later and you know that. I know you don't want to talk about it, but it's true.

RICK: *(Retelling the old story, with feeling.)* People have been trying to buy this place all my life. They first tried when Pa died. Old Cope was ready to buy, too. Funny how things work out. Cope was a good man. He and Pa were life-long friends. Died in his eighties still running his farm. I found him, at the steering wheel of his tractor, stiff as a board. Had to pry him loose. He died a—

MAGGIE: *(Interrupting. With great care.)* Papa? *(It's time to talk.)* This is a springboard for Chris. They're showing a great deal of confidence in him.

RICK: *(Pause.)* So, who is this "big, company man" that wants to buy my farm?

MAGGIE: It's Chris, Pop.

RICK: *(Beat.)* The two of you in the market for a farm?

MAGGIE: Well, not quite. He's the agent, Papa.

RICK: *(Disappointed.)* Oh . . . I thought . . .

MAGGIE: He's just the bank's representative for this company that buys and leases farmland.

RICK: I see.

MAGGIE: Chris and I have been looking into possibilities for some time.

RICK: *(Cynically.)* I see. You mean if I fell under the tractor or got bit by a rabid skunk?

MAGGIE: Papa . . . you promised.

RICK: Yes, I did.

MAGGIE: Anyway, Chris made a few inquiries and . . . some people popped up. The bank thinks it's a win-win and ordered him to run with it.

RICK: *(Sullen, barely managing his patience.)* Why did you keep this a secret? Afraid I'd stop you? I feel like I'm coming out of the dark. You didn't say anything about how much progress you've made.

MAGGIE: I'm not trying to keep anything from you. I did want to surprise you with Chris. If he was working the deal, I didn't think you'd mind as much.

RICK: *(Smoldering.)* You could have told me.

MAGGIE: I am, Pop. Things are just now coming together.

RICK: Going to shake hands, sign papers, and show up with a moving van?

MAGGIE: You know full well that I keep an eye on the farm. I always told you that if a possibility came up, you'd be the first to know.

RICK: And what is this?

MAGGIE: A prospect. That's all it is, a prospect. You promised you'd listen. At least hear me out. *(Cautious.)* Now . . . If you wanted. And I say if. If you give the go-ahead . . . we could have the farm sold possibly within weeks? Nothing is ever a sure thing, but this is as close as you get. These folks are more than interested. Things could happen very quickly. Odds are, we could close within the month. You'll never have to work again. You can move to Amarillo. Move in with us. Chris will set you up a retirement fund. It's perfect! It's not like people are lining up to buy farmland! Do you know how many farms are subsidized by the government just to sit idle? And we don't know how long this interest rate will hold.

RICK: I know that.

MAGGIE: If you intend to sell anytime within the next few years, this will be your best offer.

RICK: It's just happening too fast.

MAGGIE: It's the nature of this business. Who would've thought we'd have a buyer so quickly?

RICK: What about the house?

MAGGIE: I don't know. They'll do whatever they do. *(Pause.)* I know it's hard. It's hard for me. I grew up here, too. You know? But you'll be close to us and . . . *(Long pause.)* well I might as well tell you now. I don't think there's going to be a better time. *(Pause.)* I'm pregnant.

RICK: *(Pause.)* You know for sure? I mean it's . . . it's . . .

MAGGIE: It's for certain, Papa. Next April. I'm sorry. This is not how I wanted to tell you. Thing's are just happening so fast.

RICK: You're having a baby?

MAGGIE: *(Nods.)*

RICK: *(Nods.)*

(Silence. He goes to her and holds her.)

RICK: *(Quietly, contemplative.)* Ever wondered what if?

MAGGIE: Like what?

RICK: Wonder if your mother was still alive? What would have happened?

MAGGIE: You mean, what if my brother had lived, if he would have become the farmer you always dreamed of? Like I didn't?

RICK: Baby, I'm not implying anything. Just . . . what if? I wonder how things would've played out. No, Chris is a good man. But . . . wonder if you had of stayed with that Palmer boy. He farms those ten sections in the north county and owns the feed and seed store . . .

MAGGIE: *(With growing pressure from genuine concern.)* It's time to deal with it. Papa, you have to understand that. The price will never be better, you have a buyer, and I need my daddy with me. Like it or not, you're at the age you have to think about such things like retirement. You've worked every day of your life. Want to play "what if"? What if you never realize that you can't keep up with these demands? That you can't farm anymore? I know how much you love this place. I do, too. But . . . you'll die for it.

RICK: Baby, I'm only seventy-two. I'm not about to pass on anytime soon.

MAGGIE: That's right, but if I can't get you to talk about it now, I'm going to drive up one day and you'll be out there, slumped over your tractor plowing in circles.

RICK: *(Distracted and annoyed, looking down the drive way.)* What's this? Who's that pulling up the driveway? At this time of day?

MAGGIE: Must be lost.

RICK: Listen, Mag. I promised to listen and I have. These are things I have to think about. And I will. But you want an answer right now and I just can't give you one.

MAGGIE: This offer won't be on the table very long. It's good for now. The clock is ticking.

RICK: You're clock is ticking. Mine stopped running years ago.

(Toni enters. She is in her early seventies, a pretty woman who maintains herself well and is dressed fashionably for a long drive and a walk on a farm. Her makeup and apparel are immaculate. She is soft-spoken and demure but confident in her demeanor and character.)

RICK: And as I said, I'll think about it.

MAGGIE: *(Helpless.)* Papa!

TONI: Excuse me.

RICK: *(Pressured, wheeling on her, barking impatiently.)* What! *(Realizing his error and recovering quickly.)* I'm sorry. Can I help you, ma'am?

TONI: Yes, I was looking for Rick Childress . . . *(Recognizing him.)* Rick? Is that you?

(Rick stops but doesn't immediately recognize her.)

TONI: I'm sorry about the hour, but I knew it was my best hope to catch you. It's been a lifetime, hasn't it?

RICK: Toni?

TONI: Yes. It's me underneath all this wear and tear but it's me nevertheless. I do hope I'm not intruding. I know it's a surprise that I pop in without warning. I hope you don't mind.

(Silence.)

MAGGIE: Hi, I'm Maggie, Maggie Falls, his daughter. Of course we don't mind. You know my father?

TONI: Yes, I'm Toni Childress . . . *(Beat.)* an old friend. I am so pleased to meet you.

MAGGIE: *(Confused.)* Are we related? *(Looking to Rick for a clue to what's going on.)*

RICK: *(Recovering.)* We go back a long time.

MAGGIE: *(Realization.)* Oh! Toni! Oh, my! You're . . . you're Papa's . . .

RICK: This is . . . uh . . . this is Toni . . . my . . .

TONI: I'm Rick's first wife.

MAGGIE: *(Embarrassed and feeling very self-conscious.)* Well . . . Mrs. Uh . . . Toni . . . I don't even know what to call you.

TONI: Toni's fine.

MAGGIE: *(Nervous, babbling.)* I am so sorry. I feel silly. Quite frankly, I'm dumbfounded. Papa was never very forthcoming about those days, and I can't pry anything out of him if it's not his idea in the first place.

TONI: Oh, I can just imagine.

(The three stand and stare at each other, unsure what to do next.)

MAGGIE: *(Breaking the spell.)* Oh! . . . excuse my lack of manners. Wouldn't you like to come inside?

TONI: If you don't mind, I'll just stay out here. I've been driving so long, it feels good to stretch my legs. I can't believe I'm really here.

MAGGIE: *(Still in doubt, wondering.)* I can't either. Can I get you something?

TONI: If I could trouble you for some water?

MAGGIE: Sure, no trouble at all.

TONI: Do you still use the well?

MAGGIE: Sure do. Won't take long.

(Maggie exits into the house. They both stare at each other self-consciously but can't believe they are really there. They laugh to break the tension.)

TONI: It is so good to see you.

RICK: I'm surprised you recognized me?

TONI: It wasn't too difficult. *(Pause.)* Isn't today full of surprises? *(Rick nods.)* I bet I'm the last person you thought you'd see.

RICK: Yeah.

TONI: You don't mind?

RICK: No. Of course not.

TONI: How have you been?

RICK: Me? *(Searching.)* Life on the farm. Nothing changes. It just takes longer to do the same old thing.

TONI: I fully understand.

RICK: So, what brings you all the way out here?

TONI: I admit, I'm not just passing through. I've really wanted to see the farm . . . and you again after all these years. I'm with some friends on one of those tours to Santa Fe. Coming back, we stopped in Amarillo for the night, to see the musical in Canyon. Since I've seen it several times, I got this bright idea and rented a car and here I am. I hope I'm not interfering. I know it's presumptuous to just drop in after forty-some-odd years without warning.

RICK: *(Sarcastically, with humor.)* You're lucky I'm still alive.

TONI: I checked the phone book. You're still listed. I took that as an omen. *(They laugh.)*

RICK: So, you never changed your name?

TONI: Rick . . . I never remarried. There were prospects, but I was never seriously interested.

RICK: Children?

TONI: *(Amused.)* I don't see how.

RICK: *(Sheepishly.)* I'm not thinking. I guess not. Your brother and sister?

TONI: They're in Dallas, both with families. *(Silence.)*

RICK: Boy! A lot of water under the bridge. *(Pause.)* So? You?

TONI: Um . . . Dad's sporting goods store expanded into a sports equipment chain which was a perfect opportunity for me to start out at the top. I was the buyer. Imagine me, going to market buying football helmets. But, I enjoyed it and I got to travel.

RICK: Like you always wanted.

TONI: Getting older, we started talking retirement and found a buyer for the stores. Now, I'm involved with several organizations doing volunteer work and a group of friends and I travel. That probably sounds perfectly dreadful to you, doesn't it?

RICK: No. It's what you want to do.

TONI: I do and I'm having a ball. And you? Still working the farm?

RICK: Oh, yes.

TONI: Same old Rick. *(No response from Rick. Remorseful.)* Oh . . . I didn't mean that. I hate even mentioning it. *(Pause.)* I feel like I'm at a high school reunion.

RICK: *(Laughing.)* It is a little awkward, isn't it?
(They laugh.)

TONI: Your daughter is lovely.

RICK: Thank you. You noticed she didn't get her looks from me.

TONI: No I didn't.

RICK: She's looking more like her mother every year.

TONI: Is your wife a local girl?

RICK: Aggy? No, she, um . . . was a native Kansan. She came down here for a job. That's how we met. She took one look at the farm and fell in love. I came as a bonus, depending on your point of view. She moved in and took over.

TONI: *(Pause.)* Did she . . . is she . . .

RICK: She passed away when Maggie was five.

TONI: Oh. I'm sorry. How did she . . .

RICK: She died in childbirth. *(Beat.)* We lost them both.

TONI: I'm so sorry.

RICK: There, for a while, life was pretty tough.

TONI: She must have been very special.

RICK: *(Pause.)* Yeah . . . I never thought I'd feel that way again. You know?

TONI: I know.

RICK: She had the toughest hide of anyone I ever met. She had to put up with me. If anything, that woman had perseverance. She never quit.

TONI: Like I did.

RICK: *(Quickly to her, innocent.)* No, no, no . . . what I meant was she didn't let me get away with anything. *(A pause.)* And that little girl's cut from the same mold. She had to be tough to put up with me as a mother and father.

TONI: It must have been difficult.

RICK: It's been fun. Maggie was born and raised a farm girl. Then she fell in love with medicine. She's a nurse in Amarillo. That's where she met my son-in-law.

TONI: *(Sitting on the porch.)* And you lost your farmhand.

RICK: *(Sitting, ready to change the subject. Her appearance is intriguing but troubling.)* And what brings you to this corner of nowhere? It's a long drive just to say hello. Something on your mind?

Toni: *(Half-joking, feigning the question.)* I just wanted to try my hand at farming again.

(They laugh.)

RICK: *(Realizing her feint but patient.)* I bet I could keep you busy for a few days.

TONI: I bet you could. *(Moving away, willing a partial answer but not ready for full disclosure.)* But . . . after so many years, I wanted to see what happened here. I have so many memories . . . *(Staring off across the landscape.)* I could have found this place in the dark. It's just as I pictured. And I knew I was getting close when I saw a dead raccoon on the highway near a hand-painted sign advertising fresh jerky.

RICK: Never buy jerky at a roadside stand.

(They laugh.)

TONI: And you're still growing cotton.

RICK: That's right.

TONI: You never expanded?

RICK: Played with some things. Never felt comfortable.

TONI: Like sugar beets?

RICK: *(Smiles.)*

TONI: *(Regarding the fields.)* Looks to be about a month from harvest?

RICK: *(Moving to her.)* Very good, I'm impressed. About a month, yes.

TONI: I didn't forget everything I learned from five years as a farmer's wife. *(Seeing the new house in the distance.)* And, what is that house? Which house do you live in?

RICK: That one. That's the house I built for Aggy.

TONI: Modern conveniences?

RICK: Air conditioning, microwave oven, dishwasher, satellite dish . . . just like real people.

TONI: I'm impressed. I half imagined you had succumbed to heat prostration in this old house by now.

RICK: I still love this place. I'm over here every day, using the barn and out buildings.

TONI: So, Mr. Childress . . . how long are you going to keep her going? What are your future plans?

RICK: Well . . . tomorrow I plan to wake up. That's all the plans I have for now. *(They laugh.)*

TONI: Are you just going to farm forever?

RICK: If Maggie has anything to do with it, I'll soon be in Amarillo, retired. And, I just found out she's expecting.

TONI: Your first grandchild?

RICK: Now, she's putting on the pressure for me to sell the place and move near her. The time's right, the money's right, and the deal is on the clock. I just haven't had a chance to get used to the idea. I don't know.

(Maggie enters from the front door. She is visibly upset, struggling to control her emotions. She carries a glass of water and a prescription bottle. She gives the glass to Toni.)

MAGGIE: I'm sorry it took so long.

TONI: Not at all, thank you.

MAGGIE: I decided to snoop around . . . after I found this. *(She reveals the prescription bottle. To Rick.)* Have you got something you want to tell me?

RICK: *(Matter-of-factly.)* It's mine.

MAGGIE: Well, obviously it's yours.

RICK: Yes, it is.

MAGGIE: Papa, I'm a nurse. I know what this is for.

TONI: What is it, dear?

MAGGIE: Lanoxin! It's for a heart condition.

TONI: *(Concerned.)* Rick?

MAGGIE: Papa? What is this all about?

TONI: What's it for?

MAGGIE: It's not for curing the problem, that's for sure. It treats the symptom. It just helps him live with it. Papa?

RICK: *(Moving away.)* It's nothing serious . . . a little angina, that's all.

MAGGIE: *(Facing him.)* Nothing serious, Papa? A "little"? Angina doesn't go away like a headache.

RICK: I wasn't feeling very well so I went to the doctor.

MAGGIE: And hell froze over. I'm surprised you know one.

RICK: I've had a family doctor for years. I thought I was having some stomach problems. I had been taking a powder, but they didn't help anymore. He prescribed these and told me to be a good boy and I'm feeling much better.

MAGGIE: Do you have any other prescriptions I don't know about? Are you taking nitroglycerin? Surely he prescribed that.

(Rick reaches into his shirt pocket and shows Maggie.)

MAGGIE: *(Maggie taking the bottle.)* It's full.

RICK: I haven't needed any.

MAGGIE: None?

RICK: He gave them to me as a precaution.

MAGGIE: Papa, why didn't you tell me?

RICK: Because I knew how you'd react.

MAGGIE: This is serious.

RICK: *(Trying to laugh it away.)* I'm fine. I've never felt better. I'm watching my diet for the first time in my life and I walk to the highway every morning. I even bought walking shoes!

MAGGIE: You can't panhandle me. I know what I'm talking about. *(To Toni.)* This is the type of thing I've worried about for some time. I've tried to talk to him about it, but—

TONI: I know. I can just imagine.

RICK: Would you two stop talking about me as if I wasn't here?

MAGGIE: You know what I'm going to say because I've said it before *(To Toni.)* A man his age doesn't try to run a farm this size by himself. Last month, he left half a section unsprayed. He got to the end of a row and just came home.

RICK: *(Defensively.)* It was the end of the day.

MAGGIE: Four o'clock and a half full tank?

RICK: *(Losing patience and moving away.)* Yes, I'm getting old. No, I'm not a doddering old fool.

TONI: She didn't say that, Rick.

RICK: *(Fuming.)* That's what it sounds like. To hear her side of the story, I'm wondering in circles and can't find the barn. I know where this is going. I have years of farming ahead of me.

MAGGIE: *(Irritated, following him.)* Maybe, all things being normal. *(Holding up the prescription bottle.)* But after this . . .

(There is a moment of awkward silence. Feeling intrusive, Toni excuses herself to the house.)

TONI: If you don't mind, I need to step inside a moment.

(Neither respond and she exits.)

RICK: Why did you have to bring this up now? In front of her?

MAGGIE: *(Angry, growing increasingly emotional.)* You know what? I don't care.

RICK: You're overreacting.

MAGGIE: Excuse me?

RICK: *(Attempting to placate her.)* The doctor said I was in great shape. Yes, I have a heart problem, or rather a heart inconvenience, his words, not mine. Now that we have the blood pressure finally under control, I feel better than I have in months.

MAGGIE: *(Stunned.)* Blood pressure?

RICK: *(Caught.)* Yeah.

MAGGIE: Where is that prescription?

RICK: *(Pause.)* In the truck. I hate it. It can't do anything without stopping every fifteen minutes to go to the bathroom. After a while, it zaps my strength and I don't have the energy to get off the porch.

MAGGIE: *(Exasperated.)* That's the medicine working, Papa!

RICK: Give it a rest, Mag!

MAGGIE: *(Incredulous.)* You won't make any attempt to understand. Nothing is going to change. A bad heart only gets worse. An old man only gets older. A plowed field always goes back to nature.

RICK: *(Fed up.)* Well, just be sure not to throw dirt in my face yet. If you haven't noticed, I'm still breathing.

(He exits behind the house. Maggie, frustrated, watches him go. Toni, at the front screen door for the last several exchanges, enters on the porch.)

MAGGIE: Well, that went well.

TONI: Did you really think it would?

MAGGIE: *(Gaining control.)* I guess not. I knew better. You can't corner him and expect him to listen and be reasonable.

TONI: "Being reasonable" depends on one's perspective.

MAGGIE: *(Momentarily defensive.)* You think I'm being unreasonable?

TONI: *(Sitting on the porch steps.)* It's none of my business, Maggie. I'm sorry. It's not my place to say anything.

MAGGIE: No, no, no . . . it's just . . . I need help. *(Sitting next to her.)* I'm at my wits end. I don't know what to do. If you have any ideas . . .

TONI: All right . . . no, I don't think you're being unreasonable. But, look who you're dealing with. He's being asked to sell his first love. I loved the way he used to put it. When a major decision was to be made, he would say, "I'm at the end of the row." He didn't know whether to start the next section or turn the tractor toward home.

MAGGIE: You'd think the decision is clear.

TONI: You would. But that's the woman talking . . . mother knows best. If "he" would only listen and do what I ask, everything will be OK. But there's more to it. There's another woman involved. Don't you see? The farm, this place, she's a part of who he is and you must consider her.

MAGGIE: *(Intuitively.)* That sounds like a real life experience. Is that what happened?

TONI: That's pretty close.

MAGGIE: So, you regret leaving?

TONI: I used to lie awake nights wondering. Several times I almost returned. But . . . I couldn't. During those first years, I was tormented by "what if."

What if those hard times had been fruitful? What if the drought hadn't happened? What if I hadn't persuaded him to try a new crop? What then? Could our marriage only work in good times? Was I that shallow? Could I have come back? Would my pride let me? Would his?

MAGGIE: Papa never talked much about it until I was old enough to ask the right questions. He'd say something about a "previous life," that's what he'd call it, and one day I asked him what it meant. Like before, he'd talk around it but I was older and kept asking until he told me about you.

TONI: I hope he wasn't too unkind.

MAGGIE: It was never that way. I knew it was a very painful experience, but for both of you. He always wanted to know about you, but could never muster the courage to find out.

TONI: That man.

MAGGIE: *(Forming an idea.)* Will you help me?

TONI: Well, I'll do whatever I can.

MAGGIE: Great! Would you talk to him?

TONI: Me?

MAGGIE: I tell him he's dying, he's got to sell his home, and I'm pregnant. What do you think?

TONI: Yes, I can see how he's a trifle overwhelmed.

MAGGIE: That's for sure.

TONI: I don't know what help I'll be.

MAGGIE: Just talk to him.

TONI: Just talk?

MAGGIE: You're my last hope. *(Rising.)* I'm leaving. He won't come back until I do. He's probably not angry anymore, but he won't like me for a few hours. Bye, now. It's great to finally meet you. And thank you.

TONI: But . . . Maggie?

MAGGIE: You'll be fine. Will I see you again?

TONI: Who's to say? I hope so.

(Maggie exits.)

TONI: *(To herself.)* If he doesn't throw me off the farm. *(Toni is left alone and moves across the front yard, looking over the landscape and glancing back at the corner of the house. Rick appears.)* You're safe. Maggie left. She thought you needed some time.

RICK: She's a smart kid.

TONI: She's a wonderful young woman.

RICK: I think so . . . but she can get under my skin faster than a sand flea. She's the best part of what I've done here.

TONI: She thinks you're pretty special, too.

RICK: I sometimes wonder how she'd turn out having a mother. Talk about an incompetent, bungling old fool. Imagine me having to raise a daughter alone.

TONI: You didn't have any help?

RICK: *(Remembers.)* An old friend of mine *(Beat.)* Rafael . . . his wife would watch her when she was young. Later on, she'd spend most of the day with me. She was a born farmer. I always hoped to hand the farm over to her . . .

TONI: And your wife?

RICK: Aggy walked onto the farm and took over. It seemed . . . natural.

TONI: And . . . you loved her.

RICK: I couldn't help it. I'd look up and there she'd be. She had me going to movies in town or we'd go to Lubbock or Amarillo for special things. I really enjoyed it. Time passed and she couldn't see why we weren't engaged. I finally said OK and we got married the next weekend. One year later and Maggie was born. Three years later and . . . well, that was that.

TONI: Outside of the obvious, what are you thinking?

RICK: Outside of the obvious? I love my life. I want to keep working. Always have. You know what I want? I want to be as young as this place needs me to be. I want to be as young as I think I am. I wish my body would agree with my brain and allow me to work from dawn to dusk regretting the day was over . . . "just earth, sky, and me."

TONI: And you feel cheated?

RICK: It's not fair, is it? I finally feel like I've gotten good at it. Just look at all I've learned. I can read signs for weather, when and how to plant, feed, harvest and when to fold and run for my life. Why is it that experience makes you so old? And now I look at it all and think, all of this may be gone in five years.

TONI: It all sounds so sad . . . so final.

RICK: As it should be . . . just leave it alone and allow things to take their course.

TONI: That is a decision, Rick . . . to do nothing.

RICK: I suppose it is.

TONI: I know. I have personal experience.

RICK: What do you mean?

TONI: My decision to come here . . . oh, it's been in on my mind for years. There were times I almost wrote you a letter. Many times I almost called.

RICK: Why didn't you?

TONI: Because doing nothing is safe. *(Making good on her promise, she subtly argues Maggie's case.)* So, let me play the devil's advocate for a moment.

RICK: OK.

TONI: Forty odd years ago, you had a dream. You made all decisions, looked after every detail. You've spent a lifetime making that dream become reality. The farm is a testament to that. So . . . maybe it's time you accepted it.

RICK: Quit while I'm on top?

TONI: Yes.

RICK: Retire?

TONI: Well, yes . . . but more. Maggie has some dreams of her own.

RICK: You mean, maybe it's time I focus on what she wants?

TONI: What's best for her now? After all, that baby will need a grandpa. Think of the ballgames or dance recitals. Why, there will be school plays, Thanksgivings, and Christmases when a grandpa is needed. Besides, think of what fun you'll have.

RICK: *(Moving, talking as much to himself as to Toni. He grows more emotional though out this speech.)* But retire? What would I do? Be a doting granddaddy twenty-four hours a day? There's nothing in Amarillo. I could go to the park and feed pigeons or play dominos with the other old hasbeens. I dunno. But, if it's the best thing for Maggie I guess I should try. Is that my lot now? What am I supposed to do? How do I walk away from this, the only life I've ever known?

TONI: *(Feeling guilty.)* I've upset you. I'm sorry. It's not my place. I simply promised Maggie I'd speak with you on her behalf. She was hoping . . . well, if it wasn't coming from her . . .

RICK: I know. *(Beat.)* When we were young, these decisions didn't seem so difficult.

TONI: We were more passionate about life.

RICK: And idealistic . . . everything would work out . . . even in the midst of a crop failure, I always knew we'd be OK.

TONI: I didn't. Oh, don't get me wrong. I had faith in you. But since leaving here, I have the peace of knowing where my next meal was coming from. *(They laugh.)*

RICK: Those were trying years.

TONI: They made us grow up, didn't they?

RICK: *(Carefully.)* I always wanted to know what happened to you, after you went home. Was it as hard for you as it was for me?

TONI: Oh, Rick, it was awful, terrible . . . terrifying.

RICK: I know. There were times I wanted to die.

TONI: Yes, me, too. I'd wake up in the mornings and just lie there . . .

RICK: Hoping it was all a bad dream.

TONI: Exactly. And you were the lucky one.

RICK: Me?

TONI: You had the farm. You had a reason to get out of bed. I didn't. Finally, my dad came to my rescue and put me to work.

RICK: Selling football helmets.

TONI: Baseballs, basketballs, volleyballs, soccer . . . every kind of ball imaginable. *(They laugh.)* I know more about sports equipment than I thought possible. I fell in love with my work. I traveled to New York and LA rubbing elbows with professional athletes and celebrities. It was such great fun. I even watch games on television. I've become quite an armchair quarterback. *(They laugh.)*

RICK: So . . . you did what you wanted to do.

TONI: It seems I did.

RICK: I'd love to hear your stories.

TONI: I have a million of them.

RICK: That would be nice about now.

TONI: *(With great insight.)* This is hard for you, isn't it?

RICK: Maggie can be very persuasive.

TONI: Rick, can I be very honest with you? I know I have no right to butt in—

RICK: You go ahead. I need someone who can be objective.

TONI: I want to ask you something.

RICK: OK.

TONI: I don't want you to take it in the wrong way.

RICK: All right, Toni, ask your question.

TONI: Rick, where do you want to die?

RICK: I see. I didn't expect that.

TONI: You're at a crossroads. You see, in a long series of life-changing decisions, this could be the last. And this one will be final. You know that.

RICK: *(Pause.)* It always comes back to this place, doesn't it? I dunno. My grandfather passed away under that tree over there. My dad died in his bed in that house. Old Copeland died harvesting in that field near the road. I guess I just always accepted the fact that I'd be here when that time came. I never questioned it. I just made peace with the idea that someday I'd slump over whatever I was doing and go to sleep. *(Beat.)* But Maggie's scared. And now she knows about my heart. The doctor is confident if I follow his directions. And, I will. It's not like I don't know anything about it! Over the years, if something affected the farm, I learned all about it so I'd be prepared to act. Well, my heart qualifies. But I've never seen her like this. *(Pause.)* Maybe if I sold the place and moved to

Amarillo, she won't worry so much. With a baby on the way, she doesn't need to be concerning herself with me. Suddenly, I feel awful guilty and selfish. *(Pause.)* OK, so I move to Amarillo. She'll feel better. She'll be happy. *(Beat.)* Fine.

TONI: You still haven't answered my question. You are so close to selling this farm for Maggie's sake. If that's what you want to do, then do it.

RICK: Is that wrong?

TONI: It's not for me to say. Oh, it's admirable. People retire everyday for far more trivial reasons. Some regret their decisions. Others find entirely new lifestyles.

RICK: You?

TONI: I have total freedom to go and do whatever I want. That's the freedom I chose to have.

RICK: About forty years ago you wanted to go and do things we couldn't afford. I always felt guilty.

TONI: Don't. Not now. Look how far we've come.

RICK: Well, driving over a hundred and thirty miles to pay your respects does raise a few questions.

TONI: *(Collecting her thoughts.)* It all began here. This was such a big part of my life. Somehow, at some time, I needed to see where it started and answer some questions. Do I wish I had a husband and children and maybe grandchildren? Some days I think about it. But those were the decisions I made. After I got over leaving here, those things just weren't important. I loved what I did.

RICK: So what's the problem?

TONI: It's those nagging questions over the years that plague you. You know what I mean?

RICK: What would have happened if?

TONI: You, too?

RICK: Me, too.

TONI: And what have you come up with? *(Her elemental question.)* Did we do all right?

RICK: *(Laughing.)* After those first ten years, I swore off romance. I figured that part of my life was over and it was just between this place and me.

TONI: Is that when Aggy came?

RICK: I had a lot of hurt and pain tucked away. She opened the wounds up, helped me heal. She gave me friends and a lovely daughter. Shared in success of the farm and a sense of accomplishment and peace I never had. When we lost her *(Pause.)* it was tough. Was a hard time. But, it was different.

TONI: And Maggie . . .

RICK: Maggie . . . yes, we had Maggie.

TONI: Then . . .

RICK: Then?

TONI: Then, we did all right, didn't we?

RICK: Toni, I cherish that part of my life with you. I wouldn't want to live through it again, but, I don't regret it one day. But . . . you had to leave. I know that.

TONI: And you had to stay.

RICK: I finally understood. It just took me a while.

TONI: It took me a while too.

RICK: *(Sitting with her on the porch.)* And you? That's what this visit is all about, isn't it?

TONI: I would have been miserable here. I would have made you miserable. I would have missed the life I made for myself.

RICK: Then, yes. I think we did all right. Funny, huh? Look at us. Aren't we the wise ones? I guess years and perspective will do that for you. *(Very carefully, matter-of-factly.)* But through it all, and after all this time *(Pause.)* I never . . . I never *(Trying to find the words.)*

TONI: I understand . . .

RICK: Let me finish. *(Beat.)* I never stopped loving you either.

TONI: *(Shaken.)* I can live with that . . . I feel the same way.

RICK: *(Taking her hand.)* Are you all right?

TONI: *(Tearfully.)* I'm glad I came. It's good to be here. I want no regrets.

RICK: Oh, I have a few.

TONI: You do?

RICK: The day I left the tractor in gear and tore the guts out of that old barn. *(They laugh.)*

TONI: *(Serious again.)* You know, you still haven't answered my question.

RICK: I was hoping you'd forget.

TONI: So far, you've decided what you think is good for Maggie and you told me that you wish you were young enough to keep working this farm from sunup to sundown and be hungry for more. So, now, Mr. Childress, answer my question.

RICK: Where I want to die?

TONI: And whatever you say, you must be happy with it. You have to know it's your choice and no one else's. Let me say this. Inside this old husk is the young man who could laugh at a roadrunner chasing grasshoppers, or a puppy flushing its first covey of quail. I saw him dance in a thunderstorm and race dirt devils in his pickup. Where is his happiness now, old man?

RICK: I always thought it was here. But, yes, I'm getting old. At least that's what my body is telling me. And I get tired *(Pause.)* so tired. *(Struggling.)* Is it really over? When I die, this place will be here. This may not mean much to anyone else . . . and it doesn't matter. It means something now, to me. They'll look back and say, once upon a time, there was . . . there was the most beautiful farm . . . and it was mine . . . and after all is said and done, that's what matters.

(At this point they are both seated on the front porch steps, next to each other. Rick can't seem to contain his emotions any longer. He struggles to. But finally lets go. With his head down, Tony reaches over to him, taking her into his arms. He effortlessly and naturally leans over into Tony's arms. She holds him.)

TONI: What does a man do when he outlives his dreams?

RICK: *(Recovering.)* I do love this place.

TONI: Your dreams aren't over.

RICK: *(With understanding and resolve.)* Nope. And I still have a harvest. And I have a new crop to plan for next year. And by then, I should have a new grandchild. And maybe . . . just maybe . . .

(Incidental music cue.)

TONI: What?

RICK: Maybe, he'll be a farmer.

(They quietly laugh as the last rays of sun fade They look deeply at each other for a long moment. She understands that he answered the question. She acknowledges.)

TONI: The sun's going down. I have to leave.

RICK: Walk you to your car?

TONI: *(A sudden afterthought.)* No . . . I want to look back and see you . . . here.

RICK: The way it should be?

TONI: The way it is.

RICK: *(Quietly.)* All right.

TONI: *(Offstage.)* I want to come back.

RICK: Invitation's open. *(A matter-of-fact statement rather than a suggestion.)* Harvest . . . is a good time. The best of times.

(He watches her leave, then mounts the porch. He then turns and faces out, looking over the fields. He looks deeply. He sees his parents, his grandparents, his loves, his life, his choices. He takes a deep breath, savoring it as if it were his last. He perhaps smiles, he perhaps laughs. He's at peace. The light fades.)
(Blackout.)

END OF PLAY

NEIGHBORHOOD 3: REQUISITION OF DOOM

Jennifer Haley

For Mom, Dad, Betty, Bill, Ashlee, Carson, and Garrett. I love you, my family.

PLAYWRIGHT'S BIOGRAPHY
Jennifer Haley is a Los Angeles–based playwright whose plays include *Froggy, Gingerbread House,* and *Dreampuffs of War.* Her work has been presented and developed at the Actor's Theatre of Louisville Humana Festival of New American Plays, Summer Play Festival, and hotINK in New York City, PlayPenn in Philadelphia, Brown/Trinity Rep Playwright's Repertory Theatre in Providence, Annex Theatre in Seattle, and Refraction Arts at the Blue Theater in Austin. Haley holds an MFA in playwriting from Brown University, where she was awarded the Joelson Prize in Creative Writing and the Weston Award for Drama. She is a 2008 resident of the MacDowell Colony and Millay Colony for the Arts.

ORIGINAL PRODUCTION
World premiere in the 2008 Humana Festival of New American Plays at Actors Theatre of Louisville, directed by Kip Fagan. Developed with the assistance of New York University's hotINK International Festival of New Play Readings, Seven Devils Playwrights Conference, a project of id Theatre Company at the Alpine Playhouse in McCall, Idaho, and the Brown/Trinity Playwrights Repertory Theatre in Providence, Rhode Island. Cast and crew of the Actors Theatre of Louisville production was as follows:

CAST
STEVE, DOUG, TOBIAS . . . . John Leonard Thompson
LESLIE, VICKI, BARBARA, JOY . . . . Kate Hampton
TREVOR, RYAN, JARED, ZOMBIEKLLR14/BLAKE . . Robin Lord Taylor
MAKAELA, KAITLYN, MADISON, CHELSEA . . . . Reyna de Courcy
WALKTHROUGHS . . . . William McNulty

Scenic Design . . . . Michael B. Raiford
Costume Design . . . . Jessica Ford
Lighting Design . . . . Brian J. Lilienthal
Sound Design . . . . Benjamin Marcum
Properties Design . . . . Doc Manning
Fight Supervision . . . . Lee Look

Stage Manager	Bethany Ford
Production Assistant	Sara Kmack
Dramaturg	Amy Wegener
Casting	Cindi Rush Casting

PRODUCTION NOTES

Most of the play should be staged abstractly, in the netherworld of a video game or modern-day suburbia. Realistic elements may be added to Scene 9 so that we feel we are somewhere recognizable and comfortable, and we imagine, for a little while, that none of what's happened previously in the play is real.

The language should be spoken as it appears on the page. However, the line breaks represent the briefest of pauses, should be emotionally motivated (not robotic), and sound almost natural. The walkthroughs may be voiceovers or spoken by the actors.

A knowledge of MMORPGs, or Massive(ly) Multiplayer Online Role-Playing Games, such as World of Warcraft, is helpful in understanding this play. For a look at production photos, or for more information about online role playing, avatars, and gamers gone wrong, visit www.jenniferhaley.com/neighborhood.html.

SCENES

1 Kitchen: It is fun for the actress playing Makaela to use a whispery, gravelly monster voice on *i'm coming to get you for real.*

2 Front door: There may be a whiff of sexual attraction between Leslie and Steve.

4 Pool: Doug is not a calculated sadist . . . his behavior arises from fear.

5 Gameroom: Chelsea is on a PlayStation or Xbox. When her team members' headsets go out, she can use her game controller to send text messages to them via the game. Jared logs into the game using a computer.

7 Driveway: This is not a case of physical incest.

8 Street: Look at the movement of AFK (away from keyboard) characters in World of Warcraft for zombiekllr14.

The Final House: This is an actual episode of CSI: The violence should be very dramatic, unbelievable, and loud. Perhaps stupidly spurting blood, like in a video game. Look at the killing of harpies in World of Warcraft.

CHARACTERS

FATHER TYPE (STEVE, DOUG, TOBIAS)
MOTHER TYPE (LESLIE, VICKI, BARBARA, JOY)
SON TYPE (TREVOR, RYAN, JARED, ZOMBIEKLLR14, BLAKE)
DAUGHTER TYPE (MAKAELA, KAITLYN, MADISON, CHELSEA)

SETTING

The virtual reality of a video game or suburbia.

TIME

The present.

NEIGHBORHOOD 3: REQUISITION OF DOOM

1 WALKTHROUGH

the house you want is third from the left
as you face the cul de sac
all the houses look the same
be careful

move toward the house slowly
you will hear the sound of your
footsteps
in the street
do not walk too fast

as you approach the house
you will see on the sidewalk
a Claw Hammer

pick this up
you will need it later

like all other houses
this house will have a
flesh colored brick façade
and a welcome mat in front of the door

hint: if you kneel down and
take a closer look at this mat
you will see the word
"welcome" becomes
"help me"

enter the house
on your right is a set of
saloon doors
push through these
and enter
the kitchen

1 KITCHEN

MAKELA: you want a coke

TREVOR: OK

MAKAELA: shit
    we don't have any
    my brother
    inhaled them

TREVOR: that's OK

MAKAELA: so then i just have stupid stuff
    like grape juice
    want some
    grape juice

TREVOR: OK

MAKAELA: only
    he left like an inch
    in the bottle

TREVOR: that's OK

MAKAELA: no it's not
    i'm going to
    rip his balls off

TREVOR: i mean
    i don't need grape juice

MAKAELA: well nobody needs grape juice
    it'd just be nice
    otherwise we've got milk
    you want some
    milk

TREVOR: no thanks

MAKAELA: it's Chocolate Milk

TREVOR: OK

MAKAELA: it's like we're
    eleven
    again

TREVOR: that's the last time i had it
    when i was over here
    my mom doesn't buy
    Chocolate Milk

MAKAELA: your mom

TREVOR: what

MAKAELA: doesn't she sell
  makeup
  or something
TREVOR: vitamin shakes
MAKAELA: what are those
TREVOR: shakes with vitamins
MAKAELA: can you e lab or ate
TREVOR: it's like powder
  you add water
  you make a shake
  you drink it five times a day
MAKAELA: does it taste good
TREVOR: no
MAKAELA: why do you take it
TREVOR: my mom says it gives you
  everything you need
MAKAELA: does it work
  are you getting
  everything you need
TREVOR:
MAKAELA: i always see
  a bunch of cars
  in front of your place
TREVOR: she has meetings
  at the house
  she gives
  demonstrations
MAKAELA: isn't it like a
  pyramid scheme
TREVOR: what's that
MAKAELA: you know
  you get a bunch of people
  there are all these levels
  everyone tries to get to the next
  level
  tries to get to the
  top
  like scientology
  or the mafia

TREVOR: my mom
    is not
    in the mafia
MAKAELA: she doesn't know
    you're here
TREVOR: she's gone
    this afternoon
MAKAELA: it's the first time i've seen you
    on the bus
TREVOR: she drives me
MAKAELA: i'm getting a car soon
TREVOR: what kind
MAKAELA: the brand new kind
TREVOR: but what make and model
MAKAELA: i don't know
    tyler
    my brother
    just got a hummer
    it's actually his second
    hummer
    he totaled the first one
    almost killed someone
    so my dad got him another
    i want something that costs the same price
    as two fucking hummers
    like maybe a jag
TREVOR: you think your dad
    will get you a jag
MAKAELA: maybe
    if i act like a giant jerk
    who's totally circling the drain
    he'll buy one to try to
    save me
    otherwise
    it'll probably be
    a toyota
TREVOR:
MAKAELA:
TREVOR: still

MAKAELA: yeah
    then i could drive you to school
TREVOR: my mom
    drives me
MAKAELA: wouldn't you rather
    i mean
    it's high school
TREVOR: you don't have the car yet
    so you can't drive me
    so there's no point in discussing it
MAKAELA: no point in discussing it
    OK dad
TREVOR: just
    didn't you say your brother has an xbox
MAKAELA:
TREVOR:
MAKAELA: do you want a vicodin
    my brother's a candy man
    i know where he
    keeps his stash
TREVOR: won't that
    slow my reflexes
MAKAELA: haven't you
    done it before
TREVOR: no
MAKAELA: you should ask mummy
    for a sip of her
    special shake
TREVOR: she doesn't make
    special shakes
MAKAELA: she doesn't get
    that many people over for
    vitamins
TREVOR: look
    i didn't come over here to
    do drugs
    or listen to you insult my mom
    i thought we were playing
    a game

MAKAELA: that's the only reason you came over
   you barely said hello to me in four years
TREVOR: so i'm saying
   it now
MAKAELA: yeah cuz i have
   an xbox
TREVOR: i wanted to
   it's just
   you know
MAKAELA: what
   your mom
TREVOR: no not my mom
MAKAELA: she stopped letting you out
   cuz you got so cute
TREVOR: look shut up
   makaela
   i stopped coming over
   cuz you're such a flippin know-it-all
   i don't have to take this crap
   i'm leaving
MAKAELA: we've got Neighborhood 3
TREVOR:
MAKAELA:
TREVOR: you've got Neighborhood 3
MAKAELA: it's tyler's
   but i know where he
   hides it
TREVOR:
MAKAELA:
TREVOR: OK
   but my mom
   doesn't stop me
MAKAELA: OK
TREVOR: OK
MAKAELA: i have to sneak into
   his room
TREVOR: i'm dying to play Neighborhood 3
MAKAELA: ha
   that sounds like something out of a horror movie

like you're about to play this video game
and you think it's just a game
but actually it's real
but these teenagers don't know it
but the audience knows it
and this one kid's like
i'm dying to play
and it's like ooooo foreshadowing
TREVOR: i've been watching cody play
MAKAELA: so he's your contact
TREVOR: he's got all the walkthroughs
so you know what to look for
in the game
MAKAELA: bet cody doesn't have Chocolate Milk
bet that's why you came
over here
TREVOR: he came on to me
MAKAELA: no
way
cody came on to you
TREVOR: i think so
he kept saying how good i was with the joystick
and they're not even called joysticks
anymore
MAKAELA: i can't believe it
he's so hot
next time i see him
i'm gonna tell him
i'm pretty good
with a joystick
TREVOR: are you
MAKAELA:
TREVOR:
MAKAELA: i could be
TREVOR: well let's turn on the game
and find out
MAKAELA: wait
are you
what are you

TREVOR: the game
     what are you
MAKAELA: nothing
     i'll set it up and
     you can play
TREVOR: you're not going to play
MAKAELA: nah
TREVOR: do some split screen with me
MAKAELA: no
TREVOR: why not
MAKAELA: this game's fucked up
     it maps out
     your own Neighborhood
     how creepy is that
TREVOR: are you kidding
     it's sweet
     it's the best use of satellite technology i can think of
MAKAELA: oh now he's excited
TREVOR: how can you not think it's sweet
MAKAELA: there's no point to it
TREVOR: sure there is
     you have to keep getting to the next
     level
     you have to get to the
     top
MAKAELA: and then what
TREVOR: you're out
     you're free
     you've beat everything and
     nothing can hurt you anymore
MAKAELA: my brother beats the shit
     out of those things
     he gets online
     and plays with his friends
     the sicker the game
     the more they like it
     he whacks those Zombies
     to smithereens
     and spends a little too much time with them
     after they're dead

TREVOR: sometimes it's fun
    to be sick
    sometimes you need a place
    to be sick
MAKAELA: that's not the only place
    he's sick
    you don't know much
    about my brother
TREVOR: he plays
    at cody's house
MAKAELA: what
TREVOR: tyler
    he's almost almost at
    the Last Chapter
MAKAELA: have you been
    hanging out with him
TREVOR: they won't let me
    play the game
    they keep calling me
    a noob
MAKAELA: what else
    do you do
    with them
TREVOR: what do you
    mean
MAKAELA: any of that other
    sick shit
    any of their missions
    in the Neighborhood
TREVOR: missions
MAKAELA: maybe your mom
    would want to know about this
    would want to know about her
    beautiful vitamin shake boy
    what if i told
    your mom
TREVOR: you say a fucking word to my mom and i'll
MAKAELA: what
    slice my titties off

like they do the girl Zombies
in the game
TREVOR:
MAKAELA:
TREVOR: you're nuts
MAKAELA: just leave
TREVOR: you're the one
who invited me
MAKAELA: i didn't know
you'd got so twisted
TREVOR: it's only
a game
MAKAELA: oh right trevor
don't tell me
you've never seen it
TREVOR: seen what
MAKAELA: one of those things
like
reach out
TREVOR: what things
MAKAELA: in the game
while you're hacking it
reaches out with what's left of its
hand
and gurgle
i'm coming
to get you
for real

2 WALKTHROUGH

drink the
Chocolate Milk
to replenish your
Sugar Rush
exit the house and
advance down the street
slowly

remember
all action
must appear
unhurried
the goal
during the daytime
is to blend in

two blocks down
on your right
look for the house
with a Garden Gnome
in the front yard

use your Hammer
to break the Gnome
inside you will find a
Pink Post-it Note
with three numbers on it

add this to your inventory
and proceed
up the sidewalk

2 FRONT DOOR

STEVE: hi there
    hi
LESLIE: yes
STEVE: i'm sorry i
    accidentally kicked
    your Garden Gnome
LESLIE: oh
STEVE: it's just
    his head
    i've got some
    superglue
LESLIE: no that's

STEVE: you might want to keep him
    out back
    i don't think Garden Gnomes are
    acceptable
    to the Neighborhood Association
LESLIE: are you with
    the Neighborhood Association
STEVE: no i
LESLIE: oh i
    thought you were a
    representative
    come to give me another
    warning
STEVE: no i'm
    from down the street
    i'm
LESLIE: of course
    halloween
STEVE: halloween
    yes
    i was in the gorilla suit
    until
LESLIE: yes
    i remember
STEVE: i sometimes get
    carried away at
    block parties
LESLIE: well this one was
    unseasonably warm
STEVE:
LESLIE:
STEVE: steve
LESLIE: leslie
STEVE: you have
    twins
    right
    both
    of them
    were there

the wolfman and
cinderella
LESLIE: the hunchback and
tinkerbell
STEVE: tinkerbell
oh right
my daughter was
freddy krueger
LESLIE: oh i didn't know
that was a
girl
STEVE: sometimes neither do we
LESLIE:
STEVE: uh so
i'm home from the office
early today
i went in the house
and couldn't find my daughter
chelsea
my wife is
taking a break from
the family
so i'm kind of
holding down the fort ha ha
and
well
um
LESLIE: i'm sorry
but
STEVE: yeah
it's hard
LESLIE: no
we're having
a party
for my husband
when he gets home
i'm cooking
buffalo wings
STEVE: a party

oh
that's nice
that's really nice
well i won't
take up your time
i just um
let me ask you real quick
have you heard about these
online video games
the kids are playing
LESLIE:
LESLIE: why do you
ask
STEVE: my only daughter
chelsea
is hooked on one
Neighborhood
something
i don't know
but when i say
hooked
i guess i'm
putting it mildly
she basically plays this
every waking moment
from the time she gets home from school
to the time she goes to bed
if she goes to bed
we bought her a
high speed gaming computer
for christmas
we thought that would make her
happy
we didn't know
we'd never see her again
she gets online
and plays this character
with other people online
playing characters

some of them
are her friends
but some of them
for all i know
could be pedophiles
they conspire for hours
on that instant message
and conference calls
they run around a Neighborhood
that looks very much like
ours
butchering Zombies
who look a whole lot like
us
but let's see
what am i worried about
i'm worried that
she's not making real friends in the
real world
the way she looks
no one at school will
talk to her
when i was a kid
i made bombs out of firecrackers
and my folks thought i was
possessed
and of course they were
overreacting
and i've threatened to
remove the computer
but i don't know if it is the computer
or if it's
i'm a
corporate manager
i manage people at all levels
and when they're not up to task i just
fire them
but you know
you can't fire your only kid

even when she comes out of her room
looking like some kind of
monster
LESLIE:
STEVE: i'm sorry
of course
your party
LESLIE: no let me
come outside
my daughter
madison
plays this game
STEVE: really
LESLIE: i can't get her to
come to dinner
we used to think it was
anorexia
until i figured out i had to
set the food down
right in front of her
STEVE: that's what i do
i pick chelsea up
a burger
every day
on my way home from work
LESLIE: i circle back
for the dirty dishes
she screams when i
make her stop for half a minute
to clean drippings
out of the keyboard
STEVE: her mom and i were dating
by her age
but she's never mentioned
a single boy
LESLIE: i'd be terrified to see
what kind of date
she'd bring home
STEVE: she won't allow me
in her room

LESLIE: she calls me
    leslie
    she won't call me
    mom
STEVE: what about taking
    the computer away
LESLIE: she'd just go to
    someone else's house
STEVE: that's what i thought
    i'd be in our house
    alone
LESLIE: we'd never see her
    we want to see her
    it's hard enough
    with her father
STEVE: it's his
    birthday
LESLIE: no
    no
    not that kind of
    party
    he's a judge
    a federal judge
    he has to decide
    right and wrong all the time
    it's really quite stressful
    i'm hoping it will
    end soon
    i hear her talking to
    the other players
    something about
    the Last Chapter
    they're almost at
    the Last Chapter
    doesn't that sound
    promising
STEVE: i thought
    your daughter was
    tinkerbell

LESLIE: it was dark
    at the block party
    you didn't notice
    the hoofprints
    on her chest
    she went as
    tinkerbell bride of satan
STEVE:
LESLIE:
STEVE: i came home
    and found her gone
    i looked on
    her computer
    this game is
    quite sophisticated
    it uses global positioning
    to map out the Neighborhood
    there's a key for points of
    Zombie infiltration
    several houses
    including mine
    and yours
    are red
LESLIE:
LESLIE: so
STEVE: i want to talk
    to madison
LESLIE: she's on her
    game
STEVE: she may know
    where chelsea is
LESLIE: i can't
    disturb her
STEVE: we don't know what they're
    really up to
LESLIE: tonight is already
    very hard
STEVE: i don't know anymore
    what's serious

what if this is
serious

LESLIE: i know serious
i know serious
you think i don't know
serious

STEVE: no i

LESLIE: they're making me do this tonight
his friends from work
this wasn't my idea
everyone coming over
to tell him he's drinking
it's so stupid
he knows he's drinking
he'll think this is
my idea and then
i don't know
i don't know
i don't know anything anymore

STEVE: i'm sorry
i guess
this is not a good night
here's your
Gnome

LESLIE:

STEVE:

LESLIE: i liked
the Gnome
everyone else in the family
hated him
but
he was always so cheerful
on the front lawn
i'd sit down next to him
and put my hands
on his cheeks
when it's warm out
they're warm
when it's cold out

they're cold
the logic
is so appealing
when it's warm out and turns cold
his cheeks are still warm
so you have a history
but only a recent history
just the past hour
instead of the crushing history
of your lifetime
or your country
or hominids
STEVE: i'm sorry i
kicked him
i've got some
superglue
LESLIE:
STEVE:
LESLIE: no
STEVE: no
LESLIE: i think
his time
is up

3 WALKTHROUGH

enter the house
you will find yourself in a
living room
with white walls and a
white carpet

turn to your left
proceed up the stairs
and enter the
bedroom

across the room
is a closet

warning: do not enter
this closet
unless you picked up the
Weed Wacker
in Chapter Four

instead
on the nightstand
you will see the
Glass of Red Wine

drink this

when you exit
the bedroom
and go back
down the stairs
you will notice a pool of
blood
on the carpet

you have just moved through
a secret wormhole
in the Neighborhood
you are now in a house
on the opposite side
of the subdivision

3 LIVING ROOM

VICKI: did you get what you were
    looking for
KAITLYN: yes thank you for letting me in
    his room
VICKI: hopefully he won't find out
    we were in
    his room
    unless he has some
    hidden camera

KAITLYN: i don't remember
     a camera
VICKI: i'm kidding
     although i wouldn't be surprised
     he's always been into
     gadgets
KAITLYN: yeah
VICKI: i don't know what he has in there
     he keeps it such a big
     secret
     but we've always pledged
     to protect his
     privacy
KAITLYN: uh-huh
VICKI: well this will be
     our
     little secret
KAITLYN: um
     i should be going
     but thank you again
     mrs. prichard
VICKI: vicki
     it's still vicki
     and it's no problem
     i'm glad you found
     what you were looking for
     it's so good so good to see you again
KAITLYN: it's good to see you
     too
VICKI: we really miss you
     around here
KAITLYN: yeah
     me too
VICKI: my husband and i
     thought you were really
     good for him
KAITLYN: thanks
     but i should
VICKI: do you want to sit down
     for a minute

KAITLYN: oh
VICKI: i could get you a coke
or even a Glass of Wine
i'm having a Glass of Wine
only if you think
your mom wouldn't mind
KAITLYN: no she lets me
have Wine sometimes
it's just i
VICKI: i don't expect
tyler
to get home anytime soon
KAITLYN: OK
i guess i could
for a minute
VICKI: great
great
sit down
let me get you
a glass
did you notice we reupholstered the loveseat
KAITLYN: it looks nice
VICKI: thank you
it was not cheap
KAITLYN: no it looks
nice
VICKI: i went back and forth on the material
i just couldn't decide between
stripes or oriental
it doesn't seem like a big decision
but it affects the whole room
these things that seem so small
have such enormous consequences
here you go
KAITLYN: thank you
VICKI: so
kaitlyn
how's school
KAITLYN: fine

VICKI: what electives
     are you taking
KAITLYN: graphic design
VICKI: really
     on the computer
KAITLYN: oh yeah
VICKI: wow
     they teach you such
     great things now how
     are the grades
     still good
KAITLYN: i guess
VICKI: you know
     even though
     we got him that hummer
     tyler's grades took a downturn
     when you two split up
KAITLYN: oh
     i'm sorry
VICKI: no
     no
     it's not your fault
     i just think he was
     upset
KAITLYN:
VICKI: i mean
     you were the one
     to break up
     with him
KAITLYN: sort of
VICKI: that's what
     he said
KAITLYN: we weren't
     hanging out much
     anyway
VICKI: but
     when he wasn't on
     his computer
     i thought he was
     with you

KAITLYN: i mean
   sometimes
VICKI: almost every night of the week
KAITLYN: no
VICKI: well where could he
   have been
KAITLYN: probably
   with his friends
VICKI: you mean the olson boys
KAITLYN: he's not really
   friends with them
VICKI: those are his
   best friends
KAITLYN:
VICKI:
KAITLYN:
VICKI: it was strange to see his room
   i haven't seen it in months
   we bought that bed
   when he was five years old
   one morning i went in
   and his feet were poking
   off the end
   and they were
   hairy
   i said it was time
   for a new bed
   but that was when
   he sealed off the room
   and like i said
   i want to give him
   a place of his own
   to be himself
   isn't that good
   i'm not the kind of parent
   to read her son's diary
   if boys really keep diaries
   maybe he has a
   what is it called

a blog
even if it was online
i wouldn't read it
not that i'm too savvy
with the internet
he's playing that
game now
that takes up
all his time
when he's not out with his friends
i'm just trying to
something's different
do you think
gosh
do you think it's
drugs

KAITLYN: maybe that's
part of it

VICKI: he has those
red eyes
but that's just marijuana
right

KAITLYN: not like
that kind of
red

VICKI: you mean
something harder
something like
it was on dateline
oxycontin

KAITLYN: maybe not even
drugs

VICKI: he has a great imagination
he gets into trouble
with the Neighborhood Association
but so would a saint
i mean
who cares about the stupid golf course
it was strange

to see those posters
on his walls
but all the boys
have posters like that
with skeletons
and Zombies
and blood
right
VICKI:
KAITLYN:
KAITLYN: i think you should go through his room
VICKI:
KAITLYN:
VICKI: what do you think
　　i might find
KAITLYN: do you remember
　　that Cat
VICKI: what Cat
KAITLYN: the hendersons
　　Cat
VICKI: wasn't it
　　hit by a car
KAITLYN: you didn't hear
　　how they found it
VICKI: how did they
　　find it
KAITLYN: it was
　　still alive
　　even though
VICKI: stop
　　i don't know what
　　this has to do with
　　my son
　　we give him
　　everything
　　he needs
　　this Wine is
　　too sweet
　　it's making me

sick
i suppose i do need to let you
get home
i'm so glad you
stopped by
say hello
to your mother
for me
i see her in the
grocery store
all the time
and we keep making plans to
get together
but we just can't seem to
get together
you only live a few blocks over
so i don't know
what it is
but tell her i really will
call her
and we really will
get together
KAITLYN: OK
thanks for the
wine
and letting me
in
VICKI: of course
of course
come back if you need
anything else
what was it
that you needed
KAITLYN: sorry
VICKI: from his
room
KAITLYN: just something
of mine
he took

VICKI: something
　　like
　　what
KAITLYN: it's
　　private
VICKI: oh
KAITLYN: i mean
VICKI: no that's
　　OK
　　of course i
　　respect that
KAITLYN:
KAITLYN: did you know
　　this house
　　is the mirror opposite
　　of mine
VICKI:
KAITLYN: if you divide the Neighborhood
　　along the line of the sewage ditch
　　and fold it in half
　　my room
　　would be right on top of
　　his room
　　so we'd see each other
　　through the ceiling
　　which is kind of how
　　we got together
　　when i needed to escape
　　my mom
　　i could lie in bed
　　and look through the ceiling
　　down at him in his bed
　　looking up through the ceiling
　　and we just sort of
　　knew each other
　　he started playing
　　that game
　　it uploads floorplans
　　from the Neighborhood Association

he showed me a map
of the subdivision
and the wormhole
between our rooms
there are wormholes
all over
the Neighborhood
he said
one of them connects
your imagination
in the game
to what happens
in life
for real
he's got like
obsessed
with finding
that wormhole
it's not just
the Cat
vicki
i think you should go through his room

VICKI: his father's
a real estate agent
i quit my job
to be home for him

KAITLYN: if you don't
look at something
it can sort of
blow up
don't you want to know what's in his

VICKI: no
he needs the right
to his own
privacy
and we give him
everything
he needs

4 WALKTHROUGH

before you are through
back away
from the Cat
do not let the mewing
deter you

leaving it
half alive
will boost your
Ruthless Ratings
which will help you
in future combat

continue down the street
casually
one block up
you will see a house
with a flagstone path
leading to
the back

take this path
to a wooden gate
use your Hammer
to smash the lock
enter the backyard
and proceed to
the pool

4 POOL

DOUG: it's OK son
    things die
    Snickers had a
    good life
RYAN:

DOUG: we don't really know what happens
     when something dies
     Snickers could be with us
     right here
     right now
     we could even say
     hello Snickers
     you were an awesome cat
     i'm sorry you got hit by that
     hummer
     at least it happened fast
     we should all hope to be
     so lucky
RYAN:
DOUG: as henry david thoreau said
     i went to the woods
     because i wished to live deliberately
     to front only the
     essential facts of life
     and not when i came to die
     discover that i had not lived
RYAN: Snickers didn't go to the woods
DOUG: well he went into the bushes a lot
RYAN:
DOUG: look
     ryan
     we've all been affected
     by the death of Snickers
RYAN:
DOUG: it reminds us of our own mortality
     and i know that can be scary
     as inderpal bahra said
     we are afraid to live
     but scared to die
RYAN:
DOUG: death comes to everyone
     think of it as something really democratic
     like our country
RYAN: or as warren leblanc said

life is like a video game
everyone must die
DOUG: who is warren leblanc
RYAN: he got caught up in this game called manhunt
and killed his fourteen-year-old friend
with a Claw Hammer
DOUG:
RYAN:
DOUG: that's not quite
what i mean
look
ryan
we need to do something about this
crying
everyone has had a
good cry over Snickers
now it's time to dry our eyes
lift the shades
and let in the sun
do you think you can do that
RYAN:
DOUG: you're not a child anymore
part of growing up is realizing
there's a lot of pain in this world
and taking responsibility for your life
means you don't let it destroy you
and you don't let your behavior
increase the pain and fear
for everyone else
RYAN:
DOUG: your mother wants to put you
on antidepressants
do you want to be put
on antidepressants
RYAN: um
DOUG: i didn't think so
we don't need drugs
to repair ourselves
the answer is within us

our personal power
is greater
than we realize
you've always been a good son
we depend on you to keep us in
good spirits
now
we've given you
a break on your chores
since Snickers passed
but i think reinstating them
will help take your mind off things
as henri matisse said
derive happiness in oneself
from a good day's work
so
ryan
you know the grind
clean the filters
skim the leaves
and replace the chlorine tablets
OK

RYAN:

RYAN: i don't like
    the Barracuda

DOUG: it helps us
    keep the pool clean

RYAN: i don't like
    the way it moves

DOUG: what are you
    ten years old
    it's not as though it's
    alive

RYAN: maybe not the way we think of
    life

DOUG: well i guess we have
    two options here
    we could turn it off
    or

you could practice getting over
your fear of it
which would you rather do
RYAN:
DOUG: which would be the
brave
thing to do
RYAN:
DOUG: look
RYAN: i just don't want it
going
while i'm cleaning the
pool
is that so
fucking
hard
DOUG:
RYAN:
DOUG: is there something else
besides Snickers
RYAN:
DOUG:
RYAN: it's just
something
in the Neighborhood
DOUG: what
RYAN: i don't know
i don't think Snickers
was hit by a hummer
DOUG: your mom saw it
pulling around the block
RYAN: i just don't
the way Snickers looked
it just
didn't look
like a car
did that
DOUG: what did it
look like

RYAN: i've been playing this
        game
        at blake's house
DOUG: we have seen a bit
        less of you
RYAN: and we
        there's this part with this
        Cat
        and we
        we
        i didn't think
        it was
        real
DOUG: what was
        real
RYAN: that
        it would
        Snickers
        dad
        listen
        there's something
        in the Neighborhood
        something's
        coming
DOUG:
RYAN:
DOUG:
RYAN:
DOUG: do you remember
        what i was saying
        about personal power
        being a wonderful thing
        well it works both ways
        personal power
        can do great damage
        when it's negative
        you're beginning
        to remind me

of my sister
every morning
when she woke up
you'd hear this
wail
up above
this wail
would sound
and you'd think
here she comes
she'd appear
at the top of the stairs
with her pigtails all twisted
her mouth wide open and wet
hair sticking to the mucus on her cheeks
she'd come down the stairs
one pajama foot
after the next
dragging her yellow blanket behind her
plunking down and
down and
closer and
closer
her howls sounding
louder and
louder
god
nothing will scare you more
than your own family
as charles manson said
from the world of darkness
did i loose demons and devils
let me tell you
son
don't you dare
bring something like that
into this house

5 WALKTHROUGH

once you've vanquished
the Barracuda
open the filter
behind its mouth
you will find a
Lime Post-it Note
with four numbers on it
add this to your inventory
and exit the backyard

the only way
to escape the Neighborhood
is to enter the
Final House
you must enter the
Final House
before the Neighborhood
is overrun
by Zombies

proceed past the
pocket park
to the house with the
open garage
if you have any available
light weapon slots
turn to the
gas grill
and pick up the
Barbecue Fork

enter the house
through the back of the garage
and find yourself in
the gameroom

5 GAMEROOM

JARED: come on
      madison
      it's going to start
MADISON: i'm coming
JARED: no
      come on
      now
MADISON: i said
      i'm coming
JARED: you always say that
      it's never true
      he's on his way home from work
      he'll be here any minute
MADISON: i'll be right
      there
JARED: i'm not mom
      don't feed me bullshit
      she went through a lot
      to pull this together
      don't you it's more important
      than your game
MADISON: we're almost at
      the Final House
JARED: you worked on
      what you're going to say to him
      didn't you
MADISON: did you
JARED: sort of
MADISON: what are you
      going to say
JARED: i asked you first
MADISON: i'll just tell him
      he's totally fucked up
      and he's fucked
      everyone in the family up
      so he should fucking stop
      fucking everyone up

hey shithole
get off me
fucking Zombie
how about some gut raping
with my garden spade
JARED: you're not
supposed to be
angry
MADISON: that's been made
perfectly clear
by that douche
from the facility
JARED: he's trying to get everyone together
in the living room
he told me
to come get you
MADISON: well you tell him
i'm coming
JARED:
MADISON:
JARED: i'm going to tell dad
that time he forgot to pick me up
from baseball practice
really
um
hurt
i was standing
on the sidewalk
and all the other dads
were picking up their kids
until everyone was
gone
except for me
with my mitt
and it turns out
he was at that bar
in the strip center
he totally
forgot

MADISON: oh he'll cry
        with his big red eyes
        and everyone
        will feel sorry
        for him
JARED: don't you
        feel sorry for him
MADISON: i'm surrounded by Zombies
        where the fuck is my
        team
JARED: what if he
        can't help it
MADISON: look i stayed home
        didn't i
        everyone else
        is at cody's house
JARED: i think you're like him
        i think you're
        hooked
MADISON: oh who was sleeping like
        two hours a night to play
JARED: i gave it up
MADISON: not until the end
        you were almost in
        the Final House
JARED: yeah dude
        it creeped me out
MADISON: what did
JARED: you're almost there
        you'll see
MADISON: i can't get
        any closer
        hello
        chelsea
        come in chelsea
        where are you guys
JARED: i think we play
        to get away from him
        like he's trying

to get away from
whatever he's trying to
get away from

MADISON: like us
foreclosing

JARED: what do you mean
foreclosing

MADISON: hello
he drank up
all our money

JARED: how do
you know

MADISON: i went in the study
i needed some dough
i went through their records
mom opened a new card
to pay for his fancy rehab
where are they

JARED: madison
would you stop
for a moment
playing that

MADISON: they better not have
ditched me
why does everyone
ditch me

JARED: for a moment
would you stop
and look at me

MADISON: no fucking way
they went in
they went in the Final House
they went in without me
now i'll never
get in
i can't do it
on my own

MADISON:

MADISON:

MADISON: you have to
  log in
  and help me
JARED: i'm not playing that
  anymore
MADISON: jared
  i need you
  you're my twin
JARED: just stop
  and do it
  later
MADISON: i'm not stopping
  anymore
  i'm not stopping
  for him
  you've got the computer
  it will only take a second
JARED: there's something
  wrong
MADISON: you've got
  the circular saw
  and the lawn darts
  pleeeeeeeeaaaasee
JARED: no
MADISON: pleeeeeeeeeeeeeeeaaaaaaaasse
JARED: no madison
MADISON: please please please please please please
  you have to help me or i'll die
JARED: he'll be home any minute
  we don't have time
MADISON: i don't care
  i hate him
  i hate him
  he's messing even this up for me
JARED: this is nothing
  don't you care about
  anything that
  matters
MADISON: hold up

chelsea's online
why isn't she using
oh
she says her headset is dead
JARED: besides
with the game
there's something
MADISON: weird
tyler found a Zombie
in the Final House
that looked like
his mom
JARED: what'd he do
MADISON: he pwned her with the Barbecue Fork
they're freaking out
chelsea's logging off
she said
don't go in
JARED: don't go in
where
MADISON: i'm not going anywhere
cuz i'll get creamed
cuz my team ditched me
shit
mother fucker
die
die
die
die
die
die
die
die
die
die
die
JARED: listen
MADISON: what
JARED: in the Neighborhood
a siren

MADISON:

JARED:

MADISON: pleeease

JARED: why don't you put
     that energy
     into this
     intervention
     if not for him
     then for us
     maybe it would be
     good for us
     to
     tell the truth
     don't you ever want to
     shout the truth
     out the window
     shout
     this is the truth
     this is the truth
     this is the truth

MADISON: fuckin a
     you're gonna get us in trouble with
     the Neighborhood Association

JARED: i don't care
     come and get me
     come and get me
     Neighborhood Association
     come and get me
     for telling
     the truth

MADISON: you're not even
     saying anything
     why don't you shout this
     every night
     on his fifth cocktail
     my dad
     turns into a Zombie
     and basically tells me
     what a loser i am

what a loser son i am
so now i
slump
everywhere i go
i have such
terrible posture
i'm known at school as
The Hunchback
i still think
he's great
way deep down
i'm so glad
the man who deformed me
is taking a month at a spa
to learn he's a
beautiful being
at heart

JARED:

JARED:

JARED: i don't want to
    yell that

MADISON: yeah cuz it's
    the truth

JARED:

MADISON:

JARED: OK
    let me log in

MADISON: yaaaay

JARED: have you
    figured it out
    have you seen
    the Final House

MADISON: no
    there's like
    twenty Zombies
    in my way
    it's not
    dark enough
    if i pop out
    they'll see me

JARED: where are you
MADISON: in the pocket park
    behind the bench
JARED: i'll distract them
MADISON: don't die
    remember
    in the Last Chapter
    you can't resurrect
JARED: you telling me now
    about this game
MADISON: oh my god
    you're running right
    out in the open
    right
    in front of them
JARED: hurry
    madison
MADISON: this isn't a
    suicide mission
JARED: you wanted to see
    the Final House
    go on
    one block past
    the pocket park
    locate the house on the left
MADISON: how do you
    remember
JARED: oh this house
    i could never forget
MADISON: but
JARED: go
    go
    go
MADISON: i'm going
JARED: a few of them
    are peeling away
    they're coming after you
MADISON: shit
    shit
    i'm almost there

house on the left
house on the left
house on the left
is
our house
JARED: what did i tell you
MADISON: what happens
    when you
    go in
JARED: i don't know
    that's where i stopped
MADISON: i'm on the front porch
    i'm at the front door
JARED: oh man
    did you hear that
MADISON:
JARED:
MADISON: he's home

6 WALKTHROUGH

killing Zombies
will alert the Neighborhood Association
to your presence

as the job
of the Neighborhood Association
is to protect
the Zombies
consider the forces
they deploy
to be your
enemy

exit through the garage
proceed down the street
two blocks
and take a
right

in the front yard
of the first house
you will see
a newly planted crape myrtle tree
with a set of
Hedge Clippers
at its base

move toward
the tree

6 FRONT YARD

TOBIAS: excuse me
　　you're in the way of my
　　Weed Wacker
BARBARA: you already did this
　　you weed-wacked it
　　yesterday
TOBIAS: i'm weed-wacking it again
　　today
BARBARA: you do it every day
　　the grass doesn't need it
　　every day
TOBIAS: i have to keep it down
　　i have to keep the ground prepared
BARBARA: i can't
　　hear you
　　could you please turn the Wacker
　　off
TOBIAS:
BARBARA: thank you
　　i'm barbara
　　i'm from next door
TOBIAS: i've seen you
　　come and go
BARBARA: you know my son
　　cody

TOBIAS: i've seen him
    come and go
BARBARA: my husband and i
    just got home
    cody apparently had some
    friends over
    they left the game room a mess
    a different kind of
    mess
    you didn't see any of them
    come and go
    while you were here wacking your
    very short grass
TOBIAS: i just got
    started
BARBARA: but
    you don't work
    do you
    you didn't see them
    this afternoon
TOBIAS: i heard some
    screaming
BARBARA: screaming
TOBIAS: i think they were playing
    some kind of
    game
BARBARA: you mean like
    cheering
TOBIAS: i mean like
    screaming
BARBARA: like they were
    excited
TOBIAS: if by
    excited
    you mean
    frantic
    then
    yes
BARBARA:
TOBIAS:

BARBARA: why do you do your lawn
    every single day
    every day i hear that
    buzzing
TOBIAS: the grass is
    unruly
    it grows
    very fast
BARBARA: not in a day
    not that fast
TOBIAS: i notice you have
    stones
BARBARA: we filled our yard with stones
    so we wouldn't have to mow
    i am very sensitive
    to noise
TOBIAS: i'm surprised stones
    are allowed
    by the Neighborhood Association
BARBARA: we were one of the first buyers
    they wrote our contract
    without the grass clause
TOBIAS: ah the grass clause
    you have to have grass
    but keep it short
    they want it to look like everything
    is under control
BARBARA: what
TOBIAS: they want it to look like everything
    is under control
BARBARA: i can't hear you
    over the sirens
TOBIAS: everything
    is under
    control
BARBARA: they must love you
TOBIAS: i don't trim my grass
    for the Neighborhood Association
    i have to keep the ground prepared

BARBARA: prepared for what

TOBIAS:

BARBARA: you don't work
    do you

TOBIAS: i stopped finding it
    important
    i stopped finding a lot of things
    important

BARBARA: you did this
    today
    to your house
    why are the
    windows boarded

TOBIAS: have you looked at
    your son's game

BARBARA: how do you know about

TOBIAS: it's quite popular
    playing with
    real people

BARBARA: i know
    some of the people
    he plays with
    but some of them
    i don't
    it could be someone next door
    or it could be
    a pedophile

TOBIAS: or both

BARBARA: what do you mean

TOBIAS: what do you mean

BARBARA:

TOBIAS:

BARBARA: you don't have children
    do you

TOBIAS: we had a hard time
    we took some drugs
    we got pregnant with triplets
    three girls
    dead in the womb

at seven months
we buried them in the yard
under the crape myrtle tree
BARBARA: isn't that
illegal
TOBIAS: no
it's our belief
they were
Ballerinas
they died floating in a
pas de trois
at night they come out
and float through the yard
i cut the grass for their glisades
they move on to your place
to practice their grand jetés
you wake up and hear
their pointe shoes
on your stones
BARBARA: i wake up
and hear that
clacking
TOBIAS: we moved here
to raise children
and then i realized
this Neighborhood
in trying so hard to
deny fear
actually magnifies it
i could feel it
warping them
in the womb
if they'd been born
it would have warped them
into something
unthinkable
instead
they dance
for the Last Chapter

BARBARA: the Last Chapter
   that's something from
   cody's game
TOBIAS: it was hard
   getting it out of him
BARBARA: getting it out
   i thought you hadn't
   seen him
TOBIAS: not today
   last night
BARBARA: last night
TOBIAS: i caught him in
   my yard
   he was making
   a mess
BARBARA: what kind of
   mess
TOBIAS: a different kind of
   mess
BARBARA: you have to
   tell me
   i'm his
   mom
TOBIAS: we believe imagination
   creates reality
   if you fear something
   it will manifest
   if you don't face it
   it will kill you
   are you sure you're ready to
   face it
BARBARA: his father's out
   looking for him
   his father is
   an angry man
   if you're not telling us
   something we need to know
TOBIAS: are you sure you're ready to
   face it
   yes or no

BARBARA: i'm not playing
   this game
   with you
TOBIAS: then if you'll
   excuse me
BARBARA: don't you dare
   turn that on
TOBIAS: are you
   threatening me
BARBARA: yes
TOBIAS:
BARBARA: yes
TOBIAS: cody said
   in the Final House
   there's a wormhole
   once you go in
   you take your family with you
   they appear to you as
   Zombies
   and finally you can
   kill them
   without
   remorse
BARBARA:
TOBIAS:
BARBARA: do you know what the neighbors say about you
   they say you killed those girls
   you killed them and buried them in the yard
   because you were afraid
   they were going to be
   monsters
TOBIAS: monster
   who do you think
   is the monster
   i'll leave out these
   Hedge Clippers
   if you see
   your son
   don't hesitate

you may pick up the
Hedge Clippers
if you have
a proficiency
in garden tools

proceed toward a street sign
that reads "dead-end"
turn left into
the cul de sac

as night
begins
to fall
you may engage the
Run Really Fast Function

your Stealth Talent
increases by
three
Zombie Olfactory Skill
increases by
twelve

turn to the first house
on your right
you will see the
Cell Phone
in the driveway

pick this up
and move toward
the house

7 DRIVEWAY

STEVE: there you are
    i've been looking
    all over for you
CHELSEA: not now steve
STEVE: don't not now steve me
    chelsea
    get back inside
    the house
CHELSEA: i'm not staying
    i have to check on
    my friend
STEVE: what friend
CHELSEA: you don't
    know her
STEVE: it's too late
    where have you been
    all afternoon
CHELSEA: i was at
    someone's house
STEVE: whose house
CHELSEA: you come home
    every night
    in the dark
    what do you care
STEVE: i came home early
    to spend some time with you
    only to find you
    gone
CHELSEA: i have to check on
    my friend
STEVE: even when
    you're here
    all i see
    is you at the computer
    with your big bag of cheetos
    well that's about to
    end

CHELSEA: you have no idea
     what's going on
     i don't need
     your permission
STEVE: why don't you
     just call her
CHELSEA: i can't find
     my Cell Phone
STEVE: that's because i have your Cell Phone
CHELSEA:
STEVE:
CHELSEA: give it to me
STEVE: is this what you came home to look for
     it was on the kitchen counter
     lot of interesting stuff here
CHELSEA: what are you
     talking about
STEVE: fascinating
     photo gallery
CHELSEA: you looked through my
     pictures
STEVE: only
     a few
     i saw
     enough
     your dad
     may be
     a lot of things
     but one thing he's not
     is a pervert
     who are these for
     you got a
     boyfriend
     you're not
     telling me
CHELSEA: yeah
     a boyfriend
     how fucking
     quaint

STEVE: your mouth
    when did you get so
    filthy
CHELSEA: my friend's in
    trouble
    give me
    my Phone
STEVE: your Phone
    who do you think
    paid for
    your Phone
    this is a
    market economy
    i've paid for
    this house
    this Phone
    this driveway
    you're standing in
    right now
    i got the money
    to pay for it
    because i
    work
    i have something of
    value
    what do you have of
    value
CHELSEA: i am a level 90 gothic cheerleader
    with a plus 12 proficiency in the Golf Club
    i suggest
    you give me
    my Phone
STEVE: my god
    i let you do
    whatever you wanted
    after your mother left
    i've given you
    everything
    why would you take these

                        pictures
                        why chelsea
                        tell me
                        why
                        and i'll give you
                        your Phone
CHELSEA: currency
STEVE: you mean money
                        i give you
CHELSEA: in the game
                        we have our own
                        currency
                        i upload
                        photos
                        to other
                        players
                        in exchange for
                        food
                        armor
                        weapons
                        i know all about
                        the market economy
                        i know
                        what i have
                        of value
STEVE:
CHELSEA:
STEVE: get inside
CHELSEA: you said
                        you'd give me
                        my Phone
STEVE: i've done something
                        wrong
                        i can no longer
                        trust you
CHELSEA: i can't
                        trust you
                        you said
                        you'd give me

STEVE: this is not
    a debate
    this is
    an order
CHELSEA: you don't fucking
    understand
    there's something
    at madison's
    house
STEVE: what did you say to me
CHELSEA: there's something
    at madison's
    house
STEVE: you're lucky
    i can't hear you
    young lady
    over all the
    sirens
    what's up with
    the sirens
    what's going on
    in the Neighborhood
CHELSEA: oh my god
    go inside
    and lock
    the door
STEVE: what
CHELSEA: give me
    my phone
    and get
    inside
STEVE: you're the one
    who's going
    inside
CHELSEA: dad
    listen
    we were all playing
    at cody's
    we went in

the Final House
tyler found a
Zombie
that looked like
his mom
he stuck her through the eyes
with the Barbecue Fork
freaked out
ran home
and called us
screaming
get out of
cody's house
he screamed
cody's father
is after him
his house is covered in
yellow tape
there are sirens and
swat teams
from the Neighborhood Association
i'm trying to
get to madison
to tell her not to
go in
maybe she can help us
if she doesn't
go in

STEVE: stop it
right now
something is
really wrong with you
are you on
drugs

CHELSEA: keep the phone
i'll go myself

STEVE: you're not going
anywhere

CHELSEA: let go
of me

STEVE: i don't know
    why i didn't
    see this
    why i didn't
    see you

CHELSEA: let go

STEVE: maybe i never wanted to
    look
    and this is what happens
    when you don't
    look
    your family becomes
    something you don't
    recognize

CHELSEA: i'm going to
    scream

STEVE: your mouth
    a wound
    your eyes
    a ghoul
    and those pictures
    you didn't used to be like this
    my daughter
    you used to be so pretty

CHELSEA:

CHELSEA:

STEVE: i'm sorry
    don't cry
    i'm sorry
    i'm a
    monster

CHELSEA:

CHELSEA:

STEVE: why are you
    looking at me
    like that

CHELSEA:

STEVE: where did you get that
    Golf Club

CHELSEA:
STEVE: chelsea
    wait
    please
    no

8 WALKTHROUGH

    remove the
    Pink and Lime Post-it Notes
    from your inventory

    the numbers on
    the Notes
    combine to form
    a phone number

    using the
    Cell Phone
    text the words
    Final House
    to this number

    you will receive a
    return text
    that contains your
    instructions

    as darkness falls
    for good
    you must use the
    streetlights
    to track the
    Zombies
    make sure you have the
    Flashlight

    and follow your instructions
    to the Final House

8 STREET

ZOMBIEKLLR14: holy shit man
    WTF
BARBARA: don't kill me
    don't kill me
ZOMBIEKLLR14: what
BARBARA: i'm sorry i
    knocked you down
ZOMBIEKLLR14: are you a player
BARBARA: please don't kill me
    i'm trying to find
    my son
ZOMBIEKLLR14: i can't kill you
    if you're a player
    i'll lose points
BARBARA: i'm a player
    i'm a player
ZOMBIEKLLR14: then get down
    they're alerted
    to movement
BARBARA: who are
ZOMBIEKLLR14:
BARBARA:
ZOMBIEKLLR14: are you sure
    you're a player
BARBARA: i
    my name is
    barbara
ZOMBIEKLLR14: barbara
    your screen name is
    barbara
    LOL
BARBARA: who are you
ZOMBIEKLLR14: zombiekllr14
BARBARA: are you with
    the Neighborhood Association
ZOMBIEKLLR14: do i look like i'm with
    the NA

BARBARA: they're sending out
    swat teams
    you're wearing all that
    armor
ZOMBIEKLLR14: if i were with
    the NA
    you'd already be
    dead
    i'm looking for
    the Final House
BARBARA: no
    the Final House
    my son
    i think
    went in
    all the sirens
    all the houses with
    yellow tape
    no one will tell me
    what's going on
    my husband and i
    are looking for him
    he has to be here
    somewhere
ZOMBIEKLLR14: WTF
    get down
BARBARA: WTF
ZOMBIEKLLR14: what the fuck
    stay out of the
    streetlight
    i don't know how you got to the Last Chapter
    noob
    but you better not give me away
BARBARA: the Last Chapter
    what is it with
    the Last Chapter
ZOMBIEKLLR14: you're really
    pretty
    you look like

my friend's mom
i always thought
she was hot
where'd you get
that avatar
BARBARA: avatar
you sound like
my son
ZOMBIEKLLR14: you have a son
IRL
BARBARA: IRL
ZOMBIEKLLR14: in real life
are you like
old
BARBARA: what was that
in the streetlight
ZOMBIEKLLR14: the streetlights
are how we
keep track of them
BARBARA: track of what
ZOMBIEKLLR14: shit
there's like
fifty
heading this way
BARBARA: fifty of what
how do you know
ZOMBIEKLLR14: on my headset
one of my team members
told me
aren't you on
a team
BARBARA: i mean
my husband
my son
ZOMBIEKLLR14: come on
keep down
if i have to kill one
we're in trouble
BARBARA: what

have you
been killing
what's that
in your hand
a Hammer
oh my god
it's slimy
ZOMBIEKLLR14: where's your
weapon
BARBARA: i don't have a
weapon
ZOMBIEKLLR14: how'd you get
this far
BARBARA: my neighbor
tried to give me
Hedge Clippers
ZOMBIEKLLR14: oh wow
you've got the Hedge Clippers
BARBARA: no
i didn't take them
ZOMBIEKLLR14: dude
what's wrong with you
BARBARA: i thought he was
crazy
ZOMBIEKLLR14: you're the one
who's crazy
get the fuck
away from me
BARBARA: wait
where are you
going
ZOMBIEKLLR14: there are fifty of them
hot on our tracks
you're going
to give me
away
BARBARA: oh my god
ZOMBIEKLLR14: OMG
BARBARA: oh my god

ZOMBIEKLLR14: it's OMG
BARBARA: OMG
     fifty of what
ZOMBIEKLLR14: fifty Zombies
BARBARA:
BARBARA: i don't believe in
     Zombies
ZOMBIEKLLR14: AFK
BARBARA: AFK
ZOMBIEKLLR14: away from keyboard
BARBARA: keyboard
     what are you
     talking about
     what the hell are you
     talking about
     i don't believe in
     Zombies
     do you hear me
     i don't believe in
     what was that
     was that what i
     think it
     was that
     did you see that
     hey
     did you see that
     hello
     what's wrong with you
     you said there were
     Zombies
     so why don't you
     do something
     do something
     do something
ZOMBIEKLLR14: i'm back
     sorry
     i had to shut my window
     there was some woman outside screaming
     now what was i doing

oh yeah
ditching you
BARBARA: wait
i saw something
ZOMBIEKLLR14: where
BARBARA: over there
in the streetlight
ZOMBIEKLLR14: that's the only way
to see them coming
BARBARA:
ZOMBIEKLLR14:
BARBARA:
ZOMBIEKLLR14: WTF
BARBARA: what happened to
the streetlights
ZOMBIEKLLR14: the NA must have
turned them off
BARBARA: it's so dark
i can't see
anything
ZOMBIEKLLR14: where the fuck is my team
come in
KneelBeforeMe
are the lights out
where you are
BARBARA: my god
where am i
ZOMBIEKLLR14: KneelBeforeMe
where are you man
BARBARA: where am i where am i
ZOMBIEKLLR14: you better
come in
you've got
the Flashlight
BARBARA: i have a
Flashlight
ZOMBIEKLLR14: you have the
Flashlight
f'n a

turn it on

BARBARA:

BARBARA: Last Chapter
Final House
Zombies
OMG
am i in
cody's game

ZOMBIEKLLR14:

BARBARA:

ZOMBIEKLLR14: you know
cody

BARBARA: cody
is my
son

ZOMBIEKLLR14: mrs. whitestone
it's me
blake

BARBARA: blake
blake
you're
seven feet tall

ZOMBIEKLLR14: dude
i thought i recognized you
how'd cody find an outfit
that looks so much like you

BARBARA: where is he

ZOMBIEKLLR14: last time i heard
he had a fuckload
i mean buttload of Zombies after him
one of them looked like
his dad

BARBARA: OMG
i've got to
find them

ZOMBIEKLLR14: where are you going
with that
Flashlight

BARBARA: cody's in
trouble

ZOMBIEKLLR14: i need you
    i need you to get to the
    Final House
BARBARA: no
    don't go in the
    Final House
ZOMBIEKLLR14: that's the only way
    out of the Neighborhood
    i need you to follow me
    and keep the light
    in front of us
BARBARA: i can find him
    on my own
ZOMBIEKLLR14: i'm sorry to say this mrs. whitestone
    but i will waste you
    and you know
    if you die in the Last Chapter
    you can no longer
    resurrect
BARBARA:
ZOMBIEKLLR14: over there
    up one block
    let's go
BARBARA:
ZOMBIEKLLR14:
BARBARA: how do you know
    where we're going
ZOMBIEKLLR14: i called the number on the
    Post-it Notes
    i got the instructions
    from the Cell Phone
BARBARA: ewgh
    something
    dripped
    on me
ZOMBIEKLLR14: come on
    come on
BARBARA: it felt
    warm

ZOMBIEKLLR14: felt
that's some imagination you got there
mrs. whitestone
BARBARA: what is up there
in that tree
ZOMBIEKLLR14: don't worry
it's dead
BARBARA: but it looks like
someone i
ZOMBIEKLLR14: just keep
the light
in front of us
BARBARA:
ZOMBIEKLLR14:
BARBARA: did you hear that
ZOMBIEKLLR14: yeah
that was creepy
shine the light
over there
BARBARA: OMG
ZOMBIEKLLR14: WTF
it looks like
BARBARA: Ballerinas
ZOMBIEKLLR14: what are Ballerinas
doing in the game
BARBARA: don't you get it
Zombie Killer
this isn't
ZOMBIEKLLR14: holy shit
they found it
we're at the
Final House
BARBARA: it's
my house
ZOMBIEKLLR14: it's my house
BARBARA: cody
i wonder if
what's that on
the porch

ZOMBIEKLLR14: careful
BARBARA: Post-it Notes
 they're covered in
ZOMBIEKLLR14: yeah
 the blood effects are
 killer
BARBARA: are these
 cody's
 where is
ZOMBIEKLLR14: i don't know
 mrs. whitestone
 he may not
 resurrect
BARBARA: what do you mean
ZOMBIEKLLR14: my teammate
 just told me
 that Zombie that was after him
 got him
BARBARA: i don't
 no
 i don't
 no
 there must be
ZOMBIEKLLR14: when my team gets here
 we're going in
BARBARA: no
 no
 don't
 go in
ZOMBIEKLLR14: that's the only way
 out of the Neighborhood
BARBARA: that is not
 the only way
 get up
 from your computer
 get up
 from your computer
 and go talk
 to your mom

ZOMBIEKLLR14: i don't talk
    to my mom
BARBARA: tell her
    barbara sent you
    she knows me
    from when you and cody
    were boys
ZOMBIEKLLR14: she doesn't
    listen to me
    crap
    here she comes
BARBARA: tell her
    to contact
    my neighbor
ZOMBIEKLLR14: right when i'm
    about to
    go in
BARBARA: no
    do not
    go in
    maybe
    it's not
    too late
    if some of you
    don't
    go in
    maybe
    oh god
    cody
ZOMBIEKLLR14: i can't play with her
    over my shoulder
    fuck
    AFK
BARBARA: wait
    blake
    blake
    tell her
    to listen you
    talk

to your mom
talk
to each other
oh god
cody
we thought
when we moved here
we were moving
up
but all the Neighborhoods
are mirror images
all the Neighborhoods
fold onto each other
don't go in
the Final House
there are no levels
there's no moving up
there's no getting out

9 THE FINAL HOUSE

(A teenage boy sits at a computer. Light from the monitor shines on his face. He wears a headset and alternately types on the computer keyboard and maneuvers a fancy mouse with a giant tracking ball. Clothes are strewn about his room. Fast-food wrappers litter his desk.)

BLAKE: I'm here. *(Pause.)* At the final house. *(Pause.)* In the bushes by the front door. *(Pause.)* Well hurry up. *(Pause.)* My Cologne du Corpse is wearing off. They're gonna smell me. *(Pause.)* Please just get your ass over here. *(The door to the bedroom opens. A woman in a fuzzy bathrobe stands in the hall light, clutching a fast-food bag.)*

JOY: Honey? *(Pause.)* Are you still on your game? *(Pause.)* I microwaved your burger since you were too busy to eat it earlier. Do you want it now? *(He ignores her. She is used to it.)*

JOY: I'm watching a little CSI. I love how that forensic team figures everything out in the end. This episode is about a dwarf—I mean little person— who murders another little person because he's about to marry his daughter—who is normal—I mean, a person of average height. He wants his daughter to marry another person of average height so she'll have a normal family. I mean, everyone wants a normal family. So he murders the little fiance by hanging him. They even show the vertebrae going snap snap snap. At least, that's what I think was happening. You know I cover my eyes for the gory part. It's too, um, real. *(She hears something downstairs, turns her head for a moment to listen, then turns back to Blake.)* I know you're busy, but, it's a little lonely downstairs . . . don't you want to come sit on the couch with me and watch?

(He ignores her.)

JOY: Well. I offered. *(She drops the bag inside the room and closes the door.)*

BLAKE: There you are, man! I was getting lonely. *(Pause.)* Yeah, I'm ready. In a minute. Calm down. Don't you think, um . . . *(As he talks he gets up from the computer, retrieves the burger, comes back to the computer.)* Don't you think we should wait for the rest of the team? *(Pause.)* Yeah I know we can, it's just—I have to check my armor one more time. *(Pause.)* And refill my Sugar Rush. *(Pause.)* And um . . . hey, get off the porch, get back in the bushes, I'm not ready yet! *(Pause.)* I am NOT stalling—!

(Door opens.)

JOY: Honey? I thought I heard something by the front door. It sounded. Strange. I don't know, maybe I'm imagining things. You aren't—up to anything—are you? You can—tell me—if you are. I promise I won't—freak out. I'd really actually prefer some advance notice to one of those phone calls. Why don't you come downstairs, I'll make some popcorn, we can—talk—and maybe you could listen to this noise and see if you think it sounds strange. Like something coming through the walls. I never used to feel that way about this place. But now. It's like that movie. Maybe our house is built on an Indian burial ground. Maybe the neighborhood. Maybe the whole country. Oh now listen to me—being morbid—I must need another— *(She stops herself.)* It's just that thing by the front door. You wouldn't know anything about it, would you? *(Pause.)* Hey. I'm talking to you. Look at me when I talk to you!

(Blake turns his head the tiniest degree possible. Pause.)

JOY: No, of course you wouldn't. Why don't you get ready for bed. I'll bring you something to help you sleep.

(She closes the door.)

BLAKE: Fuck, she makes me insane. *(Pause.)* No, I'm not ready yet. *(He eats his burger, talking through the food.)* It's not about being a pussy you fucking douche—listen—there was this woman. *(Pause.)* I wish—no—in the game. I couldn't tell if she was a Zombie or a player. She looked like

Cody's mom and kept asking if I'd seen him. *(Pause.)* Yeah, I thought at first it was Cody being a total weirdo, but. Something was off. She kept saying, don't go in. *(Pause.)* I know it's lame, but— *(Pause.)* Look, shut up—I took care of it! That's her on the sidewalk. I bashed her head in. *(Door opens.)*

JOY: Blake, I'm sure of it. There's something out there. You're the man of the house now—you should come take a look. It's not just the noise, I saw— a shadow. In the porch light. Coming. To the front door. Hey! Are you listening to me? I am asking you a favor! It's the least you can do after everything I do for you. I cook your meals. I wash your clothes. I make sure you don't shrivel up and—die—behind that computer. The computer that was bought for you. And can you be bothered to do a single thing for me? *(Pause.)* You! I'm talking to you! I'm not just some drudge who does all your shit work! Look at me!

BLAKE: *(Without turning around.)* What.

JOY: What?

BLAKE: I said what.

JOY: Is that all you have to say?

BLAKE: What do you want me to say, Joy?

JOY: Don't call me that!

BLAKE: It's your name.

JOY: I have told you not to call me that! I have told you and told you, but you don't listen to me! You don't listen to a thing I say! And I have done— everything for you! Well let me tell you, buster, things are going to change around here. Nothing's free in this world, and it's time for you to earn your keep. I'm making a list of after-school chores and setting lim- its on your game time. Starting now. Off the computer in five minutes! *(She closes the door. Blake straightens.)*

BLAKE: Grrrw, I just got the things-are-gonna-change-around-here speech. But nothing ever does. So fuck it—let's go in. *(Pause.)* Get up here and cover me. *(Pause.)* I'm trying the front door . . . oh weird, weird . . . it's open- ing on its own. *(Pause.)* I can't see anything inside. *(Pause.)* You ready? *(Pause.)* OK. *(Pause.)* I'm in, I'm in! *(Pause.)* I'm behind the sofa, come on. *(Pause.)* Shit I saw something move. *(Pause.)* In the light of the television. *(Pause.)* I don't know—just get up the stairs—it's in the bedroom at the top. Bedroom at the top. *(Pause.)* Wait, don't open the door yet. *(Pause.)* Do you hear that? *(Pause.)* Fuck, my heart is pounding. *(Pause.)* OK, ready man. *(Pause.)* Opening the door . . . I'm . . . opening the door . . . *(Door opens.)*

JOY: Honey?

BLAKE: Not now!

JOY: I did it. I looked.

BLAKE: You said I have five minutes!

JOY: I didn't have a choice—the front door just—opened.

BLAKE: Get the fuck outta my room!

JOY: Do you remember Barbara, Cody's mom?

(Pause. For the first time, Blake turns to look at her.)

BLAKE: What about her?

JOY: She's on the sidewalk. With half her head gone.

(Blake stares at her in disbelief. Then he whirls back to the computer and jabs at the keyboard.)

BLAKE: Get out. Get out of the room get out of the house. Get out get out get out get out get out get out fuck the front door is locked.

JOY: I locked the front door.

BLAKE: Are you there man? We're in trouble!

JOY: All night I've heard sirens.

BLAKE: I'm unarmed. I dropped my hammer somewhere on the stairs.

JOY: Is this what you're looking for? I found it on the stairs.

(Blake turns around to look. Joy is holding a bloody claw hammer.)

BLAKE: Give that to me.

JOY: Does it belong to you?

BLAKE: Look, Joy—

JOY: Don't call me that! Just the fact that you're capable of calling me that. What else are you capable—of?

BLAKE: I haven't—done—anything.

JOY: What happened to Barbara?

BLAKE: You tell me.

JOY: No, you tell me. You never tell me anything anymore.

BLAKE: You never ask.

JOY: I try all the time to talk to you.

BLAKE: You don't really want to know.

JOY: This is the first time I've seen your face in so long. You never even look at me anymore.

BLAKE: I'm looking at you now.

JOY: I don't recognize you.

BLAKE: I'm your son. Give me the hammer.

JOY: I have tried to talk to you! I have tried! I want to hear you say, I know you've tried.

BLAKE: Easy, Joy.

JOY: DON'T CALL ME—

BLAKE: OK! You've tried.

JOY: Say it like you believe it. Say it like it's the truth.

BLAKE: I. Believe. You've—

JOY: NO. You don't believe me. You don't even see me. You don't see anything outside of your game. You don't see anything that's real!

(Joy realizes Blake is cowering from her. She sags.)

JOY: I'm sorry. *(Pause.)* It's so good . . . to see you, son. It's so good . . . to see your face.

(Touched, Blake nods. This is their only moment.)

JOY: I just want to . . . I just want . . . the two of us . . . It's not too late, is it? It's not too late?

(Blake shakes his head.)

JOY: I'm so sorry. So so so so so so so so so—

(She rushes toward him, arms raised. Blake, suddenly terror-stricken, wrenches the hammer from her hand and, through her screams, beats her to death.)

10 BEDROOM

(Blake shoves himself away from the computer. Shivering, he looks around the empty room.)

BLAKE: Mom?

END OF PLAY

100 SAINTS YOU SHOULD KNOW

Kate Fodor

For Lucy's grandparents

PLAYWRIGHT'S BIOGRAPHY

Kate Fodor is a recipient of the Kennedy Center's Roger L. Stevens Award, the National Theater Conference's Barrie Stavis Award, a Joseph Jefferson Citation, and an After Dark Award and is a finalist position for the Susan Smith Blackburn Prize. Her work has been produced by Playwrights Horizons, Epic Theatre Ensemble, San Jose Repertory Theatre, Steppenwolf Theatre Company, and other theaters around the country and abroad. She is a proud member of New Dramatists.

ORIGINAL PRODUCTION

World premiere presented at Playwrights Horizons. Directed by Ethan McSweeny with the following cast and crew:

CAST

THERESA	Janel Moloney
MATTHEW	Jeremy Shamos
ABBY	Zoe Kazan
COLLEEN	Lois Smith
GARRETT	Will Rogers

Artistic Director	Tim Sanford
Managing Director	Leslie Marcus
General Manager	William Russo
Scene Design	Rachel Hauck
Costume Design	Mimi O'Donnell
Lighting Design	Jane Cox
Sound Design	Matt Hubbs
Casting	Alaine Alldaffer
Director of Development	Jill Garland
Production Manager	Christopher Boll
Press Representative	The Publicity Office
Production Stage Manager	Michaella K. McCoy

CHARACTERS

THERESA: thirties
MATTHEW: thirties
ABBY: sixteen
COLLEEN: sixties
GARRETT: sixteen

SETTING

Two American towns, a couple of hours away from each other.

TIME

The present.

100 SAINTS YOU SHOULD KNOW

ACT I

Theresa is on her knees cleaning a toilet. She wears tight jeans, a tank top, and long yellow rubber gloves. She scrubs around the inside of the bowl with a plastic brush, flushes, then wipes down the seat with a rag from a bucket. The doorknob turns, the door opens, and Matthew, a priest, is suddenly there in the tiny bathroom with her.

MATTHEW: Oh, ah—

THERESA: Theresa.

MATTHEW: Theresa. I'm so sorry. I didn't realize—

THERESA: No problem.

MATTHEW: I was working, I was writing and I . . . I forgot you were here. I didn't mean to intrude on your . . . on your work.

THERESA: It's no big deal, Father McNally.

MATTHEW: Did I see you come in this morning?

THERESA: You said hello.

MATTHEW: Did I? I'm sorry. I was working.

THERESA: It's no problem. I wish I could focus the way you do. My brain is always going in three directions at once.

MATTHEW: Well, I'll let you get back to —

THERESA: Do you want the bathroom?

MATTHEW: No, no. Thank you.

THERESA: I mean, if you need the bathroom . . . I have the whole kitchen to do. I can finish later.

MATTHEW: No, no. It's all right.

THERESA: If you have to go to the bathroom, I mean . . . I still have the whole kitchen to do.

MATTHEW: Well. All right. Thank you.

THERESA: I'll just leave these things here for now. Is that all right?

MATTHEW: Of course. It's fine.

THERESA: OK, great.

MATTHEW: Thank you, Theresa.

THERESA: No problem, really.

(Theresa rises and squeezes past Matthew out the bathroom door. Matthew pulls the door closed and locks it. Blackout.)

SCENE 2

Later the same afternoon. Abby's bedroom. Posters, dirty dishes, tangled bunches of dirty laundry. Abby is lying on her bed, flipping through a magazine. She hears the front door of the apartment open.

ABBY: Mom? Mom! Mom! Is that you?

THERESA: *(Offstage.)* Yes.

ABBY: You said you were gonna leave me ten dollars and you didn't! *(A pause.)* Mom? Mom! Mom!

THERESA: *(Offstage.)* What?

ABBY: You said you were gonna leave me ten dollars and you didn't! *(A pause.)* Mom? Mom!

(Theresa appears in the doorway of Abby's room, still in her work clothes from the first scene, with a cigarette in one hand and the day's junk mail in the other. She's tired.)

THERESA: Sorry, Abby. I forgot.

ABBY: What's in the mail?

THERESA: Catalogs and bills.

ABBY: What catalogs?

THERESA: Avon and Victoria's Secret.

(Abby holds out her hand. Theresa gives her the catalogs.)

ABBY: Why were you gone so long?

THERESA: I wasn't. This is what time I always get home on Saturdays. I clean the rectory at Saint Dominic's. Eleven to three.

ABBY: What's a rectory?

THERESA: Where the priest lives.

ABBY: Was the priest there?

THERESA: Yes.

ABBY: Creepy.

THERESA: He's not too bad. He's young.

ABBY: Did he say anything about your tight jeans?

THERESA: No, Abby. God.

ABBY: Tight jeans are the devil's playground. You said you were gonna leave me ten dollars.

THERESA: I forgot.

ABBY: I was hungry, Mom. I didn't have any money to order food. Have you looked in the fridge lately?

THERESA: I brought home groceries.

ABBY: But do you know what was in the fridge when you left me here with no money?

THERESA: I don't know.

ABBY: Can you name two things that were in the fridge when you left me here with no money?

THERESA: There was yogurt, Abby.

ABBY: It's four o'clock and I haven't even had lunch yet. Can I have ten dollars?

THERESA: I brought home groceries. I'll make tuna.

ABBY: But you said I could have ten dollars, so you owe me money.

(Theresa takes ten dollars from her wallet.)

THERESA: Don't ask me again until next week.

ABBY: Plus, that yogurt said May 9th and it's May eleventh.

THERESA: Did you ever hear anything about any babysitting jobs?

ABBY: I don't know what you're talking about.

THERESA: I thought you put up flyers for babysitting jobs.

ABBY: No.

THERESA: Didn't you and Katya go to Kinko's and make flyers for babysitting jobs?

ABBY: Oh. Yeah.

THERESA: So what happened to them?

ABBY: We didn't put them up.

THERESA: Oh.

ABBY: OK?

THERESA: OK. Why didn't you put them up?

ABBY: We just didn't.

THERESA: Don't you think babysitting would be good experience if you want to be a teacher?

ABBY: I don't want to be a teacher.

THERESA: Isn't that what you said in your presentation for school, that you wanted to be a teacher?

ABBY: That was for school. You have to say something, or you get a zero. I already have fourteen zeros in that class. I didn't need another one.

THERESA: Are you going to fail social studies, Abby?

ABBY: Even if I do, they're not going to hold me back. You have to fail three subjects to get held back.

THERESA: So not getting held back is your only goal for yourself?

ABBY: You should be lucky I'm even in school.

THERESA: I just don't think that not getting held back is a really, you know, lofty ambition.

ABBY: Katya's dropping out at the end of the year.

THERESA: Great, maybe she can get a job as a cleaning lady.

ABBY: Maybe.

THERESA: The best part is scraping the shit off the inside of other people's toilets.

ABBY: Just because you fucked up your life doesn't mean Katya's going to fuck up her life.

THERESA: If she drops out of school it does.

ABBY: Katya has talents, Mom. You don't have any talents, so there's a difference.

THERESA: What are Katya's talents?

ABBY: She sings and she designs clothes.

THERESA: Tell her I'll see her at Magic Maids. She'll probably be good at scrubbing floors. She looks like a girl who has some experience providing services on her knees.

ABBY: You're really horrible.

THERESA: I guess I am.

ABBY: You look all sweaty. Why don't you take a shower?

THERESA: I'll make lunch when I get out. Do you want me to make you a sandwich?

ABBY: Sure, Mom. Let's have lunch together, and maybe you can call me a slut some more.

THERESA: I didn't say anything about you.

ABBY: If you call Katya a slut, it's really just a way to call me a slut, which you don't want to do because you don't want to think that you're a horrible enough person that you would say that about your own daughter.

THERESA: You and Katya are very different people, Abby.

ABBY: No, we're not.

THERESA: For one thing, Katya doesn't have parents to take care of her.

ABBY: Like I have parents to take care of me? Like I have a dad and we all sit down for dinner every night and eat meatloaf and he says, "So, honey, how was your day at school?" And I say, "Great, Dad, but I'm having a little bit of trouble in science." And he says, "Don't worry about that. I can help you with that tonight after we eat our fucking ice cream." Katya has her uncle, and at least he doesn't call her a slut. At least he respects her as a person.

THERESA: Why is Katya dropping out of school?

ABBY: Um, because.

THERESA: No, really. I'm serious. I want to know why.

ABBY: Well, let's see. You have two choices. You could ride a bus that smells like a barfed-up boloney sandwich to the worst high school in the state where some dumb-ass security guard searches your backpack and gets off on touching your tampons and then you could sit through some class where the teacher puts on a movie and falls asleep at his desk and it's a federal case if you ask to go to the bathroom because they assume you're going in there to shoot up or something and some guy writes "Nice Tits" on your locker in permanent marker and all the girls think you're a loser because you're not on the fucking cheerleading team. Or you could, you know, not go.

THERESA: She's pregnant?

ABBY: Oh, God, Mom.

THERESA: Do you use condoms, Abby?

ABBY: Oh, my God! I shouldn't have to listen to this just because you saw some public service announcement!

THERESA: You can come to me if you need anything.

ABBY: Oh, OK then.

THERESA: What?

ABBY: I'll just come see the world's expert on birth control.

THERESA: Sometimes I do know things you don't.

ABBY: If you knew anything about birth control, I would not be here on this earth. If you knew anything about anything, I would never have been born and I wouldn't have to be listening to you right now. I'd be a nice little star up in the sky.

THERESA: You'd be a what?

ABBY: Unborn babies are stars in the sky.

THERESA: Where'd you get that? Science class?

ABBY: No.

THERESA: That's not some kind of right-to-life propaganda or something, is it?

ABBY: It's a figure of speech, mom! It's a goddamn simile.

THERESA: It's not a simile.

ABBY: Yes, it is. English class.

THERESA: No, it's not, Ab. A simile is when you use like or as to —

ABBY: Oh my God, shut up, shut up! You act like such a fucking know-it-all!

THERESA: I know more than I did when I was sixteen.

ABBY: I hope so because if you end up having some ugly little pig baby with that hog man you bring here, you will never see me again. I will run so far away. Do you understand that?

THERESA: You want Doug to stop coming over? Is that why you're so mad at me all the time?

ABBY: I'm not mad at you. I hate you. Those are two different things. *(A beat.)*

THERESA: Oh. OK. I'm going to go take a shower.

ABBY: I think I should go and live with Grandma.

THERESA: Don't be stupid, Abby. You wouldn't know Grandma if you saw her on the street.

ABBY: Well, I just think I could use a change, so I don't think you should call me stupid for—

THERESA: I didn't say you were stupid, I'm just saying you haven't seen Grandma in like—

ABBY: I'm just saying I don't think she'd be very happy if she knew how you were raising me. I don't think she'd be very impressed with—

THERESA: I don't really give a shit what your grandmother—

ABBY: Don't swear at me!

THERESA: I'm not swearing at you.

ABBY: Don't swear at me, you stupid fucking—!

(A silence. Theresa goes to the door, then turns back.)

THERESA: This time last year, you were a nice kid, Abby.

(Theresa exits. Blackout.)

SCENE 3

The living room of Colleen's overstuffed little house. Doilies on the tables, lace cushions on the chairs, china figurines and bronzed baby shoes on the mantelpiece. Matthew, wearing jeans and a sweater, sits in a recliner that has seen better days. Colleen is on the telephone.

COLLEEN: Frank. It's Colleen here with my order. Have you got a pen anywhere? . . . I'm teasing you, Frank, because you've always got a pen behind each ear . . . Yes, one pen behind one ear, you might expect from a grocer, but you've always got two pens, Frank, one behind each ear. You can check right now if you like . . . There, you see? You've always got a pen behind each ear, sticking out from your face like a pair of horns . . . Yes, always. Now, Frank, I need to tell you that my son has arrived for a visit! He just appeared on my doorstep and I don't have a thing to feed him, so I need your help very badly. I had lovely tomatoes from you last week. Have you still got those? . . . Three pounds of them, then, please, and the usual list, with double the potatoes, double the bread, double the eggs, and double the bacon, as well as a roasting chicken about the size of a baby, and a largish tub of ice cream in a nice flavor, I think butter pecan . . . You've written it down? . . . Thank you, Frank . . . Oh, yes, he's lovely. Big, broad shoulders, doing very well . . . Yes, I'll tell him. And you say hello to Maura for me, and to that good boy of yours . . . All right, Frank. Good-bye!

(She hangs up the telephone.)

COLLEEN: Frank the grocer says hello to you.

MATTHEW: Hello, Frank the grocer.

COLLEEN: He gets lovely bacon in from one of the farms, in good thick slabs, just the way God meant for bacon to be sliced. I ordered extra so that you can have as much as you like each morning for breakfast. Did you hear me ask him for extra for you, Mattie?

MATTHEW: Yes, Ma, thank you.

COLLEEN: He takes my list like that every week, just over the phone, and then he sends the groceries over in boxes, because of my hip. It's not been easy for me to get around, you know, because of my hip and my heart. So Frank has his boy drive the groceries over in boxes. He's sixteen and just got his driving license, so he likes to do it. What would you like to do now, Mattie? Would you like to play a game of Scrabble?

MATTHEW: Sure, Ma, if that's what you'd like.

COLLEEN: Well, it's what I'd like if it's what you'd like, Mattie.

MATTHEW: All right. Yes. Let's play Scrabble.

COLLEEN: There! I thought you might like a game of Scrabble! That's why I put it out there for you. *(She sets up the board.)* It's good of me to play with you, since you always win, don't you think? You're just like your Aunt Kitty, with your seven-letter words and your triple-word scores. Oh, she'd make me angry when we were children, but what wouldn't I give to sit and have a game of Scrabble with Kitty now that there's an ocean between us? Go on, take your letters. And you go first. You've always gone first, since you were a little boy, otherwise you cried. And Kitty always went first at games when she and I were girls, because she was older, so all in all I don't think I've ever gone first in a game in my whole life, but that's all right.

MATTHEW: *(Holding the plastic bag of letters out to her.)* Here.

COLLEEN: What's that?

MATTHEW: You pick a tile without looking, and whoever's letter is closer to the start of the alphabet takes the first turn.

COLLEEN: Oh, no. I'm not one to spoil a tradition! You go. Go on, make up a word. Kitty was saying on Sunday that she and I ought to have a game of Scrabble over the telephone! What do you think? Why not? Why shouldn't we?

MATTHEW: You wouldn't be able to see each other's words.

COLLEEN: We'd have to tell each other. I'd say, "Now, Kitty, I'm making a word off of your B in butter, going down, I'm making the word belly," and then she'd put that on her board so she'd know. And she'd say, "Now, Colleen, I'm making a word off your Y in 'belly.' It's 'boyish' and the y is in the middle." Oh, we've got it all worked out, Mattie, don't you worry about us. I think it would be lovely. Except for the expense, of course! Can you imagine, an hour and a half on the telephone to Ireland for a game of Scrabble! I'd have to turn out all the lights for a month and live on toast to pay for it! Now, look at you already. How many points do you have there?

MATTHEW: Seventeen for "juiced," doubled because I went first. That's thirty-four.

COLLEEN: Because you've used a J, that's what's done it for you. I see.

MATTHEW: Put a word down, Ma.

COLLEEN: All right, all right. Let's see. I could do "cats" and get six points off of your C there, but then we'd have "juiced" and "cats," which gives me the picture of a man trying to wring the juice out of some poor, unfortunate cats! We wouldn't want that sitting on the board the whole time, would we? "Juiced" and "cats"?

MATTHEW: Not if it upsets you, no.

COLLEEN: I'll do "jest," then, for eleven points. That isn't bad at all! I've used your J, that's what's done it for me. And the score is eleven to thirty-four, so we're both in the double digits, aren't we? It's your turn now.

MATTHEW: I know, Ma. *(He places three tiles on the board.)* Smit.

COLLEEN: Did you say "smit," Mattie?

MATTHEW: Smit, which is the archaic form of smote, as in "And he smote them hip and thigh with a great slaughter." Judges 15:8. Archaic words are allowed under the rules. They're on the inside of the box. It's six points.

COLLEEN: Just six points for you? So early in the game?

MATTHEW: It's the best I could do.

COLLEEN: I don't need pity, Mattie! I hardly need for anyone to help me win a game of Scrabble.

MATTHEW: You've never won a game of Scrabble, Ma.

COLLEEN: Then why should I win today? If I lose at Scrabble, then I lose at Scrabble. It's what I do. It's in my nature. And I'll be left to it if you don't mind.

MATTHEW: All right, Ma. Sorry. Make a word.

COLLEEN: I'm not feeble-minded.

MATTHEW: No, certainly not.

COLLEEN: If anyone needs pitying, it's you. You look like a fever patient, Mattie, weak and white. I haven't said a word all this time, but I thought it the moment you came to the door —

MATTHEW: That's why I thought I'd come here and relax. *(A beat.)* I'm working hard, Ma, that's all.

COLLEEN: You heard me order all that food for you from Frank the grocer.

MATTHEW: Yes, Ma. That's great. Thank you.

COLLEEN: I'll get you fattened up a bit.

MATTHEW: OK.

COLLEEN: How long will you be staying, Mattie?

MATTHEW: I won't stay at all if it's trouble for you.

COLLEEN: Oh, no, I want you here, I do! I only wondered because I do like to plan my meals, and a roasted chicken lasts a day or two of course but—

MATTHEW: If I'm going to be in the way, I can go to the Best Western.

COLLEEN: Do you know why I always lose to you at Scrabble?

MATTHEW: Because you were educated by semiliterate nuns in a one-room schoolhouse in Galway?

COLLEEN: No, that's not why.

MATTHEW: I think it probably is.

COLLEEN: I lose to you at Scrabble because I play to keep the game going, to keep the conversation going. When I put down a word, I'm thinking about whether I've left the other person something on the board to work with. I don't try to get everything all tangled up into a corner like you do, until there's nothing left for anyone to build off of but a Q and a Z.

MATTHEW: This is meant as a sort of allegory?

COLLEEN: I'm trying to say, Mattie, that you make it hard to talk to you sometimes. Is there a better way to talk to you that I don't know about? I wish you'd tell me if there is.

MATTHEW: There's no better way, Ma. It's your turn.

(Colleen looks at her letters for a moment, and then puts them down.)

COLLEEN: I'd like you to help me with some things while you're here.

MATTHEW: That's fine. Whatever you want.

COLLEEN: I'd like to get some of the things in the attic sorted out, to begin with.

MATTHEW: Fine. We'll work on it tomorrow.

COLLEEN: I might even put a few of the things up there in the trash, though I wouldn't have dared while your father was alive. He didn't believe in the trash, your father. Every shirt he ever wore went up to that attic when he'd finally done with it, ripped, stained, or otherwise. A shirt not fit to wear one day might seem a treasure the next, depending on what the Lord had got in store for you, that's what he said about it. Shoes, as well. There must be thirty pairs of your father's shoes in that attic that would have done for mending if times got hard. Your father believed in conserving.

MATTHEW: Yes, I know.

COLLEEN: There might be one or two things up there that you'd like to have for yourself. Your father had a very fine silk homburg, you know, with a feather in the band. He bought it to wear to the church the day you were ordained. Do you remember that hat at all?

MATTHEW: Yes.

COLLEEN: It's good that you do. That hat cost seventy-five dollars. Your father pinned the bill of sale to the inside, to remind himself of the luxury. That's how proud he was of you. Proud enough to spend seventy-five dollars on a gray silk hat with a feather and pin the bill of sale inside!

MATTHEW: He didn't say anything to me about being proud.

COLLEEN: He said it with the hat with the feather.

MATTHEW: He called me strange.

COLLEEN: Don't be silly, Mattie.

MATTHEW: He said, "You were a strange boy, but your grades were good, and I guess that turned out to be worth something."

COLLEEN: He had a funny way of putting things sometimes, that's all. His own way of phrasing things. But I always told you right out, didn't I? I always told you how proud I was.

MATTHEW: Yes.

COLLEEN: I'm proud of you, Mattie.

MATTHEW: I know, Ma. Do you want to finish the game or no?

COLLEEN: Yes, all right. *(She looks at the wooden tiles on her holder, then puts a few on the board.)* There's "soul." As in the thing the Lord sees into, isn't that right, Mattie?

MATTHEW: The thing the Lord sees into is your S-O-U-L, Ma, not your S-O-L-E. That's fish.

COLLEEN: I sent you to Harvard. You went there, but I sent you there, do you understand? I filled out the scholarship forms and got you the money from Saint Agnes and worked at the Hallmark shop with the colored women. So you were the one to get the education, but I was the one to give it.

MATTHEW: You think I learned how to spell the word soul at Harvard?

COLLEEN: I think you learned to talk to your mother like this at Harvard. I think at Harvard they taught you to be rude.

MATTHEW: I'm just saying it matters, Ma. For example, I've been reading *Dark Night of the Soul*, S-O-U-L, which is very different than Dark Night of the Fish.

COLLEEN: Well, I'm not familiar with that particular work, but I do know it's not meant to be about a fish fillet.

MATTHEW: It's St. John of the Cross. He's a sixteenth-century mystic.

COLLEEN: Well, then, it's not about fish at all, is it?

MATTHEW: No. It's about——union. The ecstatic experience of union with God. It's astounding poetry.

COLLEEN: Why don't you say a bit of it for me then?

MATTHEW: Recite it?

COLLEEN: Yes, like when you were in school.

MATTHEW: All right.

COLLEEN: Go on, then.

MATTHEW: "Oh, night that joined beloved with lover, Lover transformed in the Beloved!"

COLLEEN: I'm not sure I like the sound of that, Mattie.

MATTHEW: It's about union with God.

COLLEEN: It doesn't strike the ear that way.

MATTHEW: "Upon my flowery breast, Kept wholly for himself alone, There he stayed sleeping, and I caressed him."

COLLEEN: I think you ought to stop now.

MATTHEW: You asked me to recite it.

COLLEEN: Well, I don't like the sound of it, so now I'm asking you to stop.

MATTHEW: "And the fanning of the cedars made a breeze. The breeze blew from the turret as I parted his locks; With his gentle hand, he wounded my neck And caused all my senses to be suspended—"

COLLEEN: I said stop now!

MATTHEW: " My face I reclined on the Beloved. All ceased and I abandoned myself, Leaving my cares forgotten among the lilies."

(A long silence.)

COLLEEN: I'll put the radio on, shall I?

MATTHEW: I'd rather you didn't.

(Matthew lies back on the couch and closes his eyes. After a moment, Colleen goes to him and quietly takes his glasses from his face. He jerks upright.)

MATTHEW: What are you doing?

COLLEEN: Your glasses.

MATTHEW: Please don't do that.

COLLEEN: You shouldn't wear them while you're sleeping. You'll bend them.

MATTHEW: I wasn't sleeping.

COLLEEN: You looked like you were sleeping, lying there with your eyes closed.

MATTHEW: Can I have them back, please?

(She hands the glasses to him.)

COLLEEN: You shouldn't wear them when you're sleeping.

MATTHEW: I don't.

SCENE 4

The front yard and driveway outside Colleen's house. Matthew is crossing from stage right, carrying a large cardboard box. Garrett is crossing from stage left, carrying a large cardboard box. He has pimples and his pants are too long.

GARRETT: Hi.

MATTHEW: Hello.

GARRETT: What's in the box?

MATTHEW: I could ask the same of you.

GARRETT: Sorry?

MATTHEW: What's in the box?

GARRETT: This one?

MATTHEW: Yes.

GARRETT: Um. This week's groceries. For Mrs. McNally. There are more in the car. I'm Garrett. I bring the groceries.

MATTHEW: Hence the groceries in the box.

GARRETT: Hence the groceries in the box. What's in your box? If I can ask.

MATTHEW: Seventeen pairs of brown suede shoes from the 1960s, minus the laces, with holes in the soles. There are more in the attic.

GARRETT: Oh.

MATTHEW: You wouldn't want to trade, would you?

GARRETT: *(Squinting into the box.)* How come there's no laces in the shoes?

MATTHEW: Because old shoelaces are useful for other things and are kept in a drawer in the guest bedroom.

GARRETT: Oh. *(Beat.)* You're her son?

MATTHEW: Yes.

GARRETT: You kind of look like her. Not in a bad way or anything. My mom says I look like my dad because we both make a funny squint with our eyes when we look at stuff, but I don't think I do that, so I don't think she should really say that all the time.

MATTHEW: Mothers, huh?

GARRETT: Yeah.

MATTHEW: They're always saying things.

GARRETT: Where are you going with all of those shoes anyway?

MATTHEW: I'm taking them to the trash.

GARRETT: That seems kind of sad. You know? It's like they're a collection or something.

MATTHEW: You're right. How often do you see seventeen identical pairs of brown suede shoes from the 1960s all in the same place?

GARRETT: I never have!

MATTHEW: Do you think I should display them somehow?

GARRETT: Like how?

MATTHEW: Well. I could line them up all along the driveway, so that it looks like seventeen invisible men are on their way to see my mother to ask if she's got any shoelaces they could borrow. It could be a sort of art installation, don't you think?

GARRETT: Yeah! But I wouldn't do it for real, you know?

MATTHEW: Why not?

GARRETT: Because people would probably, like, say things about you if they drove past and saw it.

MATTHEW: That's a good point.

GARRETT: So, do you eat a lot, I guess? There's so many groceries.

MATTHEW: When I'm at home on my own, I have toast for breakfast, soup for lunch, and half a ham sandwich for dinner.

GARRETT: Every day?

MATTHEW: Sometimes I have turkey instead of the ham.

GARRETT: So how come your mom got so much food?

MATTHEW: I don't know. Mothers.

GARRETT: She's a nice lady, though. She always gives me a big tip, because I'm saving up to go to Wonder World on the class trip. I have seventy dollars, but it costs one hundred and you have to pay by May 29th, no exceptions.

MATTHEW: Do you like school?

GARRETT: No. I'm not that smart at all.

MATTHEW: Do you know how to spell sole, like the sole of a shoe?

GARRETT: S-o-l-e.

MATTHEW: Very good. *(Hands him a shoe.)* And soul like the thing the Lord sees into?

GARRETT: S-o-u-l.

MATTHEW: Absolutely right. *(Hands him a shoe.)* Yours to keep. The pair.

GARRETT: I came in fourth in the third-grade spelling bee. I mean, that was a while ago, but I did.

(He jams one shoe into each of the pockets of his baggy pants.)

MATTHEW: And what did you get for that?

GARRETT: Bookmark.

MATTHEW: *(Shakes his head sadly.)* A bookmark.

GARRETT: Are you a fag?

MATTHEW: I'm sorry?

GARRETT: My dad said you were.

MATTHEW: Frank the grocer called me a fag?

GARRETT: He says he's always known it because of the way you talk.

MATTHEW: He said that?

(Garrett nods.)

GARRETT: He said the people at your church probably figured it out, and that's why you had to move back in with your mom.

MATTHEW: I haven't moved back in.

GARRETT: He said not to talk to you, but as long as he doesn't find out.

MATTHEW: I'm visiting.

GARRETT: My mom says more priests than you would think are fags. Except she calls it homosexual. And she said that's why she never sent me to church camp when I was little, even though I cried about it. She was worried about me staying overnight with a bunch of homosexual guys, which a person can really understand.

MATTHEW: I'm not gay. I'm celibate. That means I don't have sex with anyone at all.

GARRETT: I don't know if you should be talking to me about sex.

MATTHEW: Are you kidding me?

GARRETT: I just would hate to see you get in trouble.

MATTHEW: Thank you. I'm not—and I don't—Why don't you take those groceries inside now, and then hurry up and unload the car.

(Garrett picks up the box of groceries, takes a few steps toward the house, and then stops and puts it down.)

GARRETT: I have to tuck in my shirt or your mom yells at me.

MATTHEW: Fine.

GARRETT: Sorry if I insulted you.

MATTHEW: It's fine.

GARRETT: I'm, you know, interested in fags. To know what it's all about. I think I have a kind of open mind compared to some people.

MATTHEW: I can't help you.

GARRETT: OK.

MATTHEW: Go inside now.

GARRETT: OK. *(Garrett picks up the box and turns toward the house.)* Don't tell my dad I talked to you.

MATTHEW: I won't.

GARRETT: He'd be really fucking pissed.

(Garrett exits. Matthew looks after him for a moment, still holding the box of shoes.)

SCENE 5

That evening, after dinner. Matthew sits on the couch in Colleen's living room, reading. Colleen enters, wearing a bathrobe, and begins to straighten the room. She picks up Matthew's empty wine glass from the coffee table.

COLLEEN: I like to see you sitting there reading. What are you looking at tonight?

MATTHEW: Volume IV of the 1965 Encyclopedia Britannica. I found it in the attic.

COLLEEN: Oh, the Encyclopedia Britannica! I wonder where the rest of it's gone. We bought the whole set. Some time ago now, maybe forty years.

MATTHEW: Maybe in 1965.

COLLEEN: That sounds about right, yes. It's interesting material they put in encyclopedias, isn't it?

MATTHEW: Yes, Ma.

COLLEEN: With all of your theology and philosophy, it is just possible that you've missed out on learning about one or two more everyday things that are still very interesting. How plants make food and why the sun is hot and how airplanes fly. The things that make the world go round. What are you reading about now?

MATTHEW: Goats.

COLLEEN: There, you see. It isn't often we get to just sit quietly of an evening and learn what there is to be learned about goats. They may be lowly creatures, they may not be a subject for great thinkers, but the Lord made them, and where would we be without them?

MATTHEW: I agree.

COLLEEN: God made goats, Mattie.

MATTHEW: I said I agree, Ma.

COLLEEN: They've got sideways eyes, haven't they? Go on, say something related to goats.

MATTHEW: "You shall not boil a young goat in its mother's milk."

COLLEEN: That's from the Encyclopedia Britannica?

MATTHEW: That's from the Bible.

COLLEEN: What on earth sort of person needs to be told not to boil an animal in its own mother's milk?

MATTHEW: People get up to all kinds of things. That's why there have to be rules.

COLLEEN: I was looking to learn what goats eat and how long they live, that sort of thing, Mattie.

MATTHEW: Goats eat grass, weeds, and shrubs, and they have an average life-span of ten to twelve years in the wild. At least they did in 1965.

COLLEEN: I'm sure that's not the sort of thing that changes much.

MATTHEW: I'm sure it's not.

COLLEEN: Imagine boiling an animal in its own mother's milk! If you were a mother, you would understand just how upsetting an idea it is. A young creature boiled in the milk meant to nourish it! Are you hungry at all, then, Mattie? Would you like a bowl of ice cream before bed?

MATTHEW: No, thank you, Ma.

COLLEEN: There's quite a bit left over.

MATTHEW: All right. I'll have a little.

COLLEEN: There. I thought you might. *(The doorbell rings.)* Mattie, it's the bell!

MATTHEW: I know, Ma.

COLLEEN: But it's nine o'clock! And I'm not dressed!

MATTHEW: I'll get it for you.

(Colleen exits. Matthew goes to the door and opens it. Theresa is there, wearing lipstick and a sundress.)

THERESA: Hi.

MATTHEW: Hello. What can I do for you?

THERESA: Oh, well. I know it's a little strange for me to be here, but I do have a reason. It's an errand, really. I just have something to drop off.

(A beat. Matthew looks at her.)

THERESA: I brought you something that you left.

MATTHEW: I'm sorry. Do I know you?

THERESA: Theresa! Wednesdays and Saturdays, from eleven to three. The office and the rectory. I clean them.

MATTHEW: Of course. Theresa. I'm sorry.

THERESA: Usually when you see me I'm wearing rubber gloves.

MATTHEW: No, of course. Theresa. I'm so sorry.

THERESA: That's OK. It's sort of strange that I'm here, I know.

MATTHEW: Are you all right?

THERESA: Oh! God. Yes, I'm fine. I'm totally fine. I just brought you something you left behind. I went to clean the rectory this morning, no one told me, and I was so surprised when all your things were gone. I went to the office, and the church secretary—Mrs. Tierney, that's her name, right?—she told me to just keep coming twice a week, because there was some other priest coming to stay in the rectory—from New Mexico, I think she said? So I went back and I cleaned the place, and I found this while I was vacuuming. *(She digs out a thin leather-bound book from her purse.)* It was under the bed.

(She holds out the book to Matthew. He looks at it for a moment, then takes it and tucks it under his arm, as though to get it out of sight.)

MATTHEW: Thank you.

THERESA: *Dark Night of the Soul.*

MATTHEW: Yes.

THERESA: Mrs. Tierney told me to throw it out, but I didn't feel like I could do that. So she gave me this address so I could mail it to you, but then I thought, why not just drop it off so there's no chance of it getting lost, or whatever? Damaged in the mail.

MATTHEW: Thank you. It was beyond the call of duty.

THERESA: It's no problem.

COLLEEN: *(Offstage.)* Mattie?

MATTHEW: Yes, ma?

COLLEEN: *(Offstage.)* Is there someone at the door?

MATTHEW: Yes, Ma. *(To Theresa.)* She doesn't know I left.

THERESA: I'm sorry?

MATTHEW: She thinks I'm on vacation.

COLLEEN: *(Entering.)* Hello? *(Sees Theresa.)* Hello.

MATTHEW: Ma, this is Theresa. She cleans the rectory for me.

THERESA: I brought a . . . a book . . . that Father McNally—

MATTHEW: This is my mother, Mrs. McNally.

COLLEEN: You're a maid?

THERESA: I'm a cleaner. I work for Magic Maids.

COLLEEN: Are you in some sort of trouble?

THERESA: No, I—

COLLEEN: Do you need money?

THERESA: No. Well, yes. I mean, who doesn't need money? But I just brought a book . . . I thought Father McNally might need it while he was here.

COLLEEN: Do you need the book, Mattie?

MATTHEW: It's nice to have it, yes.

COLLEEN: *(To Theresa.)* You'd better come in and sit down.

THERESA: Oh, no. That's all right.

COLLEEN: You should rest and have something to eat. It's nearly two hours' drive.

THERESA: No, no really. Thank you, though.

MATTHEW: Theresa will want to be getting home before it gets too late, Ma.

COLLEEN: It's dark already. I don't see the difference if she stays for half an hour. And it isn't safe to be driving when you're hungry.

THERESA: I'm not hungry.

COLLEEN: Just sit down, right here. I don't turn travelers away from my home. We weren't expecting you, so you must forgive me. You're not offended that I'm in my dressing gown, are you?

THERESA: No.

(Colleen exits to the kitchen.)

THERESA: I'm so sorry. I didn't mean for this to turn into—

MATTHEW: It's fine.

THERESA: I guess I didn't think it through all the way.

MATTHEW: It's fine.

THERESA: What did you do with all your other books?

MATTHEW: The church is storing them for me.

THERESA: You have so many.

MATTHEW: They're in storage.

THERESA: You know before, when you asked me if I was all right?

MATTHEW: Yes.

THERESA: Well, I don't go to church.

MATTHEW: OK.

THERESA: And I don't pray.

MATTHEW: OK.

THERESA: But I've been thinking, and I guess I have some questions. About God. And how you . . . how a person . . . you know, how you're supposed to—I mean, I guess I have some questions about God and maybe prayer.

MATTHEW: You can make an appointment at the church. There's a visiting priest, Father Regan from New Mexico.

THERESA: I was thinking if you weren't too busy, maybe you could—

(Colleen enters. She puts a plate of food in front of Theresa.)

COLLEEN: Here you are, then. A bit of roasted chicken.

THERESA: *(Without looking at it.)* Thank you. It looks good.

SCENE 6

Outside Colleen's house, the same evening. Abby is only partially visible to us, squatting behind a tree. She is listening to her Walkman and rapping along, badly. We hear the music over speakers. Garrett enters.

GARRETT: What are you doing? Hey! You! Stop that! What are you doing? Hey!

ABBY: Fuck you! Get off me! Get back!

(She pushes her headphones off and the music stops.)

GARRETT: No, no, I'm not anyone bad! I'm sorry. It's just—what are you doing?

ABBY: What does it look like I'm doing?

GARRETT: Urinating!

ABBY: Bingo.

GARRETT: But you can't urinate here.

ABBY: That's OK. I'm done.

GARRETT: You can't just urinate on somebody's private property.

ABBY: I did. I did just urinate on somebody's private property.

GARRETT: Are you from around here?

ABBY: No, thank God. I'm waiting forever for my stupid mother to get done giving some book to some priest.

GARRETT: In the house?

ABBY: No, in the woods. They formed a secret society and they worship bears and raccoons. Yes, in the house. Jesus.

GARRETT: Why didn't you just go to the bathroom in the bathroom in the house?

ABBY: I would not set foot in that crappy little house if I hadn't peed in six months. I'd sooner piss in a pot of poisonous snakes.

GARRETT: Um. OK.

ABBY: Also? I'm just bad.

GARRETT: On purpose?

ABBY: Yeah, I'm bad on purpose. Who are you?

GARRETT: Garrett.

ABBY: Is this your house?

GARRETT: No.

ABBY: Then you're a trespasser, so you're bad, too.

GARRETT: No, I just came to talk to Father McNally.

ABBY: Well, get in line, I guess. That's the one my mother's talking to.

GARRETT: I'll come back later. I had a question for him, that's all.

ABBY: If God exists, why does he let all those babies starve to death in Somalia? Is that your question?

GARRETT: No.

ABBY: And how come people say things like, "God was really watching over me because my car flipped over and caught on fire and I got these bad burns but I didn't die." If God was watching over them, how come their car flipped over and caught on fire in the first place? Is that your question?

GARRETT: No.

ABBY: Things to think about, though, right?

GARRETT: You must get really good grades in school.

ABBY: Wrong. I'm flunking four classes. But I am very smart.

GARRETT: I can tell. That's your mom's car?

ABBY: No, that's George Bush's car. He's inside, too.

(A beat. Then he gets it.)

GARRETT: That's funny.

ABBY: Thanks.

GARRETT: I got my license this year.

ABBY: You got your walking license?

GARRETT: Um?

ABBY: You're walking.

GARRETT: Oh, yeah, I don't have a car. But I drive all the time. My dad lets me drive his car to deliver the groceries from his store to old people and handicapped people and stuff.

ABBY: Sounds like a pretty wild time.

GARRETT: It's all right.

ABBY: I don't have a car, either. I don't have anything I need. I think life is crap.

GARRETT: Maybe you have depression, like on the commercials.

ABBY: Maybe.

GARRETT: If you feel unusually sad for an extended period of time or have lost interest in activities that you used to enjoy, you may be suffering from depression.

ABBY: Are you a doctor?

GARRETT: I just watch a lot of TV.

ABBY: I guess so.

GARRETT: I pay attention to the commercials because sometimes I think I might be suffering from depression.

ABBY: Have you lost interest in activities you used to enjoy?

GARRETT: Yes.

ABBY: Like what?

GARRETT: A lot of things. Baseball, baseball cards, NASCAR, NASCAR cards, fishing with my dad.

ABBY: So. You grew up. You're not supposed to like those things anymore. Fishing with your dad? Come on.

GARRETT: Those things used to make me happy when I was little.

ABBY: That's because little kids are stupid.

GARRETT: And now I just feel bad all the time.

ABBY: Yeah. Well. *(Beat.)* I'll tell you what helps.

GARRETT: What?

ABBY: Drugs. Ecstasy, yaba.

GARRETT: I don't know. I do take Ritalin, though.

ABBY: You can snort that. Crush it up and snort it.

GARRETT: I'd be kind of nervous to do that.

ABBY: Right. Of course you would.

GARRETT: I drink.

ABBY: No, you don't.

GARRETT: Yes, I do. It helps with my depression. I don't really have any friends.

ABBY: You don't say.

GARRETT: So I just kind of walk around and drink when I get bored.

ABBY: Are you drunk now?

GARRETT: Not very.

ABBY: You've been drinking, though?

GARRETT: Some.

ABBY: No, you haven't.

GARRETT: Yes, I have.

(He pulls a bottle from his pocket.)

ABBY: Holy shit. Look at that. Yes, you have.

GARRETT: I told you. I walk around and drink.

ABBY: You wanna share a little of that with me? *(Garrett hands Abby the bottle. She takes a swig and smiles at him.)* Thanks.

SCENE 7

Colleen's living room. Theresa hasn't touched her food.

COLLEEN: Was there traffic for your drive?

THERESA: Oh, no. Not much.

MATTHEW: Listen, I'm sorry. I'm very tired and—

COLLEEN: You can't go to bed when there's a guest, Mattie!

THERESA: It's OK. I don't mind.

COLLEEN: It's rude!

THERESA: It's fine. I should be going anyway. I should have just mailed the book. I don't know what I was thinking.

COLLEEN: *(To Theresa.)* You haven't eaten.

MATTHEW: I'm very tired, Ma.

COLLEEN: Well, go on, then. Go on. It's rude, but go on.

MATTHEW: Thank you for the book.

THERESA: It's no problem. I'm sorry I—

MATTHEW: It's fine.

THERESA: Good night, Father McNally.

MATTHEW: Good night. *(Matthew exits up the stairs.)*

COLLEEN: Oh, it is so difficult to be a mother!

THERESA: Yes. *(Theresa stands and picks up her purse.)*

COLLEEN: Do you have children?

THERESA: I have a daughter.

COLLEEN: Just the one?

THERESA: Yes.

COLLEEN: Mattie's my only child as well. My sister Kitty used to feel sorry for me because of it, but now Mattie's a priest and one of Kitty's is dead and another's been let go of his job at the garage because of his drinking, so now I feel sorry for Kitty. Things have turned around that way. How old is your daughter?

THERESA: She's sixteen.

COLLEEN: And where is she this evening?

THERESA: In the car.

COLLEEN: Just sitting out there all by herself?

THERESA: She's got a Walkman and a video game. You can leave her like that for hours, like a brain in a jar.

COLLEEN: Wouldn't you like to bring her inside to have a bit of roasted chicken?

THERESA: She doesn't eat food, really. Only things called Whopper or, you know, Taco Supremo.

COLLEEN: Oh, children are terrible!

THERESA: They can be.

COLLEEN: You see the way Mattie's gone off to hide from me in his room again? He doesn't like conversation, that's why he runs off like that. He never has. The nuns at his school used to squeeze his arm until they left purple marks in the shapes of their fingers and they'd say, "You'll speak, child, you'll speak!" but he wouldn't say a word to them. Does he talk to you?

THERESA: To me? No. I mean he says good morning. He's always polite.

COLLEEN: Well, that's no trouble, is it?

THERESA: I guess not.

COLLEEN: It isn't any great accomplishment to say good morning.

THERESA: Well, no.

(A beat. Colleen speaks quietly.)

COLLEEN: Do the people at the church like Mattie?

THERESA: I'm just the cleaner. I don't know.

COLLEEN: You're not a member of Mattie's congregation?

THERESA: No, I don't actually go to church.

COLLEEN: Oh. Well, some people don't, I suppose. But you clean the church?

THERESA: I clean the rectory and the church office. I work for Magic Maids.

COLLEEN: Well, do you know if he's all right, then? He turned up here unannounced and said he was taking a vacation, but he's already had his vacation this year. He went to Italy and saw the famous paintings and sent me a postcard.

THERESA: I don't—I mean, I'm sure he's fine—

COLLEEN: So I'm wondering if the people at the church like Mattie, because I worry that he can be difficult.

THERESA: Well, I'm just the cleaner, but I think he's wonderful.

COLLEEN: You think he's wonderful?

THERESA: Yes, I really do.

COLLEEN: Oh. Oh, dear. I see.

THERESA: What do you see?

COLLEEN: You drove such a long way to come and see him. My husband did the same with me when we were courting. He said he'd found a pink button in his car and thought it would be mine, and he drove three towns to give it to me. Now you've done the same with Mattie's book.

THERESA: No, no—I just came to ask him about something, that's all.

COLLEEN: I thought you came to give him his book.

THERESA: I did. But I thought while I was here—

COLLEEN: My son isn't permitted to be with a woman, you understand.

THERESA: Oh, God, no—

COLLEEN: You may not be aware of this, because you aren't a member of the church, but a priest is called to single-heartedly devote himself to our Lord.

THERESA: Yes, yes, I know. I didn't come to—

COLLEEN: So my son belongs to God, you see.

THERESA: Of course. Of course he does.

COLLEEN: My son belongs to God!

SCENE 8

Colleen's driveway. Abby and Garrett pass the bottle.

GARRETT: Tonight I might stay out all night, because my parents are in Minnesota because my aunt had an operation. I can do whatever I want for three days.

ABBY: You'll get bored wandering around all night by yourself.

GARRETT: I might want to see the sunrise or something.

ABBY: You don't have one single friend to hang out with?

GARRETT: Not really.

ABBY: That's rough. *(A beat.)* Hey, where'd you get those shoes?

(He is wearing the pair of Mr. McNally's brown shoes from the 1960s that Matthew gave him.)

GARRETT: I won them.

ABBY: You won them?

GARRETT: Yeah.

ABBY: Where, Homeless Man Jeopardy?

GARRETT: They're antiques from the 1960s. They might be valuable.

ABBY: You're funny. If you lived in our town, you could hang out with me and my friend Katya. We'd take you everywhere with us, like our pet. Wouldn't that be fun?

GARRETT: Is your friend Katya nice?

ABBY: She's a total bitch. But she's nice to me. And I could tell her to be nice to you.

GARRETT: Do you have other friends, too?

ABBY: Yeah, but she's the only one I trust.

GARRETT: Do you have a boyfriend?

ABBY: No. I sleep around.

GARRETT: *(Laughing.)* That's not true.

ABBY: I don't know if you're the best judge of character. I don't get the feeling you get out much.

GARRETT: I look at pornography.

ABBY: *(Gasps.)* Oh, my God, not *Playboy*! Not *Penthouse*! You don't look at ladies' titties, do you?

GARRETT: No.

ABBY: Worse?

GARRETT: Yes.

ABBY: Stuff about girls with big butts, maybe? Do you like that stuff?

GARRETT: No.

ABBY: Worse? Worse than big butts?

GARRETT: Yes.

ABBY: Nothing is worse than big-butt pornography!

GARRETT: No, there's worse.

ABBY: Like what?

GARRETT: Never mind.

ABBY: Come on, like what? *(Beat.)* Garrett. I am your only friend. Tell me what you look at.

GARRETT: No, it's nothing.

ABBY: I am the last person in the world to ever judge anything that anyone else does. If it feels right, do it. That's my motto. And that's why people confide in me. And that's why you can, too.

GARRETT: Stuff about guys sometimes.

ABBY: Oh. *(Beat.)* You look at magazines?

GARRETT: I look on the Internet.

ABBY: You have your own computer?

GARRETT: I use my dad's.

ABBY: Oh. Well, try not to let him catch you doing that.

GARRETT: This is what I wanted to ask Father McNally about. You know, whether it's OK.

ABBY: You wanted to ask a priest whether it's OK for you to be looking at gay guys having sex on the Internet? That was your big plan for coming here?

GARRETT: I mean, I know it's not OK. But whether it makes me a fag in the eyes of the Lord.

ABBY: I think in the eyes of the Lord, it probably doesn't exactly make you straight.

GARRETT: Every time I do it, I feel really bad about it, but then I just do it again.

ABBY: OK. I'll tell you what to do.

GARRETT: What?

ABBY: Drink six shots, stand on your head, and say fourteen Hail Marys. You shouldn't say fag by the way. It's not correct.

GARRETT: Homosexual.

ABBY: Gay.

GARRETT: OK.

ABBY: Gay as a big fruit salad. That's you. Drink up.

GARRETT: I'm not.

ABBY: Not what?

GARRETT: Gay as a salad.

ABBY: A big fruit salad.

GARRETT: I don't want to be gay as a big fruit salad. I want to meet a nice wife someday.

ABBY: Then repent! Put your underwear on your head and say eleven Hail Marys! *(Waving her hands like a TV preacher.)* Holy moly, holy moly, little baby Jesus!

GARRETT: Does your family, like, go to church or anything?

ABBY: My mom doesn't believe in church.

GARRETT: You can kind of tell.

ABBY: When I was little, she told me Jesus was just a nice story that it makes some people happy to hear, like Babar.

GARRETT: Who's Babar?

ABBY: This elephant who wears a bow tie and becomes king of the jungle.

GARRETT: My dad would probably get mad if he found out we were friends.

ABBY: We'll probably never see each other again.

GARRETT: But I'm saying if we were friends, my dad wouldn't like it.

ABBY: You know what makes me mad, though?

GARRETT: What?

ABBY: So, my mom, she told me all this stuff when I was little about how the stuff in the Bible was a nice story, and it helped some people to believe in it, but really it was like Babar, and random shit just happens, and some of it's bad, so we all have to try to take care of each other the best we can here on earth. Right? Fine. But then a couple of days ago, I walk by her door, and she's watching some holy moly preacher on TV, and the guy goes over to some lady in a wheelchair, Yi and he goes like this *(She puts her hands on Garrett's shoulders, then on his head.)* and the lady in the wheelchair gets up and starts walking and the guy is going, "It's a miracle, it's a miracle, praise Jesus, Amen!" and my mom, in this quiet little voice, she puts her hands in the air and she goes "Amen." I mean, can you believe that? *(Puts her hands in the air.)* "Amen." I couldn't even believe it.

GARRETT: Lots of people believe in God.

ABBY: That's not even God, though. That's some guy in a toupee. Anyway, my mom doesn't believe in God.

GARRETT: It kind of sounds like she does.

ABBY: But she doesn't.

GARRETT: My mom does.

ABBY: Yeah, well I hate to even think about what your mom must be like. Oh, my God, I would rather die than meet your mom.

GARRETT: I never met anyone who didn't believe in God.

ABBY: Do you?

GARRETT: I definitely don't not believe in God.

ABBY: You definitely don't not believe in God?

GARRETT: Yeah.

ABBY: So you do believe in God?

GARRETT: I definitely don't not.

ABBY: OK. Here you go then: Holy moly, holy moly, you're healed from being as gay as a pineapple upside-down cake!

GARRETT: Stop that.

ABBY: Take five shots, take off your clothes, stand on your head, and say ten Hail Marys! Go! Holy moly, holy moly, I mean it. Do it. *(She hands him the bottle.)* Take five shots. *(He hesitates, then takes them as she counts.)* One . . . two . . . three . . . four . . . five. Now take off your clothes! *(He begins to unbutton his shirt. She laughs and claps her hands.)* Hallelujah! *(Blackout.)*

SCENE 9

Out of the darkness, large black-and-white images appear, one by one. They are photographs: delicate gelatin silver prints of tall, pale, handsome men, completely naked. Below the pictures, Matthew is getting ready for bed. He has taken off his shoes and unbuttoned his shirt.

MATTHEW: *(To the audience.)* These are the pictures that Mrs. Tierney, the church secretary, found in my study. They've given me three months to think about them. Three months to pray and to contemplate while a visiting priest from New Mexico tends to my congregation, and then I'm to meet with the bishop and explain myself. *(He looks at the pictures.)* They're by George Platt Lynes, a photographer who worked in New York City in the 1930s. He photographed movie stars for magazines, but he also took pictures—he also took pictures like these ones. I hadn't ever heard of him until I found a book called *George Platt Lynes* in the public library. I was looking in the L's in the art section for Lorenzo Lotto, who painted the lives of the saints on the walls of the Suardi chapel in Trescore in 1524, and I found George Platt Lynes instead. I don't think any patron of our local library had ever looked at the book before I did. The edge of each page peeled away from the next one as I turned it, the way they sometimes do in books that have never been read, as though you were breaking into something that's meant to stay sealed. *(A beat.)* I ripped the pictures out of the book. I took the book to a long table in the back of the library, away from the DVDs and the Internet access stations to a place that's meant for reading and so is always utterly deserted, and I ripped out the pages I wanted. I don't know what came over me. I'm careful with books. I don't approve of dog-earing pages to mark your place. Not even that. And when I'm reading a book, I hold it open only three-quarters of the way, so as not to crack the binding. But I ripped out the pages and folded them into my pocket, and at home, I opened them and smoothed them with my hands. I think I took them because I felt somehow, just momentarily, at the quiet table in the library, that God was in the pictures. There is a line of thought that goes that beauty is God's goodness made visible, that it's in objects of beauty that we see the beauty of the Lord reflected. When God called me to service, he called me through beauty. In the church, there was incense and quiet. Dark wood. Masses and requiems. I went to talk to Father Michaels, and his study smelled of books, and bits of colored light from the stained glass windows were thrown across the floor like someone had spilled a handful of rubies, and I thought, "For wisdom is better than rubies, and all the things that may be desired are not to be compared to it," and those words were my calling. So one can be called to God by beauty. But I know, also, now, that one can be called away from God by beauty. The Church teaches that as priests we are sanctified: that is, literally, separate, set apart for sacred use. I'm set apart. I'm set aside. I'm lonely. When I look at the pictures, I inhabit the bodies of the men; I don't look at them as objects of desire; I become them, just as a beginning step before even thinking about desire. I feel for the first time since I was a child what it might mean to have a body. Maybe even what it might mean to have a body in relation to another person's body. I look at the pictures, and those lines from St. John of the Cross come to me out of nowhere. "With his gentle hand he wounded my neck. And caused all my senses to be suspended." I didn't even know that I knew them, and suddenly they're all I can find in my head no matter what else I'm looking for. "Upon my flowery breast, Kept wholly for himself alone, There he stayed sleeping, and I caressed him." I know that it's supposed to be about God, but I just can't seem to hear it that way anymore.

(*Blackout.*)

SCENE 10

Abby's voice is heard in the darkness as she pounds on Colleen's front door.

ABBY: Mom? Mom! Mom!
    (*Lights up as Colleen opens the door on Abby and Garrett. Garrett is in his underwear and is bleeding from a gash on his cheek. Abby is carrying his clothes.*)
THERESA: Abby, what's going on?
ABBY: We need a Band-Aid or something.
COLLEEN: (*To Garrett.*) Good Lord, what's happened to you, child?
ABBY: (*To Theresa.*) Can you wash out his cut?
THERESA: Who is this?
ABBY: Just some kid I met.
THERESA: What happened to him?
ABBY: He fell.
GARRETT: I'm Garrett.
THERESA: What happened to you?
GARRETT: I fell out of a tree.
THERESA: You hit the ground?
ABBY: No, Mom. He didn't. He grew these big, beautiful wings and he just flew and flew and—

THERESA: Have you been drinking, Abby?

GARRETT: I have. Sort of a lot.

THERESA: Oh, God. *(To Colleen.)* Can he come in and sit down?

COLLEEN: Yes, he'd better. He's Frank the grocer's boy.

THERESA: Are you dirty? You're all dirty. Put this down before you sit on the couch. *(She opens a magazine and puts it on the couch. Garrett sits on it.)* Let me see that cut. *(To Colleen.)* I'm so sorry. I should never have brought her here. I don't know what I was thinking.

ABBY: I didn't do anything.

THERESA: Abby, be quiet please.

ABBY: Well, what are you sorry for? I didn't fall out of a tree.

THERESA: *(To Garrett.)* And you, what were you thinking climbing a tree with all of that booze in you?

GARRETT: Abby said I should, ma'am. It was part of my ceremony.

THERESA: Oh, I see. What kind of ceremony, Ab?

GARRETT: It isn't her fault I fell! I was going like this *(He waves his hands around.)* to show off. That wasn't part of the ceremony.

COLLEEN: Put your clothes on!

GARRETT: I don't know where they are.

ABBY: They're right here.

COLLEEN: *(To Garrett.)* Well, put them on, child.

(Abby hands Garrett the clothes, and he pulls on his shirt, still sitting on the couch.)

COLLEEN: *(To Theresa.)* Should I get Mattie, do you think?

THERESA: No! No, just—Do you have a first aid kit?

COLLEEN: I might have something upstairs. I'll see what I've got. *(She starts up the stairs.)* You're a good boy, Garrett. I always tell Frank. I can't imagine what you've gotten yourself mixed up in. *(She exits.)*

THERESA: Put your pants on, OK?

(Garrett stands up to get into his pants and lurches forward, catching himself on the coffee table.)

THERESA: Jesus Christ. Sit down, sit down. Did you hit your head when you fell?

GARRETT: Yeah, I hit it pretty hard, I guess.

THERESA: Where? *(Garrett gestures to the back of his head, and she feels the lump.)* Are you dizzy?

GARRETT: I have to say I'm pretty dizzy.

THERESA: You're not going to throw up, are you?

GARRETT: I have to say I think I might.

THERESA: Abby, get a bowl.

ABBY: Who, me?

THERESA: Yes, get a bowl from the kitchen.

ABBY: What kind of bowl?

THERESA: Just look around for a big metal bowl, or bring the trashcan or something.

ABBY: You want me to bring the trashcan?

THERESA: Abby, go!

ABBY: God.

(Abby exits.)

THERESA: You might have a concussion. I'm going to have to call your parents, you know. Believe me, I don't want to, I'm not very good at this kind of thing, but I'm going to have to.

GARRETT: Please don't call my parents.

THERESA: I'm going to have to.

GARRETT: I'm not supposed to be here.

THERESA: Well, maybe you should have thought of that before. I mean, I hate to sound like this, I hate to sound like somebody's mother, but maybe —

GARRETT: I'm not supposed to be near Father McNally! I'm not supposed to be—anything! I'm not supposed to be anything! *(He starts to cry.)*

THERESA: Shit. What's your phone number?

GARRETT: I can't remember.

THERESA: Oh, please. Please give me a break for just a minute here. You need to see a doctor. I'm not a doctor. I'm barely even a grown-up, so let's call your mother, who is probably a nice grown-up lady. What's your phone number?

GARRETT: Honestly, honestly, I'm trying to remember it. It has eights.

THERESA: It has eights?

GARRETT: Yeah. Eights and, I don't know. Maybe threes? A bunch of eights and then just like a couple of threes.

THERESA: Jesus. Are you all right? Don't put your head down. Look at me. Gary? Garth? Shit. Gavin? Gavin! Look at me.

(Abby enters with a large cut-glass punchbowl.)

ABBY: Yikes. Is he OK?

(Garrett slumps onto the floor.)

THERESA: *(Calling up the stairs.)* Father McNally! Father McNally, I need help!

END OF ACT ONE

ACT II
SCENE 1

A hospital waiting room: scuffed floor, fluorescent lights, Formica chairs. Noises from a loudspeaker. It's past midnight. Matthew, dressed in his priest's collar, leans against a wall, his hands folded in front of him. Abby sits Indian-style in a chair, chewing gum. They are alone in the room.

ABBY: So, are you really a priest?

MATTHEW: Yes.

ABBY: What do you have to do?

MATTHEW: I'm sorry?

ABBY: For your job? What do you have to do?

MATTHEW: It's a mix of things. I celebrate Mass. I try to be of service to God's people, whatever that entails from day to day.

ABBY: You get paid?

MATTHEW: Yes.

ABBY: Cool. Can I ask you a question?

MATTHEW: OK.

ABBY: How come people say things like, "God was really watching over me because my car flipped over and caught on fire and I got all these bad burns but I didn't die." If God was watching over them, how come their car flipped over and caught on fire in the first place?

MATTHEW: Do you really want the answer?

ABBY: Is it long?

MATTHEW: Yes.

ABBY: Can you summarize?

MATTHEW: The Lord provides Grace in the face of our suffering. He doesn't promise to deliver us from suffering.

ABBY: But do you know what I mean? I think maybe I could be religious or whatever if it made any sense, but it doesn't make any *sense*. You know?

MATTHEW: Where did your mother go?

ABBY: She's talking to the police. She has to help them try to find Garrett's parents. They're in Minneapolis or Minnesota or something. Which one's the state?

MATTHEW: Minnesota.

ABBY: Minnesota. That's a whole state so, you know, good luck finding two little people.

MATTHEW: I'm sure they left some contact information with someone.

ABBY: I guess. *(Beat.)* So, how do you decide to become a priest?

MATTHEW: You don't really decide. God calls you. It's a voice you hear that isn't your own.

ABBY: Seriously?

MATTHEW: Yes.

ABBY: OK. You want gum?

MATTHEW: No thanks.

ABBY: Like literally a voice? Like it's coming out of that loudspeaker? Like, "Be a priest, Be a priest!"

(The loudspeaker crackles. Abby jumps.)

LOUDSPEAKER: Paging Doctor Galena to cardiology. Galena to cardiology.

ABBY: Holy shit! That scared me! I thought I was getting my calling! Didn't you? *(Beat.)* OK. Sorry. Like, literally a voice?

LOUDSPEAKER: Doctor Galena, cardiology.

MATTHEW: No, I guess not literally a voice.

ABBY: 'Cause it'd be kind of funny if it was a voice. Don't you think?

MATTHEW: Some people hear voices.

ABBY: Some people are in loony bins.

MATTHEW: Some of the saints heard voices.

ABBY: What's a concussion exactly?

MATTHEW: A concussion is when the brain gets knocked against the inside of the skull and the brain tissue ruptures.

ABBY: Ew. Really?

MATTHEW: Yes.

ABBY: It's not bad, though, right? Like, really medically bad.

MATTHEW: It can be sometimes.

ABBY: But it doesn't have to be. It's not always really bad.

MATTHEW: No.

ABBY: Is this kid going to die, do you think?

MATTHEW: I don't think so, no.

ABBY: But he could?

MATTHEW: I don't think there's any reason to think that.

ABBY: I hate that!

MATTHEW: I'm sorry?

ABBY: "I don't think there's any reason to think that." Just say yes or no!

MATTHEW: I can't say yes or no, because I don't know the answer.

ABBY: Then say, I don't know!

MATTHEW: I think he's going to be fine.

(A long silence.)

ABBY: Do you think the cafeteria's still open?

MATTHEW: I don't know.

ABBY: What time is it?

MATTHEW: 12:40.

ABBY: I'm gonna go see.

MATTHEW: All right.

ABBY: You want coffee or something?

MATTHEW: Yes, actually. Thank you. *(A beat.)*

ABBY: You have to give me some money, though. To get it with. I don't really have any money.

(Matthew takes a ten dollar bill out of his wallet and hands it to her. She takes it and turns to go. At the door, she turns back.)

ABBY: Can I ask you a question, though?

MATTHEW: Yes.

ABBY: I'm serious, because you're a priest.

MATTHEW: OK.

ABBY: Is there evil?

MATTHEW: Yes.

ABBY: There are evil people?

MATTHEW: It's more that there's good and evil in each of us. We're all capable of committing evil, but we're also all forgivable.

ABBY: You believe that?

MATTHEW: It's the central notion of the Church.

ABBY: I didn't push that kid out of the tree or anything.

MATTHEW: I don't think anyone even vaguely suspects that you did.

ABBY: OK. *(A beat.)* You want milk or whatever in your coffee?

MATTHEW: Milk, no sugar.

(Abby looks at the ten dollar bill in her hand.)

ABBY: You mind if I get myself a snack or something? Nothing big. I don't have any money on me.

MATTHEW: You can keep that.

ABBY: Really?

MATTHEW: Yes.

ABBY: Thanks. *(Matthew nods. Abby looks at him.)* The thing is—that kid. He was so—I liked him, that's the thing, I liked him. He was nice. But he was such a loser, you know? I had to mess with him a little bit. And when he fell and his head hit the ground really hard like that and bounced back up again? It was satisfying. I liked it. That's gotta make me a bad person, don't you think?

MATTHEW: Do you want to pray for forgiveness?

ABBY: *(Laughs.)* No.

MATTHEW: Why not?

ABBY: Because there's nobody there. I mean, I know that for a fact, and so I could do it anyway, just to make myself feel better, but it'd be fake. *(Beat.)* I'm just trying to say, do you think I'm a really bad person?

MATTHEW: We're all bad in some ways. And we're all forgivable.

ABBY: By God?

MATTHEW: By God.

ABBY: That doesn't help me.

MATTHEW: That's what I have to offer you.

ABBY: Well, whatever. I mean, thanks. I'm going to the cafeteria.

(Abby exits into the hospital's hallway. After a moment Theresa enters through swinging doors leading from the nurses' station.)

THERESA: What time is it?

MATTHEW: It's about 12:40.

THERESA: It's late.

MATTHEW: Is the boy awake yet?

THERESA: No.

MATTHEW: Did they find his parents?

THERESA: They're in Minnesota visiting a relative. According to the neighbors, they always leave their contact information with the store's assistant manager, but he's not easy to find on a warm spring night. They're looking for him in every bar in town. *(She sits, takes out a cigarette, remembers where she is, and puts it back.)* Where's Abby?

MATTHEW: She went to the cafeteria.

THERESA: Is it still open?

MATTHEW: I don't know.

THERESA: The police want to talk to her about the accident.

MATTHEW: That's just a formality, I'm sure.

THERESA: This was totally her fault. I absolutely blame her for this.

MATTHEW: Accidents have no blame attached to them. That's the definition of an accident.

THERESA: I would beg to differ. I would say a girl who gets a kid like that drunk and has him dangling out of a tree so she can laugh at him is in some way responsible for whatever happens next. Do you have any gum?

MATTHEW: Sorry, no.

THERESA: It's cold in here, huh?

MATTHEW: A little.

THERESA: It's good to see you in your collar. It's comforting.

MATTHEW: It itches, to be totally honest.

THERESA: It looks nice, though. It's a comfort to the rest of us.

MATTHEW: Well, I'm glad.

THERESA: They give priests all kinds of nice clothes to wear. Like all the drapey purple things for church.

MATTHEW: Vestments.

THERESA: Vestments. That's a nice word.

MATTHEW: It's from the Latin vestio, "to clothe." So it just means clothes, really.

THERESA: It sounds a lot nicer, though. The church has a lot of nice words, doesn't it?

MATTHEW: Like flabello.

THERESA: What's flabello?

MATTHEW: A flabello is a big feather fan at the end of a long handle that you wave to keep the bugs off the Eucharist bread.

THERESA: Really?

MATTHEW: It's one of my favorite words.

THERESA: I think you're a good priest.

MATTHEW: I haven't really done anything all night except stand here.

THERESA: I went to one of your services.

MATTHEW: You did?

THERESA: I heard the speech you gave.

MATTHEW: The homily.

THERESA: The homily. It was really beautiful. The whole service was beautiful, but my favorite part was hearing you talk.

MATTHEW: Why did you come to church?

THERESA: I don't know. Everything's so hard lately. Abby and—just everything. So I thought maybe—I don't know. I just got the idea. I really love cleaning the rectory.

MATTHEW: That seems unlikely.

THERESA: No, I do. All the papers and the books and the dark woodwork. I like the way you fold your socks. I mean, not that I look in your dresser or anything, but just when there's something and I'm putting it away . . . It's nice that you take care with things. It reminds me of my parents' house.

MATTHEW: They're careful people, your parents?

THERESA: Yeah. They're logicians. In Michigan. U of M. Or maybe they're retired. I don't know.

MATTHEW: Your parents are logicians?

THERESA: I know, weird, right?

MATTHEW: No, no. I just—they're logicians?

THERESA: Yeah, you know like, if X and Y, then P, but if X but not Y, then Q. My dad used to say things like: "Being done with one's book report is a necessary but not a sufficient condition for being permitted to watch an hour of television. That is, incomplete homework means no television, but completed homework does not necessarily mean television, because your behavior throughout the day has to be factored into the equation." *(She shrugs.)* That's just the way his mind worked.

MATTHEW: You didn't—You weren't interested in—?

THERESA: No. It seemed like such a lie: if this, then that. I had my own hypothesis about the world, which was basically, whatever the fuck happens, happens and we'll probably never know why. Then I got pregnant with Abby when I was in high school and that was pretty much the last straw for my parents. Imagine: you spend all your time thinking up these complicated rules about exactly what will happen under exactly which circumstances, and then your own daughter turns out to be . . . you know, so much not what you expected. *(A beat.)* I'm sorry. Did I say the F-word back there?

MATTHEW: It's fine.

THERESA: It is?

MATTHEW: Yes.

THERESA: Thanks.

MATTHEW: Did your parents throw you out?

THERESA: They wanted me to go live with my thousand-year-old grandmother and finish high school, but I just left. Don't laugh, but I followed the Grateful Dead. Abby and I followed the Dead, and I dropped a lot of acid and she ran around naked with all these other little naked kids and got tangles in her hair. I was looking for something enormous and expansive, but somehow I ended up with this little scrap of a life. I mean, this little nothing thing. You could just vacuum it up with the Dustbuster and it'd be gone. It's nothing at all.

MATTHEW: You have your daughter. She seems like less of a scrap and more of a handful. If you don't mind my saying so.

THERESA: I've got nothing for her. I mean—I've really got nothing—no stuff, no money, no ideas, no plans. She hears my boyfriend call me names he shouldn't call me when we fight. *(Beat.)* But sometimes lately, since I've been cleaning the rectory, I've been thinking a little bit about God, which is something I really never did before. I mean really never. And then, during your homily, you spoke so beautifully about, you know, humility, and I've been thinking, maybe the state of having nothing and feeling so used up, maybe that's sort of the state God wants me in, not so full of all my ideas about myself and what a rebel I am—but, you know, kind of— ready to listen. Do you think that's true?

MATTHEW: I really don't know.

THERESA: Does somebody know? Is there somebody else I could talk to?

MATTHEW: There are lots of people who think they know, and all of them like to talk.

THERESA: I brought the book because I wanted to talk to you. When all your stuff was gone so suddenly, just like that, I got scared. I guess I felt kind of like maybe you were supposed to be my path to God, and by snatching you away like that, He was telling me He'd thought about it and He didn't want me after all.

MATTHEW: I just had some things going on in my life. I just needed a break. I don't think you should feel like—

THERESA: No, no! I didn't mean to sound like you're just some sort of device in my own—

MATTHEW: No, I just. I don't think you should take it as some sort of message.

THERESA: Your homily was really beautiful.

MATTHEW: It's just something I wrote. There isn't anything holy in it necessarily. I wouldn't want to mislead you.

THERESA: You made me want to learn how to pray.

MATTHEW: Well, I think that's something you should, you know, pursue.

THERESA: My grandmother gave me this book when I was maybe eight. She was the only one in the family who really did the church thing, and the book was called *Saints You Should Know*, something like that. *100 Saints You Should Know*. It was a really, really boring book, but there was one saint in it I loved, because she had my name—Saint Therese—and because they also called her the Little Flower of Jesus, and in the picture, they showed her with roses all around her. And after I heard your homily, I thought maybe my Little Flower would be the right place to start, maybe she would remember me and she would help me somehow. So I looked her up on the Internet. She's the patron saint of florists and of tuberculosis—so really. I mean, she's a good saint. And I found something she said. She said, "For me, prayer is a surge of the heart, a cry of recognition and love." And I thought, well, that's what all those drugs were about, and the sex. A surge of the heart and trying to find some kind of—some kind of recognition and love. *(A beat.)* So, I wanted to, you know, ask you: What is prayer for you?

MATTHEW: I haven't prayed for a long time.

THERESA: Since you came to stay here?

MATTHEW: Since before then. Weeks. I mean, I've said the words, but I haven't prayed.

THERESA: I don't really understand why you left.

MATTHEW: They asked me to.

THERESA: Forever?

MATTHEW: For three months.

THERESA: Did you do something wrong?

MATTHEW: Maybe.

THERESA: Was it something like what's in the newspapers? About priests? I don't mean to be prying. I just—

MATTHEW: I had some pictures. I'm supposed to pray about them. Contemplate.

THERESA: Pictures of children?

MATTHEW: No.

THERESA: Oh, OK. Pictures of grown-ups?

MATTHEW: Yes.

THERESA: OK.

MATTHEW: I got them from the library. They were by a photographer called George Platt Lynes. They were in an art book. A big book called *George Platt Lynes.*

THERESA: Well, that's art then.

MATTHEW: They were nudes.

THERESA: Yeah, I got that. But, I mean, God made the human body, didn't he? So isn't it only right to think it's beautiful?

MATTHEW: Not in this way, I don't think, no. Not for me.

THERESA: But what did you *do* that was wrong? You didn't do anything. Did you?

MATTHEW: Thoughts can be wrong.

THERESA: Can they?

MATTHEW: Yes.

THERESA: I don't know.

MATTHEW: I think all the time about . . . I think about . . .

THERESA: Sex?

MATTHEW: No. *(A beat.)* I don't know.

THERESA: People are sexual beings. Men especially. I think it's a totally natural thing.

MATTHEW: There's not a lot of touching in this kind of life. I don't really touch anyone, and no one touches me, which is OK, because I'm not very comfortable with being touched.

THERESA: I could touch you. *(Beat.)*

MATTHEW: I don't know. I don't think . . .

THERESA: I don't even mean . . . I just mean . . . I rub Abby's head. Sometimes. When she'll let me. *(Matthew doesn't move.)* It's not a good thing, never being touched. They do experiments on monkeys. Little baby monkeys. They stop eating if nobody touches them for a long time. Sometimes they die. *(He takes a few steps toward her.)* Sit down here. *(She gestures to the floor by her feet, and he sits.)* This is what Abby does when we're watching TV. Once in a blue moon, when she's speaking to me. She just sits at my feet, like this, and leans her head back. *(He doesn't lean his head back, but that's all right.)* And I go like this.

(She runs her fingers through his hair. When he doesn't move or flinch, she does it again and again. He is barely breathing. She does it again and again. The room is silent except for the humming of the fluorescent lights above them. She keeps going. It isn't sexual, exactly, but it is intimate. They keep their eyes focused straight ahead of them, and she does it again and again. Then the door opens and Abby enters, carrying a loaded cardboard tray. Matthew stands and moves back to where he'd been, against the wall.)

ABBY: OK, so the cafeteria's closed, but there's an all night Taco Bell right in the building. I got a few different things: I got a Mountain Dew Baja Blast, which is a special kind of drink only available at Taco Bell, but that's for me. And I got two coffees and I got some stuff to eat. These are Club Chalupas; they're for me. And Mom, I got you just a soft taco, because I know you think Taco Bell is gross or whatever. And *(To Matthew.)* honestly, I didn't get you anything, because you seem like a just-coffee kind of guy, but I'll go back if you want. *(She hands him his coffee.)*

MATTHEW: Thank you.

THERESA: Did you pay for all this, Abby?

ABBY: He gave me money.

THERESA: Did you bring any change?

ABBY: He said I could keep it.

THERESA: Give Father McNally his change, Abby.

ABBY: It's only like about three dollars.

THERESA: Well, then give it to him.

ABBY: All right. *(To Matthew.)* Here. Three dollars and fourteen cents. *(She begins to count the money out, slowly and dramatically, into his hand.)*

THERESA: And don't be obnoxious. Father McNally is a priest, so show a little respect.

ABBY: What's to respect if Jesus is like Babar? I'm supposed to respect a man who worships a made-up elephant in a hat? *(To Matthew.)* I mean no offense to you, but—come on, Mom.

THERESA: The police want to talk to you about the accident. There was a policewoman at the nurses' station. Go see if she's still there.

ABBY: I don't want to talk to the police.

THERESA: Too bad.

ABBY: Am I in trouble?

THERESA: It depends what you did, I guess.

ABBY: I didn't do anything.

THERESA: Then you should be fine.

ABBY: An adult should come with me.

THERESA: Since when do you need an adult?

MATTHEW: I'll take her.

THERESA: Would you?

ABBY: I want to finish my food.

THERESA: Just go and get it over with.

MATTHEW: Come on. I'll take you. It's only a formality, for their report.

(Abby exits with Matthew, reluctantly. Theresa takes a cigarette out of her purse, looks at it for a while, then lights it and smokes it furtively. After a few moments, Matthew reappears. She drops the cigarette quickly into her coffee cup to put it out.)

THERESA: Where's Abby?

MATTHEW: With Officer Norwitz.

THERESA: Is she in trouble?

MATTHEW: I don't think so.

THERESA: OK.

MATTHEW: They want me to go in with the boy.

THERESA: Go in with him?

MATTHEW: Go in to be with him.

THERESA: To sit with him?

MATTHEW: To pray for him.

THERESA: Why? *(A beat.)* Oh, my God, why?

MATTHEW: I think he's—They said he's not as stable as he was.

THERESA: You're going to go in?

MATTHEW: Yes. They asked me to.

THERESA: This is bad, isn't it?

MATTHEW: I don't know.

THERESA: You're going to go in now?

MATTHEW: I have to.

THERESA: OK.

(Blackout.)

SCENE 2

Colleen's living room, later that night. It's dark except for a small lamp on a table by her armchair, where she sits dozing. Matthew enters.

COLLEEN: Mattie, is that you?

MATTHEW: Yes, Ma.

COLLEEN: I sat here all night listening for your tires on the gravel, just like when you were in school. Do you want a drink?

MATTHEW: No.

COLLEEN: How's the boy? How is Frank's boy? Is he going to be all right?

MATTHEW: He died, Ma.

COLLEEN: No!

MATTHEW: He did, Ma. He died.

COLLEEN: But it was just a little fall.

MATTHEW: There was bleeding in the brain.

COLLEEN: I don't believe it.

MATTHEW: It happens sometimes.

COLLEEN: Poor Frank. Oh, poor Frank. He loved that boy, Mattie. They went fishing together all the time.

MATTHEW: You should call him tomorrow and find out about the funeral.

COLLEEN: And Maura? What will Maura do now? You don't recover from something like this, Mattie. No matter how long. You don't ever recover all the way.

MATTHEW: She'll have to find a way to go on. There isn't any choice, is there?

COLLEEN: I'm glad you were there at the hospital. Did you sit with Frank and Maura? Did you pray with them?

MATTHEW: They're on a plane coming home from Minnesota.

COLLEEN: They weren't with the child?

MATTHEW: No.

COLLEEN: The boy died on his own?

MATTHEW: I was there.

COLLEEN: You gave him his last rites, then?

MATTHEW: Yes. *(A beat.)* No.

COLLEEN: Why not?

MATTHEW: I couldn't remember them.

COLLEEN: You don't know what to say for the last rites?

MATTHEW: I know what to say. "Incline Thine ear, O Lord, unto our prayers, wherein we humbly pray Thee to show thy mercy upon the soul of Thy servant, whom Thou hast commanded to pass out of this world, that Thou wouldst place him in the region of peace and light, and bid him be a partaker with thy Saints."

COLLEEN: Why didn't you say it for him then?

MATTHEW: I just couldn't remember, in the moment. The machines were making noise, and there were doctors going in and out looking frantic.

COLLEEN: What did you do, then? What did you do for him?

MATTHEW: I held his hand.

(Colleen looks at him carefully. He might be crying.)

COLLEEN: I'm glad that you were there with him, in any case. It's good that you were there.

MATTHEW: I did the best that I could do.

COLLEEN: Mattie?

MATTHEW: What?

COLLEEN: You're not going back to the church, are you?

MATTHEW: I don't think they want me, Ma.

COLLEEN: Why wouldn't they want you? Have you done something wrong?

MATTHEW: Maybe.

COLLEEN: There's been a misunderstanding of some kind, that's all it is. We'll find a way to sort it out with the monsignor and the bishop. Whatever it is. I'm going to help you. I'm very good at getting people sorted out, you know that. We'll place a phone call in the morning, and we'll get it all straightened out, whatever it is.

MATTHEW: It's not like that, Ma.

COLLEEN: You let your mother help you now, Mattie.

MATTHEW: It isn't something you can do anything about.

COLLEEN: You don't want to go back, do you?

MATTHEW: No.

COLLEEN: That seems— *(She catches her breath.)* wasteful!

MATTHEW: I don't feel as though I have a choice

COLLEEN: There's always a choice in life.

MATTHEW: I don't know if I love God properly anymore.

COLLEEN: All men of faith have doubts, Mattie. Pray on it.

MATTHEW: I'm not finding prayer very useful.

COLLEEN: What do you need, then?

MATTHEW: Love.

COLLEEN: God loves you.

MATTHEW: Sex.

COLLEEN: Don't you dare say that word to me like that!

MATTHEW: You watch television, Ma. You hear that word all the time.

COLLEEN: Don't you dare look me in the face like that and say that word! This is about that girl, isn't it? The maid.

MATTHEW: No.

COLLEEN: She fancies you.

MATTHEW: No.

COLLEEN: I told her to leave you be, but I could see that she was wily. Did she do something to you? Did she talk you into something?

MATTHEW: This isn't about sex, Ma.

COLLEEN: You've just told me it is! You've just said it was! You said so yourself! Did you lie to me, then?

MATTHEW: I guess I don't know. I just—I have a longing, Ma.

COLLEEN: I don't much like the word longing, either. I don't think that's a good or wholesome word! *(Beat.)* A longing for what, Mattie?

MATTHEW: A surge of the heart, a cry of recognition and love.

COLLEEN: What about God's love? What about the love God has for you?

MATTHEW: Sometimes I feel God like a gentle hand on my back, guiding me. I really do.

COLLEEN: Of course you do.

MATTHEW: But that's not much. A fatherly hand on one's back isn't much to serve as one's whole life's experience of intimacy and love, is it?

COLLEEN: God puts his hand on you and it isn't *enough*?

MATTHEW: I don't think it's enough, no.

COLLEEN: Why did you come here?

MATTHEW: Where could I go? I don't own the house I live in. I have no lover, no wife, no family except you. Where was I supposed to go?

COLLEEN: What do you want from me?

MATTHEW: Please, Ma. I'm your son.

COLLEEN: You tell me you don't love God, you don't love the Church. You don't want to do the work that God called you to do and that I raised you to do. And you want me to stand here and pour out love for you? In return for what? What should I love you for?

MATTHEW: For nothing, Ma! For nothing! That's what you're supposed to love me for. If you find me drunk in a ditch, you're supposed to lean down and wipe the spit off my chin and tell me you love me because I'm your son.

COLLEEN: *Drunk in a ditch?*

MATTHEW: I'm just saying, Ma—

COLLEEN: I don't know what you're saying!

MATTHEW: I'm just saying I want it for free.

COLLEEN: Well, I think that's selfish. I do. And I'm going to bed now because I don't want to look at you. *(She starts toward the stairs, then turns back.)* You should pray.

MATTHEW: I told you, Ma—

COLLEEN: You should pray.

SCENE 3

Abby's bedroom. Theresa and Abby enter, back from the hospital. Theresa is propping Abby up.

THERESA: I know you're tired. I'm sorry I had to wake you up.

ABBY: I'm OK.
(Abby rubs her eyes, looks around the room dazed. Theresa sits on the edge of the single bed.)

THERESA: Come on, sit down. *(Theresa sweeps a pile of magazines off the bed and onto the floor to make room for her, and Abby sits.)* Take your shoes off.

ABBY: When I was little and I used to fall asleep in the car, you used to carry me inside and take my shoes off and put me under the covers.

THERESA: I remember.

ABBY: Sometimes I'd fake it so you wouldn't make me brush my teeth.

THERESA: *(Pulls back the covers on the bed.)* Get on in.

ABBY: I feel really bad about that kid, Mom.

THERESA: So do I. We'll talk about it in the morning.

ABBY: I feel so bad.

THERESA: I know. Get under the covers now.
(Abby gets in, still in her clothes, and closes her eyes.)

ABBY: I should take off my makeup. I'm gonna get zits.

THERESA: It's fine for one night.

ABBY: I read an interview with Amber Valletta, and she said even if she gets home and it's really late and she's kind of drunk or whatever, she always washes her face because it's the most important thing you can do.

THERESA: It's fine for a night, Ab.

ABBY: Do you know what I wish more than anything?

THERESA: What?

ABBY: I wish I could be clean and good.

THERESA: I think you can be clean and good.

ABBY: No, I mean—like something totally different. Like Grandma.

THERESA: Like *Grandma*?

ABBY: Yeah. How she sits up all straight and folds her hands, and she doesn't do things that are sloppy or stupid.

THERESA: When was the last time you even saw her, Abby?

ABBY: When I was seven.

THERESA: I don't remember.

ABBY: We went to the cafeteria at Nordstrom's and Grandma got me ice cream in this little blue bowl but then you got mad at her and we had to leave and I couldn't finish it.

THERESA: Well, sorry. She can be hard to deal with.

ABBY: She said you smelled bad.

THERESA: I don't want to talk about this.

ABBY: She said you smelled like sex and cigarettes and you said, "Not in front of Abby," and she said, "I wish you would say that to yourself sometimes, Theresa! I wish sometimes you'd think a moment and say to yourself, 'Not in front of Abby' before you do the things you do." And you got mad and pulled me up by my arm and we had to go.

THERESA: Well. I guess I repressed that one. Sorry you didn't get to finish your ice cream.

ABBY: I just wish I could be all straight like that sometimes. With my hair all neat and my clothes all clean.

THERESA: That's just money, Abby. It doesn't make you good.

ABBY: It's not, though. It's like she knows she's OK and she's not gonna mess up. She doesn't even have to worry about it. You can see it in her face, like in that picture.

THERESA: What picture?

ABBY: The one where she has on the green suit and she's getting an award and some guy is shaking her hand.

THERESA: Where did you see that picture?

ABBY: I have it. I found it when we were moving.

THERESA: You have it?

ABBY: In my wallet.

(Theresa reaches down for Abby's purse and pulls out her wallet. She finds the picture, takes it out, and looks at it.)

THERESA: I don't think you should be carrying this around with you.

ABBY: I want it.

THERESA: Why?

ABBY: I just like it to look at.

THERESA: Why?

ABBY: I like it. What's she getting the award for?

(Theresa peers closely at the picture, then shrugs.)

THERESA: I don't know. It's something from the university. They liked to show her off because they hardly had any women. They gave her plaques all the time.

ABBY: I like that suit.

THERESA: You do?

ABBY: It's elegant.

THERESA: Yeah, well, she missed out on a lot of things, being so elegant. And I think she knew it, too. But she'd put on a new suit and somebody would give her a prize, and she'd feel like she ruled the world for a little while. A plaque. So what? It's not a whole lot to get by on when you think about it. I don't think it's good for you to be carrying this picture around like some kind of holy relic.

ABBY: Please, Mom!

THERESA: OK, OK. *(Theresa hands the picture to Abby, who looks at it carefully.)* You miss her?

ABBY: I don't know. I just think sometimes—she might be able to help us.

THERESA: *(Quietly.)* I don't think she can, Ab. I think we have to try to fix this on our own.

ABBY: I'm always fucking up. *(A long silence. Abby waits for an answer from Theresa.)* I'm always fucking up, Mom.

THERESA: There are a lot of things we could fix.

ABBY: I'm so sorry about that boy!

THERESA: It wasn't your fault.

ABBY: It happened because I don't know how to act right! I don't know how to be good! I'm mean to people, Mom! I'm mean!

THERESA: Abby. Abby.

ABBY: It was like I was being nice to him, but I was being mean to him at the same time.

THERESA: Abby.

ABBY: I can't believe I did that to someone!

THERESA: He fell. It was an accident.

ABBY: But it happened because I'm so mean.

THERESA: No, it didn't. It happened because he was drunk and not so coordinated to begin with, and because shit happens. Really terrible, horrifically awful shit just happens.

ABBY: It wasn't my booze.

THERESA: You told me that already.

ABBY: I know you think it was, but he had it. He was walking around drinking. He had a bottle in his pocket.

THERESA: OK.

ABBY: Do you believe me? *(A beat.)* Mom!

THERESA: Yes, Ab. I believe you.

ABBY: A lot of the time it seems like you don't believe me even when I'm telling the truth.

THERESA: I said I believe you, Abby.

ABBY: You should.

THERESA: I do.

ABBY: Because sometimes I'm not lying.

THERESA: A lot of the time you're lying.

ABBY: Maybe not as much of the time as you think, though.

THERESA: Well, how am I supposed to tell the difference?

ABBY: I don't know.

(Theresa looks at her watch, closes her eyes, and lies back across the foot of the bed.)

THERESA: I want to be different, too, you know.

ABBY: Different how?

THERESA: I don't know. But better.

ABBY: Like Grandma?

THERESA: No. Something else.

ABBY: Is that why you've been watching that God show on TV?

THERESA: Yes.

ABBY: They're liars on those shows, Mom.

THERESA: I know. But that doesn't mean there isn't something out there worth trying to find.

ABBY: Like what?

THERESA: A surge of the heart. A cry of recognition and love.

ABBY: What does that mean?

THERESA: I don't know. It has to do with God. Or maybe just some kind of spirit or—connectedness or something.

ABBY: I don't believe in that. *(A beat.)* Are you going to fall asleep there?

THERESA: Maybe. Do you mind?

ABBY: No.

SCENE 4

*Colleen throws open her bedroom door and stumbles out onto the landing in
her nightgown. Her hair is down; her arms and legs are bare. Matthew has
been sleeping on the couch. He jerks upright.*

COLLEEN: Mattie! Mattie! Mattie!

MATTHEW: What's going on? What's the matter?

COLLEEN: I was sleeping, and I woke up, and I couldn't stop thinking about
Frank's child. I don't know how a person survives that kind of loss. How
does a person survive?

MATTHEW: I don't know, Ma. They'll find their way.

COLLEEN: I just couldn't stop thinking about it. What a terrible, stupid loss it
is. I woke up and remembered what happened, and it felt like a shock
through my heart. My heart isn't strong, Mattie. It can't take that sort of
thing.

MATTHEW: Do you want me to call the doctor?

COLLEEN: No.

MATTHEW: Do you want a glass of water?

COLLEEN: No. I'm all right now.

MATTHEW: You should go back to sleep, then.

COLLEEN: Yes, all right. I'm sorry I woke you.

MATTHEW: Good night, Ma.

COLLEEN: Mattie!

MATTHEW: What is it?

COLLEEN: I want to pray for the boy.

MATTHEW: All right.

COLLEEN: Will you help me do it?

MATTHEW: All right.

   (Colleen kneels. Looks up at him.)

COLLEEN: I didn't know you were so lonely.

MATTHEW: I'm all right.

COLLEEN: I know what lonely is, with my husband dead six years. I wouldn't
wish it on my son.

MATTHEW: Do you want to pray for the boy?

COLLEEN: What's the prayer for funerals, for sending him to God?

MATTHEW: The prayer of commendation.

COLLEEN: Come here and kneel down with me.

   (Matthew kneels next to her.)

MATTHEW: Go forth, Christian soul, from this world
        In the name of God,
        The almighty Father who created you,
        In the name of Jesus Christ,
        The son of the living God,
        Who suffered for you,
        In the name of the Holy Spirit,
        Who was poured out upon you.
        Go forth, faithful Christian.
        May you live in peace this day.
        May your home be with God in Zion.
        May you return to your Creator,
        Who formed you from the dust of the earth.
        May you see your Redeemer face to face.
COLLEEN: Amen.

END OF PLAY

SPAIN

Jim Knable

PLAYWRIGHT'S BIOGRAPHY

Jim Knable's plays have been produced at MCC Theater, NYC's Summer Play Festival (2006), The Woolly Mammoth Theatre, Soho Rep, Playwrights Theatre of New Jersey, New Jersey Rep, Actor's Express in Atlanta, Phoenix Theatre of Indianapolis, Yale University, and New York University. He has commissioned and produced touring educational plays for Playwrights Project and The Hangar Theatre. He began his playwriting career as a teenager, winning the California Young Playwrights Contest three times and the National Young Playwrights Contest twice. His other plays include *Green Man, The Rapier of Europa, Othamlet,* and *Emerson High.* Knable is also a songwriter and leader of the New York City band The Randy Bandits, who released the CDs *Redbeard* in 2006 and *Golden Arrow* in 2009.

ORIGINAL PRODUCTIONS

Spain received its professional premiere on December 10, 2001, at the Woolly Mammoth Theatre Company, Washington DC, Howard Shalwitz, artistic director, Kevin Moore, managing director. The production was directed by Tom Prewitt. The stage manager was Margie Hasmall, with the following cast:

CAST

BARBARA	Emily Townley
CONQUISTADOR	Chris Lane
ANCIENT ET AL.	Sarah Marshall
JOHN ET AL.	Andrew Wynn
DIVERSION	Katie Barrett

The sets were by Robin Stapley, lights by Lisa Ogonowski, costumes by Rosemary Pardee, sound by Dave McKeever, and props by Linda Evans. Dramaturg was Mary Resing.

Spain received its New York City Premiere on July 18, 2006, at The Summer Play Festival, Arielle Tepper, producer and founder. The production was directed by Jeremy Dobrish. The stage manager was Alexis R. Prussack, with the following cast:

CAST

BARBARA	Stephanie Kurtzuba
CONQUISTADOR	Michael Aronov

```
ANCIENT ET AL.  . . . . . . . . . . . . . . . . . . . . . . . . . . . . . Lisa Barnes
JOHN ET AL.  . . . . . . . . . . . . . . . . . . . . . . . . . . . David Rossmer
DIVERSION  . . . . . . . . . . . . . . . . . . . . . . . . . . . . . . . . Barb Pitts
```

The sets were by Dustin O'Neill, lights by Michael Gottlieb, costumes by Jessica Ford, and sound by Jill BC DuBoff.

Spain received its Off-Broadway premiere on October 10, 2007, at MCC Theater, New York City, Bernard Telsey and Robert LuPone, artistic directors, William Cantler, associate artistic director, Blake West, executive director. The production was directed by Jeremy Dobrish, the stage manager was Alexis R. Prussack, with the following cast:

CAST

```
BARBARA  . . . . . . . . . . . . . . . . . . . . . . . . . . . . . Annabella Sciorra
CONQUISTADOR  . . . . . . . . . . . . . . . . . . . . . . . . . Michael Aronov
ANCIENT ET AL.  . . . . . . . . . . . . . . . . . . . . . . . . . . . . . Lisa Kron
JOHN ET AL.  . . . . . . . . . . . . . . . . . . . . . . . . . . . . . Erik Jensen
DIVERSION  . . . . . . . . . . . . . . . . . . . . . . . . . . . . . Veanne Cox
```

The sets were by Beowulf Boritt, lights by Michael Gottlieb, costumes by Jenny Mannis, sound by Jill BC DuBoff, and props by Jeremy Lydic.

CHARACTERS

BARBARA: A woman in her thirties

CONQUISTADOR: A barbarous man in armor in his thirties or forties

ANCIENT: Also Old Man, Roman, Lawyer, Monk, Psychiatrsit, General. A woman in her fifties playing men's roles.

DIVERSION: A woman in her thirties. A little older than Barbara. No wiser.

JOHN: Barbara's husband. Also Guitar Player, Shepherd, and Horse.

SETTING
America. Sort of.

TIME
The present. Sort of.

SPAIN

ACT I

Barbara and Conquistador are on opposite sides of the stage, unaware of each other.

BARBARA: The heart of Spain is gold. Warm. Welcoming. Culture and cultures mixing, glowing in the high heat of the noonday sun.

CONQUISTADOR: The discovery of the New World marked a major turning point in my life. It opened up doors, gave me options I never knew I had. I found a genuine sense of purpose. I really felt like I was doing something for a change.

BARBARA: The soul of Spain.

CONQUISTADOR: Conquering. It is a great feeling. Meeting uncivilized people. Killing them, making them your slaves, what not.

BARBARA: Roosters.

CONQUISTADOR: For the first time in my life, I felt good about myself. My parents were proud of me. My wife wanted to sleep with me all the time.

BARBARA: Flamenco.

CONQUISTADOR: She told me I had become so much more virile. It was true.

BARBARA: The sweet sea smell of Barcelona.

CONQUISTADOR: My sexual appetite was insatiable. And I sated it quite often. Usually with my wife.

BARBARA: Red and Black and Yellow.

CONQUISTADOR: Ah, the New World, the new me.

BARBARA: Ferdinand and Isabella.

CONQUISTADOR: This helmet.

BARBARA: Picasso.

CONQUISTADOR: This beautiful shiny thing.

BARBARA: Gaudi.

CONQUISTADOR: Sometimes at night, I just sit on my bed and hold it on my lap.

BARBARA: Dali.

CONQUISTADOR: Trace the engraving. Look at my face in the reflection.

BARBARA: Lorca.

CONQUISTADOR: Who else gets to wear something like this?

BARBARA: Art.

CONQUISTADOR: The Spanish blood is strong in our veins.

BARBARA: Music.

CONQUISTADOR: We go places and name them.

BARBARA: Fire in the belly. Nothing else like it.

CONQUISTADOR: And in the heat of battle. On my horse. This God-like thing on my head. I swing my sword down. I feel so . . . good. Really and truly good. Blessed.

BARBARA: I have never been to Spain.

CONQUISTADOR: And afterwards. Wipe off the blood, get off my horse, stick my feet in the new earth, drink with my friends, maybe rape a prisoner.

BARBARA: I don't know Spanish.

CONQUISTADOR: This is what I was made for. I believe that. Look at me. This is who I am. I love myself.

BARBARA: The heart of Spain is gold.

(A guitar player appears, playing a fast Spanish dance song. Barbara dances in place, facing the audience. Conquistador does the same. They stop. The guitar stops.)

BARBARA: I first hallucinated him shortly after my husband of five years left me for some slut with a boob job.

(Lights reveal Conquistador sitting on a sofa with his feet up.)

BARBARA: He was sitting on my sofa with his feet up. His funny metal boots on my coffee table. I was not attracted to him in the traditional sense. I knew immediately he was not a real human being. He looked like one, smelled like one; when he talked I heard his voice like I'd hear anyone else's. But he was quite obviously a delusionary fragment of a repressed childhood primal picture book memory, nothing more. I asked him: Who are you?

CONQUISTADOR: They call me El Tigre.

BARBARA: I asked him: Why are you here?

CONQUISTADOR: I do not know. It is a great mystery to me.

BARBARA: I asked him: What century are you from?

CONQUISTADOR: Sixteenth, year of our Lord, bless us and protect us, amen.

BARBARA: I did not ask him about his profession. Obviously he was a Conquistador. A real Spanish conquistador. Luckily, he spoke English. I did ask him to take his metal boots off my coffee table. And if I could take his sword and helmet.

CONQUISTADOR: *(Taking his boots off the coffee table.)* I will hold on to them, thank you.

BARBARA: And then I said: Where exactly were you before this and how do you think you got from that place to my apartment?

CONQUISTADOR: It is a strange story.

BARBARA: I called in sick to work. *(To him.)* I want to hear it.

(Guitar Player strums.)

CONQUISTADOR: Well . . . *(Stands.)* It was a raid like any other. Screaming, burning dwellings, what not. We rode through this . . . I suppose you could call it an alley or street . . . past the charred huts and dead Indians. And we came to an odd structure. A temple of sorts. We had seen it from a distance. A pyramid of sorts. Very tall, many steps. We all liked the look of it and decided not to destroy it. We would instead use it to throw a festival. It was perfect. I got off my horse with the others and climbed all those steps. I could hear my men behind me. Clomp, clomp, clomp. The air grew cooler, the breeze blew lightly. I came to a portal. An entrance. Inside, a fire was glowing. I walked in. I saw an ancient sitting before the fire.

(Conquistador walks left, into a new space. An implied fire is on the ground. An Ancient sits before it. Silence. Ancient and Conquistador look at each other.)

ANCIENT: *Buenas noches.*

(Conquistador draws his sword and prepares to strike. He stops, suddenly, to correct.)

CONQUISTADOR: *Buenos días.*

ANCIENT: *Buenas noches, Señor.*

CONQUISTADOR: *No. Buenos días. (Pointing outside.) Días.*

ANCIENT: *No, Señor Tigre. Buenas noches.*

CONQUISTADOR: At which point there was a bright flash of light like lightning and I saw a vision. A man on a skeleton donkey. A monkey's head on his neck. A crowd of men in white robes and hoods surrounding him. And then I became the man with the monkey head and the white hoods fell. All their eyes glowed red. And lion claws reached out from white sleeves to touch me. And I closed my eyes and heard a voice.

ANCIENT: In the Mayan Calendar, days, weeks, and months are counted as are all numbers with dots and lines. And on this day of the four dots and two lines, there is predicted a shift in the very nature of time and continuity. That is to say, this raid of our culture was prophesied, and you are now to become the vessel of higher perception due to the fact that I already know everything and the rest of the village is dead.

(Stage left goes black.)

CONQUISTADOR: And then another flash of light and I found myself sitting on your furniture. *(Beat.)* Where am I?

BARBARA: We call it the United States of America.

CONQUISTADOR: America?

BARBARA: Yes. Look. Did I hear you say burn and kill people?

CONQUISTADOR: Savages.

BARBARA: Your sword. Oh God.

CONQUISTADOR: Blood of the savages. I would have washed it if I knew I was coming.

BARBARA: Suddenly I feel ill.

CONQUISTADOR: Plague?

BARBARA: Conscience. What an awful hallucination.

CONQUISTADOR: You are having a vision now?

BARBARA: I like Spain. I love Spain.

CONQUISTADOR: Good, I won't have to kill you.

BARBARA: But you represent everything I hate about Spain and mankind in general.

CONQUISTADOR: I don't understand you.

BARBARA: You are symbolic of fear and repression and colonization and everything evil.

CONQUISTADOR: Evil?

BARBARA: But I love Spain. Jesus. Why couldn't you have been Lorca or Picasso. Well no, not Picasso.

CONQUISTADOR: I am not evil.

BARBARA: Cervantes.

CONQUISTADOR: I am all good.

BARBARA: Dali.

CONQUISTADOR: I love myself.

BARBARA: I don't want to deal with this right now.

CONQUISTADOR: I'm not even going to rape you.

BARBARA: And that's when I left.

(Black on all but Barbara and Diversion, her best friend.)

DIVERSION: Barbara, I'm worried about you.

BARBARA: You're always worried about me.

DIVERSION: I'm always concerned. Now I am worried, this is worry.

BARBARA: You don't believe me?

DIVERSION: I do. I truly believe you are delusional.

BARBARA: But why him? Of all the delusions . . .

DIVERSION: Do you need to come live with me?

BARBARA: What?

DIVERSION: Being alone so suddenly. You're not used to being alone. And the circumstances.

BARBARA: I don't want to live with you.

(Beat.)

DIVERSION: Why not?

BARBARA: I have a place. I live in a place. I'm OK.

DIVERSION: You're having conversations with conquistadors!

BARBARA: I shouldn't have told you.

DIVERSION: Why not? I'm your best friend.

BARBARA: It's not like I'm doing harm to myself.

DIVERSION: You're missing work.

BARBARA: I hate work.

DIVERSION: No, you don't.

BARBARA: I do. I really do. I'm sick of escrow folders and phone calls to buyers and Roman with his roaming hands. I want to quit.

DIVERSION: Quit? Quit and do what?

BARBARA: Go to Spain.

DIVERSION: You're obsessive.

BARBARA: You should encourage me.

DIVERSION: You don't even know Spanish.

BARBARA: Maybe the Conquistador will teach me. *(Silence.)*

DIVERSION: I have to get back to work. Do you want me to say anything to Roman?

BARBARA: No, no. I already told him I was sick in bed.

DIVERSION: That's not the only place you're sick.

BARBARA: Go back to work. I'll call you tonight.

> *(Diversion disappears. Lights shift. Conquistador is sitting with his helmet in his lap on the sofa. He looks at his face in its reflection. Barbara stands above him.)*

BARBARA: You're still here.

CONQUISTADOR: Yes.

BARBARA: What are you doing?

CONQUISTADOR: Spending time with my helmet. It makes me feel peaceful.

BARBARA: Your helmet?

CONQUISTADOR: Yes. Look. Come look.

> *(Barbara walks cautiously over to Conquistador and sits beside him on the sofa. They look at the helmet together.)*

BARBARA: What are these designs?

CONQUISTADOR: Beautiful, no?

BARBARA: Yes. But what are they?

CONQUISTADOR: Tigers. *(He looks up at her and smiles.)*

BARBARA: El Tigre.

CONQUISTADOR: Sí. *(Silence.)*

BARBARA: I know that if I touched you, I would actually feel you.

CONQUISTADOR: I do not understand.

BARBARA: I know it without even trying. And I know I don't want to try.

CONQUISTADOR: To try what?

BARBARA: To touch you.

(Conquistador looks at her. He places his hand on her breast.)

CONQUISTADOR: Like this?

BARBARA: *(pushing his hand away quickly.)* Don't. I don't want that.

CONQUISTADOR: I am beginning to.

(Barbara stands and moves away from him.)

CONQUISTADOR: Do not be afraid. I would not dishonor you without your permission.

BARBARA: You're a killer and a rapist.

CONQUISTADOR: Only with savages.

BARBARA: They're not savages, they're human beings, and you wiped them out of existence.

CONQUISTADOR: Where is your husband? *(Silence. Conquistador holds up a photo frame with a picture of Barbara and a man in it.)* This painting. I found it in your bedroom. Very true to life, especially for a miniature.

BARBARA: It's a photograph. I'm not going to explain what that is.

CONQUISTADOR: This is your husband, is it not? *(Beat.)*

BARBARA: It was.

CONQUISTADOR: He's dead? *(Beat.)*

BARBARA: Yes.

CONQUISTADOR: He was killed in battle?

(Barbara laughs. Conquistador looks at her.)

BARBARA: John never fought a battle in his life.

CONQUISTADOR: He was lame?

BARBARA: Yes, he was very lame. Lame, boring, cowardly, lying, cheating.

CONQUISTADOR: How did he die? Did somebody kill him?

(Barbara looks at his sword.)

BARBARA: I killed him.

CONQUISTADOR: You?

BARBARA: Sure. I found him with another woman and killed both of them. *(Silence.)*

CONQUISTADOR: Hm. Good. Did you kill them in sleep?

BARBARA: No. I killed them in the heat of their passion.

CONQUISTADOR: Good. Good.

BARBARA: You approve?

CONQUISTADOR: I would do the same to my wife if I found her with another.

BARBARA: Would you rape her first?

CONQUISTADOR: *(Repulsed.)* No. No. She's my wife.

BARBARA: Give me that picture.

(Barbara holds out her hand. Conquistador hands it to her.)

CONQUISTADOR: Why do you still keep it?

(Barbara looks at him. She smashes the frame against the table, takes out the photo, and rips it to shreds. Silence.)

CONQUISTADOR: You are not going to stomp and spit on it?

(Beat. Barbara does so.)

CONQUISTADOR: How do you feel?

(Barbara looks at him.)

BARBARA: Savage.

(Blackout. Light on Ancient.)

ANCIENT: In the Mayan culture, the Ancient occupies a position of supreme wisdom beyond all comprehension. Ancients are destined to be ancient from birth. But to become Ancient, you must live long enough.

You must be brave.

You must master yourself.

You must go past the words, through imagination.

You must act out the ritual.

You must then choose to go beyond it.

(Lights up on the full stage. Barbara has Conquistador's sword. She is practicing sword thrusts, lunging in place while Conquistador stands behind her, steadying her arm, his other arm at her waist.)

CONQUISTADOR: Good. It is in your nature.

BARBARA: It is?

CONQUISTADOR: I am sure you dealt a swift and cruel death to your husband.

(Barbara stops.)

BARBARA: What am I doing?

CONQUISTADOR: Reliving the death blow. You thrust your sword into him, his blood spilled in rivers on the ground. His head went rolling down the stone steps.

BARBARA: I don't have stone steps.

CONQUISTADOR: You took your bloody revenge at the peak of his betrayal.

BARBARA: Betrayal. Yes, right, I did.

CONQUISTADOR: Did he see you come in?

BARBARA: No. No, not at first. She saw me. She screamed. The sword went through his back and came out his chest. His mouth fell open. This is horrible. Am I saying this?

CONQUISTADOR: Yes, yes, tell me more.

BARBARA: I never killed anyone.

CONQUISTADOR: It is a great feeling, is it not? The power.

BARBARA: Power. Yes. Having the power to . . . kill him. Kill him.

(She thrusts.)

CONQUISTADOR: Yes!

BARBARA: Stab him through the heart!

CONQUISTADOR: It is beautiful!

BARBARA: Destroy him!

CONQUISTADOR: You have so much Duende! You are so strong!

(She stops.)

BARBARA: I am? I have what?

CONQUISTADOR: Duende. I want to take my armor off with you.

BARBARA: I don't think that's a good idea.

CONQUISTADOR: You would like to remove it for me.

BARBARA: We'd better keep the armor on in this relationship.

CONQUISTADOR: I am holding you around the waist.

BARBARA: Yes.

CONQUISTADOR: Why are you letting me?

(Barbara pulls out a phone and speaks out to Diversion.)

BARBARA: And I couldn't really answer. But there was no denying it. Since he came, I had destroyed my husband's picture, allowed him to put his cold hand on my breast, and held his sword.

(Diversion is lit, standing with a phone while the Ancient gives her a meta-physical shoulder massage.)

DIVERSION: You touched him.

BARBARA: We've touched each other.

DIVERSION: You're not supposed to be able to touch delusions.

BARBARA: That's what I'm trying to tell you. This is turning into something else.

DIVERSION: Roman asked about you.

BARBARA: Are you hearing me?

DIVERSION: He asked if you were really sick or if you were planning to quit soon.

BARBARA: I don't care.

DIVERSION: I told him he would have to ask you himself tomorrow. When you come in.

BARBARA: Do you want to meet the Conquistador?

DIVERSION: I'll be right there.

(Barbara hangs up. Dark on Diversion.)

CONQUISTADOR: You can communicate with spirits?

BARBARA: What?

CONQUISTADOR: You were not talking to me, but when you were talking I thought I heard a small voice near us.

BARBARA: I was using a telephone. It was invented by Alexander Graham Bell. It lets people talk to each other without them having to be in the same place.

CONQUISTADOR: Why would anyone want to do that?

BARBARA: I don't know.

CONQUISTADOR: I do not feel that you have told me exactly where I am.

BARBARA: This is the future. You're a few hundred years past where you were before this.

CONQUISTADOR: Are you part of my vision?

BARBARA: You are part of mine.

(A doorbell rings. Conquistador jumps back and grabs his sword.)
It's all right. That was my doorbell. It's Diversion.

CONQUISTADOR: I don't understand.

BARBARA: My best friend. Diversion.

CONQUISTADOR: What does that mean?

BARBARA: Don't worry about it. You're about to meet her.

(Barbara opens the door. Diversion steps in and yells at seeing the Conquistador. He yells back. Stunned silence.)

DIVERSION: My God.

BARBARA: I told you.

DIVERSION: I'm seeing your delusion.

BARBARA: Two people can't see the same delusion.

DIVERSION: Can I touch him?

BARBARA: Can she?

CONQUISTADOR: Please.

(Diversion touches him.)

DIVERSION: Oh! My God. Look at him. His metal is cold.

BARBARA: His hands are cold.

DIVERSION: What about his face?

BARBARA: I don't know.

(Diversion reaches out and touches his face. She holds her hand there.)

DIVERSION: Oh . . .

BARBARA: Cold?

DIVERSION: Warm. Hot. Burning. *(Diversion pulls her hand back gently.)* Where did you come from?

CONQUISTADOR: It is a strange story.

DIVERSION: I want to hear it.

(Conquistador looks at Barbara.)

BARBARA: Go on. Tell it. I'll get us drinks. What would you like?

DIVERSION: Jim Beam on the rocks.

BARBARA: I'll be right back.

(*Barbara exits. Guitar strums.*)

CONQUISTADOR: It was a day like any other. Roaming the green fields of my countryside. Alone on my stallion. Crossing short wooden bridges over brooks. I came to a grove of trees and bushes. Beneath one tree sat an old man. I swung off my horse and stood before him.

(*Conquistador walks; lights follow him. The Ancient sits on the ground, leaning up against an implied tree.*)

CONQUISTADOR: *Buenos días.*

ANCIENT: *A las cinco de la tarde.*

CONQUISTADOR: *Que?*

ANCIENT: *El niño come naranjas.*

CONQUISTADOR: And all at once there was burst of light and I saw a vision. A woman dressed in a flowing white gown, her hair falling down on her shoulders. Floating above the earth. Her lips move as if to speak, but I hear nothing. A dew drop. A lily shaft open. The crowning of a boy eating oranges. And then another burst of light and I was here. And the woman I knew in her white dress was dressed like a man.

(*Lights up on stage right. Barbara stands nonplussed with two drinks.*)

BARBARA: That wasn't the story you told me.

DIVERSION: It was beautiful.

BARBARA: What happened to killing and raping everybody?

(*Conquistador just looks at Barbara.*)

DIVERSION: Barbara. Don't offend him. He would never do that. He is a knight. A noble knight.

BARBARA: He's a conquistador!

DIVERSION: You are his Dulcinea. You are his lady in white.

BARBARA: What happened while I was in the kitchen?

CONQUISTADOR: I told the story of my journey here, my lady.

BARBARA: My lady? Now I'm my lady?

DIVERSION: He is quite obviously in love with you.

BARBARA: What happened to you? You were against this whole thing being real at all.

DIVERSION: People can change.

BARBARA: Stop. Stop.

(*Barbara passes the drinks off to Diversion and walks up to Conquistador.*)
What have you done to my friend?

CONQUISTADOR: I told her my story.

BARBARA: Why does she get a different story than I do?

CONQUISTADOR: She is a different woman.

BARBARA: So she gets the pretty story about countrysides and brooks and I get the pillaging and burning story. She gets a woman in a white dress and I get you on a skeleton donkey with a monkey head? I'm the one in mourning for something! I'm the one who needs soothing!

CONQUISTADOR: Mourning?

BARBARA: I'm stranded. I'm alone. My husband left me for a slut with a boob job.

CONQUISTADOR: You killed your husband and his lover.

DIVERSION: Barbara?

BARBARA: I didn't kill them. I just told you I did to make myself feel good.

(Silence. Barbara and Conquistador look at each other.)

CONQUISTADOR: Did it feel good?

BARBARA: Yes.

DIVERSION: What is he talking about, Barbara?

(Beat. Barbara turns to Diversion.)

BARBARA: He's talking about murder. He's talking about lust. He's talking about wind that blows over the heads of the dead. He is a cruel, barbaric man with a bloody sword at his waist, a hundred angry souls at his heels and desire stronger than anything you've ever known in his heart.

DIVERSION: Am I dreaming?

BARBARA: You don't belong here.

DIVERSION: Does he?

BARBARA: Yes. But only as I want him.

DIVERSION: Barbara, am I losing my mind?

BARBARA: No. You're the sane one. Go home and pretend you dreamt this. Leave the drinks for us. Go.

(Diversion exits. Barbara looks at Conquistador.)

BARBARA: What are you, really?

CONQUISTADOR: What do you believe?

BARBARA: I don't know what to think.

CONQUISTADOR: Do not think.

BARBARA: Who do you think I am?

CONQUISTADOR: I am not thinking.

BARBARA: A woman in man's clothing? A vision?

CONQUISTADOR: Yes.

BARBARA: Which story is true?

CONQUISTADOR: Both.

(A brilliant flash of white light. The Ancient stands and sings with the Guitar Player. The Guitar Player in Spanish, the Ancient in English. As they sing Barbara begins removing Conquistador's armor with his help and silent instruction. This is not erotic. It is simple.)

GUITAR PLAYER:

En mita del mar
había una piedra
y se sentaba mi compaerita
a contarle sus penas
Tan solamente a la Tierra
le cuento lo que me pasa,
porque en el mundo no encuentro
persona e mi confianza

ANCIENT:

Out in the sea
was a stone.
My girl sat down
to tell it her pains.
Only to the Earth
do I tell my troubles,
for nowhere in the world
do I find anyone I trust.

(Conquistador stands in his sixteenth-century underwear. Barbara motions for him to sit on the floor by the table. She pulls a bottle of whiskey out from under the table, drinks from it. He drinks. She drinks. He drinks. She reaches under the table and pulls out a large travel book. She opens it and shows it to Conquistador.)

BARBARA: It's been my fantasy for a long time.

CONQUISTADOR: Spain.

BARBARA: I wanted to go there with John. I wanted that to be the place where we found love again. I wanted a country to love.

CONQUISTADOR: You want love.

BARBARA: Wanted.

CONQUISTADOR: And now?

BARBARA: Tell me what it feels like to kill someone.

CONQUISTADOR: You already know.

BARBARA: A whole civilization. What is that like?

CONQUISTADOR: It is like nothing else.

BARBARA: It makes you feel strong.

CONQUISTADOR: Yes.

BARBARA: Because they can't defend themselves against your weapons.

CONQUISTADOR: Yes.

BARBARA: And you can do anything you want with them?

CONQUISTADOR: Yes.

(Barbara drinks.)

BARBARA: Cut off their heads.

CONQUISTADOR: Of course.

BARBARA: Disembowel them.

CONQUISTADOR: Certainly.

BARBARA: Cut off their balls.

CONQUISTADOR: Occasionally.

BARBARA: You ride into town with your men, in your armor; you all stink like horses . . .

CONQUISTADOR: Horses, oh yes!

BARBARA: The villagers stare up at you terrified, helpless, you don't even see them as human . . .

CONQUISTADOR: Villagers?

BARBARA: The weak, the peasants . . .

CONQUISTADOR: Peasants, pthuh . . .

BARBARA: Then what?

CONQUISTADOR: Kill the peasants!

BARBARA: Yes! You hit your heels on your horse and ride through them, swooping your sword, hacking, slashing . . .

CONQUISTADOR: *(Suggesting.)* Chopping?

BARBARA: Chopping up and down! You take up a fiery lance, you hurl it through the air, it soars, fire trailing, down into the hut where the men hold ceremonies; it bursts into flames.

CONQUISTADOR: Many, many flames!

BARBARA: You burn it all down, you leave nothing standing. The dirt roads run muddy with blood.

CONQUISTADOR: Muddy blood.

BARBARA: You drink the blood, your mouth is red, you run, screaming battle cries, killing everything in your path, even your own men, your lust consumes you.

CONQUISTADOR: You are very good at this.

BARBARA: You burn with death and pain, painless pain because you feel nothing but overpowering joy, you spin your arms and wave your sword and stand on top of all the bodies, like a mountain, you stand on top and breathe in the smell of torn-out flesh!

(Conquistador drinks.)

CONQUISTADOR: Yes, all that. I do that. This drink is good. What is it?

BARBARA: Whiskey. John drank it, his bottle.

BARBARA: *(Gleefully, with him.)*   CONQUISTADOR: *(As before with the portrait.)*
Why do I still keep it?   Why do you still keep it?

(She takes another swig and hurls it offstage. Crash! They laugh.)

BARBARA: I could destroy everything. The couch. We bought it together.

(She goes to the couch and tears into the pillows, hurling them, violent and crazy. Conquistador helps some, but is no match for her fury.)

BARBARA: What else? More pictures? I have more pictures. Dishes? The sheets? His smell still on them. Everything here we had together, I could destroy everything!

CONQUISTADOR: You are amazing.

BARBARA: I could destroy, myself, I could destroy . . . I could . . . *(She flops down on the remains of the couch.)* Too much, too fast. Spinning.

CONQUISTADOR: Spinning. Yes, spinning your arms.

BARBARA: Room spinning. Can't look. Too much . . . *(She collapses.)*

CONQUISTADOR: Barbara?

(Lights rise on the Ancient, fall on Conquistador and Barbara. While the Ancient talks, he changes into a very corporate looking business suit.)

ANCIENT: In the Mayan culture, a sacred ritual is not just acted, it is lived.

Sometimes it is necessary to be violent.

Sometimes it is necessary to make a sacrifice. *(Pause.)*

You must take him to the temple, tie him to the rock.

Hold the point of the blade over his heart and then . . . push it in.

There will be screaming and spattering of blood.

No one likes to be sacrificed.

But then the sky opens up along a bright white crack. The moon is invented. The dark grass of hills holding trees waves in sea green, the whole of souls goes spinning; and names are remembered. Empires fall. Countries lose their borders. Anything is then possible.

(Light falls on Ancient. Rises on Conquistador and Barbara. Morning. They are sleeping, passed out on the floor. A key in a lock is heard. A door swings open. John [the Guitar Player] walks on carrying a guitar in a case and a trunk full of his clothes. He looks spent and dejected. At first he does not see Barbara and Conquistador. He lays down his load and flops onto the couch. Now he notices the bodies. He peers at them inquisitively. He notices the armor lying near the table.)

JOHN: Barbara? Barbara?

BARBARA: *(In sleep.)* John?

JOHN: Barbara, I'm back. I'm sorry I left you. What is this man doing on the floor and why is there armor in our house?

BARBARA: John? *(She wakes.)* John?! *(Sitting bolt upright.)* John?!!

JOHN: You wouldn't believe what I've been through. And now this. Christ, what a strange world.

BARBARA: What are you doing here?

JOHN: Yolanda dumped me for some guy with big muscles and no neck. I realized I made a mistake leaving you. I came back. I hope you can forgive me. Do you want to tell me who this guy is?

BARBARA: You're gone.

JOHN: I'm right here.

BARBARA: I killed you.

JOHN: Honey, I think you're still a little bit asleep.

BARBARA: I walked in on you and the slut with the boob job having sex in our bed and I slaughtered you both.

JOHN: Barbara, I'm right here. I'm alive. Yolanda's alive. I wish she was dead, but she's alive. You're in the middle of a dream or something.

BARBARA: Spain.

JOHN: What?

BARBARA: Spain. *(Barbara stands.)*

JOHN: You want to talk about Spain right now? Why don't you go splash some water on your face. Would you like me to make coffee?

(Barbara walks over to the armor and picks up the sword.)

JOHN: What are you doing? Jesus, what the hell is that?

BARBARA: Spain. *(Barbara puts the point of the sword against John's chest.)*

JOHN: Honey, what are you going to do here? Kill me?

BARBARA: Sure.

(Barbara drives the sword into John. Lights go white. A phone rings. Black.)

BARBARA: Hello?

(Lights back on. Diversion stands next to Roman [Ancient] stage left. Diversion holds the phone. Barbara stands calmly with the sword at her side, her dead bleeding husband on the sofa and the Conquistador passed out on the floor.)

DIVERSION: Barbara, it's me. I'm standing here with Roman. We're both worried about you.

BARBARA: Concerned?

DIVERSION: Worried. I had the strangest dream about you last night. I was telling Roman about it. Why aren't you coming into work?

ROMAN: Let me talk to her.

DIVERSION: Roman wants to talk to you.

ROMAN: Barbara, look, I'm not angry with you for lying about being sick. You're obviously going through some period of mental instability resulting from being rejected by your husband. I understand. I've read lots of books where that happens. But we need you here, Barbara. We need you in Escrow, we need you on the phone, we need your magic touch. I think it might even help you with your feelings of worthlessness to come in and make yourself busy. I've heard that it's good for people in your state to keep going to work and, in fact, work even harder than usual to make up for the emptiness in their lives. And look, Barbara, I don't want to have to threaten you, but if you don't come in by tomorrow, I'll fire you. So why don't you come in today. What do you say?

BARBARA: I quit.

ROMAN: Barbara, don't do this.

BARBARA: If I came into that office, I would hack all of you to pieces with a long and blood-stained Spanish sword.

ROMAN: Maybe you should think about this for a little while. I'll call back tomorrow.

BARBARA: If you call me, I'll track you down and murder your whole family.

ROMAN: Jesus, Barbara, you've really gone off the deep end, haven't you.

BARBARA: Yes.

ROMAN: Well. We'll miss you.

BARBARA: Thanks. Put Diversion on, would you?

ROMAN: No problem. *(Handing Diversion the phone.)* For you. *(Roman walks off.)*

DIVERSION: What's going on here, Barb?

BARBARA: I'm going through some very important changes.

DIVERSION: Yeah? That sounds positive.

BARBARA: I just quit my job.

DIVERSION: Barbara!

BARBARA: It was easy. It felt good. Just like when I drove this sword into my husband's chest. That's the thing I've realized, you know? It's so easy to simply do these things.

DIVERSION: What are you talking about?

BARBARA: Do you remember your dream from last night? The one with me and the Conquistador? Where he told you what you wanted to hear and I told you the way it was. That really happened. Things like that really happen. Do you understand? No, you probably don't. Why don't you just pretend I'm crazy.

DIVERSION: I think you need help, Barbara.

BARBARA: Good, good.

DIVERSION: I know you have a thing against shrinks, but this guy I've been seeing lately . . .

BARBARA: I don't care about your personal life. Go give Roman a blow job or something.

DIVERSION: Barbara!

BARBARA: You can use my desk if you like.

DIVERSION: I can't believe . . .

BARBARA: No, you can't. Good-bye.

(Barbara hangs up. Dark on Diversion. Conquistador is sitting up at this point, watching Barbara. She nods over to John. Conquistador looks at him inquisitively.)

CONQUISTADOR: Dead.

BARBARA: Dead.

CONQUISTADOR: Who is he?

BARBARA: Husband.

CONQUISTADOR: Again?

BARBARA: Yeah.

CONQUISTADOR: You killed his ghost.

BARBARA: Sure.

CONQUISTADOR: My head hurts.

BARBARA: You have a hangover.

CONQUISTADOR: Barbara?

BARBARA: *(Jarred at hearing him say her name.)* Yeah?

CONQUISTADOR: Why am I still here? *(Beat.)*

BARBARA: Beats me. But do me a favor. Don't talk like a real human being.
(Barbara starts to walk off.)

CONQUISTADOR: Where are you going?

BARBARA: Wash the blood off.

(Barbara exits. Conquistador looks at John. John opens his eyes and talks nonchalantly to Conquistador.)

JOHN: I met Yolanda in a snowstorm. I was walking home from the Metro. She was all bundled up like an Eskimo, getting her mail I guess. Very cute. I said something stupid like: Nice snowstorm, huh? She laughed. Her breath was hot. It puffed. Then she said: Do you want to come inside? And I thought she was kidding. She couldn't even see my face and I couldn't see hers. But then she took my hand and led me in. All we knew were each other's voices, but she just brought me into her house. And I started to take off my coat but she stopped me, wouldn't even let me take down the hood. Not yet, she said, and she reached down to her pants and unbuttoned them. And I did the same with mine. And then both of us were standing with no pants or underwear in our big coats and hoods, all bundled up on top. And she pulled me against a wall and we did it like that. The coats, you know, they were squeaking against each other. I put the hole in my hood next to the hole in hers and we breathed on each other. It was like hiding under a blanket. It was wonderful. When it was over, she said: I will if you will. And we both took off our coats and hoods and laughed and laughed and laughed. Not because we knew each other. Because we didn't. But then we tried to.

And I left my wife with all her books about Spain and all her misery and boredom. But then something went wrong. Something always goes wrong. And here I am. Who are you?

CONQUISTADOR: They call me El Tigre. Do you know that you're dead?

(Beat. John looks down at his body and the blood on his shirt.)

JOHN: How did that happen?

CONQUISTADOR: Your wife stabbed you.

JOHN: Christ. When?

CONQUISTADOR: Before I woke up.

JOHN: I'm dead?

CONQUISTADOR: Yes.

JOHN: I don't feel dead.

CONQUISTADOR: If she finds you alive, she'll kill you again.

JOHN: Where is she?

CONQUISTADOR: Washing your blood off her hands.

(Beat. John jumps up.)

JOHN: I tried, right?

(Conquistador shrugs.)

JOHN: Good luck.

(John runs to his suitcase and guitar, grabs them, and leaves. Barbara enters, refreshed. Conquistador looks at her. Barbara looks at the empty couch.)

BARBARA: Where is he?

CONQUISTADOR: He left.

BARBARA: He was dead!

CONQUISTADOR: I told him.

BARBARA: What did he say?

CONQUISTADOR: He told me the story of how he met his lover. *(Beat.)*

BARBARA: Did he leave through the front door or did angels come and get him or something?

CONQUISTADOR: Front door.

(Barbara grabs the sword and charges out the front door. Conquistador sits on the sofa. Ancient enters and sits next to Conquistador. Conquistador notices but is not surprised.)

CONQUISTADOR: What am I doing here?

ANCIENT: Being useful.

CONQUISTADOR: When can I leave?

ANCIENT: When you're done.

CONQUISTADOR: Done what?

ANCIENT: Participating in a ritualistic experiment.

CONQUISTADOR: Who are you?

ANCIENT: Ancient.

CONQUISTADOR: Besides that.

ANCIENT: Old man.

CONQUISTADOR: Why do I have two different memories of how I got here?

ANCIENT: They're the same.

CONQUISTADOR: Why won't Barbara sleep with me?

ANCIENT: Because you told her you're a rapist.

(Barbara enters, sword in hand, out of breath. She sees the Ancient.)

BARBARA: Now what.

CONQUISTADOR: Did you find him?

BARBARA: No. I frightened the neighbors. I think someone is going to call the police.

ANCIENT: You must be Barbara.

BARBARA: Yeah. What are you?

CONQUISTADOR: He's the one who sent me here.

BARBARA: Oh. You're all-knowing?

ANCIENT: Usually.

BARBARA: How about a little enlightenment?

ANCIENT: You are acting out a Freudian fantasy based on a Jungian nightmare, served to you by an Andalusian Mayan Soul Prophet by way of a delusionary fragment of a repressed childhood primal collective unconscious memory.

BARBARA: You talk like a textbook.

ANCIENT: I have to be going now.

BARBARA AND CONQUISTADOR: Wait!

ANCIENT: You'll see me again.

BARBARA: What are we supposed to do?

ANCIENT: Whatever you want.

BARBARA: Is my husband dead or alive?

(Ancient shrugs.)

BARBARA: Is any of this really happening?

(Ancient nods.)

BARBARA: Why him?

(Silence. Conquistador looks at her, a little hurt. Ancient shakes his head.)

BARBARA: Am I a murderer?

ANCIENT: No.

BARBARA: Is he?

ANCIENT: Good-bye. *(Ancient walks off.)*

BARBARA and CONQUISTADOR: Wait!

(Silence. Barbara and Conquistador look at each other.)

BARBARA: Put your armor back on.

(Lights move to Diversion, who is speaking with her implied psychiatrist.)

DIVERSION: He was dressed in shiny silver metal. It curved around his chest, rose at his shoulders, fell in patterns down his back. His beard was rough and brown. His face was warm, I touched it with my palm. It was so incredibly lifelike. And Barbara was there, too. She was acting crazy, like a wild animal. She tried to make him seem less good. She tried to make him take back the story about the green country and the old man. She doesn't make any sense. I tried to suggest she come in and talk to you.

(Psychiatrist [Ancient] appears.)

PSYCHIATRIST: Good. That was the right thing to do. Tell me more about the man in shiny silver. Were you attracted to him?

DIVERSION: Not in the traditional sense. There was something familiar about him.

PSYCHIATRIST: You mentioned a story.

DIVERSION: Yes. It was beautiful. He was Don Quixote. But Barbara said he was a conquistador.

PSYCHIATRIST: How do you feel about Barbara?

DIVERSION: She's lost her marbles.

PSYCHIATRIST: Are you attracted to Barbara?

DIVERSION: I don't want to think about that.

(Lights go stage right. Conquistador is back in his armor.)

BARBARA: We need to make a pact.

CONQUISTADOR: A pact?

BARBARA: A pact between you and me that says we are allies.

CONQUISTADOR: I do not—

BARBARA: Sure you do. Allies. In war. Whatever happens. You protect me, I protect you.

CONQUISTADOR: How will you protect me?

BARBARA: You've seen me in action.

CONQUISTADOR: Yes.

BARBARA: We're in whatever this is together. And I think it's a fight. I think we're fighting something. That's why you're here.

CONQUISTADOR: What are we fighting?

BARBARA: We don't know. Right? But we're here. Look. Give me your sword.

CONQUISTADOR: What are you going to do with it?

BARBARA: Trust me.

(Conquistador hands her his sword.)

BARBARA: Get on your knees.

(Conquistador does so. Barbara passes the sword from one of his shoulders to the other.)

BARBARA: I knight you in the name of the fight whatever it is. Rise.

(He does. She hands him the sword.)

BARBARA: Now do it to me.

CONQUISTADOR: I—

(Barbara gets on her knees.)

BARBARA: Do it.

CONQUISTADOR: I have never met a woman like you.

BARBARA: Sure you have. Knight me.

(Beat. Conquistador knights her.)

CONQUISTADOR: I knight you, Barbara—what is your full name?

BARBARA: Tusenbach.

CONQUISTADOR: I knight you Barbara Tusenbach in the name of Spain, Her Majesty, God—

BARBARA: The fight.

CONQUISTADOR: The fight. And in the name of Duende.

BARBARA: Duende? What's that?

CONQUISTADOR: Rise.

(Barbara rises.)

BARBARA: What's Duende?

(The sound of sirens.)

CONQUISTADOR: What is that noise?

BARBARA: Sirens. They're coming.

CONQUISTADOR: Who?

BARBARA: Our adversaries. What is Duende?

CONQUISTADOR: Everything you cannot name, but already said.

(The sirens get louder.)

BARBARA: Is this what it feels like before a battle?

CONQUISTADOR: Barbara.

BARBARA: Is this the feeling you get? Is this the Duende?

CONQUISTADOR: Barbara Tusenbach.

BARBARA: Yes, El Tigre.

CONQUISTADOR: I have never been in a battle.

BARBARA: What?

CONQUISTADOR: I have never been out of Spain.

BARBARA: What?

CONQUISTADOR: I have never killed anyone.

BARBARA: What are you talking about?

CONQUISTADOR: I wander around the green countryside pretending. I pretend. I am not even married.

BARBARA: What the hell are you talking about?!

CONQUISTADOR: I'm pretending this right now.

BARBARA: Bullshit. Bullshit. This is the truest thing I've ever felt.

CONQUISTADOR: I'm pretending. You're not.

BARBARA: What does that mean?

CONQUISTADOR: I am not a conquistador.

(A screeching of tires up to a house. A beating on the front door.)

COP VOICE: Mrs. Tusenbach! Mrs. Tusenbach, this is the police! We have you surrounded. Open up, or we'll break down your door!

(Barbara looks at Conquistador. She takes his helmet off his head and puts in on hers. She takes his sword.)

COP VOICE: Mrs. Tusenbach, we know what you've done! Let us in!

(Barbara charges for the door with a terrible battle yell.)

END OF ACT I

ACT II

An interrogation room. Barbara sits across from Lawyer (Ancient). She is dressed in an orange numbered jumpsuit.

LAWYER: Mrs. Tusenbach. Let's talk about the carving knife.

BARBARA: What carving knife?

LAWYER: The one you used to attack the policemen at your door and stab your husband.

BARBARA: The Spanish sword?

LAWYER: No. The carving knife. What were you thinking when you picked it up?

BARBARA: The sword?

LAWYER: Sure, the carving knife.

BARBARA: I wasn't thinking.

LAWYER: Were you defending yourself?

BARBARA: I was attacking.

LAWYER: You were attacking your husband and the police.

BARBARA: I was fighting with Duende.

LAWYER: Is Duende the name of the Conquistador?

BARBARA: He's not really a Conquistador.

LAWYER: Let's talk about him.

BARBARA: Who the hell are you, anyway?

LAWYER: I'm your attorney. I introduced myself when I came in. Do you remember that?

BARBARA: Who can believe what anyone says when they introduce themselves?

LAWYER: Mrs. Tusenbach, is there a history of mental instability in your family?

BARBARA: No, my family is the only family in the world that acts completely rationally.

LAWYER: You should try to answer my questions cooperatively, Mrs. Tusenbach. I'm the one who might save you from a very long prison sentence. *(Beat.)*

BARBARA: I met him shortly after my husband of five years left me for some slut with a boob job. He was sitting on my sofa with his feet up. His funny metal boots on my coffee table. I was not attracted to him in the traditional sense.

LAWYER: You spoke to him.

BARBARA: It was easy.

LAWYER: Did you think there was anything odd about the situation?

BARBARA: I told him to take his metal boots off my coffee table.

LAWYER: Other than that.

BARBARA: His sword was bloody.

LAWYER: The sword you used to stab your husband and the—

BARBARA: Yes. It was bloody. *(To herself.)* How could it be bloody if he wasn't a conquistador? I saw blood.

LAWYER: Whose blood?

BARBARA: Mayan blood. Blood of the people he had slaughtered.

LAWYER: Uh-huh. Go on.

BARBARA: How could I have seen blood if what he said wasn't true?

(Lights switch to down right. Diversion stands there holding an orange.)

DIVERSION: Barbara always was a little, you know, out there. But she controlled it. She worked hard at the office. She was very good at talking to people on the phone and dealing with Escrow. But on her lunch breaks, you know, we would talk, I was her best friend— I am her best friend, and she would say things every once in a while. "I'm feeling restless." "John doesn't pay attention to me." She had this fantasy about Spain. It started two years ago. She saw a movie or something. She started buying books. Maps. She toyed with taking a Spanish class, but she didn't have time and John was very unsupportive of the whole thing. I don't blame her for stabbing him. He was a real bastard. She shouldn't be punished too harshly for that. I was more disturbed by the other stabbing. That poor man. He was just doing his job. *(She bites into the orange skin and lets the juice run down her chin. Lights flip over to the table.)*

BARBARA: Is that a one-way mirror?

LAWYER: Depends on which side you're on.

(Barbara stands and walks over to the implied mirror, behind the Lawyer. Lights illuminate what she sees in it— the Conquistador.)

LAWYER: What are you going to do? Make faces at them?

(Barbara ignores Lawyer. She studies the Conquistador. He is dressed like an Andalusian peasant. He mirrors her in a variety of gestures. Finally, their hands meet where the plane of the mirror would be. They lock fingers. The Lawyer watches, fascinated.)

LAWYER: Barbara?

(Conquistador pulls Barbara out of the scene. Only they are lit.)

BARBARA: Where are we?

CONQUISTADOR: Green fields. Windmills. Wild horses and deep bark trees far off.

(Barbara takes a moment to look around.)

BARBARA: It's beautiful. *(Beat.)* How did you get out of my living room?

CONQUISTADOR: White light.

(Barbara studies Conquistador.)

CONQUISTADOR: Are you angry with me?

BARBARA: *(laughs.)* Jesus, you aren't a Conquistador at all.

CONQUISTADOR: No.

BARBARA: Where did you get all the fancy armor?

CONQUISTADOR: I do not know. I only know I was in it when I met you. And I had things in my head that explained it.

BARBARA: Stories?

CONQUISTADOR: Yes.

BARBARA: You see this outfit I have on? I'm in prison. What do you make of that? You show up and tell me you're a killer and I get all inspired and stab my husband with a carving knife.

CONQUISTADOR: You stabbed him with my sword.

BARBARA: That's not what they say.

CONQUISTADOR: Who?

BARBARA: The Inquisition! What does it matter what anyone calls themselves.

CONQUISTADOR: You are angry.

BARBARA: Yes. No. I was. Now I'm just jaded and world-weary.

CONQUISTADOR: A shepherd.

BARBARA: What?

CONQUISTADOR: A shepherd.

(An Andalusian shepherd [Guitar Player] is lit. He carries a staff and a guitar slung over his shoulder, on his back. Barbara and Conquistador look at him.)

BARBARA: Jesus.

(Shepherd points to his mouth and shakes his head.)

CONQUISTADOR: He is mute.

BARBARA: He looks like John.

CONQUISTADOR: *(To Shepherd.)* She is not from around here.

BARBARA: What is this place?

CONQUISTADOR: Andalusia.

BARBARA: What is this place to you?

CONQUISTADOR: My home.

BARBARA: Spain.

CONQUISTADOR: Yes.

BARBARA: This is Spain?

CONQUISTADOR: Welcome.

(Shepherd hands off his staff to Conquistador and swings his guitar into playing position. He sings.)

SHEPHERD: Si mi corazón tuviera bierieritas e cristar, te asomaras y lo vieras gotas de sangre llorar.

(Silence. Shepherd swings his guitar back over his shoulder and takes his staff back from Conquistador. He walks off.)

BARBARA: I thought he was mute.

CONQUISTADOR: He is.

BARBARA: He has a very nice singing voice for a mute.

CONQUISTADOR: He sings the deep song.

BARBARA: It was charming.

CONQUISTADOR: Siguiriya.

BARBARA: I don't know Spanish.

CONQUISTADOR: "If my heart had windowpanes of glass, you'd look inside and see it crying drops of blood."

BARBARA: I'm feeling angry.

CONQUISTADOR: Why?

BARBARA: What the hell is going on here?

CONQUISTADOR: You are where you always wanted to be.

BARBARA: Stop. Why did I see blood on your sword if you didn't kill anyone?

CONQUISTADOR: It was not truly my sword.

BARBARA: What is your real name?

CONQUISTADOR: Pepe.

BARBARA: *(disgusted.)* God.

CONQUISTADOR: The discovery of the New World marked a major turning point in my life.

BARBARA: Excuse me?

CONQUISTADOR: Conquering. It is a great feeling.

BARBARA: Stop.

CONQUISTADOR: We go places and name them.

BARBARA: Stop. Why are you saying those things?

CONQUISTADOR: I said them before.

BARBARA: You're not a conquistador anymore.

CONQUISTADOR: The heart of Spain is gold.

BARBARA: Who the fuck are you?

CONQUISTADOR: It is a wind that blows over the heads of the dead.

BARBARA: What?

CONQUISTADOR: Duende.

BARBARA: What the fuck is Duende?

CONQUISTADOR: Dónde está el duende?

(A Monk [Ancient] enters, dressed in a white robe and black scapular. New lighting, suggesting a church. The Monk gets into prayer position downstage. Barbara and Conquistador watch him.)

BARBARA: What happened?

CONQUISTADOR: Shhh. He is praying.

MONK: Dominus padre om.

Et spiritus sancti uno.

Duende, Duende, Duende.

Barbara, Barbara, Barbara.

BARBARA: What is this?

(Silence. Monk turns and looks at Barbara. Silence. He stands. He walks to her and places his hand over her heart. She is frozen.)

MONK: Dónde está el duende? What do you want?

(Silence. Barbara is in a trance.)

BARBARA: I want faces made of glass. No more soft lips or cheeks or baby smiles. I want sharp angles and gray lines. I want eyes like lifeless diamonds. I want to live touching nothing. I want to float invisible.

(Monk holds out his arms, Christlike. Conquistador walks to him and disrobes him. Underneath his robe, Monk is Lawyer. Lights shift back to the way they were at the top of the act. Back in the little room with Barbara and Lawyer. Conquistador and the monk's robe are gone.)

LAWYER: Barbara?

(Barbara stares at Lawyer.)

LAWYER: Are you all right?

(Barbara laughs.)

BARBARA: Now who are you?

LAWYER: I'm your lawyer. I think you just had some sort of episode.

BARBARA: Several, actually.

LAWYER: You said some things.

BARBARA: I bet I did.

LAWYER: You said: faces made of glass. What does that mean?

BARBARA: If my heart had windowpanes of glass.

LAWYER: Barbara, I think the next step is to bring in a psychiatrist.

BARBARA: Will that be you, too?

LAWYER: I don't think we're going to have much trouble with the insanity plea.

BARBARA: What are all these pieces?

LAWYER: Pieces?

BARBARA: Monks and Mayans and Conquistadors.

LAWYER: Yes, I completely agree. I think perhaps our meeting is done for now.

BARBARA: What's next? You know? *Dónde está el duende?*

LAWYER: Absolutely. Nothing to worry about.

(Matador [John] enters with a flourish. Barbara collapses laughing.)

LAWYER: Yes. Keep laughing. That's wonderful. This is all on tape. Nothing to worry about at all.

(The Matador looks to be sizing up Barbara as if she were a bull. She starts to play the role, making her fingers into horns and brushing the ground with her foot. Lawyer watches.)

LAWYER: Beautiful. That's . . . amazing. Keep going, don't stop.

(Barbara charges Matador and gores him. Lights shift to illuminate Diversion, dressed as a Flamenco Dancer. She dances in silence for a few moments. Then speaks and dances at the same time.)

DIVERSION: The funny thing is: I know Spanish. I've read Lorca backwards and forwards. I took Flamenco classes at the gym. But that was a phase, you know? I got over it and settled down. Now I have a steady job and pets and all the comfortable amenities of American life. So I suppose, really, I was as discouraging as John when it came to Barbara's obsession. I wanted her to get over it. It only reminded me of a way I used to be. Young. How depressing. Younger. Than now. Now I see a shrink and pay my bills on time.

(Lights shift. Conquistador leads Barbara along a narrow cliff ledge.)

CONQUISTADOR: Careful. It is a great distance down from this cliff.

BARBARA: Where are we going?

CONQUISTADOR: To the valley. Over that stream. Through those woods.

BARBARA: What is our destination?

CONQUISTADOR: My home.

BARBARA: Your house.

CONQUISTADOR: We must get there before dark.

BARBARA: What happens after dark?

CONQUISTADOR: Wolves.

BARBARA: It's strange. You're nothing like you were, but it's still you.

CONQUISTADOR: We will also have to pass through a waterfall. Up ahead, beyond that ridge.

BARBARA: Do I seem different?

CONQUISTADOR: It is always hard to understand you.

BARBARA: Other than that.

CONQUISTADOR: Yes. You keep changing.

BARBARA: Are you sad that you aren't a Conquistador anymore?

CONQUISTADOR: A little. I am glad we could meet again.

BARBARA: Oh? Why is that?

CONQUISTADOR: You help me to understand myself.

BARBARA: Oh.

CONQUISTADOR: Come. We are nearly to the waterfall.

(They exit. Light to Diversion, no longer dancing, just fanning herself.)

DIVERSION: I used to watch her at her desk. She'd stare off into space, stare like she saw something there. And then she'd come to me with her latest map or picture, some story she found, some word. I would pretend I didn't know what the words were, pretend the fantasies she had didn't used to be my own. You reach a point where fantasizing like that is just embarrassing. When it's time to look at where you really are.

(She looks down at her fan. She walks off. Conquistador and Barbara enter. This is now Conquistador's home. A mat for sleeping, not much else.)

BARBARA: This is where you live?

CONQUISTADOR: Yes. *(Beat.)*

BARBARA: I like it.

CONQUISTADOR: It is not soft like your house.

BARBARA: That's fine.

CONQUISTADOR: Would you like to sit?

(Conquistador gestures. Barbara sits. She looks at him, he looks at her.)

Are you thirsty?

BARBARA: Yes.

CONQUISTADOR: Wait here.

(Conquistador disappears. She is alone.)

BARBARA: *(calling for him.)* El Tigre? Pepe?

(Conquistador appears with two clay cups full of mead and a rolled-up piece of parchment. He sets everything down and sits.)

CONQUISTADOR: I have something to show you.

(Conquistador unrolls the parchment. It is a drawing of a conquistador on horseback.)

BARBARA: A Conquistador. Did you draw that?

CONQUISTADOR: No. It was given to me. Do you want to hear the story?

BARBARA: Is it true? Never mind, that doesn't even matter. Tell me the story.

CONQUISTADOR: I was out in the fields.

BARBARA: The lush green countryside.

CONQUISTADOR: The fields of the farm. It was planting season.

BARBARA: Of course.

CONQUISTADOR: A shadow fell over me while I bent to the earth. I looked up to see a man dressed as I have never seen a man dressed.

(General [Ancient] appears. He is dressed in a white uniform, a purple sash, white gloves, medals on his chest, and sunglasses.)

CONQUISTADOR: I asked him who he was.

GENERAL: General Don Enrique Briz Armengol.

CONQUISTADOR: I asked him where he was from?

GENERAL: Tierra de los Muertos.

CONQUISTADOR: He held out this parchment for me to take. I stood and unrolled it. The sun glowed brown off the earth. I saw this. What is this?

GENERAL: Conquistador.

CONQUISTADOR: And he told me what that meant. He spoke of the New World. Of Savages. Of noble knights on horseback claiming the land from a people destined to be conquered. Of their ladies and their power. I asked him if he was one of them.

GENERAL: No. *(General walks away.)*

CONQUISTADOR: And then the sun grew big in the sky and his white clothes blinded my eyes. When I could see again, he was gone. I was left alone in the fields with this. When I returned home that night, I looked at it again. I studied it for hours. Sometimes I could hear the sound in my head of horses' hoofs stomping or of victory cries. I could hear fire crackling. I smelled smoke. And when I put my face close, I could see a shape carefully drawn on the helmet.

BARBARA: A tiger.

CONQUISTADOR: Yes.

BARBARA: I used to sit at my desk at work and make lists of cities. Spanish cities. Barcelona, Madrid, San Sebastían: I looked them up, collected pictures. I made a book of the pictures. The cathedrals, the rolling golden hills, people laughing and drinking, playing guitars, dancing flamenco, always lit by fire all around them; people living unafraid of anything, so full of passion and life and—

CONQUISTADOR: Duende!

BARBARA: Duende.

CONQUISTADOR: Burning coals.

BARBARA: Boiling blood.

CONQUISTADOR: Purpose.

BARBARA: Action.

CONQUISTADOR: In my guts.

BARBARA: Down my spine.

CONQUISTADOR: In my center.

BARBARA: In my soul. *(Pause.)* You said I helped you understand yourself. What did you mean? How did I help you?

CONQUISTADOR: You were a better Conquistador than I ever could be. You made me remember my true self. That is who I am now.

(They drink.)

BARBARA: You wanted to sleep with me. Was that as the Conquistador or as you? *(Silence.)* Don't be embarrassed.

CONQUISTADOR: I grew excited when I touched you.

BARBARA: Obviously. It excited me a little, too.

CONQUISTADOR: Truly?

BARBARA: A little. It also disturbed me. I haven't been touched by a man other than my husband in many years. And when he touched me, it wasn't the way that you touched me. Even though his hands were warm and yours were cold.

CONQUISTADOR: I have never been so bold with a woman.

BARBARA: Have you ever been with a woman? *(Silence.)* It's all right. This drink is good. What is it?

CONQUISTADOR: Mead.

BARBARA: You made it yourself, didn't you?

CONQUISTADOR: Yes.

(Barbara smiles.)

CONQUISTADOR: What is it? Why are you smiling?

BARBARA: I really like you.

(Silence. Barbara leans across and kisses Conquistador gently on the lips. She pulls back.)

BARBARA: Have you ever felt that?

(He bows his head.)

BARBARA: Did it feel good?

CONQUISTADOR: Yes.

BARBARA: You're shivering. Close your eyes.

(He does. She kisses him again, holding him to her. Diversion appears in a separate space in her Flamenco dress, slipping it off as she talks. Underneath she wears a simple white slip. Her tone reflects this.)

DIVERSION: It was so familiar. Her desire. It was something that I thought had died in me. That I had perhaps killed. And it was dangerous, I knew it was, to be near her, because what if that thing I killed had not died and came back and made me do . . . something like what she did? It would be so easy. To wake up one morning, take all the money out of the bank, tell Roman to go to hell, buy a plane ticket or a train ticket or just drive away, give up everything I'd decided was important. Find a beach somewhere, steal a horse, ride it along the waves, poor red sangria down my throat while I rode, pour it all over my face.

(She exits.)

BARBARA: Scratchy face.

CONQUISTADOR: What?

BARBARA: Your beard. Scratchy face. It's nice.

CONQUISTADOR: Thank you.

BARBARA: Do you know what to do next?

CONQUISTADOR: Next?

BARBARA: Touch me the way you touched me before.

(Conquistador does so. They are still.)

BARBARA: It's different.

(Conquistador withdraws his hand. Barbara takes it and puts it back where it was.)

BARBARA: It's better.

(Barbara pulls Conquistador down to make love. Diversion, in her slip, rides through on the back of a Horse [Guitar Player]. She surveys the landscape.

The Ancient appears across the stage with a bottle of sangria, holds it out to Diversion, who rides towards her unquestioningly, like in a dream. She grabs up the bottle and drinks as she rides around and off. Lights rise on Conquistador and Barbara, lying in bed together, entwined peacefully.)

BARBARA: How do you feel?

CONQUISTADOR: Uhhh . . .

BARBARA: Good. That's good. You're a man, that's how you're supposed to feel.

CONQUISTADOR: How did it feel to you?

BARBARA: Good. Thank you for asking. You're a wonderful lover.

CONQUISTADOR: I do not remember doing anything.

BARBARA: You responded to everything I did. You cared about me.

CONQUISTADOR: Barbara?

BARBARA: Yes.

CONQUISTADOR: Why did you do this?

BARBARA: Because I wanted to.

CONQUISTADOR: What do we do now?

BARBARA: We lie here like this. You hold me and I feel your warmth around me. We breathe together. We tell each other how lucky we are. We talk about anything, it doesn't matter what. We look into each other's eyes and find peace, amazing peace and relief. You tell me you love my lips. I tell you I love how your arms feel around me. We make plans for the day, or the night, or the next day. We make plans for our life together. We make so many plans.

CONQUISTADOR: You are crying. Are you sad?

BARBARA: No.

CONQUISTADOR: Your husband.

BARBARA: No, it's not him.

CONQUISTADOR: Your husband.

(Conquistador is looking at John, who stands near the bed, simply watching. Barbara follows Conquistador's gaze. John wears his blood-stained clothes. He is holding the Spanish sword. He and Barbara stare at each other.)

BARBARA: What are you doing here?

JOHN: I remember the way we started out. We used to go for long walks holding hands, swinging them. And then I would pull you to me and kiss you and the wind would blow your hair all over your face and I'd brush it away and kiss you again. And the first time we were naked together and you touched me and you pulled me into you and your lips parted like an O and you sighed so softly. And the first time you told me you loved me and I loved you. What is he doing here?

BARBARA: None of your business.

JOHN: Big muscles and no neck.

BARBARA: No.

JOHN: You replaced me with him.

BARBARA: You left me.

JOHN: I'm back.

BARBARA: You're dead.

(*John raises the sword.*)

BARBARA: What are you doing? What can you possibly do?

(*John quickly stabs Conquistador.*)

BARBARA: No! NO!

CONQUISTADOR: Barbara . . .

JOHN: Barbara . . .

(*Barbara grabs the sword away from John by the blade. She looks at Conquistador, who looks up at her. She looks at John, who sinks to his knees before her and dies. Barbara goes to and holds Conquistador. He is dying.*)

BARBARA: Please no, not you, no . . .

CONQUISTADOR: Barbara . . .

BARBARA: I'm right here, it's OK, you're fine.

CONQUISTADOR: My blood . . . I am dying.

BARBARA: No, you are not, this can't happen.

CONQUISTADOR: I am going quickly . . .

BARBARA: No, you can't die!

CONQUISTADOR: The heart of Spain . . .

BARBARA: No, no, no you don't . . .

CONQUISTADOR: Red and black and yellow . . .

BARBARA: Stay with me.

CONQUISTADOR: The New World, the new me . . .

BARBARA: Please don't leave me.

CONQUISTADOR: (*Suddenly very calm, knowing.*) Barbara.

(*She looks at him.*)

CONQUISTADOR: This is what I was made for. You have so much . . . (*He dies.*)

BARBARA: (*Weakly.*) Wait . . .

(*He's gone. She holds him. A deep drum pounds offstage. It starts into a rhythmic pattern building in intensity. Gradually, orange and red light rises upstage. In the light a figure can be made out—Diversion. She is naked [literally or gesturally] and holds a long piece of red fabric that she trails behind her. Barbara looks at her, cradling Conquistador. Diversion looks back at her. Barbara lays Conquistador down gently. She stands, not taking her eyes off Diversion. She walks towards her. Diversion suddenly runs at Barbara, the red cloth flying behind her. She reaches Barbara and starts a wild chaotic dance, using the red cloth in her movement to create swooping, billowing movement, enveloping Barbara. Lights and drumming are very loud. Chaos, bright and disorienting. Barbara stands at the center of it, overwhelmed.)*

(Blackout. Lights quickly rise tightly on the Ancient, sitting in a separate space, beating a lone drum with slow intensity. Barbara enters his space, reminiscent of the Conquistador's first encounter with Ancient. She stands before him.)

ANCIENT: Buenas noches.

BARBARA: Good evening.

ANCIENT: Noches.

BARBARA: Night.

ANCIENT: Sí.

BARBARA: Who are you?

(Ancient smiles.)

BARBARA: I don't understand who you are.

(The Ancient's smile disappears.)

BARBARA: I don't understand who I am.

(The Ancient nods.)

BARBARA: Can this just stop for second? Can we just hold still for a second?

ANCIENT: Sí.

(Stillness. Barbara looks around the stage. Lights have come up. Diversion, wrapped in the red cloth, now stands near the bodies of John and Conquistador.)

ANCIENT: Do you know who they are?

(Barbara nods.)

ANCIENT: Tell it.

(Barbara gathers her strength; she goes to John's body.)

BARBARA: This is my husband. His name was John. He played guitar. He used to kiss me on the back of my neck. He would part my hair and press his warm lips . . . here. He fell in love with another woman. He fell out of love with me. *(She takes this in and turns to the body of Conquistador.)* And this is the Conquistador. His name is Pepe. He kills people. He loves himself. He makes everything up and he makes his own liquor. I fell in love with him. I fell out of love with my husband.

(Ancient beats two heart pulses on his drum. Barbara turns. Diversion has moved to her side. Barbara looks at her.)

BARBARA: This is Diversion. My best friend, Diversion. She pretends she doesn't know. She pretends she dreamt it all. She killed her soul. This is her soul.

(Ancient beats another heart pulse. Barbara looks at him.)

BARBARA: This is a textbook. This is the man in charge. This is a lunatic. This is everything I know. This is madness.

(Ancient beats the drum again. Barbara becomes aware of the audience. She takes us in.)

BARBARA: This is a woman alone in her living room. This is a human being alone. *(Silence. Barbara breathes.)* Can I just be alone? Please? Please.

(Barbara closes her eyes. The Ancient starts a drum roll. Diversion disappears. Conquistador and John rise. They take off the bed together. They bring in the sofa from Act I together and set it where it was. They take off the chairs. They bring on the coffee table. Barbara keeps her eyes shut. They all leave. Barbara is alone in her living room. Silence. She looks around. She sits on the sofa. She puts her feet up on the coffee table. She breathes. A doorbell. Silence.)

BARBARA: Come in.

(Diversion enters, dressed normally.)

DIVERSION: Hi.

BARBARA: Hi.

DIVERSION: Are you all right?

BARBARA: Yeah. Sit down here by me.

(Diversion does so.)

BARBARA: Put your feet up on the table.

(Diversion does so.)

DIVERSION: Barbara. Did something happen?

BARBARA: John left.

DIVERSION: What?

BARBARA: John left me for some woman he fell in love with.

DIVERSION: Barbara . . .

BARBARA: It's all right.

DIVERSION: All right? He left you. Aren't you devastated?

BARBARA: No.

DIVERSION: But you're all alone. It's terrible.

BARBARA: I'm going to take a trip.

DIVERSION: Spain?

BARBARA: Yes.

DIVERSION: You don't speak Spanish.

BARBARA: I'll learn.

(Blackout.)

END OF PLAY

UNCONDITIONAL

Brett C. Leonard

PLAYWRIGHT'S BIOGRAPHY

Brett C. Leonard has been a LAByrinth Theater Company member since 2003. He is the associate artistic director of London's Shotgun Theatre and the recipient of the 2008 Daryl Roth Creative Spirit Award. His playwriting credits include *Unconditional* (LAByrinth at The Public, directed by Mark Wing-Davey; Toronto's Column 13 Company), *Guinea Pig Solo* (LAByrinth/Public—the first coproduction; Chicago's Chopin Theater/Collaboraction: *Chicago Tribune's* Top 10 of 2005; and Berlin Arts Festival's 50th Anniversary at the House of World Culture), *Roger and Vanessa* (London's Latchmere Theatre 503, directed by Robert Delamere; L.A.'s Actors' Gang; Sydney's Tap Gallery), and *Scotch and Water* (London's New Company, Critics' Choice, *Time Out London*). Short plays: *Bobo an' Spyder . . .* (NY's Production Company/Australia Project, directed by Bob Glaudini), *Beauty and Light* (Chicago's Collaboraction Sketchbook '05*)*, and *Interrogation* (Sketchbook '06). Leonard's debut feature film *Jailbait*, starring Michael Pitt and Stephen Adly Guirgis, premiered at the Tribeca Film Festival, won both the Grand Jury Prize and Emerging Filmmaker Award at the Lake Placid Film Festival and is available on Warner Brothers' DVD. Leonard is currently adapting *Unconditional* for the screen for Cooper's Town Productions and Overture Films.

ORIGINAL PRODUCTION

Unconditional was produced by LAByrinth Theater Company and directed by Mark Wing-Davey with John Ortiz, artistic director; Philip Seymour Hoffman, coartistic director; and John Gould Rubin, coartistic director and executive director. It opened at the The Public Theater in New York. First preview was on February 10 and opened on February 18 with the following cast and crew:

CAST

SPIKE . . . . Chris Chalk
MISSY . . . . Anna Chlumsky
LOTTY . . . . Saidah Arrika Ekulona
GARY . . . . Kevin Geer
DANIEL . . . . .Trevor Long
JESSICA . . . . Elizabeth Rodriguez
TRACY . . . . Yolonda Ross
KEITH . . . . John Doman
NEWTON . . . . Isiah Whitlock, Jr.

Scenic Design	Mark Wendland
Costume Design	Mimi O'Donnell
Lighting Design	Japhy Weideman
Sound Design	Bart Fasbender
Production Stage Manager	Libby Steiner
Assistant Stage Manager	Libby Unsworth
Casting	Judy Bowman Casting

CHARACTERS

SPIKE: African American, midtwenties
MISSY: white, early twenties
LOTTY: African American, forties
GARY: white, late forties to early fifties
DANIEL BREEMS: white, thirty-five
JESSICA: Nuyorican, thirties
TRACY: African American, thirties
KEITH L. MOORE: white, late forties to early fifties
NEWTON COLLIER: African American, forty-nine

SETTING

New York City.

TIME

The present.

UNCONDITIONAL

ACT I
SCENE 1

A dark room. The lights should reveal as little as possible—only the necessary information. Willie King's "Terrorized" is heard throughout. Newton Collier, forty-nine, African American, is sitting in an office chair. There's a burning cigarette in his hand. On the back of the chair is a canvas shoulder bag. Under a desk is a green metal wastebasket.

In front of Newton, with his back to the audience, is an unrecognizable white man, standing on a chair. His feet and legs are tied with tape. His arms are taped behind his back. His mouth is gagged and covered. Around his neck is a noose, attached to an overhead beam. The white man squirms a bit, on and off, occasionally trying to speak, yell, beg. Newton calmly smokes while staring at the white man. Eventually, Newton stands. Pause.

He drops his cigarette. He reaches for something in the darkness. He slowly, calmly unfolds a Confederate battle flag, showing it to the white man. He reaches down and grabs the green metal wastebasket. He approaches the white man, stops three or four steps short, puts the wastebasket on the ground. He holds the Confederate flag with one hand, and with the other he pulls a Zippo lighter out of his pants pocket. He lights the Zippo. Pause. He sets the flag on fire. He puts the Zippo back in his pocket and holds the flag as it burns. He drops the flag into the wastebasket where it continues to burn. He walks back to the chair and removes a 9-mm pistol from the canvas shoulder bag. He approaches the slightly squirming, entirely terrified white man. He stops. Pause.

He points the gun at the white man's face. Pause.

He lowers the gun to his side. Pause.

He raises the gun once again, pointing it at the white man's face. He cocks the gun. Pause.

He lowers the gun. He moves to the side and points the gun at the side of the white man's head. He puts the barrel up against the white man's temple. He holds it there. He presses the barrel into the side of the white man's head. The white man struggles to stay as still and calm as possible. The Confederate flag continues to burn. Willie King continues to sing. His guitar continues to wail. Newton moves to the other side. He presses the barrel against the white man's temple. Pause.

He removes it. He uncocks the gun and puts it in his waistband, behind his back. He takes a pack of Winstons from his shirt pocket, removes a cigarette, returns the pack to his pocket, lights the cigarette with his Zippo. He puts the Zippo back in his pocket. He smokes. The flag burns. Willie King sings.

He turns and knocks the chair out from under the white man. The white man dangles. Blackout/silence.

SCENE 2

A bar. Keith L. Moore, late forties to early fifties, Caucasian, sits on a bar stool with his fifth gin and tonic, but doesn't sound or appear drunk. The only other customer at the bar, four bar stools between them, is Lotty, forties, African American. She's had a few herself. And smokes Virginia Slims, using a coffee mug as an ashtray. She doesn't look in Keith's direction. Never. Not a glance. It's as though she doesn't hear a word.

KEITH: So this one night a few years back, I'm all fucked up at this bar after a blowout at the happy home. I go by myself, as I'm wont to do, an' proceed ta get good 'n' loaded, nice 'n' pickled just right—they finally kick me out. It's a beautiful night for a drive. A nice drive home ta lovely Teaneck, New Jersey, where I was livin' at this time. And I'm INTENTIONALLY swerving all over the road, OK?, from the far left emergency lane ta the far right shoulder, back 'n' forth, for whatever reason—it was a nice night. I run outta gas. Luckily, I'm on the right hand a' my swerves so I just sorta roll easylike onta the shoulder—let the car come to a stop. I'm fucked. I'm six sheets ta the wind, I'm outta gas, I spent my last nickel on a goodnight shot a' Goldschlagger, and I left the house in a huff—without my wallet, my driver's license, without a credit card, nada. No ID. So I decide ta PUSH it. I'm gonna PUSH the car home. I'm like eight miles away. *(Beat.)* Look, at least you could try ta PRETEND you're listening. *(Beat.)* You're gonna love this part, get a big kick outta it. So I'm pushing my Pontiac Bonneville eight miles home ta Teaneck, New Jersey. I got the car door open, my right hand's on the steering wheel, my left on the frame a' the car—ya know, where the door connects with the body—an' I'm makin' like . . . like fuckin' ZERO progress, I'm sweatin' like a Zulu, and what happens but a fuckin' COP pulls over. A police officer, no partner with 'm. Nice enough guy—young guy, white guy, comes at me with no attitude or nothin', but still . . . right? I'm drunk, I don't have ID, he's sober, he has a GUN, I've been in better situations. He comes over very helpful-like. He's uh . . . this PARTICULAR officer, he's the kind fancies himself a bit of a Good Samaritan. He does what he does to protect you and protect me—to protect and serve our children—to make our streets safe—it's got nothin' ta do with the fact he dropped outta high school at fifteen, bought his GED on the Internet, and failed his firefighters' physical on six separate occasions. He's altruistic. He's an American hero. "May I help you, sir?" he asks. "No thank you, kind officer, but it's wonderful of you to take the time to care." "Are you sure? Maybe I could give you a lift or call a tow truck?" "Again I thank you, your parents must beam with pride, but I'd hate to imagine at this very moment, while others are being carjacked, beaten, and raped, your services would be wasted on a drunk trying to push his car home." "Have you been drinking, sir?" "That's how I got drunk, yes." You still with me, sweetheart? *(Beat.)* Sweetheart? *(No response.)*

So he says, "I want you to think this through before you answer . . . are you admitting to me, right now, that you have been driving this vehicle while under the influence of alcohol?" "No sir. My FATHER was a drunk driver. My MOTHER was a mother AGAINST drunk drivers. Drunk driving is simply not a part of my life. And HENCE, I decided to PUSH the car home to AVOID driving drunk—and possibly killing any late night jaywalkers." *(Beat.)* I spent three days in the can before my wife would bail me out. *(He sips his drink. He lights a Newport. He uses a coffee mug as an ashtray.)*

Ya know . . . even more than the fact that you're black—to be honest—it's the fact that you're not white. I do not like me the white women. Anything NON-white really'll usually do me the trick. Though I never really been a big fan a' Asians either—ya'd think I would—virtually hairless, nice skin—just never really done it. But definitely not white. White men or white women—I don't like 'em. I'm white. I'm extremely white. I have freckles and skin tags. I had melanoma cancer right here on my chest. But I got a face like Jude Law. Feel free ta glance over at any time. *(No response.)*

I believe all actions have consequences. I believe all consequences should be ignored if they're gonna prevent us taking action in the first place. *(Beat.)*

If I were to offer to buy you a drink, what would be your response? What if I offered ta take you home? What if I offered ta guarantee you the greatest fuck you ever had? And if in addition, I promised never ta tell another living soul anything about it? You're wearing a wedding ring. If you looked over you'd notice I'm wearing one too. But your husband isn't with you. My wife hasn't been with me in over six months. Sexually it's been longer. *(Beat.)*

You're not a kid anymore. You have grace and maturity. The way you hold and light your Virginia Slims. The way you cross your beautiful legs. The way you know exactly how far your skirt hikes when you do it. A woman your age knows what she wants, and what works best for her in the bedroom. She's not ashamed or embarrassed to ask for it. I'm no kid myself—I'm man enough to make good on your requests. I can smell your perfume from here. Sitting in a shithole like this at almost three o'clock in the morning, all alone, wearing that kind of perfume. *(Beat.)*

We could remain here as we are, removed from one another, four bar stools between us, lying to ourselves why we're here. Or we could take a shot, be honest, and make each other feel less alone in the world. Maybe we'll feel like assholes tomorrow, sure, but for tonight? I'm curious ta find out. I'm right here. I'm gonna remain right here 'til you decide ta leave with me or Charlie throws me out. And if while you're deciding, you decide you'd like that drink, the offer still stands. I got money. *(Beat.)*

I'm Keith. Maybe later you'll let me know who you are.

(Keith looks away. He takes a sip of his drink. He smokes. He stares straight ahead. Lotty continues to nurse her drink. She smokes. She looks over at Keith. She looks straight ahead once again. Four bar stools between them.)

SCENE 3

Studio apartment. Spike, midtwenties, African American, and his goth girl-friend, Missy, early twenties, Caucasian. She playfully shakes a gift-wrapped box near her ear in an attempt to figure out what's inside.

MISSY: A Cadillac Escalade?
SPIKE: No.
MISSY: A home in the Hamptons?
SPIKE: No.
MISSY: Marilyn Manson tickets?
SPIKE: Warmer.
MISSY: An engagement ring?

SPIKE: Much colder.

MISSY: *(Tossing the box to him.)* Fuck you.

SPIKE: After you open it, in the ass. *(He tosses the box back to her.)*

MISSY: Mmmm . . . *(She shakes the box near her ear once again.)* A thousand-gigabyte iPod, a hundred-inch plasma flatscreen, a Blackberry, a subscription to *Blender*—I give up . . . *(She rips open the package: A three-quarter length black vinyl jacket with a hood.)* Oh fist me baby, it's beautiful!

SPIKE: I saw that shit, soon as I saw it I was like, "nigga, that's my girl right there, nigga."

MISSY: *(While taking off her clothes.)* Dude, it's awesome.

SPIKE: Shit jumped at me, gotchyour name all over that shit.

MISSY: It's expensive though baby, isn't it? *(Missy continues to strip down to skimpy bra, panties, and her knee-high black boots.)*

SPIKE: Expensive, man, fuck the cost, fuck the consequences—this what love's all about, baby.

MISSY: *(Missy models her new coat.)* Whaddaya think?

SPIKE: *(Rubbing his crotch over his baggy jeans.)* Mmm, I think some'ns happenin' ta King Cobra.

(She runs over and jumps onto his lap, her legs straddling his. They kiss. They stop.)

SPIKE: Happy Birthday, baby.

(She smacks him across the face.)

MISSY: Sing it, bitch. Sing me my fuckin' birthday song!

(She smacks him again. He wraps his hands around her neck and begins to choke her.)

MISSY: Fuck yeah, choke me! Sing it motherfucker, sing!! . . .

SPIKE: *(Sings.)* Happy Birthday to you . . .

MISSY: . . . yeah . . .

SPIKE: . . . Happy Birthday to you . . .

(She spits in his face.)

SPIKE: . . . Happy Birthday, my Missy . . .

(She slaps him. He spits in her face.)

MISSY: Fuck yeah!

SPIKE: Happy Birthday to you.

(She pinches his nipples really hard.)

SPIKE: Mmmphh . . .

MISSY: Yeah . . .

(She pumps her hips faster, he pumps his.)

SPIKE: . . . I love you . . .
  (She spits in his face.)
SPIKE: . . . I love you . . .
  (She slaps him.)
  (Blackout.)

SCENE 4

A diner. Tracie, thirties, African American, and Jessica, thirties, Nuyorican. Coffees and chef salads.

JESSICA: He raises a finger ta you again, ya hit him with a small appliance ta the side of his fuckin' skull—tell'm run himself into a concrete wall next time he's lookin' for contact. You are nobody's doormat, Tracie—you're not his slave, you're not his geisha, you're not a nanny for the kids— you're his goddamn WIFE. I need more coffee. *(Looking for the waitress, then spotting her.)* Lookit this bitch—she out on a cigarette break—you're not eating? *(Sticking her fork into Tracie's salad.)* You gotta eat. *(She eats.)* How you gonna kick the side a' your man's head in if ya got no protein? I hate juss cuz I ask for dressing on the side, that don't mean I only want a teaspoon of it. How's yours, you gonna use yours? . . . *(Jessica grabs Tracie's dressing and pours it over her own salad, but never stops talking.)* . . . Every time they do this, and by the way—don't think it's coincidence you're black, I'm Puerto Rican—it's a blatant attempt at a subliminal obesity, heart-disease, sickle-cell anemia thing—*(To waitress, who's not in earshot.)* Cunt. *(To Tracie.)* Look, there's two kindsa men in this world— Good Men who are Bad Fucks, and Bad Men who're Good Fucks—an' other mothafuckers wouldn't know a good fuck if ya bent 'em over an' fucked 'em in the ass. But sometimes that's exactly what ya gotta do with these limp dicks—ya gotta take CHARGE, that's that. You're in a place—we've all been there—to the "Men are a buncha selfish fuckin' scumbags" place. Their problems are bigger'n yours, their complaints are more valid . . . *(As she simulates jerking off with the fork.)* . . . Blah-blah-blah . . . Fuck 'em in the mouth. He hits ya again, ya hit 'm back, that's that. This dressing sucks. This diner sucks. You shouldn't a' waited three months to tell me this, Trace, I'm your best friend. You wait cuz, why?, cuz you feel sorry for him?, he broke down in tears? Fuck him, he should cry. *(Spots waitress reentering.)* Here go this bitch now—

lookit'r—she walk like she got a ironing board stuck up her ass. *(To waitress.)* 'Scuse me—yo!—Ironing Board—we need more coffee.

SCENE 5

An office. Behind a desk sits Daniel Breems, thirty-five, Caucasian, on the phone.

DANIEL: *(Into phone.)* As much as the next guy, right. *(Laughs.)* Exactly, hummina-hummina. *(laughs.)* If it's not one thing it's another—just lookit the Japanese. *(Beat.)* Like a boomerang—ooo—watch yourself. *(Laughs.)* *(Newton enters, politely informing Daniel of his presence. Daniel motions for Newton to come in and have a seat. Newton does.)*

DANIEL: Right, exactly, or "what?", I hear ya. Look, I gotta run, man—no, yeah, no I will, no doubt. No doubt. I look forward to it. *(Laughs.)* OK, yeah, bye-bye. *(He hangs up.)* Sorry, I . . . Thanks for coming.

NEWTON: You asked ta see me. *(Beat.)*

DANIEL: You might wanna get the door.

(Newton looks to the open door.)

DANIEL: We won't be long I don't think, but . . . I'd prefer we did this in private.

(Newton hesitates, then goes to the door, shuts it, and returns halfway as:)

DANIEL: I called you in here rather than . . . I wanted to speak to you, one-on-one. Man-to-man. Have a seat.

NEWTON: *(Sitting.)* You're makin' me nervous, Mister Breems.

DANIEL: Daniel.

NEWTON: You're makin' me nervous, Daniel.

(Daniel lifts a manila envelope off his desk and holds it out to Newton.)

DANIEL: I'm sorry.

NEWTON: What is it?

DANIEL: It came from headquarters in Tulsa. It wasn't my call.

NEWTON: Tulsa?

DANIEL: In Oklahoma.

NEWTON: I know where it is.

DANIEL: Of course.

(Newton takes the envelope. As he opens it and reads the enclosed typewritten document.)

DANIEL: Personally, I've been happy with your work and feel you've been a valuable asset to . . .

NEWTON: . . . You've been here three months.

DANIEL: And what I've seen in those three months, my observations, I've . . .

NEWTON: . . . I've been here twenny-five years.

DANIEL: I know.

NEWTON: You know?

DANIEL: You've been here close to twenny-five years.

NEWTON: Twenty-five, Mister Breems . . .

DANIEL: . . . Daniel.

NEWTON: I'm almost fifty years old. How old are you?

DANIEL: I told you it wasn't my call.

NEWTON: How old are you? Please.

DANIEL: I work in Human Resources, Mister Collier.

NEWTON: Newton.

DANIEL: Newton.

NEWTON: Yes.

DANIEL: I'm just the messenger.

NEWTON: Your message sucks.

DANIEL: I agree.

NEWTON: You agree?

DANIEL: I agree.

(Beat. Newton once again looks at the document.)

NEWTON: Tulsa, Oklahoma. Shit. *(He tosses the envelope and document onto the desk.)* Why a New York City company got headquarters in Oklahoma in the first place?

DANIEL: There's a few—there's Fort Worth, Boston . . .

NEWTON: . . . It was rhetorical.

DANIEL: Look, Newton, if there's anything I can do . . .

NEWTON: . . . How about saving me my job?

DANIEL: I meant with regards to references or a letter of recommendation.

NEWTON: I work in HR, too, Mister Breems.

DANIEL: I know. *(Beat.)* I know. *(Beat.)* The layoffs are severe. There're over thirty-five hundred. More than a hundred an' fifty from the New York office alone. I'm sorry. If there's anything I can do.

NEWTON: This is about my pension, isn't it?

DANIEL: I don't know.

NEWTON: Oh, come on now, Breems, you may be the messenger, but I'm three months short a' turnin' fifty, I'm workin' here twenty-five years next month. Twenny-five an' fifty gets me my pension in full. Short a' twenny-five, short a' fifty? I get flat shit. This about money, Mister Breems, you know like I know.

DANIEL: Of course it's about money—I'm gonna have men and women comin' in an' outta here all day, all week, givin' everyone the same shit news.

NEWTON: And how many others are comin' up on collecting in full? Bein' cut short one month one end, three months the other? How many a' the thirty-five hundred just happen ta be black?

DANIEL: Is it about race or money, Mister Collier?

NEWTON: How do you differentiate between the two?

DANIEL: Mister Collier . . .

NEWTON: . . . How many are bein' robbed short a their pensions and what's the percentage that are black?

DANIEL: I'll check if you'd like.

NEWTON: Yeah, I'd like! *(Beat.)* I'd like. *(Beat.)* I'm sorry I raised my voice.

DANIEL: It's OK. I'm sorry I'm the bearer of such bad news.

NEWTON: Yeah. Thanks.

(Daniel extends his hand. They shake. Newton takes the envelope, turns, and heads for the door.)

DANIEL: I'm thirty-five years old.

(Newton stops, turns to face Daniel.)

NEWTON: Thirty-five. You're thirty-five an' I got two daughters I gotta put through college on no pension. This letter says I got two weeks ta clear my office an' get my things. I'm gonna ignore it. I'm gonna be here on my fiftieth birthday, Mister Breems. I'm gonna blow out fifty-one candles, one for good luck. I'll see you around. Thanks for the news.

(Newton exits.)

SCENE 6

Starbucks on 125th. Over coffee: Jessica and Tracie.

JESSICA: Every bully in the world's a big fat pussy underneath. At elementary school when I was growin' up there was this Italian bully kid named Ronnie Mancini who useta beat the shit outta every kid on the playground. The cafeteria, the classrooms, it didn't matter ta this little prick. So one day, there's this kid named Bruce Tompkinson—nerdy, red hair, freckles, got braces on his teeth an' he's walkin' with those whaddaya call—those two metal walker crutch-type things with the metal arm braces. Totally atrophied legs, all fucked-up, skinny like two chopsticks, but loose—not chopsticks, like a coupla lo-mein noodles, and his feet all contorted an' twisted-up-crooked an' shit, draggin' all behind him an' shit, and he's wearin' this Cub Scout uniform with lil' tassles an' ribbons on it—lil' yellow tassles an' pleated shorts, yo, this the Bronx nineteen-eighty-two— so this Ronnie Mancini, this Guinea bully kid, he comes up to'm one day—this gotta be, what, fourth-fifth grade maybe—he's already terrorized the whole fuckin' neighborhood since kindergarten—both his uncles an' ol' man are Made Men on Arthur Avenue, blah-blah-blah—how's your coffee?—my shit's always cold in this place—they put a Starbucks in Harlem it's like "fuck 'em, them niggas don't know from coffee." So this Ronnie the Dago, he walks over ta lil' crippled Brucie Tompkinson an' he steals one a' his metal walker thingies, Brucie goes down, starts crawlin' towards this chain-link fence—Ronnie Mancini meanwhile he's limpin' around all retarded-like, makin' fun a' poor lil' Brucie. Nobody ELSE'S laughin', but Ronnie Mancini can't fuckin' STOP laughin'— limpin' around, feet draggin' all over the place—makin' fun a' the physically impaired—totally fucked up—then Brucie, both arms grabbin' hold a' the fence, his little crutch danglin'—he comes sneakin', CREEPIN', like a horror movie Zombie with flaming red hair, and outta nowhere—outta fuckin' NOWHERE—with some shit he musta learned in the Cub Scouts, he takes the OTHER crutch-thing an' cracks the shit outta Ronnie right to his bully-wop-dago-fuck-head—whack—right ta the temple—blood splurtin' all over the place—NOW the other kids start laughin'—but here's the thing . . . Ronnie Mancini? This bully bitch never shows his face around school ever again—never—that's that. One lil' crack ta the side a' the brain from a redheaded cripple retarded kid an' the biggest bully in the Bronx was a bully no more. One blow, Trace— one shot.

SCENE 7

Keith's bedroom. Keith and Lotty are in bed. Lotty's head is on his chest; her eyes are closed.

KEITH: Lotty? Lotty? Naughty Lotty?
    (She snuggles closer, eyes shut.)
KEITH: I, uh . . . Sweetheart? Can you hear me? Are you sleeping? Sweetheart?
    (Beat.) I have chlamydia. You hear? *(Beat.)* I lied when I told you I had

money. *(Beat.)* I like cock. *(Beat.)* I'm still in love with my wife. All right, c'mon, let's go, c'mon—time ta get up. *(He removes her head from his chest.)*

LOTTY: What the fuck?

KEITH: I got a lotta shit I gotta do, I got a full day . . .

LOTTY: . . . So, I got shit too.

KEITH: Terrific, we have lots in common, now let's go.

LOTTY: What kind of asshole are you?

KEITH: The following morning kind, I'm sure I'm not your first.

LOTTY: No, but you're the biggest.

KEITH: Maybe you're right, let's go.

LOTTY: I know I'm right—you don't gotta confirm it for me. I was just tryin' ta get a lil' more sleep, I wasn't tryin' ta fuckin' move in with you.

KEITH: This is the part I was talkin' about, you were warned.

LOTTY: What part?

KEITH: In the bar. The part about we'll feel better at night, but come mornin' we'll feel like a coupla assholes.

LOTTY: I don't feel like an asshole.

KEITH: This's supposed ta be a one-night stand, what the fuck're we arguin' about? C'mere, gimme a kiss.

LOTTY: Fuck off.

KEITH: Gimme a big, wet, sloppy one.

LOTTY: I haven't brushed my teeth.

KEITH: The natural odors of a natural woman.

LOTTY: Where's your wife, Keith?

KEITH: Why, where's the lil' hubby waitin' for you? At home, on a business trip, the trunk a' your car, maybe?

LOTTY: He's not WAITING for me anywhere—wherever he's at that's just where he happens ta be.

KEITH: C'mon—I haven't brushed my teeth either.

LOTTY: I didn't wanna say nothin', I know.

KEITH: So you gonna come kiss me or not?

LOTTY: No.

KEITH: No?

LOTTY: No. *(Beat.)*

KEITH: All right, then. OK.

LOTTY: OK, what?

KEITH: We'll do it again sometime.

LOTTY: What gives you that idea?

KEITH: Maybe your fingernails still stuck in my back.

LOTTY: Don't flatter yourself.

KEITH: It's more honest than tryin' ta flatter you, sweetheart.

LOTTY: That right?

KEITH: That's correct.

LOTTY: You're a very selfish fuck, Keith.

KEITH: I got money if ya need me ta call ya a cab—so long as you don't live in Newark, or too far up in the Bronx.

LOTTY: Your wife was lucky ta leave you—you're an asshole.

KEITH: You're a forty-plus-year-old black woman with a pussy the size a' the Panama Canal, you shouldn't be insulting anyone . . .

LOTTY: . . . Comin' from you?! . . .

KEITH: . . . And my WIFE, by the way, isn't LUCKY! You're not LUCKY, I'm not LUCKY, who the fuck do you know that's LUCKY?! All I wanted was ta try an' make you feel a little better for a little while. I know you were able ta do that for me and I thank you, it was nice. And now, here we are in the guilt-ridden, self-loathing ugly part. I'm sorry I insulted you and your pussy—I happen ta like them both—and if there IS a touch a' blame to be had for the occasional slippage, I'll take it, fine, I got a German-Irish dick—but I thought we were more than physically compatible and I had a very lovely time. In addition, I also happen to think you're a very beautiful woman on the OUTSIDE of your vagina as well. And despite the fact that I consider myself LUCKY for the two of us having met, as nice as it was, as nice as you are . . . you're not my wife, I'm not your husband, besides that little fucked-up fact, it was great ta meet you. *(Beat.)* Are you sure I can't give you something for your cab?

LOTTY: I don't live in Newark, Keith. I don't live in the Bronx, either. I don't live in Bed-Stuy, I don't live in Harlem. I live in Westchester, in a mansion, with a half-Olympic-size swimming pool, a twelve-person jacuzzi, and a Wimbledon grass tennis court I've never stepped foot on. I don't NEED your money—but I'm gonna take it—I had ta put up lissenin' ta your bullshit all night an' all morning and believe me, my physical experience was less enjoyable than yours. Gimme a hundred dollars, I ain't takin' no yellow, I'm takin' a Limo Town Car—yellow cabs are for low-rent mothafuckers like you.

SCENE 8

Spike and Missy's studio apartment.

SPIKE: *(Offstage.)* Baby, I'm sorry, it was a mistake, listen.
(*Missy enters—desperate, frantic, out of control. She grabs a piece of aluminum foil and glass pipe. She begins to scrape the foil, trying unsuccessfully to loosen nonexistent meth residue. She unsuccessfully tries to get high, smoking nothing. Spike enters, the vinyl coat in his hand.*)
SPIKE: I love you. I said I love you!! I'm sorry. Fuckin' sorry!! Baby!! *(He grabs her shoulders.)* Baby, Relax!
MISSY: Fuck off!
(*She runs off, exiting. He follows after.*)
SPIKE: I had shit on my mind! *(He exits.)* Happy-fuckin'-birthday!
(*Blackout.*)

SCENE 9

A home office. Gary, late forties, early fifties, Caucasian, on the computer. Lotty enters, dressed as we saw her at Keith's. She stands in the doorway, looking across the room at her husband. Gary glances at her—then goes back to his computer.

LOTTY: Did they get off to school OK?
(*No response.*)
LOTTY: Did you take them or are we supposed to pick them up?
(*No response.*)
LOTTY: *(Growing annoyed.)* Did TINA take them or did you?
(*No response.*)
LOTTY: Grow up. *(She turns to exit but is stopped with:)*
GARY: Call your mother.
LOTTY: Mmph?
GARY: Call your mother.
LOTTY: Is everything all right?
GARY: I'm sure she's fine.
LOTTY: Well, wha'd she say?
GARY: When?

LOTTY: When she called.

GARY: I told you to call HER, I didn't say she called you. Call her and tell her she was right. Tell her you married the wrong man.

LOTTY: Oh, you're so fuckin' dramatic.

GARY: Am I? Am I the dramatic one, dollface? Little Miss Thang? Little Miss . . .

(She calmly flips him off and exits.)

GARY: . . . I'm not the one who stayed out all night like a two-dollar whore without a phone call!! I'm the one who drove the kids ta school, Dollface! Love of my life! MY "BEST FRIEND"! I'M THE ONE WHO FUCKIN' STAYED HOME WORRYING WHETHER YOU WERE FUCKIN' DEAD OR FUCKIN' ALIVE!!!

SCENE 10

A living room. Newton sits in the dark on his well-worn easy chair. In one hand is a burning cigarette, in the other is a stiff drink. Silence. Tracie enters. Pause. She approaches from behind. Pause. She kisses the top of his head. He doesn't respond or react. Pause. He takes a sip of his drink. She walks around, in front of him. She sits on the footstool. Long pause.

NEWTON: I put the girls ta sleep about an hour ago. We had pizza for dinner. *(Pause.)*

TRACIE: Are you OK? *(Beat.)* Baby? *(pause.)* Why are you sitting in the dark for? Mmmph? *(She turns on the lamp. Beat.)* Baby? *(pause.)* It's gonna be OK. *(Pause.)* C'mon, let's get you to bed.

(She tries to take the drink from his hand. He forcefully pulls it back.)

NEWTON: I'm not finished! *(Long pause.)* I gave them mothafuckers twenny-five years of my life. *(Pause.)* Why don't you go in by yourself. *(Beat.)* Go on. *(Beat.)* I'll be in in a minute.

(Newton turns off the lamp. Pause. Tracie gets up. She goes to kiss him on the top of his head. He pulls away. Pause. She moves toward the bedroom.)

NEWTON: Trace?

(She stops. Newton continues to stare straight ahead. Pause.)

NEWTON: I'm sorry.

(Tracie remains—watching her husband. Newton remains—seated, staring out, in semidarkness.)

SCENE 11

Jessica's apartment. Jessica is alone in bed, under the covers. With a remote control she slowly flips channels on her TV. Flip. Pause. Flip. Pause. Flip. Pause. Flip. Pause. She turns off the TV and puts the remote on the bedside table. She puts a retainer in her mouth. She puts her head on the pillow. She turns off her bedside lamp. Blackout.

SCENE 12

Keith's apartment. Keith, seated at a glass dining table, counts stacks of money. Each stack is bound by a rubber band. Beneath each rubber band is a small piece of yellow legal-pad paper with a hand-printed name and a dollar figure. In the middle of the room Spike practices his golf swing with a 6-iron.

SPIKE: You know that nigga only quarter black, right? One quarter, ya know that shit? He half Thai, quarter black, an' quarter white, or Indian, Filipino, some'n. You see this swing, man? Shit is smooth, right? Got me that Vijay swing, look—uggh—poetry—speakin' a BLACK, that nigga Vijay? He darker than I am. Mahatma Vijay. All right, watch this shit with the putter. Mandingo Vijay. Nigga, you watchin'? Keith—watch me drain this shit.

(Spike has put the 6-iron back in the bag and taken out a putter. He lines up over a ball. Keith is busy recounting stack after stack of money.)

SPIKE: Keith? You takin' notes, bro? *(He putts the ball toward and into a plastic, green putting machine—the hole catches the ball, then spits it back. Throughout, he continues.)* Uggh—dead center, baby—never up, never in—like your sex life, right Keith? Keith, you hear me? Never up, never in? I said kinda like your dick, bro—prolly whatchoo do with all that money, huh? Prolly make book so you can buy Levitra, Viagra, an' shit, ol' mothafuckah. Yo! Keith! Ai'ght nigga—countchyer lil' money then, I ain' give a fuck—wha' I care—I'm a golfin' nigga—workin' on my game. Twenny-seven feet, uugh, St. Andrews. *(He misses.)* Shit, you see that? You ain't see shit, nigga—you too busy up in yo' own shit. Fitty feet, Pebble Beach. *(lines up another.)* Ya know, I useta know a girl in high school named Levitra—true story—biggest whore on campus—prolly mighta even fucked yo' ol' ass, nigga. Where you go ta high school at, huh?

Where you go? You like from Vermont or some shit, right? Huh? Yo' ass be like Colorado—Montana, maybe—some white mothafuckah state.

KEITH: I need you to count this with me.

SPIKE: Count what?

KEITH: This stack here.

SPIKE: What about it?

KEITH: I need you ta siddown, shut the fuck up, and count along.

SPIKE: I can't count no better than you.

KEITH: I've counted this stack three times, Spike, and each time I've gotten the same result.

SPIKE: That ain't hard ta do.

KEITH: Put down the club.

SPIKE: I'm workin' on my puttin', though.

KEITH: Siddown.

SPIKE: Which stack you even talkin' 'bout anyway, lemme see . . .

(Spike takes a quick step toward Keith. Keith pulls a gun out of the open briefcase, then puts it down in front of him, on the table.)

KEITH: I said put the club away an' sit the fuck down.

SPIKE: Keith, man . . .

KEITH: . . . Siddown.

SPIKE: What the fuck you bringin' out that for, come on man . . .

KEITH: . . . I asked you nicely, I could change my tone if you want. Now sit.

(Spike moves toward the chair, across the table from Keith.)

SPIKE: I don't know why you even trippin', bro—bringin' a fuckin' gun out . . .

KEITH: . . . Gimme the putter.

SPIKE: Come on, man . . .

KEITH: . . . Hand me the fuckin' putter.

(Keith extends his hand. Spike hands the putter across the table.)

KEITH: Now sit.

(Spike sits.)

SPIKE: You actin' all fucked-up an' shit, bro . . .

KEITH: . . . Shut up. You been talkin' nonstop since you got here.

SPIKE: I had shit I wanted to tell you.

KEITH: About Tiger Woods? I don't give a fuck about Tiger Woods.

SPIKE: You like golf.

KEITH: People talk cuz they got somethin' important ta say or somethin' important to AVOID saying. There's nothing important about Tiger Woods.

SPIKE: Lotta mothafuckas disagree wi'that statement right there, Keith—lil' black kids all 'cross America for one—shit, I started playin' cuz a' him— fuckin' OPRAH'S joinin' private golf clubs now—I read about that shit, she joinin' out in fuckin' Santa Barbara—California—black men AND black sistahs joinin' private golf clubs with a buncha white fuckin' JEWS?! That ain't IMPORTANT?! That all TIGER right there, nigga. Now maybe that shit ain't important ta yo' ass, nigga, cuz maybe cuz yo' ass just happens ta be WHITE. Ya see what'm sayin'? You never even thought about that shit like that. I broke that shit down TIGHT, right?

KEITH: Tight.

SPIKE: That nigga for real, Keith, that nigga no joke.

KEITH: Terrific. *(Counting.)* One, two, three . . . I want you to do this with me—out loud, so I can hear you. Three, four . . .

SPIKE: . . . Why you so caught up with this shit—I learned ta count in the third fuckin' grade.

KEITH: Don't make me shoot you, OK? We'll try it again. One. Two. *(Looks at Spike, prompting.)*

SPIKE: Three.

KEITH: Good. Four.

KEITH AND SPIKE: Five. Six. Seven. Eight. Nine. Ten. Eleven. Twelve. Thirteen. Fourteen. Fifteen.

KEITH: I got fifteen. You get fifteen? Mmmph? Spikey? How many'd you get?

SPIKE: Whose stack is that?

(Keith pushes a yellow piece of paper across the table.)

KEITH: It says "Barton—nineteen hundred." Short four. That is your hand-writing isn't it?

SPIKE: D'joo count the others?

KEITH: They match.

SPIKE: You count 'em more than once or . . .

KEITH: . . . More than once.

SPIKE: An' they was all good, every one?

KEITH: To the penny.

SPIKE: I dunno, man.

KEITH: What?

SPIKE: I dunno, maybe . . .

KEITH: . . . Maybe what?

SPIKE: Maybe he stiffed you, I dunno.

KEITH: Maybe he stiffed me?

SPIKE: Maybe.

KEITH: Maybe Barton stiffed me?

SPIKE: Why not?

KEITH: Barton? We're talkin' about Barton, Spike.

SPIKE: I don't know WHAT the fuck we talkin' 'bout, bringin' a gun on the table an' shit—shit ain't even got nuttin' ta do with me.

KEITH: You did the collections, didn't you?

SPIKE: No, my fuckin' mother did—c'mon man, I dunno what happened— why you all up in my shit for?

KEITH: Would you rather I was up in your MOTHER'S shit? Mmmph? Or your lil' punk rock girlfriend's shit? I'll get up in that shit, Spike, gimme the word, "bro," I'd love to.

SPIKE: C'mon, man, that's my girlfriend you talkin' about.

KEITH: Yeah, an' that's my money missing.

SPIKE: That's fucked up an' you know it.

KEITH: Is it?

SPIKE: Talkin' 'bout my mother, talkin' 'bout my girlfriend . . .

KEITH: . . . Where's my four hundred dollars, Spike?

SPIKE: I got no idea.

KEITH: You got no idea?

SPIKE: No.

KEITH: Fifty, seventy-five, I let it go . . .

SPIKE: . . . Relax, bro . . .

KEITH: . . . You're young, you're stupid . . .

SPIKE: . . . I ain't stupid . . .

KEITH: . . . your girl's got a habit . . .

SPIKE: . . . My girl ain't got nothin' ta do with this . . .

KEITH: . . . I SAID TA SHUT THE FUCK UP, NOW SHUT UP! *(Pause.)* I like you. I do. I never brought it up before because I understood and I didn't care. Your girl's a drug addict and you're a dumb-ass kid. But now it's four hundred more and you lie to me when I DO bring it up. And you insult me when you lie. Tell me the truth, Spike. Tell me the truth— think long and hard—and look me in my eye. *(Pause.)*

SPIKE: I was gonna pay you back. Every cent, from the other times, too. I got Missy a vinyl coat. All black, like she like. It's got a hood in it. She loved it, bro. We fucked six times cuz a' that coat. Six times.
(Keith grabs the handle of the golf club.)

SPIKE: That's my heart right there, Keith. She my heart. It was her birthday.
(Blackout.)

SCENE 13

Daniel's office. Daniel is behind his desk, on the phone.

DANIEL: *(Into phone.)* I'm six-foot-three, well-built, two hundred five pounds, I got tight ab muscles—a nice six pack. I'm twenty-six years of age. I like both older and younger women. I'm well-endowed, a legit nine, with a nice thick head. I like to get to the gym at least four, five times a week. I like poetry. I'm a musician . . .
(Newton enters. Daniel hangs up.)

DANIEL: Mister Collier, hello. May I help you?
(Newton puts an eight-and-a-half-by-eleven-inch envelope on Daniel's desk.)

NEWTON: They're papers from my attorney.

DANIEL: Then they should be taken ta legal.

NEWTON: Well I took 'em ta you.

DANIEL: I'll walk 'em over. How you holdin' up?

NEWTON: Don't you wanna know what's inside?

DANIEL: Not really, no.

NEWTON: Why not?

DANIEL: I'm not in legal.

NEWTON: YOU'RE inside.

DANIEL: OK.

NEWTON: You—the entire board of directors: Mister Powell, Mister Robinov—Rich Green—New York, Tulsa, Boston—wrongful firing, race discrimination, age discrimination—I'm not goin' without a fight. This woulda cost y'all a helluva lot less if ya'd just done the right thing from the beginning.

DANIEL: You're preaching to the choir, Mister Collier.

NEWTON: Read the lawsuit, Daniel. I certainly hope it doesn't cause you to lose your job. Me losin' mine? Easy come, easy go, another unemployed black man. But you Daniel? Thirty-five years old, three long months behind your nice, wooden desk. Where would be the justice in that?
(Newton moves toward the door.)

DANIEL: This is a big corporation, Mister Collier.
(Newton stops.)

DANIEL: They'll tie you up so long and cost you so much—you'll lose. *(Beat.)* Look—it wasn't my decision to let you go—but it IS my job to tell you about it . . . I'm sorry. It's my job. The same job you were hoping YOU would get.

NEWTON: And if I HAD I woulda called Tulsa. I woulda gone upstairs— instead of tryin' to save my own ass. I woulda shown those men my file an' I woulda told 'em "this ain't right. This man has worked here for TWENTY-FIVE FUCKIN' YEARS—it ain't right—white, black or otherwise." Instead of tryin' to save my own job. *(Beat.)* Have a nice day. Have a nice . . . goddamn day.

(Newton exits.)

SCENE 14

A nice restaurant. A table for two. A bottle of wine, two wine glasses.

GARY: I'm sorry if I haven't been the greatest conversationalist thus far. I'm better at typing than talking I suppose.

TRACIE: It's OK. The quiet's nice.

GARY: It is kinda, isn't it?

(They sip their wine in silence—occasional, brief eye contact. Silence.)

TRACIE: What was it about my profile? Why did you respond ta me?

GARY: Your picture.

TRACIE: Yeah?

GARY: I'd be lying if I said I didn't think you were beautiful.

TRACIE: I'm not BEAUTIFUL.

GARY: I'd be lying if I said I didn't disagree.

TRACIE: I think I'm kinda pretty, sometimes, but . . .

GARY: . . . Well you're wrong. But even so, still . . . you're doing better than most, believe me. The last time I liked the way I looked was in my photo in my high school year book—when I was a SOPHOMORE.

TRACIE: I like the one you posted.

GARY: Well, thank you I suppose, but . . .

TRACIE: . . . That wasn't taken in high school.

GARY: No.

TRACIE: No. *(Beat.)*

GARY: Neither was yours.

TRACIE: No. *(Beat.)* Mine was taken last Christmas.

GARY: As good as it is—the picture?—ta be honest, seeing how you are in person? You oughtta get your money back or retroactively fire the photographer or something—it doesn't do you justice at all. Not even the half of it. *(Beat.)*

TRACIE: My husband took it.

GARY: Oh.

TRACIE: I have a husband. *(Beat.)*

GARY: I have an appointment Thursday with an attorney. I'm planning on filing for divorce. *(Pause.)*

TRACIE: Do you have children?

GARY: No. How 'bout you?

TRACIE: No. *(Beat.)* I like this wine.

GARY: I was hoping you would. I'm not really much of a connoisseur, but I . . . I'm glad. Not too fruity, not too sweet.

TRACIE: It's nice.

GARY: Yeah. It is. *(Pause.)* Your husband oughtta be ashamed of himself.

TRACIE: Oh, he's not a professional photographer.

GARY: He oughtta be ashamed of himself for a variety of reasons besides that. He oughtta be ashamed of himself for not knowing where you are right now. For not treating you well enough to make it so you wouldn't WANT to be here. I don't mean to be bad mouthing a man I've never met. Maybe I should THANK him . . . Here we are, sharing a lovely bottle of wine. *(Pause.)*

TRACIE: Have you dated many black women before?

GARY: Black and Latina exclusively.

TRACIE: Exclusively, huh?

GARY: *(With a confident shrug.)* Well, you know . . .

TRACIE: Keepin' it real, huh?

GARY: For shnizzy, for shnizoo.

TRACIE: Yeah?

GARY: "Go Tracie, it's your birthday, go Tracie, go Tracie."

TRACIE: "Go Gary, go Gary."

(They both laugh. They're embarrassed. They stop. An awkward silence. Then more laughter. And more. Then silence once again.)

GARY: Thank you for making me feel comfortable enough to act like an idiot in front of you.

TRACIE: Thanks for making me laugh. *(Pause.)*

GARY: Is your husband white?

TRACIE: No. *(Beat.)* Is your wife black?

GARY: Yes. *(Beat.)* I'm keepin' it real, you're movin' on up.

(She playfully hits him.)

TRACIE: Jerk.

GARY: Hey, I'm joking, I'm joking.

TRACIE: You're the one movin' on up, not me.

GARY: Maybe we both are. *(Beat.)*

TRACIE: Maybe. *(Beat.)*

GARY: Probably. *(Pause.)* Tracie?

TRACIE: Yes?

GARY: When was the last time your husband made love to you? When was the last time he told you how gorgeous you are? When's the last time you believed him when he told you he loved you? When's the last time you believed it without him having to say anything? *(Pause.)* I'm extremely attracted to you, Tracie. And I wonder how you feel about me. *(Pause.)*

TRACIE: When's the last time you made love with your wife?

GARY: I don't remember.

TRACIE: I don't remember the answers to any of your questions. I don't have answers anymore. I haven't had answers in a long time. I haven't been happy in a long time. I'm happy you liked my profile. I'm happy I decided to respond. I'm happy I'm sitting here across from you right now. I'm happy right now. It's been a long time, Gary. It's been a very long time.

SCENE 15

*Newton's office. Charles Caldwell's "Old Buck" blares, starting at the 1:15 mark. Two white men in ski masks vandalize Newton's office. They unfurl a Confederate flag and drape it over Newton's desk. They hang an eight-knot hangman's noose from an overhead beam. On a wall they spray paint: "*The Silent Nigger Lives, The Loud Nigger Dies,*" "*A Good Nigger's A Dead Nigger.*"*

SCENE 16

Keith's apartment. Spike is on the floor, beaten and bloody, barely breathing. Blood has spattered onto Keith's face and shirt. The bent, crooked, bloody golf club is on the floor.

KEITH: I hope your girlfriend enjoys her new coat. I hope she sleeps in it. I hope she appreciates what you've done. She won't. She won't, Spike. But it would be goddamn nice if she did. Why the fuck didn't you just ask?!

SCENE 17

Newton's office. Lights up on Newton's vandalized office as we hear Otis Taylor's "Feel Like Lightning," from the beginning of the song. Newton stands in the doorway. He looks to the noose. To the graffiti. To the Confederate flag. To the books and papers strewn about the floor. He stands frozen. He takes it in. Pause.

He enters. He takes the flag off the desk. He folds it. He picks up a chair that's been knocked over. He moves it to the hanging noose. He stands on the chair. He unties the rope from the overhead beam. He gets down from the chair. He sits in it. He looks around. He stares straight ahead, the noose in his hands. Eventually—the lights and music fade to silence and black.

END OF ACT I

ACT II
SCENE 1

Donny Hathaway's "A Song for You" is heard as lights slowly rise to reveal Newton. Alone. In his easy chair. A cigarette burns in the ashtray. A stiff drink is in his hand. He doesn't drink from it. He doesn't smoke the cigarette. He sits motionless—staring straight ahead in a dimly lit, smoke-filled room.

Music continues and lights remain on Newton as a soft, warm light slowly rises on Gary in a hotel room. He is seated on the foot of a king-sized bed. He wears slacks—but no shoes, no socks, an unbuttoned shirt. Tracie enters (from the bathroom). She wears a black negligee. She stops. She stands nervously.

Gary rises, facing her. They stare at each other. They approach. They stop a foot or two apart. Pause.

He reaches out a hand and gently takes one of hers. She reaches out her other hand and takes one of his. They slowly lean into one another. A kiss. And another. And another. He runs the back of his hand along her cheek, down her neck, onto her shoulder, kissing each body part as he goes. He moves the strap of her negligee off her shoulder. She moves it back. He kisses her neck. Then her mouth. She kisses him back. Their kissing becomes passionate. And more passionate.

The music fades to silence. She pulls away.

TRACIE: . . . I can't, please, I . . .

(Gary stops.)

TRACIE: I'm sorry. *(Beat.)* I want to.

GARY: It's OK. *(Pause.)*

TRACIE: My husband slapped me.

GARY: I'm sorry.

TRACIE: You're sorry?

GARY: Yes. *(Beat.)*

TRACIE: Three months ago. *(Beat.)* He won't let me forgive him.

GARY: We can go if you'd like.

TRACIE: I don't know what I'm doing.

GARY: Neither do I. *(Beat.)*

TRACIE: Hold me? *(Beat.)* OK? *(Beat.)* Hold me.

(He does.)

TRACIE: Tighter?

(He does.)

TRACIE: Tell me I'm beautiful.

GARY: You're beautiful.

TRACIE: Kiss me.

(He does.)

TRACIE: Again.

(He does.)

TRACIE: Again.

(He does.)

TRACIE: Again.

(He does.)

TRACIE: Again.

(They kiss. They go to the bed. The petting becomes heavier; he kisses her breasts. She stops him.)

TRACIE: Hold me.

(He does.)

TRACIE: Just hold me.

(He does. Donny Hathaway's "A Song for You" begins once again [at the 2:47 mark]. Lights remain on Tracie and Gary in bed, as they embrace.

Lights remain on Newton in his easy chair, staring straight ahead, drink in hand, burning cigarette in the ashtray.

As the song continues, lights rise on Lotty, at home, alone, smoking a Virginia Slim, reading a magazine. She glances at a bedside digital clock.

Lights rise on Jessica, alone, in bed, under the covers, blankly staring at a flickering TV screen.

Lights rise on Daniel, alone, on his bed, sitting up, reading a James Lee Burke novel.

Lights rise on Missy, alone, on the fold-out sofa-bed. She puts a cigarette out on her arm. She smokes crystal meth.

Lights on Keith and Spike. Keith sits at the glass table. Spike is bloody and motionless on the floor. Spike's cell phone rings. Music stops. Five rings. Silence. The ringing begins once again. Ring. Ring. Ring. Ring. Ring. Then stops. Daniel dials his phone, then pushes a series of buttons.)

DANIEL: *(Into phone.)* Hey, um, hey . . . this is uh . . . this is Steve, I'm . . . I'm callin' pretty late here, it's . . . it's comin' up on three-thirty almost . . . I can't sleep, so . . . I'm just looking to have a little conversation. Maybe meet at some point. I'm callin' outta New York—Manhattan—the Upper West Side. I'm thirty-two years old. I'm six-feet tall. I'm single. I'm recently divorced. It's only been official now less than four months, I'm . . . I'm just looking for conversation, I . . . I wanna talk. I'm a good listener, too. *(Beat.)* I'm lonely. *(Beat.)* Connect if you're interested. Thanks. *(He presses a button on the phone and waits.)*

(Jessica turns off the TV. She looks at her digital clock. Lotty dials her phone.)

LOTTY: *(Into phone.)* It's me again. It's almost four. Just . . . call me back, OK? I won't answer, I won't pick up. Just . . . leave a message. Lemme know you're all right. *(She hangs up.)*

(Keith rises from the table. He exits.)

(Jessica picks up the phone. She looks at a small piece of paper. She dials. She waits. She presses a few buttons.)

JESSICA: *(Into phone.)* Hi. *(Beat.)* I'm Jessica. *(She removes the retainer from her mouth.)* This is my first time calling. *(Beat.)* I don't know WHY I'm calling really, I . . . *(Beat.)* Thanks. *(She pushes a button on her phone. She waits.)*

(Keith enters with a bucket, mop, and shower curtain. He leans the mop against the table. He lays the shower curtain on the floor.)

(Lotty smokes a Virginia Slim.)

(Missy smokes meth.)

(Newton stares straight ahead.)

(Tracie and Gary sleep in one another's arms.)

(Keith rolls Spike onto the shower curtain. He begins mopping blood.)

(Jessica presses a button on her phone.)

(Daniel presses a button on his phone.)

DANIEL: *(Into phone.)* Hello?

JESSICA: *(Into phone.)* Steve?

DANIEL: This is Steve.

JESSICA: Hi.

DANIEL: Hi.

JESSICA: This is Jessica.

DANIEL: Hey.

JESSICA: Hey. *(Pause.)*

DANIEL: Wow.

JESSICA: What?

DANIEL: Nothing, no, I . . . Hey.

JESSICA: Hey.

DANIEL: I'm glad we connected.

JESSICA: I'm not sure yet. I'll let ya know.

DANIEL: Fair enough. *(Pause.)*

JESSICA: Divorce sucks, right?

DANIEL: You too, huh?

JESSICA: About two years now. It gets easier.

DANIEL: I'm all right, I guess.

JESSICA: Better than a shitty marriage, right?

DANIEL: I guess.

JESSICA: Guess? C'mon, loneliness is loneliness, we all know what that is, but you still feel it's gonna come to an end, ya know? Ya see fat ugly bald-headed people holdin' hands all the time, in public even, so ya gotta figure, shit, right? I gotta meet somebody sometime, but, yeah, I know what ya mean . . . when you're IN that marriage? A shitty marriage, nasty shitty, I hate you, I hate your body, your face, your entire fuckin' FAMILY shitty—I agree—it's like you're NEVER gettin' out—like prison, right Steve? *(Beat.)* Steve? *(Beat.)* You still there?

DANIEL: I'm here.

JESSICA: I thought I mighta ran you off maybe.

DANIEL: Nuh-uh.

JESSICA: No?

DANIEL: No.

JESSICA: Oh. *(Beat.)* That's cool.

(As Lotty exits offstage:)

DANIEL: I like your voice, Jessica.

JESSICA: My voice?

DANIEL: Yeah.

JESSICA: What about it?

DANIEL: I dunno. I like the way it sounds. *(Beat.)* You live in New York?

JESSICA: Yeah.

DANIEL: Me too.

JESSICA: I know—Upper West Side, right?

DANIEL: Right.

JESSICA: Where're you from originally, you don't sound like New York.

DANIEL: Originally, Oklahoma. I moved here about fifteen years ago—to go to NYU.

JESSICA: That's a good school, right?

DANIEL: It was all right.

JESSICA: Where do you live on the Upper West Side? You live OLD Upper West or NEW Upper West? I know bitches up in INWOOD talkin' 'bout they live NEW Upper West—Washington Heights—Dominican mothafuckas mostly—white Columbia students, too—real estate brokers sell it like that—"welcome to the NEW UPPER WEST SIDE, 163rd and Broadway"—welcome ta puttin' families been there fifty years out on the fuckin' street—senior citizens too, wha' do they care?—they got wheelchairs, Steve—fuck 'em, put 'em on the street, that's that—gentri-fyin' greedy lil' pricks. *(Beat.)* Hello? *(Beat.)* Steve?

DANIEL: You got a little anger in ya, don't ya Jessica?

JESSICA: *(apologetic, soft, almost childlike.)* Maybe.

DANIEL: Maybe?

JESSICA: A little.

DANIEL: Just a little, huh?

JESSICA: Sometimes.

DANIEL: Yeah?

JESSICA: Sometimes. *(Beat.)* I got a lotta other stuff in me too, though.

DANIEL: Like what?

JESSICA: I dunno.

DANIEL: Sure you do. Tell me. What's inside? *(Beat.)*

JESSICA: No.

DANIEL: No?

JESSICA: Not yet.

> *(Tracie wakes. She sits on the edge of the bed. She looks at Gary. Gary doesn't stir.)*
>
> *(Keith sits at the table, staring at Spike.)*

DANIEL: The OLD Upper West. Seventy-eighth and Amsterdam.

JESSICA: That's nice there.

DANIEL: Yeah.

JESSICA: I bet that means you got a good job then, right?

DANIEL: Right.

JESSICA: Don't tell me you're in real estate.

DANIEL: No. The airlines.

(Tracie exits offstage as:)

JESSICA: You get free travel? My friend's husband works for the airlines, but they never go anywhere, I think maybe Disney World once.

DANIEL: Where do you wanna go?

JESSICA: Wha' do you mean?

DANIEL: Where can I take you? Yes—I get free travel. Where do you wanna go? *(Beat.)*

JESSICA: I dunno.

DANIEL: Go on. Tell me where you've never been.

(Newton drinks.)

(Gary wakes. He looks beside him. No one.)

DANIEL: Jessica? You still there?

(Missy rocks back and forth, knees wrapped in her arms.)

(Newton drinks.)

(Keith smokes.)

DANIEL: Hello?

JESSICA: That's good you got a good job, I think. It gives a man dignity, ya know? Not his IDENTITY, but . . . his dignity. Knowing he DOES something. Knowing others DEPEND on him. Only thing you could depend on my ex for was ta piss his pants on a three day drunk. Thank God we didn't have kids, right? *(Beat.)* You got kids, Steve?

DANIEL: No.

JESSICA: Just make everything more complicated. Make it harder ta walk away.

DANIEL: Probably.

JESSICA: Definitely. Much harder.

DANIEL: Yes. Much.

(Gary looks toward the bathroom. He sees the light, he hears the sink.)

JESSICA: Hey . . . You wanna know something?

DANIEL: What?

JESSICA: I like your voice too.

DANIEL: Yeah?

JESSICA: Yeah.

DANIEL: I'm glad we connected, Jessica. *(Beat.)* Hello?

JESSICA: Why's that?

DANIEL: I dunno. I just am. I feel better.

JESSICA: You do?

DANIEL: I do.

JESSICA: Good. That's good. Me too.

(Lights to black on everyone and everything except Newton. Tracie enters, quietly, her high-heels in her hand. She starts to move for the bedroom. Before she can exit:)

NEWTON: You shoulda called. *(Beat.)* Just that you were all right. *(Beat.)* Not ta worry.

(Pause. She begins to move once again.)

NEWTON: I know where you were, Trace.

(She stops.)

NEWTON: Jessica called three times. Sayin' she couldn't getchyou on your cell. I couldn't get you either. *(Beat.)* I told the girls you were WITH Jessica. But then JESSICA? Well, she calls HERE. Our daughters, Trace . . . they asked me where their mother was. They wanted me ta call the police, and the hospitals. Worrying about their mom. I lied. I told 'em you called earlier an' I forgot. That you told me you were with Aunt Cheryl for a surprise party at her work. In case they ask.

(She moves again.)

NEWTON: What color was he, Trace? What race was this man?

(She stops. Beat.)

NEWTON: I'm not mad. It's a question. Your black man lost his job. He raised his hand. What color was he, Trace—when your black man fulfilled their cliche? *(Pause.)*

TRACIE: I should've called. *(pause.)* He was black. *(Beat.)* Goodnight. *(She exits.)*

(Newton continues to stare straight ahead. He takes a sip of his drink. Cross fade: Lights slowly down to black on Newton as they rise on the following:)

SCENE 2

Keith's apartment. Spike's cell phone is ringing. Keith moves to Spike. He reaches into Spike s pockets. Keith takes Spike's cell phone out of Spike's jeans. The ringing stops. Keith puts the phone on the table. He turns to exit. The ringing begins again. Keith turns back and answers the phone.

KEITH: *(Into phone.)* Hello. No, this is . . . listen, no! . . . no!—MISSY!?—he can't, he, listen! . . . Will you shut the fuck up, shut up! *(Beat.)* It's about Spike.

SCENE 3

Gary's home office. Gary, home from his night with Tracie, is at his computer. Lotty enters (dressed as we've seen her thus far in Act II).

LOTTY: I left you three hundred fuckin' messages!

GARY: Aren't we in the mood for exaggeration?

LOTTY: I CALL, Gary—when I'm out, I fuckin' call!

GARY: Do you?

LOTTY: Fuck you!

GARY: We don't fuck, remember? I mean, YOU fuck . . . other people you fuck, but WE? I'm busy on my computer, Lotty . . . I'm sorry I kept you up unnecessarily, everything is perfectly splendid and in order, you may go back to sleep now.

(Gary starts to type. Lotty yanks the keyboard off the desk.)

LOTTY: We have RULES, Gary!! We have fuckin' rules!!

GARY: You didn't call! Not the other night, you didn't!

LOTTY: I called.

GARY: No you didn't.

LOTTY: I FUCKIN' called!

GARY: You didn't.

LOTTY: Did to.

GARY: Did not.

LOTTY: Did to.

GARY: Did not.

LOTTY: Well get USED TO IT, then—I didn't call, I didn't call, maybe I did, maybe I didn't.

GARY: You didn't.

LOTTY: Fine, I didn't, fuck you, I didn't, an' from now on I won't. I hope you're fuckin' happy.

GARY: I am happy! I met a woman, Lotty—a spectacular woman—and the best thing about her is she isn't you. Now gimme back my keyboard—I wanna finish telling her goodnight.

LOTTY: Fuck her! *(Lotty smashes the keyboard to the floor.)* Tell your CHILDREN goodnight!

(Blackout as Otis Taylor's "Boy Plays Mandolin" is heard [starting at 1:57 mark] as lights rise on:)

SCENE 4

Tracie's/Newton's bedroom. Tracie is in bed. Eyes closed. Music continues. Newton enters. He slowly approaches. Drunk. Uneasy on his feet and in his mind. He stands over her. She doesn't stir. Newton reaches out a hand, toward his wife, as though to touch her head. He hesitates. He does not touch her. He drops his hand to his side. Pause. He turns and slowly walks away. Tracie opens her eyes. Newton exits. Tracie looks toward the door. Blackout. Silence.)

SCENE 5

Keith's apartment.

MISSY: It was my birthday . . . we were gonna fuck each others' brains out ta celebrate, ya know . . . but he got carried away or . . . he was someplace else . . . he juss . . . kept going and going—I couldn't breathe, he was choking me harder and harder. I said "diamonds," his hands around my neck. You couldn't hear. I tried to push him off, I started hitting him, punching him in the chest and his face. He stops and looks at me, lost, no idea, he has no idea what just happened. His mind was . . . He never said anything? You're his friend.

KEITH: No.

MISSY: He bought me this coat—for my birthday. It's nice, right? *(Beat.)* It looks good on me? *(Beat.)* Keith? It looks good?

KEITH: Yeah.

MISSY: Yeah?

KEITH: You look great.

MISSY: Do I?

KEITH: You're beautiful.

MISSY: You didn't call the police, did you? I don't wanna talk ta no police.

KEITH: No.

MISSY: *(While desperately, unsuccessfully searching through her bag, her pockets, dropping stuff onto the floor.)* . . . Fuck-fuck-fuck-fuck, do you have a uh, a, a, FUCK FUCK FUCK FUCK!! . . .
(Keith grabs her, tries to control her, but she continues saying fuck and trying to hurt herself.)

KEITH: Listen to me—Missy, stop, knock it off—listen—LISTEN—SHUT THE FUCK UP! *(He grabs her face.)* SHUT UP!

(She stops. He holds her arms firmly.)

MISSY: I was gonna get 'm diamonds for HIS birthday.

(He releases his grip.)

MISSY: Earrings, ya know? I'd been saving, I . . .

(She approaches Spike.)

MISSY: "Diamonds, baby. All ya gotta do is say 'diamonds'—that'll make me stop anything." He was supposed ta stop.

KEITH: I know.

MISSY: He was supposed ta fuckin' stop, he was supposed ta stop, Keith . . .

(She begins to hit Spike's dead body.)

MISSY: . . . he was supposed ta fuckin' stop! . . .

KEITH: *(Throwing her to the ground, away from Spike.)* . . . Knock it off . . .

MISSY: . . . Fuck me, Keith, will you fuck me, fuck me . . .

KEITH: . . . Cut it out, stop . . .

MISSY: *(Grabbing at his belt.)* . . . Fuck me, please, fuck me, Keith . . .

KEITH: . . . Missy . . .

MISSY: *(Pulling down her pants.)* . . . I need you to fuck me, will you fuck me . . .

KEITH: . . . Stop—Missy! . . .

MISSY: . . . Fuck me while I kiss him good-bye, fuck me, please . . .

KEITH: *(Grabbing her firmly.)* . . . Knock it off, MISSY!, STOP!! . . .

MISSY: *(Breaking down, calm.)* Please . . . Please, Keith? Please?

KEITH: *(He holds her arms. He looks her in the eyes.)* I'm not gonna call the police. We can't tell anyone. Do you understand? We need to keep this to ourselves. Whoever did this . . . OK? . . . It will be taken care of. You understand? *(Beat.)* Missy? . . . Do you understand?

(She nods, she understands.)

KEITH: Good. *(He pulls up her pants.)* When he got here . . . you were the only thing he talked about. How much he loved you. How he wanted me to make sure you know.

MISSY: I said "diamonds" but he wouldn't stop.

KEITH: I know.

MISSY: I never told 'm I loved him.

KEITH: Tell him now.

MISSY: I can't.

KEITH: Tell him now, Missy.

MISSY: I can't!

(He uncovers Spike's face as:)

KEITH: Tell him you love him.

MISSY: I can't.

> *(He grabs her and forces her down. He pushes her face into Spike.)*

KEITH: Tell'm you love your new coat. Tell'm you forgive him. Tell'm you love him, Missy. Tell him how much you love him.

MISSY: *(To Spike.)* I love you. I love you. I love you, I love you, I love you . . .

> *(Lights fade as R. L. Burnside's "Stole My Check" blasts. The song cuts to silence as:)*

SCENE 6

> *Daniel's office. Newton slams photos onto the desk. Daniel is seated on the other side.*

NEWTON: "The Silent Nigger Lives, The Loud Nigger Dies"! "A Good Nigger's a Dead Nigger"! *(From out of his shoulder bag comes the Confederate flag.)* A Confederate-mothafuckin'-flag! *(And then the noose.)* An eight-knot noose—eight knot—that a threat a' goddamn MURDER—eight knot snap a mothafucka neck three times my size! "The Silent Nigger Lives, The Loud Nigger Dies"?! Who the nigger, Mr. Breems?! You the nigger? Huh? You the nigger, Daniel?! CUZ I AIN'T NO GODDAMN NIGGER! What happens I'm in that office when they do this?! I got two daughters, Daniel!! I got two little girls. This ain't my pension no more, this the color a' my goddamn skin! And this here New York!! This New York goddamn City, this ain't no Birmingham, ain't no Selma in the sixties—this the right here, right now, mothafucker, an' whatchyou gonna do about it?! Whatchyou gonna do, Daniel? I don't want no tied-up lawsuit dead-ends, death threats—I want justice! I want my goddamn job! We gonna call Tulsa, Dan. Pick up the phone. Pick it up.

DANIEL: It's after hours, Mister Collier, there's nobody there . . .

NEWTON: . . . Tulsa's an hour behind, pick up the phone.

DANIEL: But it's past eight here, so out there it means . . .

> *(Newton pulls the 9 mm from his bag, scaring himself as much as Daniel.)*

NEWTON: . . . I said pick up the phone. Pick it up.

DANIEL: Newton . . .

NEWTON: . . . An' when we're through I want YOUR job. Not "NO" job—your job. Y'all had a choice from the beginning. Pick up that goddamn phone!

DANIEL: I need you to CALM DOWN, Mister Collier.

NEWTON: . . . WHAT?!

DANIEL: You need to calm down and take a breath.

(*Newton pistol-whips Daniel. Blackout.*)

SCENE 7

A diner. Jessica and Tracie. Tracie is eating. Jessica is not—coffee only.

JESSICA: We were on for more than an hour—women call free—we didn't exchange numbers, not yet, but . . .

TRACIE: . . . Not YET?

JESSICA: Yeah, YET.

TRACIE: I see.

JESSICA: Our talk flowed, Trace, where he's from, where he lives, stuff about my life—I'm goin' out with this guy—we already made plans.

TRACIE: No you didn't.

JESSICA: Did too—white boy from Oklahoma.

TRACIE: From a chat line?

JESSICA: Why, you want the number?

TRACIE: No thanks.

JESSICA: I'll hold on to it for ya. I'm about ta date a white guy from Oklahoma named Steve. You ever been with a white guy? You gone white, Trace?

TRACIE: Nuh-uh, no.

JESSICA: Could be "the one," ya never know—could be fulla shit too—how he looks, bad breath, broke-ass-in-debt—but I got a good feeling, Trace—I BETTER—I'm a no-longer-eighteen-year-old bank teller with about two an' a half eggs left. You got kids, you got Newton. I got assholes on the subway, I got an asshole ex-husband and I got that asshole cheatin' ex-boyfriend still working with me side-by-side at the bank. We don't even look at each other.

TRACIE: One of you's gotta get a new job.

JESSICA: I was there first. This new guy, Steve? He works for the airlines like Newt. He asked me "Where can I take you, Jessica?" You heard? "Where would you like to fly away with me?" We're gonna start he takes me ta dinner. Then I figure Cancun's suppose ta be nice.

TRACIE: Hawaii too.

JESSICA: Wherever—outta New York, somewhere warm—Anguilla maybe.

TRACIE: Angueela?

JESSICA: Anguilla. I looked it up online after we hung up—white sand, blue water, brown skin. You got your appetite back.

TRACIE: A little.

JESSICA: We'll order dessert—you like pumpkin pie or sweet potato?

TRACIE: Either one.

JESSICA: I want a family, Trace. I need to HEAR things and FEEL things . . . Where's our waitress? I swear to God we're never comin' here again. From now on it's Five-Star-Zagat-Guide, candlelight, warm weather, you, me, Newt, and Oklahoma Steve—yee-haw! *(Raising her coffee mug in a toast.)* To Anguilla.

TRACIE: *(Raising her coffee mug.)* To Anguilla.

JESSICA: I need more coffee!

SCENE 8

The bar. Keith's seated on his regular stool. Lotty's at the bar. Four barstools between them. They look out, straight ahead.

LOTTY: This time we play by MY rules. You do what I say. We go where I say we go. Not your place, not mine. I got a room. It's a shithole. There's nothing nice or fancy or high-class about it. It smells like roach spray and dead rat. I picked it out special just for you.

SCENE 9

Daniel's office. Daniel is seated. His torso and arms are tied to the chair with the rope (the noose). Newton digs through filing cabinets and drawers. He finds a gym bag. He pulls out a T-shirt, socks, sweatshirt, sweatpants, boxing wraps, and a towel. He dumps the items onto the desk. He finds scotch tape, multiple rolls. He secures Daniel's feet and legs. The door has been secured with the desk, a chair, the dead-bolt. The gun is in his waistband. He double-checks the security of the door. Daniel speaks throughout.

DANIEL: I'm from Oklahoma, yes, but not Tulsa—I'm from Edmond, a suburb outside Oklahoma City—I've been in New York more than seventeen years. My father's a liberal Democrat defense attorney FAMOUS,

Mister Collier, famous in Oklahoma for his pro-bono work in and around the community, primarily the African-American community. My mom's a grade-school teacher in the public school system in downtown Oklahoma City—my brother's married to a Mexican girl, for chrissake. What happened with your JOB, what happened with your OFFICE, it's reprehensible, Mister Collier—unacceptable and repugnant—and despite having zero involvement in either event—ZERO, Mister Collier, I repeat—I had NOTHING to do WITH, nor any knowledge OF—yet I'm willing, right here, to accept responsibility—whatever you want—for the idiotic, hateful doings of misguided members of my so-called race—I apologize! And I accept whatever you want—you want phone calls, letters—my own resignation?! We can prosecute to the fullest extent of the law—I'll access the security tapes from the hallway outside your office—I'll ask my father for help—but if you continue down THIS road, please, if you CONTINUE . . . nothing good, Mister Collier, please . . . I'm sorry . . . plea . . .

(Newton gags and tapes Daniel's mouth.)

SCENE 10

An upscale hotel room. Gary and Tracie. They dance slowly, in one another's arms, to Lizz Wright's cover of "A Taste of Honey," from the beginning of the song. A full minute.

Lights remain on Gary and Tracie as lights rise on Jessica in a nice restaurant, all dolled up and beautiful, alone at a table for two, waiting for her date with Steve (Daniel).

Lights remain on Jessica, Gary, and Tracie as lights rise on a dive shit-hole motel room. Lotty and Keith fuck. Hard, impersonal. Doggy-style, no eye contact. Between grunts and groans, they repeat, again and again, almost to themselves:

KEITH: [Diamonds, diamonds, diamonds, diamonds . . .]
LOTTY: [Yes, yes, yes, yes, yes . . .]
(Jessica waits for her date. Gary and Tracie dance. Keith and Lotty fuck.)

SCENE 11

Daniel's office. Daniel is bound, tied, and gagged. He stands on the chair with the noose around his neck—as we saw him in the opening scene of the play. Newton is now calm, collected.

NEWTON: I don't KNOW you were involved with my dismissal. The extent of your exact participation. Nor to the destruction and threats in my office. I don't KNOW. And I don't care. And more importantly, YOU don't care. Despite your protestations and your white-guilt-obsessed mommy an' daddy and Mexican sister-in-law—with all due respect, Daniel— you're fulla shit. You hate me like I hate you. When you're alone in the privacy of your own mind—you hate me. And you're afraid. As politically incorrect as that may sound to a "left-wing-liberal" such as yourself—we scare you. I scare you. My rage. My ignorance. My history. My dick. You're terrified. You don't LIKE that you are—in fact you DISLIKE it, I know—which only makes you like YOURSELF less too—bad on top a' bad. Don't worry, I won't tell anyone. But be honest, Daniel—be honest: If your sister—or daughter—or your mom, the Democratic schoolteacher—one a' them brings home a man with skin the color a my own—what would you THINK, Daniel? Mmph? What would you THINK? Not, what would you SAY? Or DO? But THINK? *(Beat.)* How would you feel on their wedding day? *(Beat.)* On the birth of the little black babies? *(Beat.)* It's OK. If it makes you feel any better, I use to feel the same way. Full a' fear and terror. And I hated my mother for all of it. For instilling in me "be kind," "be polite," "be invisible." "Don't be a Bad Nigger, Newt. No one likes a Bad Nigger." She was trying to PROTECT me, and I forgive her. But I don't forgive you. I hate you. I've hated you my entire life. But I listened ta my mom an' played nice—shuckin' an' jivin', singin' "Kum-ba-yah-God-love-the-white-man-cuz-the-white-man-love-me." No more. Today I behave on the OUTSIDE how y'all always made me feel on the inside. I'm right here. I'm not invisible. *(Beat.)* I'm the last thing you ever gonna see.
(Newton remains still, calm, smoking his cigarette. Daniel struggles. Lights to black.)

SCENE 12

Upscale hotel room. Tracie holds a diamond ring in a ring box.

GARY: You don't have to answer. I know it's insane, it's absurd and impulsive—
I know, and I don't care—I've never been impulsive in my life. I've never
felt like this, Tracie, I'm . . . I'm usually rigid, I'm organized . . . I'm even
boring most of the time, but I don't feel boring with you, I . . . I just
don't. Listen, I . . . OK . . . I don't KNOW that you're the ONE—I don't
KNOW that. One can never really KNOW. But I do know my wife
ISN'T. And I don't believe your husband is either, for you. I'm different
with you, Tracie. I'm happy. Me. You make me feel good about being
ME. I never feel good about being me, and . . . and I believe I do the
same for you. I've never been so sure of anything in my life. Tell me you
disagree and I'll leave you alone. I promise. I'll never bother you again.

SCENE 13

*Dive shithole motel room. Lotty slowly gets dressed as Keith speaks into the
motel phone.*

KEITH: *(Into phone.)* Hey, um . . . Hey . . . Katherine, it's me, it's . . . it's Keith.
If you're there, pick up. I'm sorry it's such an inappropriate hour, I . . .
I'm sorry for a lotta shit. Look . . . This is shit, Kate. It's shit. How's Eliz-
abeth? How was her party? I wish I was there, I . . .
*(Lotty has finished dressing. She exits the motel room. Keith watches as she
goes. They do not make eye contact.)*
KEITH: *(Into phone.)* I'm not asking you to change your mind, I'm just . . . I
love you both. *(Beat.)* Sorry I called so late. *(He hangs up.)*

SCENE 14

*The restaurant. Jessica, still dolled up, still alone, still waiting in vain. Ten
seconds.*

SCENE 15

The Collier's apartment. Tracie turns on a light as she enters, a bouquet of flowers in her hand. She looks around. No one.

TRACIE: Hello? Hello? Newton? Newt? April, Angie?
   (She exits.)
TRACIE: *(Offstage.)* Anybody home? Hello? It's Mommy. Mommy's home.
   (She reenters. The flowers are now in a vase. She places the vase on a table. She picks up the mail. She sits in Newton's easy chair. She begins to look over the mail. She stops. She rests the mail in her lap. She looks around the quiet, empty apartment. She looks through the mail once again.)

SCENE 16

Gary and Lotty's home. Lotty's sitting alone on the love seat. Silence. Gary enters. He hangs his coat. He puts down his keys. He looks at his wife—she doesn't look back. He approaches. Pause. He sits down beside her. Pause. He gently places his hand on hers. Pause. She turns her palm upward, into his palm. They hold hands. They don't speak. They don't look at one another. Lotty gently rests her head on Gary's shoulder. Silence.

SCENE 17

The bar. Keith is on his stool, looking out. Newton is also seated, looking out. A drink in front of each. Four barstools between them. Silence. They are clearly aware of each other's presence, but there is no interaction. They sip their drinks. Pause. Keith removes a pack of cigarettes from his shirt pocket. He removes a single cigarette. He puts the pack back in his pocket. He lifts a book of matches off the bar, strikes a match, lights his cigarette. Silence. Eventually:

NEWTON: Excuse me.
   (No response.)
NEWTON: Excuse me.
   (Keith looks over.)
NEWTON: Ya think I could get a smoke, maybe? *(Beat.)*
KEITH: You waitin' on someone? *(Beat.)* Mmph? *(Beat.)* Maybe I know 'em for ya.

NEWTON: I'm not waitin'.

KEITH: No?

NEWTON: No. *(Pause.)*

KEITH: I've never seen you in here. Maybe I know 'em.

NEWTON: Maybe not. *(Pause.)*

KEITH: I got menthol. *(Keith removes the Newports.)*

NEWTON: That's fine. *(Beat.)*

> *(Keith slides Newton the pack of cigarettes. He then slides the book of matches. Newton lights a cigarette. He slips the book of matches into the pack and slides it back to Keith.)*

NEWTON: Thanks.

KEITH: Salud.

> *(Keith drinks. Newton drinks. Long pause.)*

KEITH: You a cop? *(Beat.)* Mmph? *(Beat.)* Friend? *(Beat.)* You the police? *(Beat.)*

NEWTON: Are you?

KEITH: No. *(Beat.)*

NEWTON: Neither am I.

> *(Beat. Newton looks away, straight ahead. Keith looks away, straight ahead. Long pause.)*

KEITH: You got kids? Mmph? *(Beat.)* How many? *(Beat.)* I got one. A little girl. Betsy August Rose. *(Beat.)* She was an accident. Maybe she was, maybe she wasn't. *(Pause.)* But when she came? When she arrived, this little thing? *(Beat.)* All ya gotta do is walk through the door. *(Pause.)* I missed her seventh birthday party last week. I wasn't invited. Her mother hates me. Maybe she does, maybe she doesn't. Who knows?

> *(Silence. They drink. They smoke.)*

KEITH: *(Almost to himself.)* [Salud.]

> *(Without looking over, Keith drinks. Newton glances over. Then away. Pause.)*

NEWTON: *(Almost to himself.)* [Salud.]

> *(Newton drinks. Neither one looks to the other. They smoke. They drink. Long pause. Then music: Leonard Cohen's "Alexandra Leaving," from the beginning. The song plays ten to fifteen seconds, then continues as:*
>
> > *Lights on Missy in the diner behind the counter. She wears a waitress's apron and name tag. She scrubs the counter with a sponge. She fills a black plastic bin with dirty cups, bowls, dishes. She wipes sweat from her brow. She leans against the counter. Exhausted, sad, her feet hurt. She continues cleaning.*

During the above: lights on Jessica in her small eat-in kitchen in her nightshirt. A small TV glows. A teapot whistles. She puts a tea bag in a cup; she pours hot water. She stirs. She puts the cup on the small kitchen table. She pours a bowl of cereal. She pours milk into the bowl. She sits at the table. She watches TV. She eats cereal. She sips tea.

As Jessica sits at the table: lights on Lotty in her bedroom. She has one packed suitcase on the floor and a second partially packed suitcase on a chair. She moves back and forth, from the bureau to the suitcase, filling it with clothes. She finishes filling the suitcase. She closes it. She puts it on the floor, next to the other suitcase. She looks around the bedroom. She sits, suitcases at her feet.

As Lotty packs: lights on Gary in a nice hotel room. Seated on the foot of the king-size bed. Wearing a black tuxedo. He takes off one shoe. Then the other. He takes off his socks and puts them in the shoes. He takes off his tux jacket, his bow tie, his cummerbund. He neatly drapes them over the back of a chair. He puts the shoes beneath the chair. He untucks his shirt. He hesitates. He moves to the foot of the bed. He sits. He tries to make himself comfortable.

Lights on Tracie in a bathroom. She wears a beautiful white wedding gown. She stares at herself in the mirror. Tears flow silently down her cheeks. She wipes them away. She composes herself. She stares at her reflection.

Newton and Keith together at the bar. Missy alone in the diner. Jessica alone in her kitchen. Lotty alone in her bedroom. Gary alone in the hotel room.

Tracie opens the door of the bathroom. The door leads to the hotel room. She stands in the doorway. Gary stands and faces her. Pause. Tracie slowly moves toward Gary. She stops five to six feet away. They stare into each others' eyes, but do not touch, or move any closer.

The lights and music fade on every person, every location. Silence. Blackness.)

END OF PLAY